Maui Revealed
The Ultimate Guidebook

Andrew Doughty
Harriett Friedman

Wizard
Publications

Maui Revealed
The Ultimate Guidebook

Published by Wizard Publications, Inc.
Post Office Box 991
Lihu'e, Hawai'i 96766–0991

© Copyright 2001 Andrew Doughty & Harriett Friedman. All rights reserved.

ISBN# 0–9639429–7–2   1/3s
Library of Congress Catalog Card Number 99–71266
Printed in Hong Kong

Cataloging–in–Publication Data

Doughty, Andrew
    Maui revealed : the ultimate guidebook / Andrew Doughty and
Harriett Friedman. – 1st ed. Lihue, HI : Wizard Publications, 2000.
    304 p. : col. photos, col. maps ; 21 cm.
    Includes index.
    Summary : a complete traveler's reference to the Hawaiian island
of Maui. Maps and color photographs by Andrew Doughty.
    ISBN 0–9639429–7–2
    LCCN 99–71266

    1. Maui (Hawaii) – Guidebooks. 2. Maui (Hawaii) – Description
    and travel. I. Friedman, Harriett. II. Title.

DU 628
919.6921__dc21

All photographs (except the cover) taken by Andrew Doughty.
Cartography by Andrew Doughty.
All artwork and illustrations by Andrew Doughty and Harriett Friedman.

Cover imagery courtesy of NASA. The image has been enhanced and is copyrighted.

Pages 2–3: Honolua Bay, right side, taken from the cliffs above.

We welcome any comments, questions, criticisms or contributions you may have.
Please send to:

Wizard Publications, Inc.
P.O. Box 991
Lihu'e, Hawai'i 96766–0991
E-mail us at **aloha@wizardpub.com**
For additional information visit our web site at **www.wizardpub.com**

Dedicated to Leo Doughty, whose love of flight and adventure has left its mark, and who has always paid his dues in silence

Maui is the undisputed playground of Hawai'i. No other island has the range of activities and scenery available to you here. There's almost nothing you can't do on Maui. Hike in pristine rain forests, snorkel in an extinct crater, coast a bicycle 10,000 feet down a volcano, walk along miles of beaches, frolic under a waterfall, dive into a natural freshwater pool, lie on a black or even red sand beach, or sip a drink as the sun sets over nearby islands. Whatever fantasy you have, Maui is bound to deliver.

We first came to the islands as visitors and decided we could never live anywhere else. We now make our home in the islands and divide our time between Maui, Kaua'i and the Big Island. Most travel publishers send a writer or writers to a given location for a few weeks to become "experts" and to compile information for guidebooks. To our knowledge, we are the only guidebook writers who actually *live* our books.

We hike the trails, ride the boats, eat in the restaurants, explore the reefs and do the things we write about. It takes us one to two *years*, full time, to do a first edition book, and we visit places anonymously. We marvel at writers who can do it all in a couple weeks staying in a hotel. Wow, they must be *really* fast. Our method, though it takes much longer, gives us the ability to tell it like it is in a way no one else can. We put in many long hours, and doing all these activities makes our lives a living hell. (Yeah, right! Feel free to gag at this point.)

Longtime locals have been surprised at some of the items described in our book. We have found many special places that people born and raised here didn't even know about because that's *all we do*—explore the island. Visitors will find the book as valuable as having a friend living on the island.

We recognize the effort people go through to visit Maui, and our goal is to expose you to as many options as possible so you can decide what you want to see and do. We took great pains to structure this book in such a way that it will be fun, easy reading and loaded with useful information. This book is not a bland regurgitation of the facts arranged in textbook fashion. We feel strongly that guidebooks should present their information so that you don't have to look through every single page every time you want to find something.

If you are here on vacation, your time is extremely precious. You don't want to spend all your time flipping through a book looking for what you want. You need to be able to locate *what* you want, *when* you want it. You want to be able to access a comprehensive index, a thorough table of contents and refer to high-quality maps that were designed with you in mind. You want to know which helicopter, SCUBA, boat tour or lu'au is the best on the island. You want to find special hidden gems most people overlook. You want to be shown those things that will make this vacation the best of your life.

A quick look at this book will reveal features never before used in other guidebooks. Let's start with the maps. They are more detailed than any other maps you will find, and yet they omit extraneous information that can sometimes make a chore out of reading a map. We know that people in unfamiliar territory sometimes have a hard time determining where they are on a map, so we include landmarks. Most notable among these are mile markers. At every mile on main roads, the government has erected numbered markers to tell you where you are. We are the first to put these markers on a map so you can use them as reference points. In addition, we repeatedly drove or walked every inch of every road on the maps. This is important because many of the roads represented on existing maps have been shifted, moved or eliminated, making "current" maps obsolete. Where needed, we've drawn legal public beach access in yellow, so you'll *know* when you're legally entitled to cross someone's land. Most guidebooks have the infuriating habit of mentioning a particular place or sight but then fail to mention how to get there! You won't find that in our book. We tell you exactly how to find the hidden gems and use our own special maps to guide you.

One of the things unique to this book is the acceptance of change. We produce brand new editions of our books every two years, but in the intervening time we are constantly incorporating changes into the text nearly every time we do a new printing. We also post these changes on our web site. This allows us to make some modifications throughout the life of each edition. We don't have the luxury of making every change that happens on a weekly basis, but it does give us more flexibility than if we only acknowledged changes every two years.

As you read this book, you will also notice that we are very candid in assessing businesses. Unlike some other guidebooks that send out questionnaires asking a business if they are any good (gee, they *all* say they're good), we've had personal contact with the businesses listed in this book. One of the dirty little secrets about guidebook writers is that they sometimes make cozy little deals for good reviews. Well, you won't find that here. We accept no payment for our reviews, we make no deals with businesses for saying nice things, and there are no advertisements in our book. What we've seen and experienced is what you get. If we gush over a certain company, it comes from personal experience. If we rail against a business, it is for the same reason. All businesses mentioned in this book are here by *our* choosing. None have had any input into what we say, and we have not received *a single cent* from any of them for their inclusion. (In fact, there are some that would probably pay to be left out, given our comments.) We always review businesses as anonymous visitors and only later as guidebook writers if we need more information. This ensures that we are treated the same as you. (Amazingly, most travel writers *announce* themselves.) What you get is our opinion on how they operate. Nothing more, nothing less.

Sometimes our candor gets us into trouble. More than once we've had our books pulled from shelves because our comments hit a little too close to home. That's OK, because we don't work for the people who *sell* the book, we work for the people who *read* the book.

This book is intended to bring you independence in exploring Maui. We don't want to waste any of your precious time by giving you bad advice or bad directions. We want you to experience the best that the island has to offer. Our objective in writing this book is to give you the tools and information necessary to have the greatest Hawaiian experience possible.

We hope we succeeded.

Andrew Doughty
Harriett Friedman

Kihei, Maui

Fire, pressure, and an endless supply of molten rock: Hawaiian islands begin life amid horrific violence. (This scene still occurs on the Big Island. All the other photos in the book were taken around Maui.)

How It Began

Sometime around 70 million years ago an event of unimaginable violence occurred in the Earth's mantle, deep below the ocean floor. A hot spot of liquid rock blasted through the Pacific plate like a giant cutting torch, forcing liquid rock to the surface off the coast of Russia, forming the Emperor Seamounts. As the tectonic plate moved slowly over the hot spot, this torch cut a long scar along the plate, piling up mountains of rock, producing island after island. The oldest of these islands to have survived is Kure. Once a massive island with its own unique ecosystem, only its ghost remains in the form of a fringing coral reef, called an atoll.

As soon as the islands were born, a conspiracy of elements proceeded to dismantle them. Ocean waves unmercifully battered the fragile and fractured rock.

Abundant rain, especially on the northeastern sides of the mountains, easily carved up the rock surface, seeking faults in the rock and forming rivers and streams. In forming these channels, the water carried away the rock and soil, robbing the islands of their very essence. Additionally, the weight of the islands ensured their doom. Lava flows on top of other lava, and the union of these flows is always weak. This lava also contains countless air pockets and is crisscrossed with hollow lava tubes, making it inherently unstable. As these massive amounts of rock accumulated, their bases were crushed under the weight of subsequent lava flows, causing their summits to sink back into the sea.

What we call the Hawaiian Islands are simply the latest creation from this island-making machine. Kaua'i and Ni'ihau are the oldest of the eight major islands.

After their long journey across the seas, the island's first life-forms found nothing but stark rock to greet them.

Lush and deeply eroded, the last of Kaua'i's fires died with its volcano a million years ago. O'ahu, Moloka'i, Lana'i, Kaho'olawe—their growing days are over, as well. Maui is in its twilight days as a growing island. After growing vigorously, Hawaiian volcanoes usually go to sleep for a million years or so before sputtering back to life for one last fling. Maui's volcano, Haleakala, awakened from its long sleep and is in its final eruptive stage. It *probably* last erupted around 1790 (see box on page 137 for an explanation) and will continue with sporadic eruptions for a (geologically) short time before drifting into eternal sleep.

The latest and newest star in this island chain is Hawai'i. Born less than a million years ago, this youngster is still vigorously growing. Though none of its five volcano mountains is considered truly dead, these days Mauna Loa and Kilauea are doing most of the work of making the Big Island bigger. Mauna Loa, the most massive mountain on Earth, consists of 10,000 *cubic miles* of rock. Quieter of the two active volcanoes, it last erupted in 1984. Kilauea is the most boisterous of the volcanoes and is the most active volcano on the planet. Kilauea's most recent eruption began in 1983 and was still going strong as we went to press. Up and coming onto the world stage is Lo'ihi. This new volcano is still 3,200 feet below the ocean's surface, 20 miles off the southeastern coast of the island. Yet in a geologic heartbeat, the Hawaiian islands will be richer with its ascension, sometime in the next 100,000 years.

These virgin islands were barren at birth. Consisting only of volcanic rock, the first life forms to appreciate these new islands were marine creatures. Fish, mammals and microscopic animals discovered this new underwater haven and made homes for themselves. Coral polyps attached themselves to the lava and succeeding generations built upon these, creating what would become coral reefs.

Meanwhile, on land, seeds carried by the winds were struggling to colonize the rocky land, eking out a living and breaking down the lava rock. Storms brought the occasional bird, hopelessly blown off course. The lucky ones found the islands. The even luckier ones arrived with mates or were pregnant when they got here. Other animals, stranded on a piece of floating debris, washed ashore against all odds and went on to colonize the islands. These introductions of new species were rare events. It took an extraordinary set of circumstances for a new species to actually make it to the islands. Single specimens were destined to live out their lives in lonely solitude. On average, a new species was successfully deposited here only once every 20,000 years.

As with people, islands have a life cycle. After their violent birth, islands grow to their maximum size, get carved up by the elements, collapse in parts, and finally sink back into the sea. Someday, all the Hawaiian islands will be nothing more than geologic footnotes in the Earth's turbulent history. When a volcanic island is old, it is a sandy sliver called an atoll, devoid of mountains, merely a shadow if its former glory. When it's middle aged, it can be a lush wonderland, a haven for anything green, like Kaua'i. And when it is young, it is dynamic and unpredictable, like the Big Island of Hawai'i, but lacking the scars of experience from its short battle with the elements. Maui is unique among the Hawaiian islands because it's in its prime—young enough to show the dynamism of its volcanic heritage, yet old enough for the elements to have carved lovely lines of character onto its face. The first people to occupy the island were blessed with riches beyond their wildest dreams.

Water and plants take turns converting lava to paradise.

The ancient Hawaiians went to great effort to create temples (heiaus) for their gods. The massive Pi'ilanihale Heiau hear Hana, reclaimed from the jungle, is a particularly grand example.

THE FIRST SETTLERS

Sometime around the fourth or fifth century A.D. a large double-hulled voyaging canoe, held together with flexible sennit lashings and propelled by sails made of woven pandanus, slid onto the sand on the Big Island of Hawai'i. These first intrepid adventurers, only a few dozen or so, encountered an island chain of unimaginable beauty.

They had left their home in the Marquesas Islands, 2,500 miles away, for reasons we will never know. Some say it was because of war, overpopulation, drought or just a sense of adventure. Whatever their reasons, these initial settlers took a big chance and surely must have been highly motivated. They left their homes and searched for a new world to colonize. Doubtless most of the first groups perished at sea. The Hawaiian Islands are the most isolated island chain in the world, and there was no way for them to know that there were islands in these waters. (Though some speculate that they were led here by the golden plover—see box on facing page.)

Those settlers who did arrive brought with them food staples from home: taro, breadfruit, pigs, dogs and several types of fowl. This was a pivotal decision. These first settlers found a land that contained almost no edible plants. With no land mammals other than the Hawaiian bat, the first settlers subsisted on fish until their crops matured. From then on, they lived on fish and taro. Although we associate throw-net fishing with Hawai'i, this practice was introduced by Japanese immigrants much later. The ancient Hawaiians used fishhooks and spears, for the most part, or drove fish into a net already placed in the water. They also had domesticated animals, which were used as ritual foods or reserved for chiefs.

Little is known about the initial culture.

Archeologists speculate that a second wave of colonists, probably from Tahiti, may have subdued these initial inhabitants around 1,000 A.D. Some may have resisted and fled into the forest, creating the legend of the Menehune.

Today Menehune are always thought of as being small in stature. Initially referring to their social stature, the legend evolved to mean that they were physically short and lived in the woods away from the Hawaiians. (The Hawaiians avoided the woods when possible, fearing that they held evil spirits, and instead stayed on the coastal plains.) The Menehune were purported to build fabulous structures, always in one night. Their numbers were said to be vast, as many as 500,000. It is interesting to note that in a census taken of Kaua'i around 1800, some 65 people from a remote valley identified themselves as Menehune.

The second wave probably swept over the island from the south, pushing the first inhabitants ever-north. On a tiny island north of Kaua'i archeologists have found carvings, clearly not Hawaiian, that closely resembling Marquesan carvings, probably left by the doomed exiles.

This second culture was far more aggressive and developed into a highly class-conscious culture. The society was governed by chiefs, called ali'i, who established a long list of taboos called kapu. These kapu were designed to keep order, and the penalty for breaking one was usually death by strangulation, club or fire. If the violation was serious enough, the guilty party's family might also be killed. It was kapu, for instance, for your shadow to fall across the shadow of the Ali'i. It was kapu to interrupt the chief if he was speaking. It was kapu to prepare men's food in the same container used for women's food. It was kapu for women to eat pork or bananas. It was kapu for men and women to eat together. It was kapu not to observe the days designated for the gods. Certain areas were kapu for fishing if they became depleted, allowing the area to

Hawai'i's First Tour Guide?

Given the remoteness of the Hawaiian Islands relative to the rest of Polynesia (or anywhere else for that matter), you'll be forgiven for wondering how the first settlers found these islands in the first place. Many scientists think it might have been this little guy here. Called the kolea, or golden plover, this tiny bird flies 2,500 miles nonstop to Alaska every year for the summer, returning to Hawai'i after mating. Some of these birds continue past Hawai'i and fly *another* 2,500 miles to Samoa and other South Pacific islands. The early Polynesians surely must have noticed this commute and concluded that there must be land in the direction that the bird was heading. They never would have dreamed that the birds leaving the South Pacific were heading to a land 5,000 miles away, and that Hawai'i was merely a stop in between, where the lazier birds wintered.

Kalolopahu—Olowalu's Day of Infamy

There were numerous incidents in the first 20 years of western contact of Hawaiians killing westerners for weapons, and westerners killing Hawaiians for revenge or to demonstrate superiority. But no skirmish between Hawaiians and westerners compares to the massacre of Kalolopahu.

A dozen years after Captain Cook was killed on the Big Island, a trading ship run by a vicious, contemptible captain named Simon Metcalf stopped at the Big Island to trade goods. His ship was followed by a small six-man sloop carrying the captain's son. A chief tried to climb on board Metcalf's ship, and a crewman smacked him with a rope to prevent it. The chief was humiliated and vowed to take revenge on the next foreign vessel that came by. It was a vow that would change the destiny of the islands.

Metcalf then went to Maui and began trading. One night, north of Lahaina, a Hawaiian sneaked over to the ship, cut loose the ship's cutter, killed the guard in the boat, then dragged the small boat to shore to break it up. (The Hawaiians didn't care about the boat; they wanted the iron.) When Metcalf found out what happened, he fired his cannons into the village in rage, then kidnapped some Hawaiians who told him that people from Olowalu did it (which was true). Metcalf then moved his ship to Olowalu.

At this time, a high chieftess had declared the bay around Olowalu off limits. She was celebrating a family function, and the penalty for a commoner going into the water was to be burned alive. (Naturally, none violated the kapu.) When she finally lifted the order three days later, commoners rushed in their canoes to begin trading with the foreign ship (Metcalf's). Metcalf told all the Hawaiians to line their canoes up on the side of the ship. When they were crowded around, Metcalf unleashed his revenge. He opened fire with all his cannons (loaded with small shot) and muskets. More than 100 innocent Hawaiians were slaughtered (but not the one who had stolen the boat; he wasn't even there). The screaming and wailing went on for hours, and the natives named the place, Kalolopahu, meaning *the place of spilt brains*.

But remember the man that Metcalf's crew had smacked with a rope? He got his revenge too, beyond his wildest dreams. He didn't know about the Olowalu massacre, but as fate would have it, that first foreign vessel he found was the one with Metcalf's son. The chief and some warriors went on board on the pretense of trade, then seized the sloop, killed young Metcalf and all but one of his crew, then stripped the boat of its weapons, including a cannon. And the one person from the sloop he let live, along with a man from the senior Metcalf's ship that King Kamehameha had captured earlier, soon became Kamehameha's trusted advisors. They helped Kamehameha defeat his island neighbors using the stolen cannon and guns, starting with the battle at 'Iao Valley described on page 65. Kamehameha eventually became king of all the islands.

As for Simon Metcalf, he was unable to find his son and eventually went back to the U.S. mainland. He had no idea that his presence had forever changed the politics of the islands.

replenish itself.

While harsh by our standards today, this system kept the order. Most Ali'i were sensitive to the disturbance their presence caused and often ventured outside only at night, or a scout was sent ahead to warn people that an Ali'i was on his way. All commoners were required to pay tribute to the Ali'i in the form of food and other items. Human sacrifices were common, and war among rival chiefs the norm.

By the 1700s, the Hawaiians had lost all contact with Tahiti, and the Tahitians had lost all memory of Hawai'i. Hawaiian canoes had evolved into fishing and inter-island canoes and were no longer capable of long ocean voyages.

OUTSIDE WORLD DISCOVERS HAWAI'I

In January 1778 an event occurred that would forever change Hawai'i. Captain James Cook, who usually had a genius for predicting where to find islands, stumbled upon Hawai'i. He had not expected the islands to be here. He was on his way to Alaska on his third great voyage of discovery, this time to search for the Northwest Passage linking the Atlantic and Pacific oceans. Cook approached the shores of Waimea, Kaua'i, at night on January 19, 1778.

The next morning Kaua'i's inhabitants awoke to a wondrous sight and thought they were being visited by gods. Rushing aboard to greet their visitors, the Kauaians were fascinated by what they saw: pointy-headed beings (the British wore tricornered hats) breathing fire (smoking pipes) and possessing a death-dealing instrument identified as a water squirter (guns). The amount of iron on the ship was incredible. (They had seen iron before in the form of nails on driftwood but never knew where it originated.)

Cook left Kaua'i and briefly explored Ni'ihau before heading north for his mission on February 2, 1778. When Cook returned to the islands in November after failing to find the Northwest Passage, he visited the Big Island of Hawai'i.

The Hawaiians had probably seen white men before. Local legend indicates that strange white people washed ashore on the Big Island sometime around the 1520s and integrated into society. This coincides with Spanish records of two ships lost in this part of the world in 1528. But a few weird-looking stragglers couldn't compare to the arrival of Cook's great ships and instruments.

Despite some recent rewriting of history, all evidence indicates that Cook, unlike some other exploring sea captains of his era, was a thoroughly decent man. Individuals need to be evaluated in the context of their time. Cook knew that his mere presence would have a profound impact on the cultures he encountered, but he also knew that change for these cultures was inevitable, with or without him. He tried, unsuccessfully, to keep the men known to be infected with venereal diseases from mixing with local women, and he frequently flogged infected men who tried to sneak ashore at night. He was greatly distressed when a party he sent to Ni'ihau was forced to stay overnight due to high surf, knowing that his men might transmit diseases to the women (which they did).

Cook arrived on the Big Island at a time of much upheaval. The mo'i, or king, of the Big Island had been militarily spanked during an earlier attempt to invade Maui and was now looting and raising hell throughout the islands as retribution. Cook's arrival and his physical appearance (at 6-feet-4 he couldn't even stand up straight in his own quarters) almost guaranteed that the Hawaiians would think he was the god Lono. Lono was responsible for land fertility. Every year the ruling chiefs and their war god Ku went into abeyance, removing their power so that Lono could return to the land and make it fertile again, bringing back the spring rains. During this time all public works stopped, and the land was left alone. At the end of this *makahiki,* man would again seize the land from Lono so he could grow crops and otherwise make a living upon it. Cook arrived at the beginning of the makahiki, and the Hawaiians naturally thought *he* was the god Lono coming to make the land fertile. Cook even sailed into the exact bay where the legend predicted Lono would arrive.

The Hawaiians went to great lengths to please their "god." All manner of supplies were made available. Eventually they became suspicious of the visitors. If they were gods, why did they accept the Hawaiian women? And if they were gods, why did one of them die?

Cook left at the right time. The British had used up the Hawaiians' hospitality (not to mention their supplies). But shortly after leaving the Big Island, the ship broke a mast, making it necessary to return to Kealakekua Bay for repairs. As they sailed back into the bay, the Hawaiians were nowhere to be seen. A chief had declared the area kapu to help replenish it. When Cook finally found the Hawaiians, they were polite but wary. Why are you back? Didn't we please you enough already? What do you want now?

As repair of the mast went along, things began to get tense. Eventually the Hawaiians stole a British rowboat (for the nails), and the normally calm Cook blew his cork. On the morning of February 14, 1779, he went ashore to trick the chief into coming aboard his ship where he would detain him until the rowboat was returned. As Cook and the chief were heading to the water, the chief's wife begged the chief not to go.

By now tens of thousands of Hawaiians were crowding around Cook, and he ordered a retreat. A shot was heard from the other side of the bay, and someone shouted that the Englishmen had killed an important chief. A shielded warrior with a dagger came at Cook, who fired his pistol (loaded with small shot). The shield stopped the small shot, and the Hawaiians were emboldened. Other shots were fired. Standing in knee-deep water, Cook turned to call for a cease-fire and was struck in the head

What rice is to Asians, taro is to Hawaiians—their most important food.

from behind with a club, then stabbed. Dozens of other Hawaiians pounced on him, stabbing his body repeatedly. The greatest explorer the world had ever known was dead at age 50 in a petty skirmish over a stolen rowboat.

KAMEHAMEHA THE GREAT

The most powerful and influential king in Hawaiian history lived during the time of Captain Cook and was born on the Big Island around 1758. Until his rule, the Hawaiian chain had never been ruled by a single person. He was the first to "unite" (i.e., conquer) all the islands.

Kamehameha was an extraordinary man by any standard. He possessed herculean strength, a brilliant mind and boundless ambition. He was marked for death before he was even born. When Kamehameha's mother was pregnant with him, she developed a strange and overpowering craving—she wanted to *eat* the eyeball of a chief. The king of the Big Island, mindful of the rumor that the unborn child's real father was his bitter enemy, the king of Maui, asked his advisors to interpret. Their conclusion was unanimous. The child would grow to be a rebel, a killer of chiefs. The king decided that the child must die as soon as he was born, but the baby was instead whisked away to a remote valley to be raised.

In Hawaiian society, your role in life was governed by what class you were born into. The Hawaiians believed that breeding among family members produced superior offspring (except for the genetic misfortunes who were killed at birth), and the highest chiefs came from brother/sister combinations. Kamehameha was not of the highest class (his parents were merely cousins), so his future as a chief would not come easily.

As a young man Kamehameha was impressed by his experience with Captain Cook. He was among the small group that stayed overnight on Cook's ship during Cook's first pass of Maui. (Kamehameha was on Maui valiantly fighting a battle in which his side was getting badly whopped.) Kamehameha recognized that his world had forever changed, and he shrewdly used the knowledge and technology of westerners to his own advantage.

Kamehameha participated in numerous battles. His side lost many of the early ones, but he learned from his mistakes and developed into a cunning tactician. When he finally consolidated his rule over the Big Island (by luring his enemy to be the inaugural sacrifice of a new temple), he fixed his sights on the entire chain. In the 1790s his large company of troops, armed with some western armaments and advisers, swept across Maui, Moloka'i, Lana'i and O'ahu. After some delays with the last of the holdouts, Kaua'i, their king finally acquiesced to the inevitable and Kamehameha became the first ruler of all the islands. He spent his final years governing the islands peacefully from his Big Island capital and died in 1819.

MODERN HAWAI'I

During the 19th century, Hawai'i's character changed dramatically. Businessmen from all over the world came here to exploit Hawai'i's sandalwood, whales, land and people. Hawai'i's leaders, for their part, actively participated in these ventures and took a piece of much of the action for themselves. Workers were brought from many parts of the world, changing the racial makeup of the islands. Government corruption became the order of the day, and everyone seemed to be profiting, except the Hawaiian commoner. By the time Queen Lili'uokalani lost her throne to a group of American businessmen in 1893, Hawai'i had become directionless. It barely resembled the Hawai'i Captain Cook had encountered the previous century. The kapu system had been abolished by the Hawaiians shortly after the death of Kamehameha the Great. The "Great Mahele," begun in 1848, had changed the relationship Hawaiians had with the land. Large tracts of land were sold by the Hawaiian government to royalty, government officials, commoners and foreigners, effectively stripping many Hawaiians of land they had lived on for generations.

The United States recognized the Republic of Hawai'i in 1894 with Sanford Dole as its president. It was annexed in 1898 and became an official territory in 1900. During the 19th and 20th centuries, sugar established itself as king. Pineapple was also heavily grown in the islands, with the island of Lana'i being purchased in its entirety for the purpose of growing pineapples.

As the 20th century rolled on, Hawaiian sugar and pineapple workers found themselves in a lofty position— they became the highest paid workers for these crops in the world. As land prices rose and competition from other parts of the world increased, sugar and pineapple became less and less profitable. Today, these crops no longer hold the position they once had. The "pineapple island" of Lana'i has shifted away from pineapple growing and is looking toward tourism. The sugar industry is now dead on the Big Island, leaving only Maui and Kaua'i to grow it commercially.

The story of Hawai'i is not a story of good versus evil. Nearly everyone shares in the blame of what happened to the Hawaiian people and their culture. Westerners certainly saw Hawai'i as a potential bonanza and easily exploitable. They knew what buttons to push and pushed them well. But the Hawaiians, for their part, were in a state of flux. The mere existence of westerners seemed to bring to the surface a discontent, or at least a weakness, with their system that had been lingering just below the surface.

In fact, in 1794, a mere 16 years after first encountering westerners and under no military duress from the West, Kamehameha the Great volunteered to cede his island over to Great Britain. He was hungry for western arms so he could defeat his neighbor island opponents. He even declared that as of that day, they were no longer people of Hawai'i, but rather people of Britain. (Britain declined the offer.) And in 1819, immediately after the death of the strong-willed Kamehameha, the Hawaiians, on their own accord, overthrew their own religion, dumped the kapu system and denied their gods. This was before any western missionaries ever came to Hawai'i.

Nonetheless, Hawai'i today is once again seeking guidance from her heritage. The echoes of the past seem to be getting louder with time, rather than diminishing. Interest in the Hawaiian language and culture is at a level not seen in many decades. All of us who live here are very aware of the issues and the complexities involved, but there is little agreement about where it will lead. As a result, you will be exposed to a more "Hawaiian" Hawai'i than those who might have visited the state a decade ago. This is an interesting time in Hawai'i. Enjoy it as observers, and savor the flavor of the islands.

If you fly directly into West Maui, you'll miss the spectacular shoreline highway.

GETTING HERE

In order to get to Hawai'i, you've got to fly here. While this may sound painfully obvious, many people spend time trying to find an ocean cruise to the Islands. With the advent of jets, the long span of open ocean makes regular cruises here infeasible.

When planning your trip, a travel agent can be helpful. Their commission has been paid directly by the travel industry, though that is likely to change in the near future. The Internet is quickly becoming a great source for companies selling travel packages. If you don't want to or can't go through these sources, there are several large wholesalers that can get you airfare, hotel and a rental car, often cheaper than you can get airfare on your own. Pleasant Hawaiian Holidays (800) 242–9244, Suntrips (800) 786–8747, and Creative Leisure (800) 426–6367 are reputable providers of complete package tours. The first two are renowned for their impossibly low rates. We've always been amazed that you can sometimes get round trip airfare from the mainland, a hotel and car for a week for as low as $700 per person, depending on where you fly from and where you stay. That's a small price to pay for your little piece of paradise. Cheap Tickets (800) 377–1000 usually lives up to its name.

If you arrange airline tickets and hotel reservations yourself, you can often count on paying top dollar for each facet of your trip. The prices listed in the WHERE TO STAY section reflect the RACK rates, meaning the price you and I pay if we book direct. Rates can be significantly lower if you go through a tour company.

When you pick your travel source, shop around—the differences can be dramatic. A good package can make the difference between affording a *one-week* vacation and *two-week* vacation. Also,

look in the Sunday travel section of your local newspaper—the bigger the paper, the better.

Flight schedules change all the time, but United, Hawaiian and other airlines often have *direct* flights to Kahului from the west coast. Not having to cool your heels while changing planes on Oʻahu is a *big* plus. Otherwise, inter-island flights are like buses; you can always take the next one, and you can sit anywhere you want. Flight attendants zip up and down the aisles hurling juice at you for the short, inter-island flight. If you fly to Maui from Honolulu, the best views are *usually* on the left side (seats with an "A") coming in, and also the left side departing (for most routes). When flying to Oʻahu from the mainland, sit on the left side coming in, the right going home. Inter-island flights are done by **Aloha** (800 367–5250) and **Hawaiian** (800 367–5320). Many of the airlines are getting picky about what they allow as carry-on. Hawaiian, for example will often confiscate your reasonably sized carry-on, especially if it has wheels, no matter how small. (Unless you're in first class, of course. In that case, feel free to bring along your bed from home.)

If you're staying in West Maui, it's tempting to look at a map and decide to fly into **Kapalua West Maui Airport** for the sake of convenience. Though it *is* nearby, we still recommend flying into Kahului. That's because the drive around the coastline into Lahaina during the day is dramatic and worth the extra time. It's during your drive along the coastline to either west or south Maui that you realize that this island, more than any other Hawaiian island, has an extremely intimate relationship with the water. No other Hawaiian island has highways that embrace the ocean so much.

If you're staying in Hana, **Pacific Wings** (888) 575–4546 has pricey flights to Hana Airport from Honolulu and Kahului. **Aloha Island Air** (800) 323–3345 was considering reinstating service there at press time.

WHAT TO BRING

This list may assist you in planning what to bring. Obviously you won't bring everything on the list, but it might make you think of a few things you may otherwise overlook.

• Waterproof sunblock (SPF 15 or higher)
• Two bathing suits
• Shoes—thongs, trashable sneakers, reef shoes, hiking shoes
• Mask, snorkel and fins
• Camera with lots of film
• Warm clothes (for Haleakala trips) and junk clothes for bikes, etc.
• Light rain jacket
• Small flashlight for Haleakala sunrise
• Mosquito repellent for some hikes. (*Lotions*—not liquids—with DEET seem to work the longest.)
• Large insulated water jug; keep in car
• Shorts and other cool cotton clothing
• Fanny pack—also called waist pack, to carry all your various vacation accouterments; waterproof ones are convenient for snorkeling
• Cheap, simple backpack—you don't need to go backpacking to use one; a 10-minute trek down to a secluded beach is much easier if you bring a simple pack
• Hat or cap for sun protection

GETTING AROUND
Rental Cars

The rental car prices in Hawaiʻi are cheaper than almost anywhere else in the country, and the competition is ferocious. Nearly every visitor to Maui gets around in a rental car, and for good reason. Many of the island's best sights can only be reached if you have independent transportation.

At Kahului Airport, rental cars can be obtained from the booths to the right (as you look out) of baggage claim. It's good idea to reserve your car in advance since companies can run out of cars during peak times. Cars are also available at the Kapalua and Hana airports.

Many hotels, condos and rental agents offer excellent room/car packages. Find out from your hotel or travel agent if one is available.

If you're wondering why you can't get any radio stations, it's usually because the rental car companies push the antenna down to wash it. So when you get *da car*, pull *da buggah* out!

Here's a list of rental car companies. The local area code is 808. Some have desks at various hotels.

THE BIG GUYS
Alamo (800) 327–9633
871–6235 in Kahului

Avis (800) 321–3712
871–7575 in Kahului
874–4077 in Kihei
661–4588 in Ka'anapali

Budget (800) 527–0700
(877) 283–2468 Locally

Dollar (800) 800–4000
877–2731 in Kahului
248–8237 in Hana

Enterprise (800) 736–8222
871–1511 in Kahului
661–8804 in Ka'anapali

Hertz (800) 654–3011
877–5167 in Kahului
661–7735 in Ka'anapali

National (800) 227–7368
871–8851 in Kahului
667–9737 in Ka'anapali

Thrifty (800) 367–5238
871–2860 in Kahului

An abundance of glorious beaches, like this one at Ka'anapali, is one reason Maui is the most popular neighbor island.

THE LITTLE GUYS
Kihei (800) 251–5288
879–7257 in Kihei

Regency (877) 280–5337
871–6147 in Kahului

Word of Mouth (800) 533–5929,
877–2436 in Kahului

4-Wheel Drive JEEPs

On Kaua'i and especially the Big Island we've strongly recommended getting a 4WD vehicle, but it isn't as important on Maui. There aren't as many off-road opportunities, and there are few places where access will require one. The drive past Hana doesn't require one, despite what you may read elsewhere. A few places in remote parts of West Maui will allow 4WDs to get *slightly* closer, and the road to Blue Pool makes it kind of nice, but it's hard to justify the increased price here. If you want to splurge, spring for a convertible instead. They can be fun, especially on the Hana drive.

Motorcycles & Scooters

If you think riding a HOG is something you do at a lu'au, you may want to skip past this section. There's something about Harleys. Maybe it's the sound, or maybe the looks. But riding a Harley-Davidson around Maui is a blast. If you want to rent one to experience things on your own (freedom, after all, is what HOGs are all about), you can get them from **Aloha Toy Store** (662–0888) and **Hawaiian Riders** (662–4386) in Lahaina, **Mavrik's** (891–2299) and **Island Riders** (874–0311) in Kihei. Check out the bike first. We've seen some pretty bald tires and snotty attitudes at some, like Island Riders. Expect to pay *(gulp!)* $125 for 24 hours, about $100 for 5 hours. You can get lesser bikes, like Kawasakis, for around $90 for the day.

If you want a small guided tour, **Quality Motorcycle Tours** (242–1015) uses various bikes (no Harleys) for all day trips. It's $199; add $100 for a back seat. They

In East Maui, even the plants have plants.

also do multi-day camping tours and are *very* flexible. They'll even tour with just one person.

If you want to rent a scooter, try Aloha Toy Store (662–0888) in Lahaina, and Hawaiian Island Crusers (879–0956) in Kihei. They start at around $40 and you need a driver's license.

Exotic Cars

Maui has lots of opportunities to rent a flashy ride. Ferraris, Vipers, 'Vettes, Porsches and other sexy autos can be had—for the right price. You're looking at around $300 for a 'Vette, $450 for a Ferrari. That's *per day!* Half-day rates are available on some. Bear in mind that there are no opportunities to open them up—we have no wide open highway straightaways—but if you just want to experience the thrill of driving a fantasy car and you have a wad burning a hole in your pocket, give it a shot.

Island Riders (874–0311 in Kihei, 661–9966 in Lahaina) has a number of heart-pounding cars. Aloha Toy Store (662–0888) in Lahaina lives up to its name. Lots of grown up car toys to rent. Mavrik's Hot Rods & Harleys (891–2299 in Kihei, 661–3099 in Lahaina) also has a few trick cars.

A few driving tips...

Seat belt use is required by law, and the police will pull you over for this alone. Open roads and frequently changing speed limits make it easy to accidentally speed here. Sobriety checkpoints are not an uncommon police tactic here.

It's best not to leave anything valuable in your car. There are teenagers here who pass the time by breaking into cars. It's not a *huge* problem, but it does happen. Thieving scum used to regularly hit Honolua Bay, but that has quieted recently. When we park at a beach, waterfall or any other place frequented by visitors, we take all valuables with us, leave the windows up, and leave the doors unlocked. (Just in case someone is curious enough about the inside to smash a window.) There are plenty of stories about someone walking 100 feet to a waterfall, coming back to their car, and finding that their brand new video camera has walked away. And don't be gullible enough to think that trunks are safe. Someone who sees you put something in your trunk can probably get at it faster than you can with your key.

If you are between the ages of 21 and 25, Alamo, Dollar, Kihei and Regency are your best bets. You'll pay about $15–$20 extra for the crime of being young and reckless, but at least you won't have to take the bus. If you're under 21—rent a bicycle or scooter, or take the bus.

Buses

Maui doesn't have a typical public bus system. There's a private bus called the Shopping Express Trolley (877–7308). You can go all the way from Makena in South Maui to Kapalua in West Maui. Call for schedules. Fares aren't too bad.

Guided bus tours include 'Ekahi Tours (877–9775), Roberts Hawai'i (871–6226), Temptation Tours (877–8888), and Polynesian (877–4242)

GETTING MARRIED ON MAUI

Maui is a wildly popular place to get married. Every romantic setting from a beach at sunset, a tropical garden, or a waterfall is here for you to use as a background for your important day.

Finding a good person or company to help you isn't easy and in this particular section, we can't review the companies the way we normally would. (After all, it's not exactly practical to get married 25 times and rate the performance of a company.) That said, we *can* say that one particularly reputable source for your wedding planning is Island Weddings at (888) 824-4134 or (808) 250-4134.

Other full service wedding coordinators that are available to contact for their wedding packages are listed below. Discuss your arrangements in detail with the coordinator to avoid misunderstandings over what your ceremony will be like and what it will cost.

A Dream Wedding Maui Style
(800) 743-2777 or (808) 661-1777
A Romantic Maui Wedding
(800) 808-4144 or (808) 874-6444
A Paradise Dream Wedding
(888) 286-5979 or (808) 875-9503
Heavenly Hana Weddings
(800) 349-8887 or (808) 248-8267

Almost all the large resorts on Maui have wedding coordinators to help you arrange your wedding at their hotel. Be aware that site fees can be pretty high. Some of the more popular resorts for weddings are the **Maui Prince,** the **Grand Wailea,** the **Renaissance,** the **Hyatt,** the **Westin,** the **Embassy Vacation Resort,** and the **Ritz-Carlton.**

Obtaining a License

You can contact the State Department of Health (808) 984-8210 on Maui to obtain an application or to obtain the names of the agents on Maui. Both the bride and groom must be 18. There is no residency or blood test requirements. The fee is $50 in cash. Both the bride and groom must be present with a photo ID at the time of the appointment with the marriage license agent. The license is good for 30 days.

WEATHER

How's the weather on Maui? A picture speaks a thousand words. The photo on the cover is very typical of the cloud and rain coverage on Maui and, with a practiced eye, tells you exactly what to expect around the island. You can see how the windward areas (meaning areas exposed to the trade winds out of the northeast) get most of the clouds and how Hana is dry, but farther uphill it's cloudy, feeding the waterfalls. Kihei and Lahaina (called *leeward* areas) are warmer, drier and sunnier than the rest of the island because they are shielded from the northeast trade winds. Notice how the clouds don't go all the way to the top of Haleakala except where they are squeezed into the Ko'olau Gap; it's because of a temperature inversion around the 6,000 foot level. (The air actually gets warmer above that for a few thousand feet, causing the temperature-sensitive clouds to dissipate.) The top of West Maui Mountain is cloudy, as usual. And you can see how the northeast trade winds build up along the bottom of Haleakala, heading southwest along the flank, and are directed off into the sea near La Pérouse Bay, leaving Kihei and Wailea calmer. You can see that because the line of demarcation between calm and choppy water makes the transition almost instant and the line heads all the way to the island of Kaho'olawe and beyond. This photo is quintessential Maui trade wind weather until about 1 p.m. Then more clouds will build as the island heats up, causing the air to rise, cool and condense into clouds. The summit of Haleakala may cloud up. Wind will increase all around the island as ocean air rushes in to replace the rising air.

To get **current weather forecasts,** call 871–5054. Call 877–3611 for a **surf forecast.**

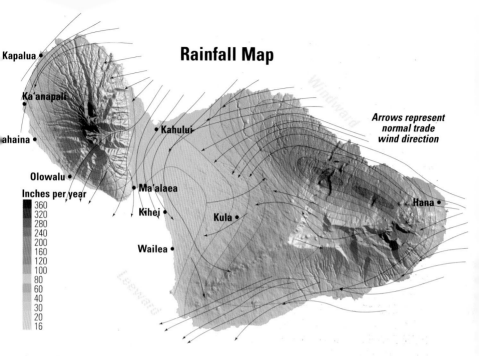

Rainfall Map

Arrows represent normal trade wind direction

Kapalua •

Ka'anapali •

ahaina •

Olowalu •

Inches per year

360
320
280
240
200
160
120
100
80
60
40
30
20
16

• Kahului

• Ma'alaea

Kihei •

Wailea •

Kula •

• Hana

The Different Weather Regions

What does all this mean? It means the weather is radically different around the island. Many times we've been at the airport in Kahului and seen people coming off the plane looking gloomy and worried. "It's so windy and rainy here," they often say. Sometimes we wish the county would erect a sign at the airport saying, *"Don't worry, da weather mo betta in Kihei and Lahaina."*

In the leeward area of **South Maui**, **Kihei** and **Wailea** will be warmer and drier. Winds that have just been squished between the two mountains will travel south along the Kihei coast veering slightly offshore, so winds will be lighter the farther down the Kihei coast you go until you get to La Pérouse Bay. There the wind from the bottom of the island can commence over the span of about 100 feet. That means mornings are usually calm from Makena to south Kihei. In the afternoon, however, onshore breezes

will form to fill the void from the heated rising air, and the trade winds that have been absent along the coast at Makena and Wailea will start wrapping around the island parallel to the coast here. This means strong afternoon winds. Winters are less windy. The sunnier and hotter it is, the stronger the afternoon winds will be. If there's heavy cloud cover over much of Haleakala, the afternoon winds will diminish. (I'm trying to avoid sounding like a weather geek, but if you understand the weather processes here, it helps you to plan your day.) High temperatures will average 80 in the winter, 86 in the summer. Nights can be cooler than Lahaina because the air that has built up atop Haleakala during the day will tumble down to the bottom. If your condo has a skylight, you may notice puffs of cool air coming down at night.

Rainfall in leeward areas is small and variable. For instance, in a recent year there were only seven days with rain in

Kihei. It was going to total 4¾ inches for the year until the last day of the year brought *another* 4¾ inches, doubling the year's rainfall tally. Other years have seen 20 or more inches of rain.

In Lahaina, Ka'anapali and Kapalua, the exact direction of the trade wind is crucial. Lahaina is usually protected from the trades. There are fewer afternoon breezes in Lahaina than Kihei, making it warmer. High temperatures are 82° in January, 88° in August and September. As you head toward Ka'anapali, at some point the trade winds that you've been protected from in Lahaina will complete their wrap around from the other side, making wind a semi-constant companion. That's good if you like cool breezes, bad if you are trying to get a golf ball from Point A to Point B. It also means that the ocean is more susceptible to whitecaps and poor visibility north of Lahaina. Kapalua, farther north, is even windier and more drizzly and has the worst weather of any of the resort areas.

Just south of Lahaina, Olowalu would normally be protected from the trade winds except for one slight detail. Its large, rain-cut valley leading to the center of West Maui Mountain connects with rain-cut 'Iao Valley on the windward side, cracking the mountain in two and making a natural diversion ditch for the wind to rip through, leaving Olowalu windy.

Kahului gets a concentration of winds deflected along the northern part of Haleakala that slither around the island here and are squeezed between the two mountains. So it's *almost always* windy in Kahului. This has made Kahului one of the greatest places on the planet for windsurfing. Big time windsurfers from all over the world make pilgrimages here.

Ma'alaea, at the south end of the valley gets a concentration of wind and dust that have been squeezed between the mountains, making it one of the windiest places on the island.

Hana is sunnier than most people think since the clouds usually form farther uphill, but it is more vulnerable to whatever the trade winds bring to the island. Most of the time Hana has beautiful weather, but sometimes systems can bring rain that can last for days, especially in the winter. The temperature is incredibly equitable. Average high in February is 78°, and the average high in September is only 84°. How's *that* for a change of season?

The summit of Haleakala has an average high of around 50° and low of 32° in February, and reaches a scorching 58° and a low of 38° in August. It's *usually* not as windy *after sunrise*, but any wind on a cold morning can cut right through you.

Upcountry areas such as Kula and Pukalani are cooler due to their elevation and less windy.

Average humidity around the island ranges from 65%–75%.

In general, windward areas like Hana and Kahului get most of their rain at night and in the early morning. Leeward areas like Kihei and Lahaina get their more sporadic rain in the late afternoon and early evening.

Ocean temperatures average 75° in February, 80° in September.

GEOGRAPHY

The island of Maui is made up of two large volcanoes called...Well, that's a little confusing. The largest mountain, on the east side, is commonly referred to as Haleakala, meaning *house of the sun.* To the ancient Hawaiians, Haleakala referred only to the summit of the mountain, not the whole mountain. In fact, as far as we know they had no name for either of the two large mountains that make up Maui. But the word Haleakala has been used so often in recent years to describe the entire mountain that it's now generally accepted. The other great mountain is topped by a small peak called Pu'u Kukui, or *hill of the candlenut tree.* A bit duller, huh? That name has never been used to describe the entire mountain so it's commonly referred to by its less-than-exotic name, West Maui Mountain. Even scholarly geology books refer to them as Haleakala and West Maui Mountain. (Some old maps label West Maui Mountain as Mauna Kahalawai, but that name was never accepted by Hawaiian linguists. We've also heard tour guides, such as boat captains, refer to West Maui as Halemahina, or *house of the moon.* Sounds so symmetric next to the house of the sun, but it's bogus.)

West Maui is the oldest of the two. Streams have cut deeply into its slopes and the results are lovely. Though you'd expect more erosion on the wet side, an accident of geology capped the wet side with more erosion-resistant lava, so big valleys aren't as prevalent as they normally would be.

Haleakala is the younger, still-active mountain. It's just over 10,000 feet high, but it wasn't always so. At one time it rose to 15,000 feet, making it the tallest mountain in the world at over 32,000 feet high (when measured from its base at the bottom of the ocean). But Haleakala is crushing itself under its own weight. Someday it will sink back into the sea. (But probably not before your trip here.) Its smoother slopes and

10,000 foot height hide an enormous volume of rock. The Hana side is a lush wonderland whose beauty is legendary. Kihei is in the dry rain shadow of the mountain, so there are few streams or eroded areas. The summit features the awesome Haleakala Crater. (Actually an erosional crater; see page 124.)

At one time, all the islands surrounding Maui formed one big island, which geologists called Maui Nui. (Meaning *Big Maui*—darned clever, those geologists.) As the volcanoes sank and the seas rose, Moloka'i, Lana'i and a now vanished island called Penguin Bank formed one island about 400,000 years ago, while Kaho'olawe and Maui formed another. Continued sinking separated the islands to today's configuration. They continue to sink, and in about 15,000 years Maui will be two separate islands. We live in an era when Maui is perfectly arranged to easily explore the two sides. Enjoy our fortunate timing.

WHERE SHOULD I STAY?

The vast majority of visitors to Maui stay on the leeward side of the island—Lahaina to the Kapalua area in the west, or Kihei–Wailea in the south. This is the exact opposite of how things were 50 years ago. Back then all the major towns were on the windward side, where rain was abundant and crops grew vigorously. Few lived on the leeward side because it was harder to grow things there. (Lahaina has been around longer than most Hawaiian leeward towns because it was a good whaling port.) But the rain that makes everything so beautiful and lush also makes short-time visitors leery. So with the advent of jets and mass travel, the heretofore sparsely populated

Maui is the only place we've ever seen where you can get waterfall fatigue. There are so many beautiful ones, like Wailua Falls here, that you start to take them for granted.

leeward sides of the islands became a magnet for travelers. Sure, the rain on the windward side makes things green, but it also means the ocean will have more runoff, the surf will be higher, and clouds will obscure the sun. On the leeward side you don't have the tropical lushness you may associate with Hawai'i, but you usually have clear weather, calm oceans, sparkling water and lots of sunshine. (And, after all, you can always *drive* to the lush areas.)

It's hard to decide *which* leeward side of the island to stay on, West or South. West Maui has more activities because it has a working harbor, and it doesn't get as windy off Lahaina in the afternoon as it does off South Maui. (Though they get plenty of wind north of Lahaina.) Activities such as submarine rides, jet skis and dinner cruises are common there, but helicopter flights are more convenient from South Maui. West Maui is more

remote, making drives to Hana, Haleakala or Kahului much longer, and the traffic can be much worse in the west. Parking in Lahaina is a mess. Also, it's hotter in Lahaina than Kihei or Wailea, though northwest Maui, like Ka'anapali and Kapalua, gets lots of cooling wind. West Maui (Lahaina) has more nightlife. South Maui has better access to Molokini, and South Maui reefs are better. West Maui has easier access to Lana'i and Moloka'i. Beaches are less crowded in South Maui, and its beach accesses don't fill up as often. Shopping is better in West Maui. West Maui's backdrop is more scenic, but it is also more densely developed. Food is better and more varied in West Maui, but South Maui has some of the most kickin' resorts. Golf is better in South Maui, and so is the diving and snorkeling. If you're traveling with kids, West Maui is more popular with families, though South Maui has two parks that are very kid-friendly. West Maui has more cheap condos, but gas and grocery prices seem higher in West Maui. Both sides are hugely popular, but West Maui has a busier and more crowded feel.

So which is better? After living here and spending countless hours exploring and experiencing both sides, in our professional opinion, we'd have to say...we don't know. Each has advantages and disadvantages that sway us back and forth. Consider the pros and cons listed above and maybe the answer will become obvious to you.

Is Maui too Expensive?

Maui has a reputation of being pricey. That's because...well, it *is* pricey. The truth is restaurants cost more here than the other islands and so do grocery stores. Anyone who says otherwise hasn't lived on the different islands. Also, many of the activities available involve giving a company money to show you something, such as boat trips, SCUBA, aerial tours, lu'aus and more. So spending time on Maui is synonymous with spending money. Some activities, like helicopters, cost more here than on other Hawaiian islands, while others, like SCUBA diving, cost less.

This doesn't mean that Maui has to put you in hock for the next decade. There are *lots* of things to do that don't involve spending a fortune, and there are some tremendous values in restaurants—if you know where to look. Some of our favorite restaurants are some of the cheapest, and we point them out in DINING. The ACTIVITIES and ADVENTURES sections have some delightful things that won't cost you a cent. Also, if you have a Costco membership or want to sign up for one, the Costco in Kahului near the airport is where most of us here buy lots of our groceries and other items. If you're here a week or more, a Costco run can save you a bundle.

That said, count on spending some dollars on this trip. Some of the paid activities are definitely worth the splurge. Others are a rip-off, and we'll try to point them out.

HAZARDS
The Sun

The hazard that affects by far the most people (excluding the accommodations tax) is the sun. Maui, at 20° latitude, receives sunlight more directly than anywhere on the mainland. (The more overhead the sunlight is, the less atmosphere it filters through.) If you want to enjoy your *entire* vacation, make sure that you wear a strong sunblock. We recommend a waterproof sunblock with at least an SPF of 15. We use lotions when hiking, and the gel types like Bullfrog when going in the water (because they stay on better.) Many visitors who get burned, do so while snorkeling. You won't feel it coming because of the water. We *strongly* suggest you wear a T-shirt while snorkeling, or you may get a nasty surprise.

Try to avoid the sun between 11 a.m. and 2 p.m. when the sun's rays are particularly strong. If you are fair-skinned or unaccustomed to the sun and want to soak up some rays, 15-20 minutes per side is all you should consider the first day. You can increase it a bit each day. *Beware of the fact that our breezes will hide the symptoms of a burn until it's too late.* You might find that trying to get your tan as golden as possible isn't worth it. Tropical suntans are notoriously short-lived, whereas you are sure to remember a bad burn far longer. If, after all our warnings, you *still* get burned, aloe vera gel works well to relieve the pain. Some come with lidocaine in them. Ask your hotel front desk if they have any aloe plants on the grounds. Peel the skin off a section and make several crisscross cuts in the meat, then rub the plant on your skin. *Oooo,* it'll feel so good!

Water Hazards

The most serious water hazard is the surf. Though more calm in the summer and on the leeward side, high surf can be found anywhere on the island at any time of the year. The sad fact is that more people drown in Hawai'i each year than anywhere else in the country. This isn't said to keep you from enjoying the ocean, but rather to instill in you a healthy respect for Hawaiian waters. See BEACHES for more information on this.

Ocean Critters

Hawaiian marine life, for the most part, is quite friendly. There are, however, a few notable exceptions. Below is a list of some critters that you should be aware of. This is not mentioned to frighten you out of the water. The odds are overwhelming that you won't have any trouble with any of the beasties listed below. But should you encounter one, this information should be of some help.

SHARKS—Hawai'i does have sharks. Most are the essentially harmless white-tipped reef sharks, plus the occasional hammerhead or tiger shark. Contrary to what most people think, sharks are in every ocean and don't pose the level of danger people attribute to them. In the past 25 years there have been only a handful of documented shark attacks off Maui, mostly tigers attacking surfers. Considering the number of people who swam in our waters during that time, you are statistically more likely to get mauled by a hun-

gry timeshare salesman than be bitten by a shark. If you do happen to come upon a shark, however, swim away slowly. This kind of movement doesn't interest them. *Don't* splash about rapidly. By doing this you are imitating a fish in distress, and you don't want to do that. The one kind of water you want to avoid is murky water, such as that found in river mouths. Most shark attacks occur in murky water at dawn or dusk since sharks are basically cowards who like to sneak up on their prey. In general, don't go around worrying about sharks. *Any* animal can be threatening. (Even President Carter was once attacked by a wild rabbit.)

In 1999 there was a famous case where a man vacationing in Maui claimed that a shark attacked and killed his wife after they were blown to another island and slipped into the water while kayaking. It made national news. What wasn't reported nationwide was that the story had huge holes in it, according to local newspaper reports, and police were never able to confirm the man's claim, leaving the case open as a "missing person." (Make of that what you will.)

PORTUGUESE MAN-OF-WAR—These creatures are related to jellyfish but are unable to swim. They are instead propelled by a small sail and are at the mercy of the wind. Though small, they are capable of inflicting a painful sting. This occurs when the long trailing appendages are touched, triggering the spring-loaded stinger, called a nematocyst, which injects poison. The resulting burning sensation is usually very unpleasant but not fatal. Fortunately, the Portuguese Man-of-War is not a common visitor to Maui. When they *do* come ashore, however, they usually do so in great numbers, jostled by a strong storm offshore, and usually land on north facing beaches. If you see them on the beach, don't go in the water. If you do get stung, immediately remove the stinger

and as much of the venom as possible with a cloth or sand. Be careful not to stimulate any inactivated nematocyst on your skin or you'll be stung some more. Remove them carefully or use white vinegar to destroy them. Then apply baking soda, diluted ammonia or alcohol and see a physician. The folk cure is urine, but you might look pretty silly applying it.

SEA URCHINS—These are like living pin cushions. They also eat coral, so we don't like them. If you step on one, or accidentally grab one, remove as much of the spine as possible with tweezers. See a physician if necessary.

CORAL—Coral is very sharp, and since it is made up of millions of individual living organisms, a scrape can leave proteinaceous matter in the wound, causing infection. This is why coral cuts are frustratingly slow to heal. Immediate cleaning and disinfecting of coral cuts should speed up healing time. We don't have fire coral.

SEA ANEMONES—Related to jellyfish, these also have stingers and are usually found attached to rocks or coral. It's best not to touch them with your bare hands.

Treatment for a sting is similar to that of a Portuguese Man-of-War.

Bugs

Though devoid of the myriad of hideous buggies found in other parts of the world, there are a few evil critters brought here from elsewhere that you should know about. The worst are **centipedes**. They can get to be six or more inches long and are aggressive predators. They shouldn't be messed with. You'll probably never see one, but if you get stung, even by a baby, the pain can range from a bad bee sting to a bad gunshot blast. Some local doctors say the only cure is to stay drunk for three days. Others say to use meat tenderizer.

Cane spiders are big, dark, and look horrifying, but they're not poisonous. (But they seem to *think* they are. I've had *them* chase *me* across the room when *I* had the broom in my hand.) We *don't* have no-see-ums, those irritating sand fleas common in the South Pacific and Caribbean.

Those annoying **midges** in South Maui are explained on page 131.

Mosquitoes were unknown in the islands until the first stowaways arrived on Maui on the *Wellington* in 1826. Since then they have thrived. A good mosquito repellent containing DEET will come in handy, especially if you plan to go hiking. *Lotions* (not thin liquids) with DEET seem to work and stick best. Forget the guidebooks that tell you to take vitamin B12 to keep mosquitoes away; it just gives the little critters a healthier diet. If you find one dive bombing you at night in your room, turn on your overhead fan to help keep them away. Local residents and resorts often rely on genetically engineered plants such as Citrosa, which irritate mosquitoes as much as they irritate us.

Bees and wasps are more common on the drier leeward sides of the island and in Haleakala Crater. Usually, the only way you'll get stung is if you run into one. If you rent a scooter, beware; one of us received his first bee sting while singing *Come Sail Away* on a motorcycle. A bee sting in the mouth can definitely ruin one of your precious vacation days.

Regarding cockroaches, there's good news and bad news. The bad news is that here, some are bigger than your thumb and can fly. The good news is

that you probably won't see one. One of their predators is the gecko. This small, lizard-like creature makes a surprisingly loud chirp at night. They are cute and considered good luck in the Islands (probably because they eat mosquitoes and roaches).

There are no snakes in Hawai'i (other than some reporters). There is concern that the brown tree snake *might* have made its way onto the islands from Guam. Although mostly harmless to humans, these snakes can spell extinc-

tion to native birds. Government officials aren't allowed to tell you this, but we will: If you ever see one anywhere in Hawai'i, please *kill it* and contact the Pest Hotline at (800) 468–4644, ext. 67378. At the very least, call them immediately. The entire bird population of Hawai'i will be grateful.

Swimming In Streams
Maui offers lots of opportunities to swim in streams and under waterfalls. It's a fulfillment of a fantasy for many people. But there are several hazards you need to know about.

Leptospirosis is a bacteria that is found is some of Hawai'i's freshwater. It is transmitted from animal urine and can enter the body from open cuts, eyes and by drinking. Around 100 people a year in Hawai'i are diagnosed with the bacteria, which is treat-

When the sugar's ready for harvest they don't exactly nuke it, but they do set it on fire. The smoke and dust wafting from sugar operations helps keep Maui cleaning people happy and employed.

ed with antibiotics if caught relatively early. You should avoid swimming is streams if you have open cuts, and treat all water found in nature with treatment pills before drinking. (Filters are ineffective for lepto.)

Also, while swimming in freshwater streams, try to use your arms as much as possible. Kicking an unseen rock is easier than you think. Also, consider wearing reef shoes or, better yet, tabis, while in streams. (Tabis are sort of a fuzzy mitten for your feet that grab slippery rocks quite effectively. You can get them at Kmart in Kahului or any Longs Drugs.

Though rare, flash floods can occur in any freshwater stream anywhere in the world, even paradise. Be alert for them.

Lastly, remember while lingering under waterfalls that not everything that comes over the top will be as soft as water. Rocks coming down from above could definitely ruin the moment.

Dehydration

Bring and drink lots of water when you are out and about, especially when you are hiking. Dehydration sneaks up on people. By the time you are thirsty, you're already dehydrated. It's a good idea to take an insulated water jug with you in the car or one of those 1½ liter bottles of water. Our weather is almost certainly different than what you left behind, and you will probably find yourself thirstier than usual. Just fill it before you leave in the morning and *suck 'em up* (as we say here) all day.

Sugar Harvesting

When a cane field is ready to harvest, they cut off water for several weeks then set the whole field on fire. A mushroom cloud of smoke and ash rises into the air, then travels downwind to harass South Maui. Once the cane has been gathered, machines plow the fields along central Maui, where trade winds are strongest, and huge clouds of dust can fill the air, looking more like Los Angeles than Hawai'i. The result for South Maui visitors (and residents) can be poor quality air when certain fields end their two year growing cycle. We don't want to overstate it. During the winter, harvesting is suspended, and during the rest of the year you may have days with no harvesting, but you can't *count* on it. The only remaining Maui sugar company, HC&S, has 37,000 acres of sugar under cultivation, nearly all in the windswept valley between the two great mountains that make up Maui. Ironically, the same conglomerate that owns the sugar company (and the main shipping company to Hawai'i) also owns many of the resorts around the island. The resorts generate *far* more profit than sugar operations, but they still insist on burning the cane and filling the air with thousands of tons of smoke and dust. By the way, in case you're wondering where the county government is in all this, it's simple. They're in Wailuku—which is upwind of all the cane fires and dust storms. So as far as they're concerned, there's no problem.

Frogs

There are some irritating visitors that first arrived on Maui in 1997 and won't leave. (Well, besides the in-laws.) They're small tree frogs that emit a whistle all night long. Cute at first, like a bird. But incessant and ultimately irritating. Most of the resorts do their best to deal with them, but there's a chance that some errant froggies may occasionally give you a long night. West Maui seems to be slightly froggier (I *swear* that's a real word) than South Maui.

Traffic

Traffic can be a problem here. West Maui traffic between Lahaina and Kapalua is notoriously bad, especially at pau hana (quittin' time). Allow extra time during that part of the day. Road work also slows things down a great deal, and on Maui, road projects seem to be measured in decades rather than months or years. In South Maui, Hwy. 31 is bad at pau hana.

Grocery Stores

A decided hazard. Restaurants are expensive, but don't think you'll get off cheap in grocery stores. Though you'll certainly save money cooking your own food, a trip to the store here can be startling. Phrases like *they charge how much for milk?* echo throughout the stores. Even items such as pineapples—*grown a mile from the store!*—may cost more here than the ones jetted to you on the mainland. Go figure. Lahaina stores seem to be the worst, but Kihei stores aren't much better. If you're stocking up, consider buying groceries at Kahului stores and at the Costco and Kmart there.

TRAVELING WITH CHILDREN (KEIKIS)

Should we have put this under HAZARDS? It's been our observation that visitors with kids are far more numerous in West Maui than South Maui, perhaps because most of the Ka'anapali resorts have such good keiki infrastructure. If you want to stay in the south, the Grand Wailea seems the most keiki-friendly.

Baby's Away (875–9030) has the usual assortment of keiki paraphernalia for rent, such as car seats, strollers, cribs, bathtubs, etc.

Kalama Park in Kihei between Welakahao and Auhana on South Kihei Road has lots of lawn, a playground, a skateboard park, inline skating park, playground and a ball field. But stay out of the nasty water here. (See BEACHES on page 160.)

Maui Go Carts (871–7619) in Kahului on Kane Street has go carts for rent for $6 per five minutes. You must be 54 inches to drive, or 36 inches to be a passenger. (Passengers are an extra $3.) Adults can ride the carts, though the tire-bound track is pretty small and will probably only thrill kids. Opens at 10 a.m. but call to confirm hours anyway.

The accommodation reviews describe the resorts with good keiki programs. By the way, if your objective was to get *away* from the kids, then maybe these resorts won't be at the top of *your* list.

Hawai'i Nature Center (244–6500) has an interactive science arcade with lots of stuff to touch, wiggle and pull. Good for kids 3–8. Entrance is $6 for adults, $4 for kids. They also have a 2½ hour rain forest walk for $25 ($23 for kids.)

In Kula, the Keiki Zoo (878–2189) makes a nice diversion for your little one. You need to make an appointment to see it. $4 per person.

Kids who want to try something more involved than snorkeling may want to try SNUBA. See page 224.

Lastly, you should know that it's a big fine plus a mandatory safety class if your keiki isn't buckled up.

THE PEOPLE

There's no doubt about it, people really *are* friendlier in Hawai'i. You will notice that people are quick to smile and wave at you here. (Those of us who live in Hawai'i have to remember to pack our "mainland face" when we journey there. Otherwise, we get undesired responses when we smile or wave at complete strangers.) It probably comes

Maui Ocean Center's aquarium in Ma'alaea is a hit with kids—and us not-so-kids.

down to a matter of happiness. People are happy here, and happy people are friendly people. Some people compare a trip to an outer island in Hawai'i to a trip back in time, when smiles weren't rare, and politeness was the order of the day. Maui has dominated the Condé Nast's Reader's Choice poll every year as the "Best Island In the World." The people are one reason.

Some Terms

A person of Hawaiian blood is Hawaiian. Only people of this race are called by this term. They are also called Kanaka Maoli, but only another Hawaiian can use this term. Anybody who was born here, regardless of race (except whites) is called a local. If you were born elsewhere but have lived here a while, you are called a kama'aina. If you are white, you are a haole. It doesn't matter if you have been here a day or your family has been here for over a century, you will always be a haole. The term

comes from the time when westerners first encountered these islands. Its precise meaning has been lost, but it is thought to refer to people with no background (since westerners could not chant kanae-nae—praise—of their ancestors).

The continental United States is called the Mainland. If you are here and are returning, you are not "going back to the states" (we *are* a state). When somebody leaves the island, they are off-island

Hawaiian Time

One aspect of Hawaiian culture you may have heard of is Hawaiian Time. The stereotype is that everyone in Hawai'i moves just a little bit slower than on the mainland. Supposedly we are more laid-back and don't let things get to us as easily as people on the mainland. This is the stereotype... OK, it's *not* a stereotype. It's real. Hopefully, during your visit, you will notice that this feeling infects *you* as well. You may find yourself letting another driver cut in front of

Ahh, August in the tropics. These poor slobs nearly froze to death watching the sunrise from atop Haleakala. Make sure you are prepared, or you won't thaw out for a week.

you in circumstances that would incur your wrath back home. You may find yourself willing to wait for a red light without feeling like you're going to explode. The whole reason for coming to Hawai'i is to experience beauty and a sense of peace, so let it happen. If someone else is moving a bit slower than you want, just go with it.

Shaka

One symbol you will see often and should not be offended by is the *shaka* sign. This is done by extending the pinkie and thumb while curling up the three middle fingers. Sometimes visitors think it is some kind of local gesture indicating *up yours* or some similarly unfriendly message. Actually it is a friendly act used as a sign of greeting, thanks or just to

say, *Hey.* Its origin is thought to date back to the 1930s. A guard at the Kahuku Sugar Plantation on O'ahu used to patrol the plantation railroad to keep local kids from stealing cane from the slow moving trains. This guard had lost his middle fingers in an accident and his manner of waving off the youths became well known. Kids began to warn other kids that he was around by waving their hands in a way that looked like the guard's, and the custom took off.

THE HAWAIIAN LANGUAGE

The Hawaiian language is a beautiful, gentle and melodic language that flows smoothly off the tongue. Just the sounds of the words conjure up trees gently blowing in the breeze and the sound of the surf. Most Polynesian languages share the same roots, and many have common words. Today, Hawaiian is spoken *as an everyday language* only on the privately owned island of Ni'ihau. Visitors are often intimidated by Hawaiian. With a few ground rules you will come to realize that pronunciation is not as hard as you might think.

When missionaries discovered that the Hawaiians had no written language, they sat down and created an alphabet. This Hawaiian alphabet has only 12 letters. Five vowels: A, E, I, O and U, as well as seven consonants; H, K, L, M, N, P and W. The consonants are pronounced just as they are in English, with the exception of W. It is often pronounced as a V if it is in the middle of a word and comes after an E or I. Vowels are pronounced as follows:

A—pronounced as in *Ah* if stressed, or *above* if not stressed.
E—pronounced as in *say* if stressed, or *dent* if not stressed.
I—pronounced as in *bee*.
O—pronounced as in *nose*.
U—pronounced as in *stew*.

If you examine long Hawaiian words, you will see that most have repeating syllables, making it easier to remember and pronounce.

One thing you will notice in this book are glottal stops. These are represented by an upside-down apostrophe ' and are meant to convey a hard stop in the pronunciation. So if we are talking about the a type of lava called a'a, it is pronounced as two separate As.

Another feature you will encounter are diphthongs, where two letters glide together. They are ae, ai, ao, au, ei, eu, oi and ou. Unlike many English diphthongs, the second vowel is always pronounced. One word you will read in this book, referring to Hawaiian temples, is *heiau* (hey-ee-ow). The e and i flow together as a single sound, then the a and u flow together as a single sound. The ee sound binds the two sounds making the whole word flow together.

Let's take a word that might seem impossible to pronounce. When you see how easy this word is, the rest will seem like a snap. The Hawaiian state fish used to be the humuhumunukunukuapua'a. At first glance it seems like a nightmare. But if you read the word slowly, it is pronounced just like it looks and isn't nearly as horrifying as it appears. Try it. Humu (hoo-moo) is pronounced twice. Nuku (noo-koo) is pronounced twice. A (ah) is pronounced once. Pu is pronounced once. A'a (ah-ah) is the ah sound pronounced twice, the glottal stop indicating a hard stop between sounds. Now, you can try to pronounce it again. Humuhumunukunukuapua'a. Now, wasn't that easy? OK, so it's not easy, but it's not impossible either.

Below are some words that you might hear during your visit:
'Aina (eye-nah)—Land.
Akamai (ah-kah-MY)—Wise or shrewd.
Ali'i (ah-LEE-ee)—A Hawaiian chief; a member of the chiefly class.
Aloha (ah-LOW-ha)—Hello, goodbye, or a feeling or the spirit of love, affection or kindness.
Hala (hah-la)—Pandanus tree.
Hale (hah-leh)—House or building.
Hana (ha-nah)—Work.
Hana hou (ha-nah-HO)—To do again.
Haole (how-leh)—Originally foreigner, now means Caucasian.
Heiau (hey-ee-ow)—Hawaiian temple.
Hula (hoo-lah)—The story-telling dance of Hawai'i.
Imu (ee-moo)—An underground oven.

'Iniki (ee-nee-key)—Sharp and piercing wind (as in Hurricane 'Iniki).

Kahuna (kah-HOO-na)—A priest or minister; someone who is an expert in a profession.

Kai (kigh)—The sea.

Kalua (KAH-loo-ah)—Cooking food underground.

Kama'aina (kah-ma-EYE-na)—Long-time Hawai'i resident.

Kane (kah-neh)—Boy or man.

Kapu (kah-poo)—Forbidden, taboo; keep out.

Keiki (kay-key)—Child or children.

Kokua (koh-koo-ah)—Help.

Kona (koh-NAH)—Leeward side of the island; wind blowing from the south, southwest direction.

Kuleana (koo-leh-AH-nah)—Concern, responsibility or jurisdiction.

Lanai (lah-NIGH)—Porch, veranda, patio.

Lani (lah-nee)—Sky or heaven.

Lei (lay)—Necklace of flowers, shells or feathers. The lokelani lei is the lei of Maui.

Liliko'i (lee-lee-koy)—Passion fruit.

Limu (lee-moo)—Edible seaweed.

Lomi (low-mee)—To rub or massage; lomi salmon is raw salmon rubbed with salt and spices.

Lu'au (loo-ow)—Hawaiian feast; literally means taro leaves.

Mahalo (mah-hah-low)—Thank you.

Makai (mah-kigh)—Toward the sea.

Malihini (mah-lee-hee-nee)—A newcomer, visitor or guest.

Mauka (mow-ka)—Toward the mountain.

Moana (moh-ah-nah)—Ocean.

Mo'o (moh-oh)—Lizard.

Nani (nah-nee)—Beautiful, pretty.

Nui (new-ee)—Big, important, great.

'Ohana (oh-hah-nah)—Family.

'Ono (oh-no)—Delicious, the best.

'Okole (oh-koh-leh)—Derrière.

Pakalolo (pah-kah-low-low)—Marijuana.

Pali (pah-lee)—A cliff.

Paniolo (pah-nee-OH-low)—Hawaiian cowboy.

Pau (pow)—Finish, end; i.e. pau hana means quitting time from work.

Poi (poy)—Pounded kalo (taro) root that forms a paste.

Pono (poh-no)—Goodness, excellence, correct, proper.

Pua (poo-ah)—Flower.

Pupu (poo-poo)—Appetizer, snacks or finger food.

Puka (poo-ka)—Hole.

Wahine (vah-hee-neh)—Woman.

Wai (why)—Fresh water.

Wikiwiki (wee-kee-wee-kee)—To hurry up, very quick.

Quick Pidgin Lesson

Hawaiian pidgin is fun to listen to. It's like ear candy. It's colorful, rhythmic and sways in the wind. Below is a list of some of the words and phrases you might hear on your visit. It's tempting to read some of these and try to use them. If you do, the odds are you will simply look foolish. These words and phrases are used in certain ways and with certain inflections. People who have spent years living in the islands still feel uncomfortable using them. Thick pidgin can be incomprehensible to the untrained ear (that's the idea). If you are someplace and hear two people engaged in a discussion in pidgin, stop and eavesdrop a bit. You won't forget it.

Pidgin Words and Phrases

An' den—And then? So?

Any kine—Anything; any kind.

Ass right—That's right.

Ass wy—That's why.

Beef—Fight.

Brah—Bruddah; friend; brother.

Brok' da mouf—Delicious.

Buggah—That's the one; it is difficult.

Bummahs—Bummer; too bad.

Bus laugh—To laugh out loud.

Bus nose—How one reacts to a bad smell.

Chicken skin kine—Something that gives you goose bumps.

Choke—A lot.

Cockaroach—Steal; rip off.

Cornbeef eye—Same as stink eye.

Da kine—A noun or verb used in place of whatever the speaker wishes. Heard constantly.

Fo Days—plenty; "He got hair fo days."

Geevum—Go for it! Give 'em hell!

Grind—To eat.

Grinds—Food.

Hold ass—A close call when driving your new car.

How you figga?—How do you figure that? It makes no sense.

Howzit?—How is it going? How are you? Also, Howzit o wot?

I owe you money or wot?—What to say when someone is staring at you.

Lesgo—Let's go; let's do it.

Make house—Make yourself at home.

Mek ass—Make a fool of yourself.

Mo' bettah—This is better.

No can—Cannot; I cannot do it.

No make lidat—Stop doing that.

No, yeah?—No, or is "no" correct?

'Okole squeezer—Something that suddenly frightens you ('okole meaning derrière).

O wot?—Or what?

Poi dog—A mutt.

Shahkbait—Shark bait, meaning pale, untanned people.

Shaka—Great! All right!

Shredding—Riding a gnarly wave.

Sleepahs—Flip flops, thongs, zoris.

Stink eye—Dirty looks; facial expression denoting displeasure.

Suck rocks—Buzz off, or pound sand.

Talk story—Shooting the breeze; to rap.

Tanks eh?—Thank you.

Waddascoops?—What's the scoop? What's happening?

Yeah?—Used at the end of sentences.

MUSIC

Hawaiian music is far more diverse than most people think. Many people picture Hawaiian music as someone twanging away on an 'ukulele with their voice slipping and sliding all over the place like they have an ice cube down their back. In reality, the music here can be outstanding. There is the melodic sound of the more traditional music. There are young local bands putting out modern music with a Hawaiian beat. There is even Hawaiian reggae. Hawaiian Style Band, the late Israel Kamakawiwo'ole (known locally as Bruddah Iz) and Willie K are excellent examples of the local sound. Even if you don't always agree with the all the messages in the songs, there's no denying the talent of these entertainers. If you get a chance, stop by **Tropical Disc** (874–3000) in Kihei at Dolphin Plaza, **Groove 2 Music** (661–4101) in Lahaina Cannery Mall, or **Borders Books** (877–6160) at the Maui Marketplace in Kahului. All have good selections.

THE HULA

The hula evolved as a means of worship, later becoming a forum for telling a story with chants (called mele), hands, and body movement. It can be fascinating to watch. When most people think of the hula, they picture a woman in a grass skirt swinging her hips to the beat of an 'ukulele. But in reality there are two types of hula. The modern hula, or hula 'auana, uses musical instruments and vocals to augment the dancer. It came about after westerners first encountered the Islands. Missionaries found the hula distasteful, and the old style was driven underground. The modern type came about as a form of entertainment and was practiced in places where missionaries had no influence. Ancient Hawaiians didn't even use grass skirts. They were later brought by Gilbert Islanders.

The old style of hula is called hula 'olapa or hula kahiko. It consists of chants and is accompanied by percussion only and takes years of training. It can be exciting to watch as performers work together in a synchronous harmony. Both men and women participate, with women's hula being softer (though no less disciplined) and men's hula being more active. This type of hula is physically demanding, requiring strong concentration. Keiki (children's) hula can be charming to watch, as well.

BOOKS

There is an astonishing variety of books available about Hawai'i and Maui. Everything from history, legends, geology, children's stories and just plain ol' novels. **Borders Books** (877–6160) at the Maui Marketplace in Kahului has a dazzling selection. Walk in and lose yourself in Hawai'i's richness.

THE INTERNET

Our web site, **www.wizardpub.com** has recent changes, links to cool sites, the latest satellite weather shots, calendar of events, and more. We also show our own aerial photos of most places to stay on Maui, so you'll know if oceanfront *really* means oceanfront. It has links to every company listed in the book that has a site—both those we like and those we recommend against. For the record we don't charge a cent for links (it would be a conflict of interest), and there are *no advertisements* on the site. (Well…except for our own books, of course.) We've been asked why we don't list web sites and e-mail address in the book. Linking from the site makes more sense. Nothing is more mind-numbing than seeing URL addresses in print.

If you're on-island and need web access (to check your mail, etc.), most of the big resorts have business services available for around $20 an hour. **Hawai'i Online** (800 733–5638) can arrange unlimited local Internet access for $10 a week. Call them in advance. **Postal Plus** (891–8585) in South Maui and **Westside Copy & Graphics** (662–3450) in West Maui offer Internet services by the minute.

MISCELLANEOUS INFORMATION

Traveler's checks are usually accepted, but you should be aware that some merchants might look at you like you just tried to offer them Mongolian money. You should also know that the Discover Cards seem to be less welcome here than other destinations. *Many* places will not accept it.

It is customary here for *everyone* to remove their shoes upon entering someone's house (sometimes their office).

If you are going to spend any time at the beach, woven bamboo beach mats can be found all over the island for $1–$2. Some roll up; some can be folded. The sand comes off these easier than it comes off towels.

It's a good idea to get your photos developed here. That's because developers are more familiar with the colors. (Just try to get a black or red sand beach to look right from a mainland developer, and you'll see what I mean.) If you don't want to pay retail-retail, try Longs, Costco or Kmart. Most have cheap one-hour service and are surprisingly good. Most will redo the photos to make the color right.

Around the island you'll see signs saying VISITOR INFORMATION or something similar. Allow me to translate. That's usually code for WE WANT TO SELL YOU SOMETHING.

If you want to arrange a lei greeting for you or your honey when you disembark the airplane at Kahului Airport, Ali'i Leis (808) 877–7088 can make the arrangements for around $20. Nice way to kick off a romantic trip, huh?

A WORD ABOUT DRIVING TOURS

Maui is split into geographic regions. We are well aware that some regions, such as SOUTH MAUI, aren't geographically accurate. Hey, don't blame us; we didn't invent these names. Other regions, like the "North Shore" are also strangely worded, since it's not where you'd think. It refers to the Hana Highway coastline, not the real north shore of the island. But this is how people here refer to the areas, so who are we to argue? The inside *front* cover shows how the tours are labeled.

Most main roads have mile markers erected every mile. Since Hawai'i is mostly devoid of other identification signs, these little green signs can be a big help in knowing where you are at a given time. Therefore, we have placed them on the maps represented as a number inside a small box 16. We will often describe a certain feature or unmarked road as being, "⁴/10 miles past the 22 mile mark." We hope this helps.

For directions, locals usually describe things as being on the *mauka* MOW-kah side of the road (toward the mountains) or *makai* mah-KIGH (toward the ocean).

Beaches, activities and adventures are mentioned briefly, but described in detail in their own separate sections.

Found nowhere else in the world...Maui is home to many endemic species, such as this silversword.

Little known Olivine Pools are proof that there is still much to discover in West Maui.

West Maui—playground of the rich and famous? Those are the words that could have described this area hundreds of years ago, when Hawaiian royalty spent considerable time frolicking in West Maui waters and sampling its delights. Today, West Maui serves as a playground for the rest of us. Calm waters, some great beaches, limitless activities and an exciting, dynamic town, West Maui delivers on its legacy of fun.

Whether you're staying in West Maui or just visiting, there's only one road in and out—Hwy 30, which changes its name to Hwy 340 once you get past the populated areas. We'll describe it as most see it, coming from Central or South Maui going clockwise.

MA'ALAEA TO LAHAINA

Between the 7 and 8 mile markers you'll see a road on the left leading to **McGregor Point and**

Lighthouse (actually a beacon). This is a good place to watch a sunset or look at whales during the season (mid-December through mid-May). Past the 8 mile marker is the more popular **scenic lookout.** In addition to a beautiful view of South Maui, it's a well-known whale-spotting place. In fact, there must be an underwater sign for the whales, because they seem to approach this area a lot. Maybe it's a scenic lookout for them, too, where they can come and observe us humans in our natural habitat. Morning and early afternoon bring more spottings, since the light winds produce less choppy seas, making the behemoths easier to spot.

Less known is the good snorkeling and diving below the lookout. See BEACHES on page 159 for more.

Highway 30 is a modern, two-lane highway. In the old days (which anthropologists define as any time

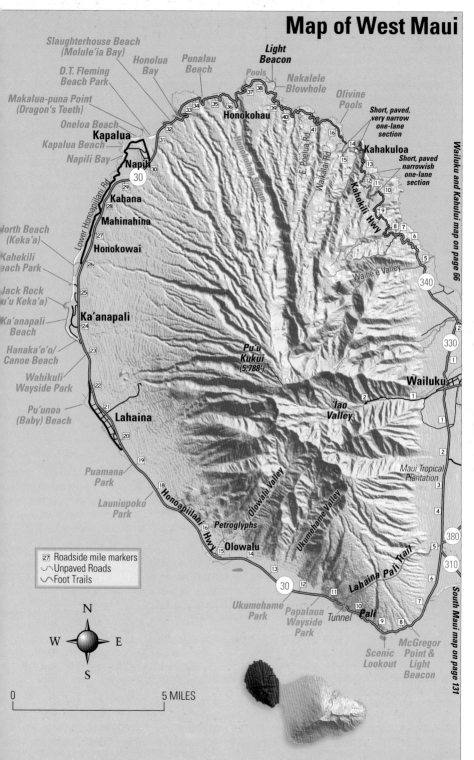

Map of West Maui

Slaughterhouse Beach
(Molule'ia Bay)
Honolua Bay
Punalau Beach
D.T. Fleming Beach Park
Light Beacon
Pools
Nakalele Blowhole
Olivine Pools
Makalua-puna Point (Dragon's Teeth)
Oneloa Beach
Honokohau
Short, paved, very narrow one-lane section
Kapalua
Kapalua Beach
Kahakuloa
Napili Bay
Napili
Short, paved narrowish one-lane section
30
Kahana
Mahinahina
Kahekili Hwy
North Beach (Keka'a)
Honokowai
Kahekili Beach Park
Jack Rock (Pu'u Keka'a)
Waihe'e Valley
340
Ka'anapali Beach
Ka'anapali
Hanaka'o'o/Canoe Beach
330
Pu'u Kukui (5,788')
Wahikuli Wayside Park
1
Pu'unoa (Baby) Beach
Wailuku
Lahaina
'Iao Valley
2
1
Puamana Park
1
Launiupoko Park
Maui Tropical Plantation
2
Honoapiilani Hwy
Olowalu Valley
3
Petroglyphs
4
Olowalu
Ukumehame Valley
380
310
Lahaina Pali Trail
6
Ukumehame Park
Papalaua Wayside Park
30
12
11
Tunnel
10
Pali
9
7
Scenic Lookout
8
McGregor Point & Light Beacon

Lower Honoapiilani Rd
Honokohau Stream
E. Edelua Rd
Waikilai Rd

27 Roadside mile markers
Unpaved Roads
Foot Trails

N
W E
S

0   5 MILES

Wailuku and Kahului map on page 66

South Maui map on page 131

© 2000 Wizard Publications

From the shoreline highway, it's easy to pull off the road and lose yourself in an idyllic setting.

female robber named Kaiaupe. She would lure men to get friendly with her at the edge of the pali, then kick them over the cliff and rifle their body for valuables (a practice that was named Ka-ai-a-Kaiaupe in her honor). So if you see a woman hitchhiker with a big *K* embroidered on her clothes…you might want to pass.

Descending to sea level, you'll find yourself constantly stealing glances toward the water. Views up the mountain are also scrumptious, and you'll probably want to pull over around the 13 mile marker and take them in.

At the **14 mile marker** you'll see lots of cars. This area is listed in virtually all visitor information as having some of the best snorkeling on the island. Don't waste your time. That's *way* out of date. Runoff (perhaps from the old sugar operations) has created cloudy water with terrible visibility. Farther offshore it's good, but the shoreline snorkeling usually stinks. See BEACHES for more.

At the 15 mile marker is the pea-sized town of **Olowalu**, the site of the massacre described on page 16. It's also here that you'll find Maui's best **petroglyphs**. In an era before pen and paper, the best way to record your thoughts was to scratch them on lava rock. At this site, pre- and post-contact Hawaiians left their artistic impressions in the smooth lava.

before TVs had remote controls) there was a narrow, winding road along West Maui. Parts are still visible in places, such as near the tunnel. It's possible to awkwardly scramble up to the old road and walk along it (if you're so inclined). You get an idea of how something as "permanent" as a road can be quickly consumed by nature, even on this dry side of the island. This part of West Maui is called the **Pali** (cliffs) and soon gives way to a shoreline highway.

In ancient times there was a legendary

(These have been augmented recently by mindless mutts leaving their more modern thoughts.) To get there, enter at the 15 mile marker, drive past the Olowalu General Store, then right, left and right. (The latter is marked by a water tank and the dirt road is lined with telephone poles.) It's less than a mile, and the petroglyph rocks are obvious by the abandoned guard-rail. This is private land (from a defunct sugar company), but we've never heard of problems accessing it. Be careful walking around as the platform is an OSHA nightmare.

Back on the highway, more ribbons of beach come and go. Parks like **Launiupoko** dot the shoreline. Though the valleys up mauka are beautiful, there are no roads to the center of West Maui, and only a few private subdivision roads penetrate a short distance. The farthest inland you can go up is on Lahainaluna Road in Lahaina. From there the view of Lahaina is peaceful and broad.

LAHAINA TOWN

Lahaina is the only town in all of leeward Maui with a *real* downtown. If

NOT TO BE MISSED!

someone told you to meet them in downtown Kihei, you wouldn't have any idea where they meant. Same goes for Wailea, Kapalua, Ka'anapali or Napili. Though it's only 1½ miles long, downtown Lahaina is well-defined and bursting with things to see and do.

The biggest problem with Lahaina is that it's crowded. And even when it's not crowded...*it's crowded.* A secluded stroll along Front Street is about as likely as likely as a snowy day in Miami. But Front Street has an electricity that defies explanation. No matter how much you curse

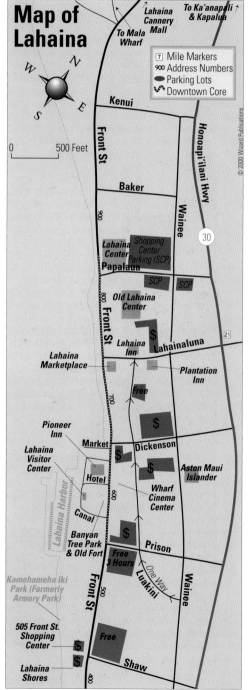

Map of Lahaina

To Ka'anapali & Kapalua
Lahaina Cannery Mall
To Mala Wharf

7 Mile Markers
900 Address Numbers
Parking Lots
Downtown Core

© 2000 Wizard Publications

Kenui

Front St

Honoapi'ilani Hwy

0   500 Feet

Baker

900

Wainee

30

Lahaina Center
Shopping Center
Parking (SCP)
Papalaua

SCP   SCP

800
Old Lahaina Center

Front St

$
Lahaina Inn   Lahainaluna

21

Lahaina Marketplace

Plantation Inn

Free

700

Pioneer Inn
$
Market   Dickenson
Lahaina Visitor Center
$
Hotel $
Wharf Cinema Center

Lahaina Harbor

600

Aston Maui Islander

Canal

$
Banyan Tree Park & Old Fort
Free 3 Hours   Prison

Kamehameha Iki Park (Formerly Armory Park)

Front St

500

Luakini
One Way
Wainee

505 Front St. Shopping Center
$
Free

$
Lahaina Shores

400

Shaw

its popularity, you can't deny Lahaina's charm. It's busy, tacky, weird and wonderful. It's full of old world character and new world annoyances. It manages to energize and relax at the same time. If you visit West Maui without strolling along Front Street (abiding by that old Yogi Berra axiom, *"Nobody* goes there anymore; it's too crowded") then you missed out on more than you think. Because for all its faults, Lahaina works.

Lahaina should be viewed as an event, not a place. You *do* Lahaina. You go there to eat, shop, walk and gawk. Lots of activities, especially boating-related, are centered around Lahaina. (This was, after all, an old whaling port.)

Ironically, as a place to stay, Lahaina lacks many of the things that make West Maui special. Namely good, clean beaches, cool breezes and a slow pace. Plus, there are relatively few places to stay in town. (Nearly all West Maui accommodations are north of Lahaina, in Ka'ana-pali, Honokowai, Kahana, Napili and Kapalua.) Of course, what it lacks in some areas it makes up for by having a better night life, tons of restaurants and a more happenin' feel.

Lahaina means *cruel sun.* According to one legend there was a chief named Hua many generations ago who, in a tiff, killed all his priests. Drought soon followed and villagers referred to the area as the land of the cruel sun. Today, that ever-present sun is the very thing that attracts people from all over the world, though it can get pretty hot in the summer.

Parking in Lahaina is a *bugga!* If anything can bring on that old fashioned mainland road rage, this is it. Lahaina is woefully under-equipped in the parking department (though fully staffed in the *enforcement* department). The county makes a tidy sum from unsuspecting visitor naïveté. One hour spots next to two hour spots and unmarked spots have

Believe it or not, this is one single tree. Banyan Tree Park in Lahaina seems to go on forever. But you gotta wake up pretty early in the morning to find—and film—it this empty.

created a cash bonanza for the ever-hungry county coffers. Even at night, big brother is watching. An example: There's a three-hour lot near the harbor, but if you park there at 5 p.m. for a sunset cruise and return at 8:10, you may find that the ever-efficient parking paratroopers have targeted you for a fee. Be very careful or you'll end up paying for some new carpet at City Hall. Here are a few tips:

Parking is free on Front Sreet for two hours if you can get a stall, and yes, they *do* keep an eye on your car. In front of Banyan Tree Park it's only one hour. There are several pay lots marked on the map. If you're having a hard time finding *any* spots in Lahaina, the pay lot on Dickenson near Wainee seems to fill up later than other lots. Don't forget to try the free lots shown on the map. They're usually full, but you may get lucky. (I don't mean it *that* way.) If you're doing an early morning boat trip, look at the free Luakini Street lot first.

Your best parking opportunities are in the morning. Arrive in Lahaina between 9 a.m. and 10 a.m. and you stand a reasonable chance of getting a street-side stall. You'll also find the shops and street much less crowded.

There is a huge four-hour lot at Lahaina Center. It's free if you buy something at the center. We guess that technically means that you could park there and walk the town, picking up a bottle of water at ABC before you leave. But we *know* you'd never do anything so sneaky.

While strolling around town, your personal tastes will dictate which shops and attractions work for you. Additional attractions, all labeled on the map, include the old courthouse (where they have a detailed brochure describing all historic sites in town), **Banyan Tree Park** (an incredible must-see tree that encompasses an entire park), **Baldwin House** (the oldest house on the island) and the **old prison** (called Hale Pa'ahao, or "stuck in irons house"). It's kind of interesting to visit this last site, made with coral walls, to get an idea of the kind of crimes that people were imprisoned for in the 1850s. They include "profanity, furious riding, adultery and fornication (the second most common offense), refusing to work on the road, giving birth to bastard children, lewd conversation, and affray." (We had to look that last one up; it basically means disturbing the peace.)

While strolling Front Street, you'll notice that activity salesmen are unusually aggressive. Lines like, *You folks have any questions? Ya need some coupons? Want to make a free phone call?* or *Interested in any activities?* are sales speak for *I want to sell you something* or *Want to see a timeshare presentation?* See ACTIVITIES on page for more on Activity Brokers.

The **Domed Theater** (661–8314) on Front near Lahainaluna is a large, semicircular screen showing a couple of specially made movies. The best is *Hawaii: Islands of the Gods,* a 40-minute movie showcasing the islands (mostly Kaua'i) with some dazzling aerial photography. Probably worth the $7 fee for the novelty and sights.

You'll also find the **Sugar Cane Train.** *(Yawn.)* See page 206 more for that thrilling *(not)* trip of a lifetime.

And the best show we've ever seen in Hawai'i, **Warren and Annabelle's** (see NIGHTLIFE on page 276) is on Front Street near Papalaua.

KA'ANAPALI TO KAPALUA

Ka'anapali was part of a large sugar

The sunset torch lighting ceremony at Black Rock is followed by a plunge into the ocean.

plantation when the sugar company's board met in 1956 and hatched a plan that would soon be repeated around the globe—the master planned destination resort, the first in Hawai'i. The large land owners had their pick of where to put the resort, and they chose the fantastic **Ka'anapali Beach** here as their showcase to the world. It opened in 1962 and has been admired ever since.

A Real Gem

Half a dozen fancy resorts line the beach. There's a wonderful paved **beachside path** that runs the entire resort area. It's an excellent place to stroll at sunset and can take an hour or more. Beach access, including the free garage between the Sheraton and the Ka'anapali Beach Hotel, are shown on the map. You can also park at the Whalers Village Shopping Center. Any

shop will validate if you spend $10. (Heck, you can practically knock that out with one scoop at Häagen-Daz.)

A Real Gem

Separating the two halves of the great beach is **Black Rock**. As mentioned earlier, Hawaiian volcanoes fall asleep for up to a million years before awakening for a last series of eruptions. West Maui had only four small eruptions during its final days. Black Rock was one. (Another is the rock where the Olowalu petroglyphs are located.)

The ancient Hawaiians believed Black Rock, which they called Pu'u Keka'a, was the jumping off point for their spirits or souls, called 'uhane, leaving this world. Each island had such a point. When Hawaiians died, it was here that their soul would leave this life and join their ancestors forever. If there was no

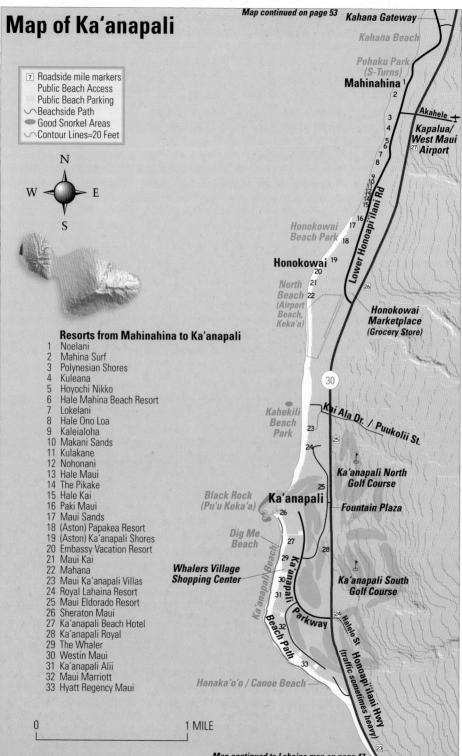

Map of Ka'anapali

Legend:
- 7 Roadside mile markers
- Public Beach Access
- Public Beach Parking
- Beachside Path
- Good Snorkel Areas
- Contour Lines=20 Feet

Map continued on page 53

Kahana Gateway

Kahana Beach

Pohaku Park (S-Turns)

Mahinahina 1

Akahele

Kapalua/ West Maui 27 **Airport**

Lower Honoapi'ilani Rd

Honokowai Beach Park

Honokowai 19

North Beach (Airport Beach, Keka'a)

Honokowai Marketplace (Grocery Store)

30

Kai Ala Dr. / Puukolii St.

Kahekili Beach Park

Ka'anapali North Golf Course

Black Rock (Pu'u Keka'a)

Ka'anapali

Fountain Plaza

Dig Me Beach

Ka'anapali South Golf Course

Whalers Village Shopping Center

Ka'anapali Beach Path

Ka'anapali Parkway

Halelo St.

Honoapi'ilani Hwy (traffic sometimes heavy)

Hanaka'o'o / Canoe Beach

Resorts from Mahinahina to Ka'anapali

1. Noelani
2. Mahina Surf
3. Polynesian Shores
4. Kuleana
5. Hoyochi Nikko
6. Hale Mahina Beach Resort
7. Lokelani
8. Hale Ono Loa
9. Kaleialoha
10. Makani Sands
11. Kulakane
12. Nohonani
13. Hale Maui
14. The Pikake
15. Hale Kai
16. Paki Maui
17. Maui Sands
18. (Aston) Papakea Resort
19. (Aston) Ka'anapali Shores
20. Embassy Vacation Resort
21. Maui Kai
22. Mahana
23. Maui Ka'anapali Villas
24. Royal Lahaina Resort
25. Maui Eldorado Resort
26. Sheraton Maui
27. Ka'anapali Beach Hotel
28. Ka'anapali Royal
29. The Whaler
30. Westin Maui
31. Ka'anapali Alii
32. Maui Marriott
33. Hyatt Regency Maui

0   1 MILE

© 2000 Wizard Publications

Map continued to Lahaina map on page 47

Some say that West Maui beaches are getting a bit crowded.
This couple at Kahekili Beach Park knows better.

'aumakua, or family spirits, to receive them, they would wander around the area, attaching themselves to rocks, and generally causing mischief. That's why it's considered unwise to take any rocks from this area. You may bring back a spirit itching to get back home.

The snorkeling around Black Rock is excellent. See page 157 for more.

Kahekili was the last king of Maui. He was utterly fearsome looking, with tattoos almost blackening one side of his body from head to foot, but completely clean on the other. He loved the sport of lele kawa (cliff diving), and legend states that he had once jumped from as high as 350 feet. Though terrifying to look at (even Captain Cook made reference to his scary appearance in his logs), he had a tiny, weak voice (sort of an ancient equivalent of Mike Tyson). This is the man that Kamehameha fought so hard to defeat when he conquered all the

islands. It was only years later that Kamehameha learned Kahekili was actually his father. **Kahekili Beach Park**, a great beach north of the 25 mile marker, is one way islanders remember him.

We should alert you that grocery stores in West Maui are renowned for their *hurt me* prices. Prepare for the stomping of your life the first time you go in for some milk here (which they may run out of!).

Also, allow for traffic when driving to Lahaina in the afternoon from Ka'anapali or Kapalua. Pau hana (end of work) traffic can be a problem, at its worst between Ka'anapali and Lahaina.

There are dozens of condos north of Ka'anapali. This is where the more reasonably priced West Maui accommodations are found. Unfortunately, many of the beaches north of Ka'anapali are unpleasant for the same reasons listed for North Kihei on page 160. The first good beach is **Napili Bay**, described

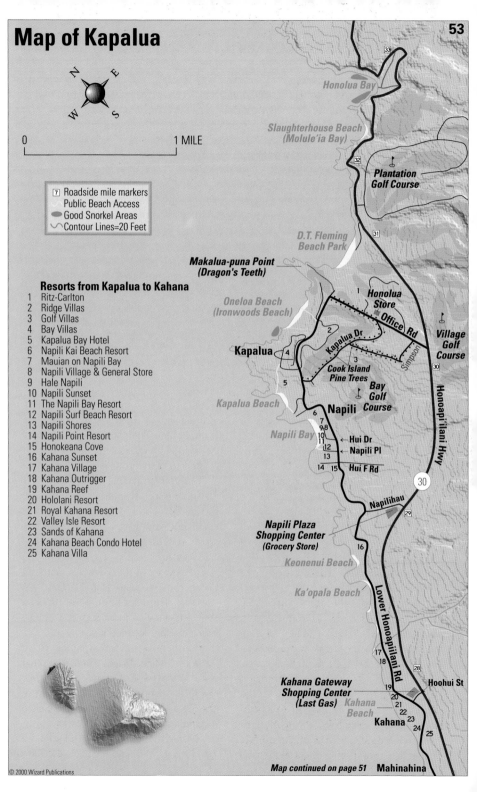

Map of Kapalua

N E W S

0 ———————— 1 MILE

7 Roadside mile markers
Public Beach Access
Good Snorkel Areas
Contour Lines=20 Feet

Honolua Bay

Slaughterhouse Beach
(Molule'ia Bay)

Plantation
Golf Course

D.T. Fleming
Beach Park

Makalua-puna Point
(Dragon's Teeth)

Honolua
Store

Office Rd

Village
Golf
Course

Resorts from Kapalua to Kahana

1   Ritz-Carlton
2   Ridge Villas
3   Golf Villas
4   Bay Villas
5   Kapalua Bay Hotel
6   Napili Kai Beach Resort
7   Mauian on Napili Bay
8   Napili Village & General Store
9   Hale Napili
10 Napili Sunset
11 The Napili Bay Resort
12 Napili Surf Beach Resort
13 Napili Shores
14 Napili Point Resort
15 Honokeana Cove
16 Kahana Sunset
17 Kahana Village
18 Kahana Outrigger
19 Kahana Reef
20 Hololani Resort
21 Royal Kahana Resort
22 Valley Isle Resort
23 Sands of Kahana
24 Kahana Beach Condo Hotel
25 Kahana Villa

Oneloa Beach
(Ironwoods Beach)

Kapalua

Kapalua Dr

Cook Island
Pine Trees

Bay
Golf
Course

Napili

Kapalua Beach

Napili Bay

← Hui Dr
← Napili Pl

Hui F Rd

Honoapi'ilani Hwy

30

Napilihau

Napili Plaza
Shopping Center
(Grocery Store)

Keonenui Beach

Ka'opala Beach

Lower Honoapiilani Rd

Hoohui St

Kahana Gateway
Shopping Center
(Last Gas)

Kahana
Beach

Kahana

© 2000 Wizard Publications

Map continued on page 51 **Mahinahina**

Dragon's Teeth at Kapalua are bizarre lava formations that owe their existence to the wind and sea.

under BEACHES on page 154. (Ah, and what a good beach it is...)

Sugar has been the symbol of West Maui since before the American civil war. All who grew up here lived their lives in its shadow. A single company dominated all commerce here. Ironically, it was a German company that ran the sugar operations until WWI when an irritated U.S. government seized the company and sold it to Americans. (In an *eat this* gesture to the Germans, they named it American Factors and their retail stores were named Liberty House.)

The waning days of the 20th century brought an end to sugar here. Now in the early years of the 21st century, nobody really knows how the previously green slopes will look for the next few years. Longtime sugar workers are moving on to other industries, sometimes pineapple. The large mill off the highway is being sold. Ironically, pineapple contributed to the demise of sugar here. Sugar is an intensely thirsty crop, and

the sugar company was never able to get as much water as they needed, in sharp contrast to HC&S's water bounty in Central Maui. Their single best source of water dried up when their water supplier decided to start growing pineapple and cut them off from their source.

Farther north, **Kapalua** is an incredibly manicured oasis of green in this windswept part of the island. The gardening bill must be immense because no dead leaf goes unpunished. *Expensive* is the operative word at these resorts. Some of the beaches, such as Kapalua Bay, are excellent. The wind can be a problem here, and it's also more prone to drizzle than any other leeward resort area.

Where Lower Honoapiilani Road becomes Office Road, there's a little road turnout with a parking lot. Walk toward the shoreline and a long point of lava separates two large beaches. Called **Makalua-puna Point,** it's worth the 5-minute walk along the grassy edge of the golf course. The lava is different than most Hawaiian lavas. Light colored, dense and fine grained, bleached white in some areas, it flowed during the dying days of the West Maui volcano. Salt spray on the upwind side has etched the lava into thrusting shapes known as **Dragon's Teeth**. Other areas on the point have other types of lava objects embedded in them. In some lava rocks the ocean has eroded holes completely through them. Walk over to the left (west) side and look at Oneloa Bay, often calm and protected on the nearest side.

The huge **lawn** in front of Dragon's Teeth has a tumultuous history. The Ritz Carlton Hotel inland was *supposed* to be an oceanfront hotel. The lawn was to be its location. The only things standing in their way were approximately 2,000 ancient Hawaiians buried in the area. The developers began digging up the graves and when the Hawaiian community learned of it, they began a series of emotional protests. Nearly 900 remains were dug up before common sense prevailed, and the hotel decided to relocate the buildings and reinter the bones in 1990. A state law was enacted after this to prevent such a thing from ever happening again.

PAST KAPALUA; OVER THE TOP

Like the highway past Hana along the bottom of Haleakala, the drive along the top of West Maui suffers from a long out-of-date reputation. Chances are you'll read that the road is not passable in a rental car. Free tourist brochures need to update their write-ups. Years ago the road was nearly impossible to drive. Poor pavement gave way to no pavement, and the narrow spots would make a stunt driver sweat. But today the road is much better. The real caveats are the two sections where it is one-lane. About 1½ miles of the highway are a *very* narrow paved one-lane road, and another 2½ miles a narrow*ish* one lane.

The Green Flash

Ever heard of the green flash? No, it's not a super-hero. We'd heard of the green flash for years before we moved to Hawai'i. We assumed that it was an urban myth, or perhaps something seen through the bottom of a beer bottle. But now we know it to be a real phenomenon, complete with a scientific explanation. You may hear other ways to experience the green flash—but this is the only *true* way.

On days when the horizon is crisp and clear with *no* clouds in the way of the sun as it sets, you stand a reasonable chance of seeing it. Avoid looking directly at the sun until the *very last* part of the disk is about to slip below the horizon. Looking at it beforehand will burn a greenish image into your retina, creating a "fool's flash" (and possibly wrecking your eyes). The *instant* before the last part of the sun's disk disappears, a vivid flash of green is often seen. This is because the sun's rays are passing through the thickest part of the atmosphere, and the light is bent and split into its different components the way it is in a rainbow. The light that is bent the most is the green and blue light, but the blue is less vivid and is overwhelmed by the flash of green, which lingers for the briefest of moments as the very last of the sun sets.

For a variety of reasons, including our latitude, Hawai'i is one of the best places in the world to observe the green flash. But if you aren't successful in seeing the real green flash, try the beer bottle method—at least it's better than nothing.

Like a jet engine firing seawater into the sky, Nakalele Blowhole rocks when the ocean rolls.

There are some turnouts on these stretches, but timid drivers may want to evaluate if this is for them. (If two cars meet where there's no turnout, etiquette dictates that the *uphill* driver needs to back up.) Just drive the one-lane portions very slowly.

For what it's worth, we think this is one of the least appreciated drives on the island. It's like the Hana Highway without the traffic. Though nowhere *near* as lush as the Hana drive (nor as long), the windswept charm of this almost forgotten piece of Maui make it worth the drive—if you can stand the curviness and the narrow sections. Along the way are some unforgettable sights, including one we discovered that amazed us with its perfection.

Our description assumes you will be driving this section from west to east, in a clockwise direction. We strongly suggest you do it this way for several reasons: The sights are better from that direction. Also, drivers rarely discover the road from the Wailuku side, so most traffic, sparse when compared to Hana traffic, will be flowing with you. Blind corners seem more blind when driving from Wailuku. Lastly, when on a narrow road, it's more comforting to be on the *inside* lane. Passengers can get uncomfortable when you're on the outside lane as you would if you came from Wailuku.

There are still some popular attractions past Kapalua. There's the *lovely sounding* **Slaughterhouse Beach** near the 32 mile marker with its concrete steps down to the shoreline, and, near the 33 mile marker, **Honolua Bay** with its outrageous snorkeling in the summer and monstrous waves in the winter. Both are worth stopping for if your destination is the water. Both are described further under BEACHES. A dirt road along the sea cliffs after you've climbed above Honolua Bay past the 33 mile mark offers a tremendous view of Honolua.

At times you'll see a yellow/orange stripe in the lava cut by the road or erosion. These are deposits of ash from the island's youth. At that time huge volcanic explosions covered much of the mountain in ash that was then covered with lava flows. Though quiet now, West Maui was very violent in its younger days.

Still one last beach remains along this stretch, though you'd have a hard time finding many visitors or even locals who know about it. Called **Punalau Beach,** the dirt access road is $\frac{7}{10}$ mile past the 34 mile marker. It's surprisingly uncrowded during the week. Past here you won't find any sand beaches until you reach the other side of the West Maui mountain at Wailuku.

The road begins its sinuous 25-mile trek to central Maui from here. Dynamite coastal views are common. Now, 25 miles might not seem very far, but you're likely to drive slow and stop often, so don't assume you'll be there in an hour. There are countless places to pull over and gawk at the untamed shoreline—sometimes from cliffs above, sometimes from along the shore.

Past the 36 mile marker is the village of **Honokohau.** There's a road that leads to the back of the valley, but expect plenty of stink-eye if you try to go. They don't seem too neighborly there. (By the way, wave if you see a big guy sitting on the highway bridge here eating a banana. He's there *a lot.*)

Exactly ½ mile past the 38 mile marker is a wide turnout backed by rounded boulders. About 1,200 feet from the road (and 205 feet below you) is one of the more spectacular sights in West Maui. Called the **Nakalele Blowhole,** the ocean here has undercut the shoreline, pounding underneath the lava shelf, where it spits through a man-sized hole in

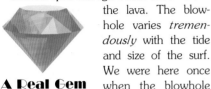

A Real Gem

the lava. The blowhole varies *tremendously* with the tide and size of the surf. We were here once when the blowhole wasn't blowing a thing. Zero water was issuing from the hole. Four hours later we returned and found the blowhole shooting 70 feet into the air every few seconds with such vicious, explosive force it made the ground tremble, and we were convinced the earth was going to split beneath our feet. It was like a jet engine rocketing seawater into the air with amazing fury. High tide is your best bet and high surf adds to the fury. The local newspaper has tide information on page 2.

Remember, this is wilderness. There's no guard-rail to stop you from shrinking the gene pool should you use bad judgment and fall into the hole. If the blowhole is pumping (which is quite common in the winter), get as close as common

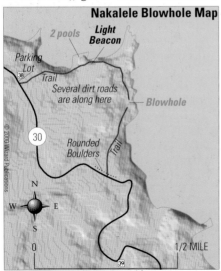

Nakalele Blowhole Map

2 pools
Light Beacon
Parking Lot
Trail
Several dirt roads are along here
Blowhole
30
Rounded Boulders
Trail
N
W E
S
0
1/2 MILE
© 2009 Wizard Publications
38
39

sense dictates. It's hard to predict which waves will make it scream. Huge waves sometimes produce nothing, while wimpy-looking waves sometimes surprise you. The area to the left (west) of the blowhole is some of the most amazing looking landscape you'll ever see. It looks like an alien war zone where combatants fought with acid. Over countless eons, billions of tons of sea spray have shot through the blowhole and been blown on the wind. The spray attacks the fracturous rocks on contact, literally eating the land, and the results are never to be forgotten. Rock hounds will enjoy seeing how the elements have tortured the rocks into various bizarre and jagged formations.

If the blowhole isn't overly angry while you're there, you'll notice a whole community of life living off this phenomenon. Crabs tempt the ocean by lining the steamy hole during pauses, eating algae growing on the sides, in constant danger of being swept away from a wave. Primitive-looking blennies (also called rockskippers since they can leap from pool to pool) live their whole lives in the 3 inches of water that remains from the splashes that shoot out of the hole. There's a natural lava viewing ledge above the blowhole, but you are still in the potential wet zone there.

The trail starts at the turnout mentioned above and goes down toward the ocean slightly to the left. (It's not the more obvious-looking road cut slightly to the right; see map.) While on the trail, take note of the huge amount of olivine encrusted in much of the lava rock. We've found dime-sized specimens of this semi-precious gem in the area. If you're interested in a longer, more beautiful hike to the blowhole, see page 191.

This is probably a good time to warn

you of the mindless cows that often wander onto the road. Cows aren't known for their smarts, but they seem especially clueless along this route, so be on the lookout for them.

Almost ⁴⁄₁₀ mile past the 40 mile marker is a small turnout on the ocean side. It presents a truly kickin' view along the coast. If the blowhole is pumping, you'll see the results from here. The ocean is directly beneath you, and you don't need to go more than 10 feet from your car. Another ²⁄₁₀ along the highway is an even better lookout about 100 feet from the larger pullout. The coastline unravels beneath you. Look for the blowhole back the way you came. It's below and slightly to the left of a light beacon near the point. Of course, no surf means no blow.

Many of the boulders in the area have been undercut by wind and salt and seem precariously balanced.

One mile past the 40 mile marker (yet ½ mile before the 41 mile marker—*go figga!*) the road opens up around a corner exposing the majestic 636-foot high **Kahakuloa Head** off in the distance. More on that later. At that corner there's a 5 minute trail that leads to a point with a commanding view. The real oddity on this point is the crumbling remains of an old Pontiac Grand Prix. Its presence seems inconceivable here. There's no way it could have been driven or rolled out onto the point. Let us know if you figure it out.

If you notice a strange feeling in your lungs about now, there's a technical reason for it. It's called perfectly clean air. The air here has drifted over the landless

When you reach the mushroom rock, you've reached a spectacular place to watch the ocean's fury.

Pacific for many weeks. Skies are often crystal clear along this part of the island. So when you're at a sea cliff, suck in a deep breath; this is as clean as air can get.

Soon the road changes and the pavements get a bit rougher, telling you that you've driven from a well-tended state road (Hwy 30) to a less-cared-for county road (Hwy 340). The state thanks you for your tax dollars (and the county wonders where their share is). Mile markers will start later at 16 (which is faded).

About 9/10 mile past the 41 mile marker, you'll find a turnout and trails leading toward the shoreline. One leads to a **mushroom-shaped rock.** From there, you'll find one of the best places in West Maui from which to observe the beautiful ferocity of the ocean during high seas. The unchecked pounding violence has tortured and scarred the helpless lava into a fantastic array of grotesque and wonderful shapes and textures. It's mesmerizing from this secluded spot to watch the creation and destruction happening at the shoreline. Be careful on the trail down, it's slippery when wet. The ocean is 175 feet below you. 4WDs can go much of the way.

This area has some very nice hiking, though less structured and often trailless. Just stop at any particularly inviting piece of shoreline and dig in. One very nice hike from here is described under Hiking on page 192.

Before the 16 mile marker, on the mauka side of the road, is the **Bellstone.** This large, round boulder can make a mildly metallic clank if you hit it at the right spot on the mountain side. Odds are, however, you'll simply look like some fool mindlessly whacking on a rock.

Right after the Bellstone is a dirt road on the ocean side. (It's almost kitty-corner to a dirt road on the mauka side with

gate leading inland—see map.) Drive or walk the short distance toward the ocean (veering to the right at the second intersection), and you'll come to some nicely placed rock platforms 150 feet above the shoreline. (See map on page 62.) People occasionally go there and then turn around because some maps erroneously label the area as containing the Nakalele Blowhole. Until now, however, few, if any, realized what they were missing below.

When you write guidebooks for a living and actually *do* and experience the things you write about, you get used to discovering exciting new things. But we were unprepared for the grand perfection of this totally unexpected oasis, which, until now, has never appeared in print. Judging by its pristine appearance when we found it, we'd say that not more than a handful of people on the island even knew about it.

We're calling it the **Olivine Pools** because of its precious gem-like quality,

the color of the area, and the ample amounts of a semi-precious gem called olivine encrusted in

A Real Gem the surrounding lava and sandstone. They are numerous natural lava swimming pools ensconced in an ancient lava shelf, offering an outrageous and usually very safe place to swim with the restless ocean pounding at you on three sides. It's reminiscent of the Queen's Bath on Kaua'i but far more grand and with more pools. The setting is as idyllic as any we can imagine. One of the pools is extremely deep and cool with a natural step to enter and exit. From this pool, your vantage point to the ocean caldron beyond makes you feel snug and smug. Another pool is just deep enough to sit in, which makes it shallow enough for the afternoon sun to occasionally heat it to about 90 degrees in the summer. Another pool has only one way in and out. Reef shoes are fine, but we've walked around barefoot and not had a problem since the lava is pretty smooth and there are no nasty sea urchins to kill your feet. It can be slippery, however. Perched above the pools is an amazingly flat platform, a perfect place to stretch out your towel to sun yourself. Natural lava steps lead to the pools themselves.

As the tide rises, splashes from the ocean may trickle into some of the pools and flow from one to another, sometimes forming small waterfalls. As far as we've observed, only very high surf at high tide or heavy rain seems to ruin the area. Observe for yourself to see if conditions are good. (Unusually high surf, above 12 feet, could spoil it during *all* tides.) There's a small blowhole off to the side that rarely does much, and next to it is the hole that most of the water drains into to return to the ocean. (Be careful around the hole; falling into it would be a *big* problem!) This area tends to be windy, though it's partially blocked by some lava. Sometimes, especially during the summer, it can get windy enough that you'll want to blow off this attraction (so to speak).

We have no doubt that when we do our second edition we will no longer find the Olivine Pools completely devoid of people as we have in the past. *Great!* You can't imagine how good it makes us feel to share this discovery with people. It seems tailor-made for recreation and, until now, it was unused.

From the pools, take a look at the unusually intriguing lava formations around you. Some look like lava chessmen sentries. Above the pool is one rock formation that looks like a lava admiral's chair facing the ocean.

To get there from the rock platform

Some deep, some shallow, the Olivine Pools are a calm playground in a stormy sea.

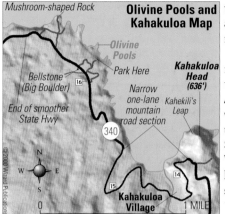

Mushroom-shaped Rock

Olivine Pools

Bellstone (Big Boulder)

16

Park Here

Kahakuloa Head (636')

Narrow one-lane mountain road section

Kahekili's Leap

End of smoother State Hwy

340

N
W   E
S

0   1 MILE

15

14

Kahakuloa Village

overlook, look down the cliff and to your left for a lava bench below you. You should see a heart-shaped pool on the lava bench. There is barely detectable trail (which should get more pronounced soon) leading down to the bench. Footing can be awkward and a little slippery. Since we are the first to reveal this, please be certain to bring everything out that you bring in. Also, it's easy to sunburn in the placid pools, but we're worried that too much suntan lotion may harm the pools. Try to refrain if you can while in the water. Though it's tempting to bring back rock souvenirs, you should know that Hawaiians strongly believe that any rocks that leave the islands bring bad luck due to a curse from the volcano goddess Pele. True or not, we can tell you that we've personally received numerous rocks from readers of our Big Island book that were mailed to us after they experienced a string of bad luck after returning. So it's up to you, but we advise you to leave everything where you find it.

Sometimes, especially in the winter, heavy rains can wash silt into the pools. This, coupled with high surf, can cause the pools to form one, large, silty pond

that you'd never recognize from our above description. When spoiled like this, nature usually cleans it up within a week.

Soon the highway gets narrow—*very* narrow—as it descends along the side of the mountain. Skittish passengers may *hate* this 1½ mile part. (We've seen some who had expressions as if they had just unexpectedly bungee-jumped into hell.) Soon enough you reach **Kahakuloa Village.** This tight-knit community is isolated from the rest of the island, though some here commute to work out in the "real world." The small, blue wagon as you enter the the village has pretty good shave ice. Several other vendors later, after the bridge, as you are leaving and the road is just beginning to ascend, a lady at the stand on the left next to a wet-looking taro patch makes the best banana bread on the planet. Makes my mouth hurt just writing about it. (Hmm, raising the bar pretty high, aren't we?)

As you're leaving Kahakuloa town, you ascend the valley walls on the narrow road. At the top the road is a turnout, if your nerves are shot and you want a nice view of the village and bay. After this the road widens, you'll see a fence and gate with a path through a cattlestop leading down between the 636-foot high **Kahakuloa Head** (which means *the tall lord*) and a 547-foot high hill to the right called Pu'u Kahuli-'anapa. The short trail between the hills offers some good views of the back side of Kahakuloa Head towering above you.

If you're feeling adventurous, from near the cattle guard you could make your way to the top of the hill to the right. It's fairly steep and you won't pick up the cattle trails until toward the top. We've hiked to the top and the views are second to...well, one, actually. You see, the much steeper Kahakuloa Head to your left has a summit that can only be reached by a death-defying, 'okole-squeezing, nail-biting scaling of the crumbly rock wall. Thanks, but no thanks. But while exploring this area from the air in an ultralight I discovered something quite impressive. At the peak of the mountain are *two folding lawn chairs.* Someone apparently loves nothing better than to climb this beast in order to relax at the top while enjoying the views. Whoever you are, *bruddah,* you've earned it!

Part of Kahakuloa Head used to be called **Kahekili's Leap.** Why? Because the 18th century Maui King Kahekili used to sometimes reside up here, according to legend. At a place part of the way down (but over 200 feet above the ocean) he would regularly dive into the water, then climb back up the cliff face for his breakfast.

After Kahakuloa Head you'll pass **Kaukini Gallery.** They have a decent selection of island-made jewelry, crafts and art (plus a restroom). Prices are expensive.

Just after the 11 mile marker is the sharpest hairpin turn we've ever seen. Look as you're approaching it, and you'll see that the upper road is almost literally on top of the lower road. (We've tried photographing it but can't get a good vantage point.)

Just after the 10 mile marker is the **Bruce Turnbull Studio and Sculpture Garden,** an apt description. Their hours are squirrely, and it's common to find them closed, but, if open, the area is replete with wood and bronze sculptures and it's worth a stop.

At the 9 mile marker you've crested at 1,000 feet. It's all downhill from here. Soon you see the **Aina Anuhea Garden and Waterfall.** We must have passed this place a dozen times until we found it open. Though nice folks, all you get for your $4 per person fee is one couple's small, private garden, manmade falls and some fruit. Only for those who are *really* into gardening.

Past the 8 mile marker is something you probably haven't seen on this side of the island—*a waterfall.* **Lower Maka-maka'ole Falls** is visible from several turnouts, keep an eye for it. It is a multi-tiered falls and is refreshing after all the dryness you've seen. Its name means *without friends.* (How sad.)

One last thing. For some odd reason, as you're pulling into Wailuku after the long drive, the last 1/10 mile of this road is one way—the *wrong* way—at the Vineyard intersection, and you're given no warning. We've seen some terribly close calls here as tired drivers plunge into oncoming traffic.

WEST MAUI SHOPPING

West Maui, or more specifically Lahaina, has the best and most extensive shopping on the island. The prime areas are along **Front Street** and at **Lahaina Cannery Mall.**

At the Lahaina Cannery some notable stores are **Escape to Maui, Honolua Surf Co.** and **Serendipity** for clothing. Antique Maui maps are available at **Lahaina Printsellers. Hats Galore** lives up to its name.

For shopping on **Front Street** in downtown Lahaina, park at one end (see map), enjoy lunch at the other end, and start back again. On some weekends there's homemade craft items sold under the Banyan Tree. The Visitors Center at the Old Courthouse also has some Maui souvenirs for sale.

There's way too many shops on Front Street to list, but some notable stops include **Dan's Green House** on Prison Street for those lava rock plants that you've probably seen on many tables around the island. Across from the Banyan Tree is **The Wharf Cinema Center. Tuna Luna** and **Quilts 'n Kitchen** are some notable stops for island made gifts.

There are tons of art galleries on Front Street. Make sure you leave time to peruse some of them.

In Ka'anapali, **Whalers Village** is a beachside shopping center with lots of designer names (and prices). There are also a number of places to get Maui-made items, including **Martin & MacArthur. Reyns** sells its own aloha shirt designs and ladies dresses. Some other clothing stores worth a peek are **Hilo Hattie Island Collections, Honolua Surf Co.** and **Crazy Shirts. Sandal Tree** has a large assortment of cool and comfortable footwear.

Kapalua has various resort shops. Actually, the best deal on things will be at the **Honolua Store** on Office Road. Pineapples, foodstuffs and even aloha shirts are a pretty good deal here.

There's a **Farmers Market** at Honokowai, in the **Hawaiian Moons** parking lot, M, W & F, 7 a.m.–11 a.m.

See page 139 for information on the **Shopping Express** trolley.

Best Bets

Best Hike—Blowhole thru Acid Warzone

Best Hidden Gem—Olivine Pools

Best Deal on Pineapple—Honolua Store

Best Baked Goods—The Bakery

Best Sunset Stroll With Your Shoes On— Ka'anapali Beach Path

Best Sunset Stroll With Your Shoes Off— Ka'anapali Beach

Best Breakfast for Cheap Cheap—Honolua Store

Best Beach To Start Your Day—Kahekili

Best Place to Watch a Guy Jump Off a Rock—Black Rock from Sheraton at Sunset

Best Place to See the Ocean Explode— Nakalele Blowhole

Best Banana Bread (on the planet)—Last Stand in Kahakuloa

Best Place to Watch the Whales—From Lawn Chairs on top of Kahakuloa Head (But how do you get there?)

Best Place to find Golf Balls While Snorkeling—Oneloa Beach

Best Place to Kiss Off Snorkeling—14 Mile Marker

Best Place to Waste Your Money—Sugar Cane Train

Best Place to Go to Have Your Bones Surgically Removed—Overnight Trip to Lana'i's Manele Bay Hotel

Best Lu'au—Old Lahaina Lu'au

Best Beach to Frolic—Napili Bay

Best Protected Beach—Kapalua

Best Place to See Just How Narrow a Road Can Be—Highway Segment Going Toward Kahakuloa

Best Pizza—BJ's (without the tomatoes)

Best Snorkeling—Right Side of Honolua Bay When Calm, or Black Rock from Sheraton Side

Best Parking Job—Car Over Bar at Hard Rock Cafe or the Abandoned Grand Prix on Cliff mentioned on page 59

Best Way to Recapture Mainland Road Rage—Trying to Park in Lahaina

Best Place to Sandblast Your Da Kines— D.T. Fleming Beach

Best Swimming Pool—Hyatt

Best Place to Lose Your Voice—Yelling at the Person Next to You at the Waterfall Bar at the Hyatt

Best Tree—Banyan Tree Park

Best Evening Show—Warren & Annabelle's

Ho'okipa Lookout is a great place to sit and watch big surf come crashing in.

Central Maui is your introduction to the island. You'll land here. You'll shop here. You'll also come through here when you head to Hana, up to the top of Haleakala, or return from a West Maui drive. But with all that exposure, few people come to Central Maui just to see Central Maui. It's like the *Denver Airport* of Maui. Everyone passes through, yet few look around. But don't blow it off completely. Central Maui does have some reasons to stop and stay a while.

Since there's no logical way to organize this area, we're going to describe it in a scattershot manner.

WAILUKU

The county seat, center of power and, most important, home to a few good restaurant bargains. (How's *that* for a reason to come here?)

Think of it as a once-

grand hub of island activity that's now in the shadow of Kahului, often forgotten, and showing its age. There is a certain charm to Wailuku, but not enough to lure many visitors. Too bad. In its day, Wailuku was quite a place: where sugar barons wined and dined, island leaders made important proclamations, and people came from all over to be entertained. One part of town is known as **Happy Valley,** even to this day. The origin is uncertain, but the age-old rumor says it's related to the fact that the area was known for its collection of bordellos. (Hard to imagine in sleepy little Wailuku.)

Most people simply drive through Wailuku on their way to **'Iao Valley** and the **'Iao Needle.** This was a sacred burying place for chiefs and the location of Maui's last giant battle for supremacy.

The king of the Big Island was Kamehameha

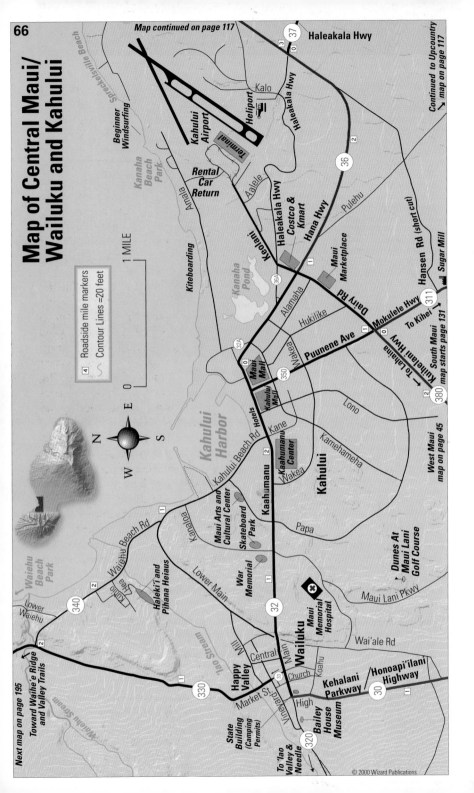

Map of Central Maui/Wailuku and Kahului

66

Map continued on page 117

Haleakala Hwy

Continued to Upcountry map on page 117

Next map on page 195

Toward Waihe'e Ridge and Valley Trails

Beginner Windsurfing

Spreckelsville Beach

Kanaha Beach Park

Kaloa

Kahului Airport

Heliport

Terminal

Rental Car Return

Haleakala Hwy

Anala

Aalele

Keolani

Kiteboarding

Kanaha Pond

Costco & Kmart

Hana Hwy

Maui Marketplace

Pulehu

Hansen Rd (short cut)

Sugar Mill

1 MILE

Roadside mile markers

Contour Lines =20 feet

Alamaha

Hukilike

Dairy Rd

Mokulele Hwy

To Kihei

South Maui map starts page 131

N
W — E
S

Waiehu Beach Park

Lower Waiehu

Maui Mall

Wakea

Puunene Ave

350

To Lahaina

Kuihelani Hwy

380

Kahului Harbor

Maui Mall

Lono

West Maui map on page 45

Waiehu Beach Rd

Kanaloa

Kahului Beach Rd

Hotels

Kane

Kamehameha

Kahu'i

Kilihau

Haleki'i and Pihana Heiaus

Maui Arts and Cultural Center

Skateboard Park

Kaahumanu Center

Kaahumanu

Wakea

Kahului

Lower Main

War Memorial

Papa

Dunes At Maui Lani Golf Course

340

Kahu

Maui Lani Pkwy

'Iao Stream

Mill

Happy Valley

Central

Church

Main

Wailuku

Maui Memorial Hospital

Wai'ale Rd

330

State Building (Camping Permits)

Market St.

High

Vineyard

Koahu

Kehalani Parkway

Honoapi'ilani Highway

Bailey House Museum

320

To 'Iao Valley & Needle

Waiehu Stream

© 2000 Wizard Publications

the Great. In 1790 he decided that the time was right to invade Maui (again). After he had personally killed the leading chief of Maui, his forces swept into Kahului and Wailuku. The two sides were fairly equal except for one thing: the cannon Kamehameha had nabbed from the seized sloop belonging to Metcalf's son. (See page 16.) With this cannon, which the natives affectionately nicknamed Lopaka (Robert), and some captured (though now happily compliant) westerners as advisors, Kamehameha was able to utterly annihilate the Maui forces.

They steadily rolled Lopaka along the rocky trails into 'Iao Valley, backing the troops into a corner, and proceed to murder almost everyone. Many of the women and children had been moved higher up the cliffs and witnessed their loved ones die as Robert, loaded with shells and sometimes rocks, blasted away. The carnage was so great the bodies clogged up the stream. Even by Hawaiian standards of the time, the killing was appalling. The natives called the battle Ka-'uwa'u-pali (clawed off the cliff) and Kapaniwai (damming of the waters).

Today 'Iao is a peaceful, beautiful valley. It seems impossible to imagine the death that once permeated the area. The valley stream is lovely and there are short trails looping around the bottom. The 'Iao Needle is a prominent point sticking up from the valley. It's actually the end of a long, winding knife-edge ridge. (If you saw it from the side, you'd probably call it the 'Iao Plate.) This valley is what remains of the central caldera (crater) of the West Maui volcano.

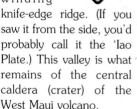

NOT TO BE MISSED!

Also nearby, if you have kids, they may like the Hawai'i Nature Center on your left on Hwy 320. See page 36 for more.

For the cerebral oriented, the Bailey House Museum (244–3326) is the former mid-19th century home of missionary

The 'Iao Needle and stream make a splendid diversion in Central Maui.

Edward Bailey. His home, now a museum, is a good place to check out artifacts from the past—such as a century-old surfboard, Hawaiian stone tools, spinning wheel, Hawaiian bible, quilts, dresses almost two centuries old, and even more surprising items such as an opium scale and pipe. Bailey was also a painter, and his renditions of Maui in the 1800s are interesting. Entry fee is $4, $1 for kids. On Main Street on your way to 'Iao Valley. Closed Sunday.

Also in Wailuku are the remains of the Haleki'i and Pihana Heiaus. These were former luakini temples (places of human sacrifice). The view from this strategic hill is impressive. You can see all of Wailuku and Kahului. As you gaze from the top of the heiau, your views of the mountains are mixed with views of the surrounding houses, creeping close to the heiau. Instead of houses, what did the ancient priests see when they looked from here? Houses...and taro. This area was called Na Wai Eha, or Four Waters, and was one of the largest taro-growing areas in the state. The streams around here provided abundant water, so it would have looked similar to rice fields but with broad-leafed taro instead of rice. Thousands of Hawaiians lived here. Instead of shingles, they had thatch. Instead of a two-car garage, they had a two-canoe shed. But this area has always had lots of people.

The heiau park is not well maintained by the state, which is surprising, given how few ancient relics there are on Maui. (Well, except for the county council.)

To get there, take Waiehu Beach Road to Kuhio to Hea. (See map on page 66.)

KAHULUI

People who live here find themselves coming to Kahului all the time. What do they come for? Malls, movies, restaurants and—most important on an island where things cost a lot—Costco.

Kahului is where people come to take care of business. The biggest mall, Ka'ahumanu Center on Hwy 32, is a big draw. And Maui Marketplace on Dairy Road is where you'll find Borders Books, the island's biggest sporting goods store, and a surprisingly good food court called Kau Kau. If you visit Maui Mall, the Paper Airplane Museum (877–8916) is definitely worth stopping for. In addition to the greatest collection of paper airplanes we've ever seen, they have tons of aviation related photos, articles, models and more.

Finding someplace in Kahului is easy, if you know one thing: Midas Mufflers is on Wakea and Hukilike. Why in the heck are we telling you this? Because every small town has a place like this. *The thing* that everything is relative to. Call up a business in Kahului and ask where they are, and, if it's not on a main street, invariably the response will be, *"You know where Midas is? Well, you take a left..."* We don't know why; it's just the way it is.

Kahului is nearly always windy. And on those few occasions that it's not windy—it's *real breezy*. If you've rented a large vehicle, like a minivan, it often feels like someone's outside rocking your car.

THE VALLEY OF SUGAR

This is the reason Maui is called the Valley Isle—the large flatland separating East and West Maui. This area is dominated by only one thing—*sugar*. A single company—HC&S—is growing all that sugar you see, all 37,000 acres of it. Before people came to these islands, a thin, dryland forest existed here. The Hawaiians quickly cut down the trees when they discovered the island and the

Sugar, sugar, everywhere. This tall grass requires one ton of water to make one pound of sugar.

area became a barren desert, after which the Hawaiians had little to do with it. When western man arrived, he saw an opportunity to grow sugar in this unused region and began building ditches to bring water to this thirsty land. Today, the broad valley between the two great volcanoes is an ever-waving field of green bisected by the three highways.

At one time, all of the islands surrounding Maui formed a single large island. Then the ocean rose and the land sank to isolate each of the volcanoes into different islands. The valley separating East and West Maui is the last land bridge remaining, and its days are numbered, too. Given the present sinking rate, East and West Maui will be separate islands in about 15,000 years when this landbridge disappears. (Gives the realtors something to worry about, huh?)

On Honoapi'ilani Hwy (30) heading toward the west side, you'll find **Maui Tropical Plantation** (244–7642) between the 2 and 3 mile markers—60 acres of assorted tropical fruits and plants. The sign says entrance is free. What that *means* is that you're free to spend money in their gift shop or see a small display of various agricultural crops. To see the rest you need to pay $8.50 and ride the tram. (No walkers.) The place seems more geared to tour buses (not surprising since the big tour bus company was an owner at press time). The tour can be marginally interesting, but it's definitely *not* a must-see.

If you drive along Hwy 311 on your way toward South Maui, you'll pass by Maui's ugliest sight (except for the line at the rental car counter when you're late for your flight home). A sugar mill looking like it belongs more in the 19th century (which is when it was built) belches steam and sometimes black smoke into the air. The smoke is from the burning of bagasse, the fiber remaining after sugar has been removed from sugarcane. They produce all of their electricity that way and sell the excess to the local electric company. At the corner of Hwy 311 and Hansen Road you'll find the Sugar Museum. It has everything you ever wanted to know about sugar harvesting and refining, but were afraid to ask. It's $4 for admission and they have lots of relics and artifacts. You'll feel hot and stuffy just *looking* at the outfits that field workers used to wear in the hot sun.

Along 311, the Maui Raceway Park between the 4 and 5 mile markers is often a happening place on weekends. (Ignore any errant HC&S NO TRESPASSING signs. They date back to when the *friendly* sugar company leased this government land. Today it's county land and you *are* allowed access.) The Navy built the landing strip during WWII to land some of their carrier planes. Lots of the bunkers they dug into the ground still dot the area. Later the area was used by the sugar company for their crop dusters. Today, even smaller planes (the remote control kind) are flown out there. Sometimes they'll let you fly them through the use of a buddy box (so they can take over before you crash it). They also have drag races on weekends, go cart races, motocross races on the dirt portion and other recreational activities. The state granted the land to the county at press time, so its uses will evolve over time. You may find little going on there during the week; hard to say.

PA'IA

If you're heading in the direction of Hana, the last town you'll visit is Pa'ia. This town has accomplished something few Hawai'i towns can claim: It has become an attraction without any attractions other than itself. No great views, no waterfalls, no scenery, no big institutions like an aquarium. Pa'ia's sights lie in its character—and characters. The odd and bizarre add color to Pa'ia like no other Maui town. An example—one morning we saw the following: A guy with a feather stuck in the top of his head (not his hat), a 90-year-old couple on a Harley (she was driving), a woman whose entire body was covered with tattoos, one gentleman with more dirt in his dreadlocks than a medium sized canefield, one guy having a serious argument with himself (and losing), and a guy in a hard hat carrying a full-sized cross. (Unfortunately, we *just missed* the naked woman painted green doing her Christmas shopping at the various shops.) Welcome to Pa'ia, where it's *still* the Age of Aquarius, and shoes are always optional in the streets. It's not a quiet town (even the name means *noisy* in Hawaiian), but it's unique.

Residents along these windward towns are so used to the frequent, short passing showers that they don't even seem to notice when it starts to rain. They often just go about doing exactly what they were doing, oblivious to the falling drops.

In addition to people-watching, Pa'ia is probably second only to Lahaina in shopping. Though not as large, the selection is eclectic. Stores like Bead Heaven and Hemp House are situated near surf shops and the area's best stocked liquor store. Everything has its own flavor. For instance, instead of a Big & Tall store, you have Big Bugga Sportswear. Even men, who normally don't like shopping, may like wandering Pa'ia. And the town has some surprisingly good restaurants.

Up Baldwin Avenue Holy Rosary Church, across from Pa'ia School is a beautiful birch and glass building. They also have a nice memorial to Father Damien of Moloka'i, the priest who worked at the leprosy colony described on page 146.

While in Pa'ia, wave bye-bye to that

last stoplight. If you're heading toward Hana, you won't see another light until you've almost completely circumnavigated Haleakala to Kula, 100 miles around.

Leaving Pa'ia, the Ho'okipa Lookout just before the 9 mile marker is a perfect place to watch the surf. When it's pounding, there's no better place to be than along this shoreline. Breakers can pound with such ferocity in the winter that it makes the ground tremble. Much of the year, expert windsurfers and kitesurfers (see page 228) ride the waves after 11 a.m., often streaking faster than the wind, and it's quite a sight to see. Wind is so predictable here—and it runs almost parallel to the shore—that it's considered the single best beach in the U.S. to windsurf.

CENTRAL MAUI SHOPPING

Kahului is where residents do much of their shopping. The large mall here is Queen Ka'ahumanu Mall on Hwy 32 in Kahului. You'll find big department stores as well as many local businesses that offer island-made gifts and clothing.

Also on Hwy 32 you'll find Maui Mall with some interesting places to stop. Have a homemade sherbet–type treat called Guri Guri at Tasaka's, check out the beautiful glass bottles at Crystal Dreams and stop at the Paper Airplane Museum mentioned previously.

If you enjoy big outdoor swap meets, Maui's biggest is on Saturdays from 7 a.m. to noon. Park off Kamehameha and Puunene streets. The entrance is on Puunene next to the post office. They have lots fresh fruits, baked goods and flowers, as well as coffees, T-shirts and other locally made items. 50¢ admission charge. A Farmer's Market takes place at Kahului Shoppping Center, Wednesdays at 7:30 a.m.–1 p.m.

Costco and Kmart are at the corner of Hwys 380 and Dairy Road (See map.) You'll want to stop here to stock up on food if you're here for a few days or more. Kmart sells inexpensive film, sunblock, T-shirts and reef shoes.

The town of Pa'ia is one of the more interesting places to shop on the island. You'll find an outstanding selection of beers at the Wine Corner, as well as a couple of bead shops and even a place to buy hemp products (the Hemp House). Not all of Pa'ia's business owners are early risers, so you may find some that don't open until 11 a.m. Regardless, some of the shops we've found to be worth a look are Jaggers and Baisa Rose Boutique; both have a good selection of island-style clothing and gifts. If you like antiques, stop by the Pa'ia Trading Co. There's public parking on the left side of Baldwin Avenue and a parking lot on the mauka side as you enter town.

Some other shops you may want to stop for are Big Bugga Sportswear or Moonbow Tropics for fine men's and women's clothing. In the window of Island People across the street there's a small impressive fountain with an atomizer that resembles dry ice.

BEST BETS

Best Food Value—Kau Kau Food Court at Maui Marketplace
Best Paper Use—Paper Airplane Museum
Best Exotic Food—Saigon Café
Best Restaurant View—Mama's Fish House
Best Place to Watch Windsurfers Race the Wind—Ho'okipa Beach Park
Best Treat—Rocky Mountain Chocolate at Maui Marketplace
Best Place to Find Weird People Doing Odd Things in a Strange Way—Pa'ia
Best Place to Watch Remote Control Planes Fly—Maui Raceway Park

If heaven had a highway...

The road to Hana is without question the most famous and desired drive in all Hawai'i, the crown jewel of driving. It's been compared to driving through the garden of eden, a slow, winding road through a lush paradise that you always knew existed—somewhere.

If you're in a hurry to get to Hana, you're missing the point. Unless you're staying the night in Hana, you probably won't spend much time there. You're heading somewhere else. (Those who spend the night in Hana will have more time to sample its delights.) At the risk of sounding like a Chinese fortune cookie, fulfillment lies in the journey, not the destination. The whole reason to drive along this route is to see the Hawai'i of your dreams, the tropical fantasy that becomes reality along the way. This is a drive through wonderland, and the only thing at the end—is the end of your discovery. As you drive,

don't feel the need to hurry up to get "there," because you may find that there is no there there.

If you're going to be staying in Hana for a couple of days (which we *highly* recommend), then you'll have a chance to see and do much of what the following two chapters present. But if you'll be seeing this part of the island on a one-day tour (as most do), then you won't have a chance to experience even a third of the things we've discovered on the road around Haleakala. If you're a one-dayer, we suggest you read through the following two chapters before you leave so you can prioritize the things that interest you most. For instance, if you're looking to get a photo of *you* under a waterfall but don't want to get beaten up by the water and don't want to walk far, then consider the photo-sized falls on page 105. If you're looking for a once-in-a-life-time photo op of you at the top of a waterfall, check out the Infinity Pool on page 109. Maybe you want to do some bodysurfing at the best beach on the island for it. Then Hamoa Beach on page 98 is what you want. If you want to see a drop dead gorgeous view of the coast, make sure you take Nahiku Road on page 88. If you want to dig your toes in a genuine volcanic black sand beach, then Wai'anapanapa on page 93 is a must see. Or maybe swim in a freshwater cave. Page 93 is where you'll find it. Want to see crazy fools make daring leaps into the water? Gotta check out page 84. Want to take a powered hang gliding flight along the coast? You need to see Armin on page 186. Or maybe you want to visit a beautiful waterfall by the ocean. Blue Pool on page 90 is *da bugga*. This is just a small portion of what's available. The point is, you can't do it all, so decide which adventure is most important to you.

The road to Hana is two lanes with lots of one-lane bridges. Tourist literature says there's 600 turns, though I don't know exactly how they classify a turn since the road is never straight. (Your steering wheel *certainly* changes direction more than that.) Whether you find the Hana Highway wild or tame depends on your experience. We've noticed that people who have lived most of their lives in flat areas—where a straight line *really is* the closest distance between two points and you can always see what's a mile in front of you—find the constant winding road and blind turns unnerving. Those of us who grew up with crooked roads find it a joy. We once met some visitors from the midwest who were highly adventurous. They skydived, flew ultralights and thought nothing about jumping off the 60-foot bridge over 'Ohe'o Gulch into the water.

But they refused to drive the Hana Highway again because it "made them nervous." Ironically, they were traveling with timid couch potatoes who grew up in Northern California and loved the "relaxing feel" of the highway. So I guess it depends on what you're used to.

CAN A RENTAL CAR GO ALL THE WAY?

There are many myths associated with the Hana Highway. Let's dispense with the biggest and most entrenched.

Myth—You can't drive a regular car all the way around Haleakala, you need a 4WD vehicle and high clearance past Hana, and even if you could it would violate your rental car agreement.

Fact—The road past Hana is nearly always perfectly driveable and *may* not violate your rental car agreement. You *don't* need high clearance or 4WD. Years ago, the road to Hana was a tortuous drive. The sadistic pavement was full of potholes and ill-conceived pothole fills beating up you and your car along the way. But today, the road to Hana is smooth, though a winding and narrow two lanes much of the way. *Yeah, but what about the part past Hana?* Well, 14 miles past Hana, after the 38 mile marker (the number sequence is altered at Hana), the road goes from regular pavement to gravel that is *graded every week,* according to the county transportation engineer we spoke to. After less than 5 miles of gravel it becomes blacktop again, textured rough from countless poor patch jobs. After 13 miles of bumpy blacktop the smooth highway returns. *Very* rarely, extremely heavy rains may close the road at one point where a normally dry stream crosses the road, but it is usually reopened as soon as they can get a crew out there.

Most rental car contracts we've seen restrict you from using the car on "unpaved" or sometimes "unimproved" roads and don't mention the road to Hana specifically. In the past that language certainly covered the latter part of the road. But now those terms don't sound as if they apply. After all, the paved portion would seem to be legitimate, and the gravel portion is certainly "improved" constantly. Besides, if it were so bad, how come large tour buses are able to drive all the way around? Even the national park at 'Ohe'o Gulch posts a notice saying the road is "passable for *all* vehicles." The fact is, the second half of the road has a very out-of-date reputation and all the free magazines and maps that tell you otherwise need to have their people drive it for themselves. Even if you are violating your rental car agreement, what does that mean? According to the rental car companies we contacted, it means the extra insurance you took out *may* not cover you there (and you may not want to pay for that anyway because your own personal car insurance may cover you) and it means they won't come get you if you get into trouble.

Driving all the way to Hana and then turning around (which the vast majority of visitors do) means missing the windswept back of Haleakala in the late afternoon. The way the light casts deep shadows in the water-scoured gulches, the incredibly expansive views of the coastline, the impossibly blue sky against the brown and red upper slopes of the volcano, the angry, wind-ravaged seas, and the utter lack of civilized development—these are the things that make a drive along the bottom part of the island worthwhile. It won't look like the Hana drive; you just *saw* that. It will pass from Eden-like lushness to the land of sun and wind. It's hard to believe that the backside is part of the same mountain.

DRIVING THE ROAD

You definitely want to drive in a clockwise direction so you can take advantage of the sun. The Hana side is sunny in the morning, shady in the afternoon, and its waterfalls are best before 11 a.m.

It's best to start the road to Hana *early*, so you'll have time to see and experience as much as possible. Unfortunately, we're not the only ones who give this advice, so everyone else seems to be leaving early, too. On average, between 1,500 and 2,000 cars per day drive the road to Hana. Most leave Kahului between 8:30 a.m. and 10 a.m. I know, I know. You're supposed to be here on vacation, and we *really* hate to suggest something as regimented as a timetable, but let us make one recommendation. If you're not going to be staying in Hana overnight, we strongly suggest you leave early enough to be passing Kahului by 8 a.m. This lets you avoid the crowds, see the sights in good light and allows you to take your time. If you're staying in Hana, leave later when the road's more empty.

Both of these scenarios allow you to avoid being in a procession of cars. This can take away *much* for the driver. *We can't emphasize this enough.* Whether they realize it or not, drivers focus almost constantly on the car ahead. You can't help it, it's instinctive. But when no one's ahead of you, your eyes tend to sweep and record the road ahead, and then fall onto the delicious scenery. That's why we're more than happy to pull over repeatedly to allow cars to get far enough ahead, so that we can drive to Hana and enjoy ourselves. We've done informal surveys and found that people who drive behind another car didn't think the drive was *nearly* as nice as those who drove it with no one in front of them. And if you notice a long line behind you, pull over to allow the faster ones to get by. There's virtually no place for them to pass on this highway.

WATERFALLS

Everybody loves waterfalls. They seem to universally affect people with a peaceful, soothing feeling. On this drive, waterfalls near the road are easy to find. This part of Maui was tailor-made for waterfall production because it has the two necessary ingredients—constant elevation changes and lots of rain up the mountain. But many of the lovelier ones are off the road, often accessible from trails. We have identified many with this symbol.

WATERFALL ALERT!

We tried to photograph most of the waterfalls flowing about halfway between abnormally pumping and abnormally light. The only exceptions are Hanawi (we just *had* to show you what it looks like when it's really going) and Lower Puohokamoa. The others are fairly typical middle-of-the-road. Sometimes higher (usually winter), sometimes lower (usually summer).

One thing you need to understand is the extremely variable nature of waterfalls. At different times, the same falls can be an unimpressive trickle, a world-class waterfall in a lovely setting, or a brown, swollen mass of water and mud after a heavy rain. We have found most of these falls in all three states at different times. During some wet winter months, you may find more waterfalls than we mention. Sometimes, during the dry summer months, some of our favorites may shrivel to a pathetic dribble, but you'll never see fewer than six falls between Kahului and Hana if you know when and where to look.

Though many of the waterfalls flow year round, some, like Wailuaiki, flow only in the winter.

A Few Basics

East Maui Irrigation Company (EMI) has ditches that run most of the way to Hana. At times, they will turn off various falls as they divert the water to feed the thirsty cane fields in Central Maui and for some residential use. Be aware that some of these falls may be on land marked with No Trespassing signs, usually EMI's. While crossing land gates here, remember that most of it is actually a *state-owned* forest reserve, not private. EMI merely leases the water rights. Their lease is supposed to be on a revocable year-to-year permit, but at press time it was only month-to-month, so perhaps they will have the authority to prevent public access, perhaps not. (In other words, who's to know if, by the time you read this, they have a lease on the land or not?) Hunters have used the land on weekends for years. Here and under Hiking we describe several awesome hikes in this area. You may want to contact EMI in advance to get permission to hike to some of the falls. You won't be able to get permission while at the falls themselves because you'll rarely find any EMI personnel around at the falls to ask. Remember, this is a watershed. So don't do anything in the streams you wouldn't do to your *own* water supply.

Car break-ins can occur at scenic spots such as waterfalls. Though not exactly common along the Hana road, all it takes is one or two scumbags smashing windows to create a problem. So avoid leaving valuables in the car, especially visible on the seat.

Many of the businesses along this road are closed on Sundays.

Start the trip with a full tank of gas.

The car of choice for the Hana Highway is the convertible. There are many times that you'll see striking greenery above you that others will miss.

The weather on the Hana Highway is notoriously difficult to predict. Parts of it get a *lot* of rain; that's why it's so beautiful and the waterfalls so plentiful. You

Serious jungle action, brah.

can call 871-5054 for a weather update. One thing that Hana road veterans know is that as you start the drive, if you observe bad weather, it usually (but not always) gets better past Nahiku, so don't turn around assuming it will be raining the whole drive. More times than we can count we've hit heavy rain much of the way only to have it disappear just before the Hana Airport.

This stretch of road, more than any other in the state, suffers from the lemming effect. (Lemmings are rodents known for going over cliffs *en masse* because the ones in front of them are doing it.) The drive is so special that everyone's afraid of missing something, so when you pull over, you'll likely see others pulling up behind you to see what they might be missing. We are well aware that many of the sights that we've discovered—some of them never mentioned anywhere else—will soon start attracting others who pull in behind our readers. But at least *you* know what to look for, and *they* are the lemmings. And just because you see others on the side of the road, don't think they know something you don't. Odds are, they don't.

PA'IA TO HIGHWAY 360

The first part of the drive starts on Highway 36 after you've passed Pa'ia. (That town is described in CENTRAL MAUI SIGHTS.) The map on page 117 covers this first part. As you pass the 10 mile marker you'll cross **Maliko Gulch.** An older bridge and train trestle were erected ½ mile up mauka (toward the mountain) in 1913. The sugar company that built it had lots of trouble getting workers to work on the foundations. It required swinging into the 300-foot gulch on ropes, and nervous workers kept refusing to go. Finally the boss/owner of the

sugar company grabbed the rope and swung into the ravine. None of the other workers ever refused again. You see, the boss, Henry Baldwin, did it while recovering from a recent accident—where he had *lost an arm.* Baldwin had swung into the gulch armed with only...well, you know. After that no worker had the nerve to refuse to do something with two arms that the boss man had done with one. The bridge was eventually torn down to prevent indestructible teenagers from repeating the feat.

While still on Hwy 36, you'll come upon the **Maui Grown Market** past the 14 mile marker with their sign saying, "Last Stop Before Hana." Don't you believe it! There's a better place 20 miles ahead.

ON HIGHWAY 360

Soon the highway changes its name to 360 (now it's a county road) and the mile markers start at 0. The map on page 78 starts here. You should reset your odometer so you'll always have a general idea where you are, but bear in mind that the mile markers aren't always placed a mile apart like they should be. We refer to their *actual* location, not where they're *supposed* to be. So if we say something is $\frac{3}{10}$ past the 8 mile marker, check again at the 8 mile marker to see what the odometer reads.

The first half of the drive is more tightly enclosed by vegetation, so you won't get too many expansive views. There *may* be a fruit stand and lots of people just past the 2 mile marker. (It sometimes disappears.) A series of roads and trails leads to **Twin Falls,** actually six or seven waterfalls, none very spectacular compared to what's ahead. People tend to spend too much time here, because it's the first available falls, and then rush by

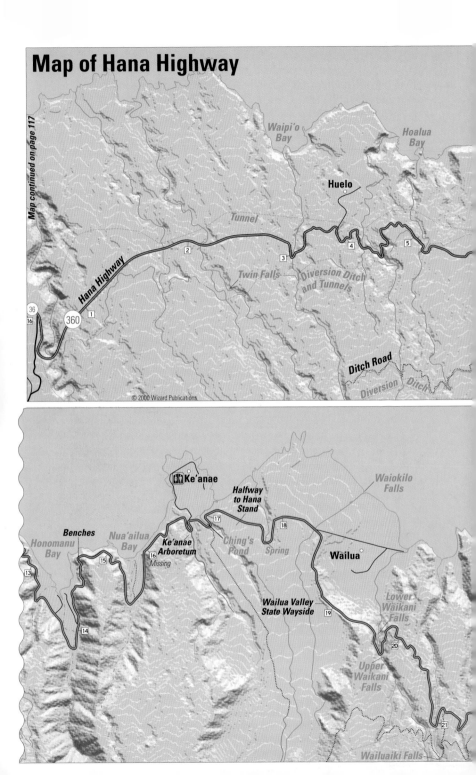

Map of Hana Highway

Map continued on page 117

Waipi'o Bay

Hoalua Bay

Huelo

Tunnel

Hana Highway

Twin Falls

Diversion Ditch and Tunnels

36
16
360
1
2
3
4
5

Ditch Road

Diversion Ditch

© 2000 Wizard Publications

Ke'anae

Waiokilo Falls

Halfway to Hana Stand

Benches

Nua'ailua Bay

Ke'anae Arboretum

Ching's Pond

Spring

Wailua

Honomanu Bay

Missing

13

15

16

14

17

18

Wailua Valley State Wayside

Lower Waikani Falls

19

20

Upper Waikani Falls

21

Wailuaiki Falls

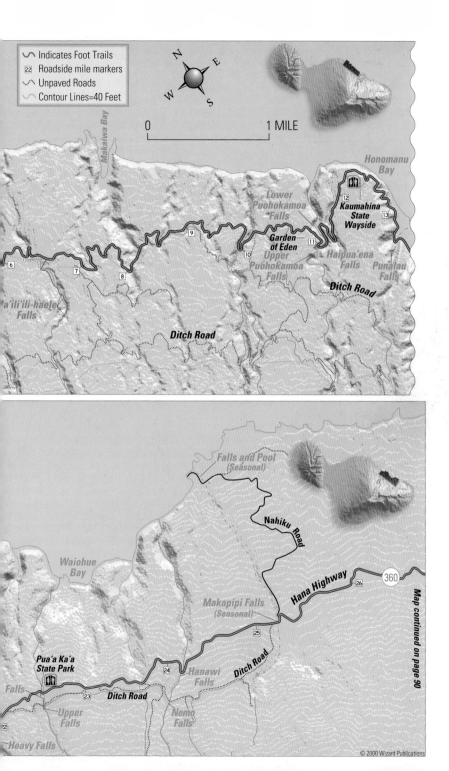

Indicates Foot Trails
22 Roadside mile markers
Unpaved Roads
Contour Lines=40 Feet

N
E
W
S

0   1 MILE

Makaiwa Bay

Honomanu Bay

Lower Puohokamoa Falls

12 Kaumahina State Wayside 13

Garden of Eden 11

10   Upper Puohokamoa Falls   Haipua'ena Falls   Punalau Falls

9

6

7

8

Ditch Road

a'ili'ili-haele Falls

Ditch Road

Falls and Pool (Seasonal)

Nahiku Road

Waiohue Bay

Hana Highway   360

26

Makapipi Falls (Seasonal)

25

Pua'a Ka'a State Park

24   Hanawi Falls   Ditch Road

Falls

23   Ditch Road

2

Upper Falls

Nemo Falls

Heavy Falls

Map continued on page 90

better opportunities. You should avoid them for the nicer, less-mobbed waterfalls later. But the fruit stand itself is pretty good. Lots of fresh fruits and excellent banana and apple bread.

Little more than a half mile past the 3 mile marker is a road marked by a faded Hawai'i Visitors Bureau sign, which leads to **Kaulanapueo Church.** Built in 1853, it's still in use and is an excellent example of 19th-century churches, though it will probably be locked when you visit. This area is called **Huelo,** and there are a surprising number of very nice B&Bs and vacation homes here.

At ⁶/₁₀ mile past the 6 mile marker is a dirt turnout. A trail leads to *four waterfalls.* Many of the waterfall trails along the highway are in this section. This one's an exception and is in ADVENTURES on page 232.

Between the 9 and 10 mile markers on the Hana Highway is the **Waikamoi Nature Trail.** Two nature loops—one about 10 minutes, the other about 30—make a pleasant place to stretch your legs a bit, but it's not a hugely compelling hike. It's good for families and you gain, at most, 200 feet. See HIKING on page 201 for more. No restrooms here.

Waikamoi Stream near the 10 mile marker is usually dry, but after a heavy rain it can be a giant caldron with a large waterfall up the mountain and a slippery trail to a smaller one. You'll know whether to bother by the amount of water flowing under the bridge.

Soon you come to the **Garden of Eden** (280–1912). Pretty tough name to live up to; it's an arboretum and botanical garden. The $5 per person entrance fee seems a little high at first, but you

Kamehameha Fights to the Death

Just before Holokai Road between the 15 & 16 mile markers (on Hwy 36) there is a hill visible a mile up mauka. This hill became famous during the time of Kamehameha, the first king to conquer all the islands. While he was here battling for Maui in the latter 1700s, the Maui king's top warrior was sent with troops to repel Kamehameha. One night Kamehameha camped at that hill and paraded his war god Ku around the camp to see how the feathers on the head of the god would look. They believed that the more erect the top feathers bristled, the better the battle would go. The feathers cooperated. The next day a fierce battle was fought beyond the hill at a place called Kokomo. Though most battles are fought by lower ranking soldiers, here Kamehameha himself fought in a battle to the death with Maui's top warrior. Kamehameha had practiced making war since he was a child, even going so far as to have some of his top men surprise him from time to time by throwing spears at him when he wasn't looking, just to keep him sharp. (He prided himself on being able to dodge or catch as many as five thrown at once.) The battle was begun as most Hawaiian battles were— both leaders on opposite sides of the battlefield hurled insults at each other to stir the other up. When the Maui warrior landed a particularly cruel blow (accusing Kamehameha of having no royal blood, but rather descending from slaves—yes, the Hawaiians did keep slaves), Kamehameha roared. Both leaders shot sling stones at each other. Then they charged each other with spears. Hand to hand, Kamehameha landed a vicious blow with his leiomanu, a club studded with shark's teeth, opening the Maui warrior's chest. The Maui warrior stabbed Kamehameha with a wooden dagger, but Hawai'i's future king finished off his opponent with his club. Maui's top warrior was slaughtered on the field of battle in front of the Maui troops. Those troops were so demoralized that the taking of Maui became inevitable.

soon realize that this is a meticulously maintained and very beautiful garden. Everything is scrupulously labeled. You can either drive it or walk a separate path. They have a picnic area with good views down the coast if you're looking for a place to eat that sandwich you brought with you, and there's a restroom. They feature a waterfall overlook on their brochure, but you actually get a better look at it from the highway just ahead.

At 8/10 mile past the 10 mile marker on the ocean side of the road is a turnout with a telephone pole and barbed wire fence. There's a path along the fence then you hop over some fence poles. Take it for a couple of minutes and you'll be treated to a particularly large waterfall that the vast majority of drivers miss. Plunging about 200 feet, **Lower Puohokamoa Falls** drops into a deep pool as drivers, blissfully unaware of its existence below, rush along on their way to Hana.

Just past the 11 mile marker is a popular place to photograph a waterfall. (Parking can be a problem; even buses stop here.) Called **Upper Puohokamoa Falls,** the small waterfall is easy to access via a short path. There's a covered picnic table overlooking the scene. The falls drop into a pool, and it's common to see people swim over to it for an action shot. Remember, the secret to shooting waterfalls is a long exposure. If your camera has adjustable shutter speeds, the longer the exposure (say around 1/10 second), the better the shot looks—if you can hold the camera still enough. If you flunked out of surgeon school because your hands shake, use a tripod. Also, see page 34 for precautions on swimming in streams. This is probably a good time to tell you that, while swimming in natural pools, use your hands as much as possible to avoid kicking unseen rocks. (Voice of experience with the stubbed toes to prove it.)

WATERFALL ALERT!

Most drivers (top) have no idea that they are passing Lower Puohokamoa Falls. A short trail takes you to this vantage point.

Above the path to the falls you may see several steep

trails leading up. They connect to a very vague and difficult trail leading upstream where another falls awaits. Not worth the effort; there are better waterfall opportunities ahead.

A half mile past the 11 mile marker there's a small turnout on the far side of the bridge and a trail that leads 30 seconds or so to a pool and waterfall called **Haipua'ena Falls**. It's worth a stop. There's another, larger falls just upstream, but the trail to the second falls, even on a dry day, has a short stretch where it's easy to fall. (An ugly fall at that.) Not worth it; stay at the first waterfall.

There's a spot a half mile past the 12 mile marker where the road opens up, exposing the very scenic **Ke'anae Peninsula**, but there's no place to pull over. In another ¼ mile there's a place where you can quasi-pull over to have a peek. What a view!

Past the 12 mile marker you come across the **Kaumahina State Wayside** with its porta-potties. Be aware the they are not as maintained as you may wish, sometimes looking more like a house of horrors. The **restrooms** at Ke'anae 5 miles ahead are usually better, though there are fewer of them. The wayside also has a series of short nature loops heading uphill from the ocean overlook.

As you cruise along, consider that cars couldn't make it to Hana from central Maui until an unpaved road was cut in 1926. Before that, Hana was isolated and quiet. Even with the new road, driving was only for the brave and the well insured. It remained unpaved until 1962. The paving job was awful, and the paved Hana Highway deteriorated until it was almost worse than the old unpaved road it replaced. The state finally did it right in the early 1980s, creating the smooth

(though still narrow) ride you enjoy today.

If you've been itching for your very own private waterfall, you *may* be in luck. One quarter mile past the 13 mile marker there's a tiny turnout on the far side of the white 1911 bridge and another one farther along the road. Even when it looks dry, there *may* be more water flowing unseen under the rocks near the highway, so it's hard to gauge the flow here. About 800 or so feet upstream is a pretty and lacy unnamed falls on the Punalau stream. (We'll call it **Punalau Falls**.) This is one of the few falls along the way that you can visit and have a reasonable chance of having it to yourself for three reasons: You can't see it from the road, it's never been written about as far as we know, and you'll have to walk on the (usually) dry stream boulders nearly the whole way. It'll take between 10 and 25 minutes to get there (depending on your rock-hopping aptitude). A pair of walking sticks is invaluable for stream walking; you'll go from being a two-legged animal to a four-legged one.

On the highway just past Punalau Falls there's a dirt road that leads to **Honomanu Bay,** though it takes you to the wrong side of the bay. (You would have to walk across the presumably low stream.) Another road just past the 14 mile marker takes you to the right (usable) side of the bay, though part of it may need 4WD clearance. The beach here is gravelly and the swimming poor, but in the early morning or late afternoon, the sun creates a magnificent golden green on the gouged-out valley walls, reminding you why you came to Hawai'i.

The present government road to Hana is by no means the first. Back in the 1500s a king named **Kihapi'ilani** decided that trips around the island were too perilous. Many of the gulches you have passed along the way were well known places for robberies, since the thieves could easily get away. So the king had trails cut and paved with smooth stream stones all around Haleakala—quite a feat at the time. It took years. (Though probably less time than the current county government seems to take these days when they repave it.) It was said that the king didn't want to be forgotten when he died. His public works project succeeded, because five centuries later he is still remembered fondly, and another public works project, Pi'ilani Highway, bears his name and the name of a 17th-century governor. His 500-year-old stone road was still visible in places until the jungle consumed the last of it in the early 1900s.

At ⁴⁄₁₀ mile past the 14 mile marker is a large turnout offering exceptional views of the valley and highway ribbon draped across the mountain. Vegetation sometimes blocks it. The turnout another ²⁄₁₀ mile ahead is better. Actually, ¹⁄₁₀ mile past that are some old, simple wooden benches. There's a skinny semi-pullout in front of them, but a real pullout just ahead. If you walk to the benches (be careful walking on the road), you'll find an amazingly tranquil view of Honomanu Bay and of the zig-zagging Hana Highway working its way up the cliffs. Take your time here and savor the smashing scene. The upper part of the valley you're looking at is full of burial sites. The old Hawaiians refused to walk there at night, believing that the spirits of chiefs buried there roamed the valley.

Off the highway just before the road into Ke'anae Peninsula is the **Ke'anae Arboretum**. While nowhere near as nice as the Garden of Eden mentioned earlier, at least this one's free. It's a partially paved path paralleling a brook with an impressive assortment of trees and plants. Unfortunately, the state does a

The raw, younger Ke'anae coastline is often a wild, frothed ocean.

poor job maintaining it, and you're likely to find few plants marked. In other words, it's kind of dumpy. It's a relaxing 20-minute walk, but not a compelling one. Their much-touted Hawaiian taro patch was nothing but weeds the last time we were there. Past the main path, a narrower, marginally interesting trail goes through a wilder, darker, more jungly terrain to a couple of very small waterfalls. Bring mosquito repellent unless you're a practiced blood-letter.

KE'ANAE TO NAHIKU

Next comes the road into **Ke'anae** Peninsula and village. (The YMCA camp you just passed has cabins for rent, see page 178.) The road hugs the coastline for a time, and at one place there's an excellent photo op with the ocean tearing through some jagged lava boulders. Very striking, especially at high tide. The impossibly blue water against the rich lushness of the Hana coast is a feast for the eyes. Farther ahead are some restrooms near the ballpark. (The ballpark has a nice open market on some Saturday mornings.) The coastline across from the restrooms is a good place to watch the waves beat up the shoreline. The land here is younger than the rest of the island, and it shows.

There's an extraordinary legend about the origin of the taro fields at Ke'anae that can't be confirmed but ties in nicely with what we know about the geology of the land. The legend states that in ancient times there was a chief who was constantly at war with the neighboring village of Wailua. At that time Ke'anae was mostly a barren lava field. The chief decided that he needed more taro-growing land and more people living in the area. So he decreed that every man,

woman and child would go to the upper valley, gather soil in baskets and fill the peninsula with enough soil to grow taro. In time, the peninsula became a prime taro-growing area. True story? Who knows? It's a legend. But what a task it would have been. Imagine hiking miles up the valley, hauling a basket of heavy dirt back, dumping it on the lava rock and heading back uphill. The definition of a thankless, Dilbert-like job!

Ke'anae was nearly wiped out by the tsunami (tidal wave) of 1946. Nearly every building was destroyed, leaving only the immovable stone church.

Back on the highway, just before the 17 mile marker, is a bridge and pullout. The path about 75 feet to the left leads down to a marvelous pool, known locally as **Ching's Pond**. The swimming is particularly good and most drivers never even see this pond. Above the narrow stream portion (just before it opens up to the pool) there's a concrete platform on the right side. We've seen daring young locals jumping (and one profoundly daring local named Dana *diving*) out and away from the cliff into the tiny part they claim is deep enough so you don't hit rocks. We're talking about a 25 foot or so drop with *zero* margin for error. *That's* what we call an 'okole squeezer. (We'll let you guess what an 'okole is.) Obviously you shouldn't do this unless you name us as beneficiaries on your life insurance.

About ⅓ mile past the 17 mile marker is a stand generally known as **Halfway to Hana.** (Actually, you're ⅔ of the way from Kahului.) They have justifiably famous banana bread (moist, sweet and tasty) that we like to review every time we travel the road. (Just to be thorough, you understand. We do it for you, only for

A cliff diver at Ching's Pond lands in the only space deep enough.

flowers and some huge elephant ears (called 'ape) in a garden setting tailor-made for a postcard (though they sometimes let the flowers overgrow). This is a **spring fed gusher,** originating here. Any pipes you see under the flowers are tapping the water, not feeding it. When they keep it well tended, it's a lovely sight.

The tiny settlement of **Wailua** is off the road not long past the 18 mile marker. This quaint community is mostly built around taro growing. (Taro is the plant Hawaiians use to make poi, the purple, less-than-tasty paste you may try—*once*—at lu'aus.) That road is dead-on straight. (Bowlers may get sweaty palms imagining the possibilities—it's strange to be driving on straight pavement again; your hands are searching for something to do.) Keep an eye on your right for a glimpse of the enormous, multi-tiered **Waikani Falls,** which drop 1,000 feet in several stages just under the highway. (You can't see the large lower falls from the highway.) Otherwise, there's not much for you in Wailua.

Just before the 19 mile marker most people blow by without even noticing the **Wailua Valley State Wayside** on the mauka (mountain) side. Take the stairs to the right to the top, and on the ocean side you'll see the quaint village of Wailua with its fields of taro beneath

you.) They also have fruits, beverages, some sandwiches and so-so burgers, very fudgy brownies and other snacks. If you're hungry, consider stocking up here for snacks. Hana has few options, and the terrible food they serve at the Hana Ranch Restaurant makes everything served at Halfway to Hana taste even better. By the way, take a peek at the house behind the stand to see if they still have all those pigs' heads hanging on the wall.

About ⅔ mile past the 17 mile mark, pull over and walk over to the white concrete bridge. Look down on the ocean side of the bridge and you see water gushing out of the mountain, surrounded by

you. Turn around and look up mauka. You'll see (clouds permitting) the Koʻolau Gap at the top of the mountain. Notice how steep the valley walls are, yet the floor is so broad and flat? This valley used to be thousands of feet deep, cutting into the very core of the volcano. It was filled in at the same time as the Kaupo Gap on the other side of the volcano. (See page 113 for the full story.) The relatively new lands of Wailua and the Keʻanae Peninsula were formed by the same flows that filled the gaps.

Many of the one-lane bridges along here are close to 100 years old. The county wants to replace them, but there's a hitch. In order to get federal (meaning your) dollars, the bridges usually need to be two-lane. (The feds don't like paying for one-lane bridges.) The problem is that Hana residents don't *want* two-lane bridges. Since the county is perpetually short of funds, it's a safe bet that some two-lane bridges are on

their way. In fact, in Kaupo on the bottom of the island before the 28 mile marker you'll notice two new expensive concrete two-lane bridges—connecting two halves of a one-lane road. We Maui residents thank you for your support.

Between the 19 and 20 mile markers there's a very popular waterfall to photo-graph called **Upper Waikani Falls**, sometimes called **Three Bears Falls** (the upper cousin to the huge falls partially visible from Wailua village). These falls vary dramatically, depending on flow. In case you're wondering, yes, you *can* get to the falls themselves. At the far side of the bridge (on the mauka side) is a fairly easy short path—it's just the first step that's ugly. At the falls, you realize that they're bigger than you thought.

The stream just before the 21 mile marker is sometimes almost dry. That's because most of the

WATERFALL ALERT!

Most people seem to think that the heavier the water flow, the prettier the waterfall. These two shots of Wàikani Falls (AKA the 3 Bears) are an example of how sometimes less is more.

water is diverted less than a ½ mile upstream. But ²/₁₀ mile past the 21 mile marker is a hunters' road called Wailuaiki. A 10-minute walk from there (at the top of the dirt road turn right) leads to a very nice waterfall and pool as well as a gorgeous valley. (See page 76 for hiking in this EMI area.) There are two more falls farther up the stream, but they're harder to reach. By the way, if there's water flowing at the highway, the real view is from about 250 feet up the road (there's a one-car turnout just up the hill), where the water that flows under the highway plunges off the cliff in a very dramatic fashion.

At ⁹/₁₀ mile past the 21 mile marker is one of the heavier-flowing falls along the coast. (It's heavy because there's no ditch upstream robbing its water) Unfortunately, it's just barely out of sight (except maybe the top as you're driving up) 500 feet inland. This whole area is part of the Koʻolau Forest Reserve, but EMI, which has the water rights, has infrastructure there that dissuades you from visiting the falls. Assuming they give you their blessing to hike to it, you'll find a trail on the right side of the stream leading most of the way to the falls. You'll have to find a way to scramble up the rock wall in front of you to get to it.

Between the 22 and 23 mile markers is **Puaʻa Kaʻa State Park**. (*That's* a hard one to say.) Two easily visited small waterfalls make good photo ops, and there are **restrooms**. The falls are often fairly light, but it's not for lack of water. If you're adventurous, we have a surprise for you. There's an awkward trail on the right side of the upper falls. It first leads to a short path to the top of the falls, but if you go past it for 5–10

squishy minutes (it's usually muddy), there's a much heavier untapped falls and pool just above the diversion ditch that's taking much of the lower falls' water. When the trail gets to the elevated waterway (viaduct), you have to walk along it (which those afraid of heights will hate), then across. Only 100 more feet upstream is your prize. The falls make an ideal photo op—you know, the *me under a waterfall* shot, if the flow's not too heavy—and it's a pretty dependable waterfall, even during the driest times. The trail goes around a hill then down to the pool.

By the way, there are boreholes in the Puaʻa Kaʻa highway bridge to answer that question that's troubled you all your life—how thick are these bridges anyway?

After the 23 mile mark you pass a couple caves, a bridge, then a larger cave. These are **lava tubes,** created when lava from volcanic vents forms a river that crusts over on top. These tubes can transport the lava for over 20 miles, losing a mere 20°F along the way. The last tube has a tree root from the tree above that snakes its way back almost to the end of the cave. Lava tubes tend to collapse over time, so young islands, like the Big Island, are loaded with them, whereas older islands, like Kauaʻi, have relatively few.

After the 24 mile marker, yet another pretty waterfall called **Hanawi Falls** awaits. It's particularly attractive. If you take a photo from the bridge, be careful. The guard-rail is shorter than it looks. There have been people who have sat on the rail for a photo, only to careen backward onto the rocks. When the flow is heavy, this becomes one of the nicest waterfalls on the whole coast. It splits around the rocks, and the portion on the left adds to the portion on the right, making it a dream.

OK, OK. I know you've probably seen a number of nice waterfalls by now. Been there, done that. But *when it's flowing,* this next one is different. Pull over on the far side of the bridge shortly past the 25 mile marker. If you walk out to the bridge (there's no walkway for you), from the middle of the ocean side look straight down. (Be *really* careful not to topple over.) You'll see something you don't normally get to see. You are *directly* above the spot where **Makapipi Falls** plunges unfettered into a large pool. Excellent vantage point as you follow the stream with your eyes as it burrows through the vegetation on its way to the ocean. Makapipi is more seasonal than most falls and is dry about half the time.

NAHIKU

Next to the falls, **Nahiku Road** leads 2½ miles down through the luxuriant community of Nahiku. If you think the road to Hana looked lush and beautiful, wait till you see Nahiku. When plants go to heaven, Nahiku must be their destination. Everything green seems so happy and healthy, you can 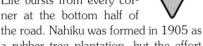 almost hear them giggling. Life bursts from every corner at the bottom half of the road. Nahiku was formed in 1905 as a rubber tree plantation, but the effort went flat a decade later.

Drive slowly; children play in the streets. Several honor-system fruit stands are usually present. Once at the bottom of Nahiku Road, you're in for a treat—a jaw-dropping view of the shoreline all the way back to Ke'anae. There's a little path on the left that leads to a variable but charming little artesian waterfall and pool, right next to the ocean. What a spot! As you stand there in your own private paradise, you can't help but wonder if there's a more beautiful place in the world. Perhaps you can't see forever, but you can see all the way to paradise. This is one of our favorite spots to sit and gaze along the Hana coast. Miles of coastline are revealed as the sound of the surf and

Hanawi Falls, when it's really pumping like it is here, is glorious even when you don't get out of your car. At other times, only the right side flows.

Nahiku Road is heaven for anything green.

the small falls make everything just perfect. A grassy area near the ocean makes a good place to have lunch.

As you depart and the road leaves the shoreline, you may think that Nahiku has delivered everything it can. But during wet months there's one surprise left. Pull the car over about 150 feet uphill from the shoreline guard-rail. The stream to your left forms a big pool with a small waterfall. (It can dry up in the summertime.) The whole setting is ensconced in an area packed with more shades of green than you ever knew existed. There was even a rope swing there when last we checked, where local children sometimes play. The scene is as wholesome and idyllic as any you may encounter. It's a flawlessly sculpted natural setting. Only the mosquitoes remind you that it's still the real world. There's a short path down to the pool.

Ex-Beatle George Harrison owns a home down here but has had neighbor problems. His neighbors were able to successfully argue that there was a public easement through his property. Neighbors, fans and the curious began sweeping through the land in droves, sparking Harrison to say that he felt that he had been "raped." His neighbors sued, claiming slander. It was tossed out by the judge as frivolous, saying the speech was "protected hyperbole" and he made the neighbors pay Harrison's legal costs. (I guess you could say George got by with a little help from his "friends.")

NAHIKU TO HANA

Back on the highway, you'll notice that the terrain is changing. It's less eroded because the land is relatively new here. You'll soon come to some food stands. One serves smoked fish (tasty but expensive) and steamed breadfruit. Another has some adequate baked goods and coffee. The small gallery is overpriced.

If you don't mind walking on beach

An idyllic Nahiku pond that looks so perfect it can't possibly be real.

boulders for about 100 yards, there's a good place to try out that waterfall frolic fantasy, because here you are in a pool with a nice waterfall on one side and the ocean on the other. It's right out of a Hollywood movie set. You probably *won't* have it to yourself, but that's OK. Called **Blue Pool** (shown on page 92), it's accessible from 'Ula'ino Road, right near the 31 mile marker. The road goes

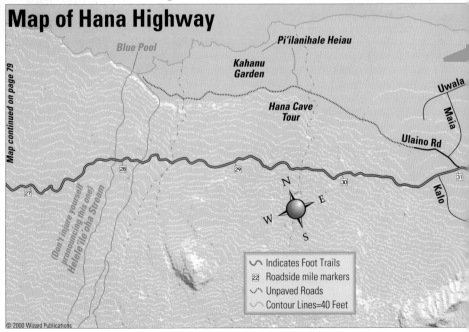

Map of Hana Highway

Map continued on page 79

Blue Pool

Pi'ilanihale Heiau

Kahanu Garden

Hana Cave Tour

Uwala

Maia

Ulaino Rd

Kalo

(Don't injure yourself pronouncing this one!) Helele'ile oha Stream

27   28   29   30   31

N
W   E
S

⌒ Indicates Foot Trails
⊞ Roadside mile markers
⋯ Unpaved Roads
⌒ Contour Lines=40 Feet

© 2000 Wizard Publications

3 miles (most of it unpaved but well graded) where it dead ends at a stream that you can usually cross without getting your feet wet. The falls (technically called Heleleʻikeʻoha Falls—now you see why everyone calls it Blue Pool) are just around the corner. ʻUlaʻino Road itself crosses two streams that are usually dry.

A Real Gem

If they're running, get out and look first. You can usually cross in a regular car unless the water is more than a foot deep. The first stream is halfway to the end of the road; the other is a short walk to the end. See map. Drive ʻUlaʻino Road slowly; dogs tend to dart out in front of you. Though there's no diversion ditch upstream, sometimes the falls at Blue Pool shrivel to a minimal flow. The photo we show on the following page is about halfway between dry and wet. (We've seen it so swollen, the blasting mist made it impossible to photograph.) While at any waterfall, remember that there's always a chance that something harder than water can fall from above.

Also on ʻUlaʻino Road is **Kahanu Garden** (248–8912), part of the National Tropical Botanical Garden. They have self-guided tours (which take around 30 minutes) between 10 a.m. and 2 p.m. for $5, and $10 guided tours at 11 a.m., Mon–Fri. The garden is set among spacious grounds, and the emphasis is on native and Polynesian-introduced plants, not ornamental flowers. The love and care is evident. They take good care of this place, and the plants are well labeled. The most extraordinary feature is not a plant at all, but rather the **Piʻilanihale Heiau** (shown on page 14). This massive temple,

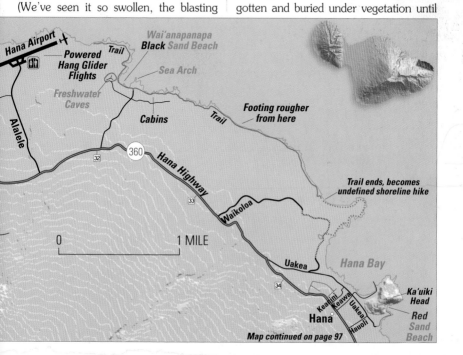

the largest in the state, was largely forgotten and buried under vegetation until

A Real Gem

Hana Airport

Waiʻanapanapa
Black Sand Beach

Powered
Hang Glider
Flights

Trail

Sea Arch

Freshwater
Caves

Alalele

Cabins

Trail

Footing rougher
from here

32

360

Hana Highway

Trail ends, becomes
undefined shoreline hike

33

Waikoloa

0   1 MILE

Uakea

Hana Bay

34

Keawa

Keanini

Uakea

Hauoli

Kaʻuiki
Head

Hana

Red
Sand
Beach

Map continued on page 97

When you're dreaming about frolicking at a waterfall, you're dreaming about Blue Pool

the garden restored it in the late '90s. The first time we saw it, we were unprepared for its immensity. When you first spot it, it looks enormous. But after you get close and go around a corner, you realize how utterly colossal it really is. It covers almost *three acres* and it took an estimated 128,000 man-days to build, starting in the late 1200s AD. The second phase was completed around 1570.

There are some nice coastal views from parts of the garden, as well as some Hawaiian stone implements and tools. Begin your walk at exhibit #4.

Near Kahanu Garden is the **Hana Cave Tour** (248–7308). See page 239 for more on that.

Back on the highway, you'll pass the tiny **Hana Airport**. If you want a thrilling adventure, consider a **powered hang glider flight** in a seated ultralight along the Hana coast. The views along the coast are unreal. See page 186 for more.

WAIʻANAPANAPA BLACK SAND BEACH

Just past the 32 mile marker is the road to **Waiʻanapanapa Park.** (Gee, that really rolls off the tongue, huh? Blew a gasket in the old spellchecker on that one. It sounds like WHY-A-NAH-PAH NAH-PAH.) The park is clean and well maintained. They even have cabins for rent. Other facilities include restrooms, showers, picnic tables and camping. It's got two other things going for it. One, there is a freshwater cave that makes a great place for a dip. Two, it has a volcanic black sand beach.

First the **spring-fed freshwater caves,** which are probably the remnants of lava tubes. There are two, though only one is suitable for swimming. The water level rises and falls each day with the tide, which the freshwater floats on. A little seawater mixes with the freshwa-

ter, meaning the water is slightly brackish but crystal clear. The temperature is very cool, though not painfully so. There are two small chambers that snake their way back a bit. A short loop trail drops three stories and circles the two caves. There's a Hawaiian legend posted on a sign near the loop trail.

If you've heard of a **volcanic black sand beach,** you may have thought they were all on the Big Island. *Au contraire.* Paʻiloa Beach here at Waiʻanapanapa Park is 100 or so feet wide and attests to the newness of the land

A Real Gem

here. The beach was formed when lava flowed and fountained into the sea near here, shattering on contact with the ocean. Fragments smashed against each other and formed the sand you see. (Don't believe books that tell you that the beach was formed by cliff erosion.) Maybe Rome wasn't built in a day, but this beach may have been, because these type of beaches are often formed in days or weeks. We've watched black sand beaches being created on the Big Island and it's an awesome sight. They usually have a short life span since the source of the sand stops as soon as the lava stops flowing. Usually within a few hundred to a thousand years they vanish as the ocean gradually sweeps the precious sand away. (White sand beaches have organic sources, like coral and shells, which are renewed.) Occasionally the sand is deposited in a perfectly shaped bay, like this one, which allows it to stay a little longer. Some lava flows nearby are 500 years old, according to a dated sample taken a mile south of here. There's a pretty coastal hike that leads to the source of all this sand. It's

Wai'anapanapa State Park has the only volcanic black sand beach (created from a lava flow) on Maui. Good facilities, freshwater caves; the only thing difficult about this park is pronouncing it.

described under HIKING on page 199.

Older islands like Kaua'i and O'ahu have no volcanic black sand beaches. (They can sometimes have the other type of black sand beaches, like the one at Hana Bay, caused when water chips flecks of lava from stream beds and piles it up onshore.) Since the sand supply here is finite, please try to refrain from taking samples back home with you, except the stowaways lodged in your bathing suit. Don't swim during high surf as currents can form in the bay.

HANA

Hana doesn't hit you, it seeps into you. Living on Maui, we had driven through Hana many times and thought we knew it well. But it wasn't until the first time we spent a week in Hana that we truly connected with it. The peace that Hana exudes can only penetrate when you're here at leisure, not on a mission. Today, Hana is one our favorite places to go to get away from the hellacious rigors of guidebook writing. (You have no idea how hard it was to write that last sentence with a straight face.) If you're on Maui for a week or more, we strongly suggest you consider spending the last couple of days in Hana.

Hana has a reputation of being a rainy place. In fact they get just over 80 inches a year at the Hana Airport, though it varies quite a bit. That may sound like a lot (actually it *is* a lot), but hidden in that number are two things you need to know. First, it's *way* less rain than what they get farther up the mountain (which is what feeds the waterfalls), and it's less than what they get to the northwest, around Nahiku. This is because Hana is relatively flat and the orographic rain engine that waters most of Hawai'i misses Hana more than most people think. (The photo on the cover is typical. Notice how Hana itself is sunny, with the clouds starting farther uphill?) Second, the great majority of the rain falls at night and early mornings due to the same effect. During the day, heavy five-minute showers also contribute to those rain numbers. Don't get me wrong. You can still come for a week and have it rain *every* day. They occasionally get monstrous rains, especially in the winter. It can happen anywhere in Hawai'i. But it's much less likely in Hana than you may guess by simply looking at raw numbers.

Things move slowly in Hana, and if you try to rush you'll only end up frustrated. Businesses may close for any reason. The only bank is open 1½ hours a day. (How's *that* for bankers' hours?)

Here are some of the things you'll want to check out near Hana.

HANA BAY

Hana Bay has a large, black sand beach. The sand source is lava eroded from a nearby stream. This is usually the safest place to swim along the coast. You can grab something to eat here (see Tutu's, page 100) and eat it at the shore.

On the north (left) side of the bay you may spot an area where the waves come in and seem to die at a certain place. Called **Ke'anini,** Hawaiian legend says there was once a visiting Tahitian chief who wanted to go surfing there. He asked the gods to give him waves, and this they did. As he was surfing two beautiful local girls saw the handsome chief from shore and fell in love with him. Competing with each other for his attention, they both removed their pa'us—skirts—the only things they wore. The chief saw them and was so startled by the sight that he stopped right there in the water, and the wave went no farther. That is why the waves always stop at that surf site today.

Little gems, like this tiny red sand pocket beach near Hana Bay (not the larger, more famous red sand beach), are here to be discovered for those not in a hurry to get to the "Seven Sacred Pools."

Sometimes forgotten Koki Beach.

On the right side of the bay is the **Hana Pier**. Nearby, there is a trail that leads 200 or so yards along Ka'uiki Hill. There's a plaque at the end of the trail marking the spot near a cave where Ka'ahumanu (King Kamehameha the Great's "favorite" wife) was born. The real reasons to take the trail are to visit a small but unknown **red sand pocket beach** that varies seasonally (not *the* red sand beach mentioned later) and to get up close and personal with the geology of this part of the island a little farther along. This hill was formed in geologically recent times when a volcanic vent sprayed lava high into the air. The hill came into being as gas-frothed lava that was caught by the trade winds and piled up here. Near the plaque area you see places where globs of lava plopped and piled up. The deep burgundy color (especially at the small beach) is from iron in the lava. It's literally rusting before your eyes. There's an isthmus

connecting the end of the trail to a small islet that houses a light beacon. During real calm seas you can cross it. One caveat: There's a small stretch of the trail near the red sand pocket beach that is in pretty poor shape, so be careful there. The cove below the end of the trail is an excellent snorkel spot, and it's common to see kayakers there.

If you ever decide that you need to make a stand somewhere, this hill is the place to do it. For generations invaders from the Big Island would capture this hill and were nearly impossible to dislodge due to the hill's easy defense. From up top they could harass area residents and plan general mischief.

RED SAND BEACH

Though we usually describe all beaches in the BEACHES section, Hana is so far that you'd never come here simply for a day at the beach. So we're deviating from our usual format and describing

Hana's beaches here. The other side of Ka'uiki Hill hides one the the area's more exotic looking beaches, **Red Sand Beach** (Hawaiian name is Kaihalulu). There's a photo on page 171. It's made from the same crumbling red and black cinders that make up the hill. The swimming is often poor except during calm seas. There's a strip of jagged lava that forms a semi-pool at the head of the beach, but it sometimes has the perverse effect during high seas and high tide of making the water more chaotic and disorienting, like swimming in a washing machine. The snorkeling opportunities are nil. To make matters worse, the trail is on the side of the hill, with loose cinders making the footing awkward in several spots. (And you wouldn't want to slip and fall down the side of the hill—regular shoes are preferred over beach shoes). Lastly, there's a strangely worded sign telling you not to trespass, then saying to use at your own risk. It also says there's no trail (which there certainly is).

This must be the most violated sign in all east Maui, because everyone, young and old alike, walks to this beach, and we've never heard of anyone being denied entry. So we often have bad swimming, no snorkeling, an awkward, potentially injurious five-minute walk, and a NO TRESPASSING sign. Is it worth going to? To us, it sure is! This is a striking beach, at least worth a look. The rainbow of colors in the lava cinders along the way, the electric blue waters outside the cove, the menacing-looking lava rock inside the bay, the ironwood trees, the layered cinder walls and the untouched beauty make this a memorable place to visit. It's popular and sometimes used by nudists. So if seeing people bearing their *da kines* is bothersome, you might want to pass on this beach.

Map of Hana

Map continued on page 91

34
360

Waikoloa

Uakea

Hana Bay

Ka'uiki Head

1

Keanini
Keawa

2

3

Uakea
Uakeaa

4

386'

Hauoli

5

6

7

Red Sand Beach

1 Hana Kai
2 Hana Cultural Center
3 Tutu's Snack Shop
4 Hotel Hana Maui
5 Hana Store
6 Hasagawa General Store
7 Hana Ranch Restaurant

51

31

'Alau Island

Koki Beach

Sea Arch

Haneoo Road

© 2000 Wizard Publications

Hamoa Beach
2nd Beach

49

N
W — E
S

48

Venus Pool

51 Roadside mile markers
Trail
Contour Lines=40 Feet

0

Map continued on page 105

1 MILE

Hamoa Beach, in the early morning, is where you'll find the best bodysurfing on the island.

To get there, park on Uakea near Hauoli. (See map on previous page.) Just before the Sea Ranch Cottages there's a large lawn area owned by the county. Walk partially across the lawn, and there's a trail on the right side leading down. When you get to the Japanese cemetery, don't walk through, but rather take the other trail to the right. It's easier to navigate than it sounds. The trail goes right past the sign telling you there's no trail. Don't hike if the trail is muddy, and be careful on the slippery cinders. All told, it's about a five-minute walk.

KOKI BEACH

It's certainly the least known and appreciated beach in Hana. It's a mixture of red and black sand (from the nearby crumbling hill) along with white sand from pulverized coral. This is a good place to sit and observe the ocean under the nearby trees with a dramatic view of the red hill behind you, a sea arch off to the left and the coconut tree-topped 'Alau Island off to the right. Swimming is unprotected and can be hazardous, except when calm. Boogie boarding can be good here. The shape and direction the beach faces makes it a good place for beachcombing. Fishing nets, Japanese net glass floats and other flotsam often wash ashore.

HAMOA BEACH

A great beach! Tons and tons of fine salt and pepper sand, some shade, show-

A Real Gem

ers, clear water and the best bodysurfing on the island make this one of the island's primo beaches. The thickness of the sand toward the middle is so great that you don't have to worry as much about stubbing your toe on rocks as at most north or east facing Hawai'i beaches. (Though it's always possible.) Toward the center of the beach the sand drops abruptly a little ways offshore, meaning that the waves tend to break at the same spot each time—exactly what you want for bodysurfing. If you've never done this before, be real careful and only do it on small waves. The ocean is unprotected here—no reef to break things up—so the waves have more power here and can drill you into the sand if you're not cautious. To bodysurf, you simply stand in place, wait for a wave to break right about where you are, and jump forward with your arms extended, turning yourself into a surfboard. I use a mask and snorkel while doing it to keep the salt out of my eyes since I wear contacts. (The mask sometimes gets torn off, so to keep from losing it, I bite down harder on the snorkel when I feel the wave coming.) Many an hour we've spent bodysurfing this beach. Don't try it during high surf; it's too dangerous. Snorkeling is marginal, and there are currents at the two ends of the beach; best to stay in the middle. Located at the south end of Haneo'o Road, there's a paved path leading down. There are other facilities that are for guests of Hotel Hana Maui, but the showers and restrooms are used by all.

Around the rocks to the right (south) is another beach which is usually deserted. Best to swim to it as the rock scrambling may be difficult.

DINING IN HANA

We normally put dining reviews in the DINING section, but we're putting them here for the same reason we put beaches here. Believe us, *nobody* drives to Hana for the food.

Hana Ranch House (248–8255)

Don't eat lunch here, don't eat lunch here, don't eat lunch here! (Enough subtlety, how do we *really* feel?) For lunch, you are the milk cow, and they are the hands. No doubt about it, you're gonna get squeezed. People think doing restaurant reviews must always be fun. But believe me, nothing is more depressing than doing the fourth review (to be *sure* you're being fair) of a place that has been so terrible the other three times.

Owned by the same large company that owns most of Hana, this is normally perceived as the only place in Hana to eat lunch. They have an amazingly bad buffet that defies description. We've seen more people leave plates full of food here than any place we've ever reviewed in Hawai'i. Cheap inedible fish, cheap beans and veggies, unpalatable rice. (How do you ruin *rice*?) They also have a half dozen items on the menu. An example is the pita sandwich—get real! You'd be better off going to the general store across the street and picking up pitas and some cat food. (What the heck, spring for Friskies.)

Outdoors they have a take-out window. It can take astonishingly long to get your food there. We waited with visiting guests there once. One ordered the burger without sauce. After *40 minutes* it came with the sauce. When he pointed this out, the counter person sniffed, "fine, scrape it off!" On a good day it's marginally edible. Also, both the take-out food and the inside restaurant feature service with a snarl at lunch.

Dinner is another matter. They do much better, though they weren't serving it every night at press time. Out come the white tablecloths, and these same people who were so indifferent at lunch become nice and friendly at night. Could it be because local residents often eat dinner here but rarely lunch? Hmm, pretty cynical, I know. Wednesday is pizza night, and locals tend to book the tables. You may walk in, see lots of empty tables, and be told you'll have to wait. The first time we ate it, the pizza tasted amazingly familiar. So we asked the waitress about the crust. *Is this the Boboli we buy at the grocery store? Yep, dats da bugga!* (But it's good.) Other nights also work better than lunch. But for the salad bar at night? It's an extra *$5* for one trip to this salad wasteland, or all the pathetic greens you can eat for $10. Breakfast is also better than lunch (though some of the prices can be offensive—$7 for French toast?!), and the setting at the outdoor tables is quite nice. Avoid the continental breakfast buffet—a complete ripoff. $7–$11 for breakfast, $10–$16 for lunch, $10–$20 for dinner.

Tutu's Snack Shop

Located at the beach at Hana Bay, this is the best place to go for lunch in Hana. Though essentially a burger shack, it is better than the horrible Hana Ranch Restaurant for lunch. Open 8–4, burgers, very good fries (when they don't overcook them), hot dogs, chili, plate lunches, sometimes teriyaki chicken, etc. Breakfast has surprisingly good breakfast sandwiches. Take the food to the little tables next to the water if it's a nice day. The service can be achingly slow, and the place is pretty disheveled. If they were anywhere else, we'd be more critical, but compared to Hana Ranch, it's lunch at the Ritz. $3–$7. By the way, the dark cliff just before Tutu's at the base of the hill was used as a bake-oven to cook the warriors taken captive here during a battle for the hill in 1782. No, they weren't eaten, and let's not hear any cracks about what the special of the day at Tutu's is, huh?

Hotel Hana Maui (248–8211)

This is Hana's version of fine dining and is mostly a dinner place, though they contemplated lunch and breakfast at press time. Resort wear is requested after 6:30 p.m. The food is pretty good. The small menu includes steak, fish, pasta and tofu. Items like the Vietnamese summer rolls make a good appetizer. Blackened "seared" ahi may be a too raw for most people's tastes. Is it overpriced? Yeah...so? Whaddayagonnado? It's Hana and your options are pretty thin.

Considered this dining guideline: Breakfast at Tutu's or Hana Ranch Restaurant, lunch at Tutu's, dinner at Hotel Hana Maui. Or, as a fallback if you're staying in Hana, pick up something cookable at Hasegawa's Store and fix it back at your hotel/condo/house.

At press time, Hana was supposed to be getting some long-needed dining competition from a new restaurant called **Hana Seafood Grill**. We don't know if it will be any good, but it certainly can't be any worse than Hana Ranch. Also, the **Hana Gardenland Restaurant** just before you came into town was closed.

ALSO IN HANA...

The **Hana Cultural Center** is a tiny museum on Ke'anini Street with a small display of Hawaiian stone tools, quilts, shells, Chinese and Japanese bottles, as well as recreations of thatched huts and a canoe shed. (Dugout canoes required serious labor and the ancients always built a garage for it.) The museum is somewhat interesting, but expendable if your time is precious.

Hina Malailena's Hana Village Marketplace is a series of market stalls built years ago but never occupied. There were rumblings at press time that, after over a decade of the bureaucratic two-step, it will finally be opening.

Maui Snorkel and Kayak Tours (248–7711 or 264–9566) has short, fun kayak/snorkel trips at Hana Bay. For

Offshore 'Alau Island.

$59 he takes you on a 2½-hour tour of Hana Bay and/or some nearby areas. Some areas have nice snorkeling, and Kevin is a good guy to lead you.

Hana Adventure Outfitters (248–7476) rents various sporting equipment, including electric bikes. But their squirrely hours seem even shorter than the bank, and they tend to not return phone calls.

Hasegawa General Store (248–8231) has the most widely diverse assortment of…stuff we've ever seen. That's the only word that describes it. Stuff. Where would you find men's dress socks? Next to the shower curtain rings, of course. And the aloha shirts? To the right of the epoxy. How about fishing spears? Across from the movie rentals. Really need some muffler tape? Turn right when you see the red cabbage; it's between the dried cuttlefish and the lawn mowers. By the way, they also have tabis, great for walking on wet rocks. (They're next to the galvanized pipe.) Some items are a decent deal. Milk was actually cheaper here than at the confiscatory Safeway in Kahului.

Other items can be breathtakingly expensive. (I remember going in for a few items once. When I checked out, the total came to $68. I was convinced that the total must represent the last few customers…*it didn't*.)

Incidentally, if your radio has faded and you miss music, 106.1 from the Big Island is the strongest signal along here.

BEST BETS

Best Food—I don't know, what did you bring with you?

Best View of Coastline—End of Nahiku Rd.

Best Bodysurfing—Hamoa Beach

Best Breakfast Experience—Eating Tutu's Breakfast Sandwich at Tables, Hana Bay

Best Exotic Beach—Red Sand Beach

Best Place for a *Cool* Dip—Cave #1 at Wai'anapanapa

Best Place to see Every Shade of Green—Nahiku

Best Place to See Cliff Diver—Ching's Pond

Best Attraction to Skip—Twin Falls or Ke'anae Arboretum

Best Breakfast on the Way—Charleys, Pa'ia

What a difference from the wet, windward side. The dry mountaintop above Kaupo is 9,000 feet high.

After the inspiring drive to Hana, what else can there be? *Plenty!* Past Hana the road goes through beautiful Kipahulu, past the 'Ohe'o Gulch (formerly called the Seven Sacred Pools) and along the bottom of the island, where jungly forest is replaced with wide open expansiveness. The road to the pools is good. Past that you have a decision to make. To go around the bottom...or not to go? The answer to that is on page 73.

KIPAHULU

If you've driven the entire Hana Highway today, it's easy to fall into a sort of beauty fatigue by now. In fact, it wasn't until we stayed in Hana the first time and drove this part of the road in the morning that we realized how utterly gorgeous it was. Only when we were fresh and had allowed

Hana to melt our bones did Kipahulu seep in. The mountains are so stunning, the waterfalls unspoiled, it's hard to believe that the highway can still deliver after all these miles. Those making the all-day drive are now getting tired. It's after noon and they are looking for the payoff at 'Ohe'o Gulch, AKA Seven Sacred Pools. But if you're lucky enough to be in Kipahulu in the morning, when the light is best, you have the highway pretty much to yourself and any waterfalls you find are yours, and yours alone.

The mile markers have changed and are now counting down. (Until 15, then they jump back to 20 and start going down again—*go figga*.) Leaving Hana, there is a surprise waiting for you, if you have time to venture to it. It's one of the largest and nicest freshwater pools on the island. Called Waioka by the Hawaiians, its physical appearance has spawned a new age name that seems to have stuck—**Venus Pool**. It looks like a painting that you would normally dismiss as being too contrived, too perfect, yet here it is. Located next to the ocean

A Real Gem

with a hala tree-capped ball of lava symmetrically dividing the sea view, you'll find numerous places that people jump from, deep water in several places, the pounding ocean just on the other side of the gravel, and some perfect areas on the mountain side from which to sit and cogitate. The aura is unforgettable. If you go in the morning or late afternoon, you'll often have it to yourself. The water is slightly brackish (salty) from the ocean but usually very clean since it is partially spring-fed and not dependent on the seasonal stream it resides in. During whale season we've seen the leviathans breaching close to shore. All told it's a five-minute walk from your car. If you're looking for a unique place to swim or ponder, this will definitely ring your WOW meter.

To get there, park on the side of the highway just past the 48 mile marker. Near the Hana side of the bridge is an opening in the fence or gate and a trail toward the ocean. Just before the path hits a weird, large, round concrete…thing (it's actually an old Portuguese bread oven), veer to the right towards the stream. Be careful of slippery rocks, and don't jump unless you've checked out what's below. (Look around to find the best place to get in and out of the water.) Avoid if the flow is too heavy from the stream.

Weather permitting, look for the Big Island peeking above the clouds. Its massive mountains, over 13,000 feet tall, are impressive to see.

Back on the highway, there may be a

Sunrise at Venus Pool. Could anything be more surreal?

small waterfall at the 46 mile marker. Then, before the 45 mile marker you'll notice a **cross** erected in memory of Helio Koaeloa, one of the earliest Hawaiian Catholic priests. The trail leading to the bottom is treacherous and not worth the bother. There's sometimes a pretty little waterfall near the sign called **Paihi Falls.**

After you cross the Wailua Stream, yet another *(sigh)* sweet waterfall called **Wailua Falls** on the next stream awaits.

(Why isn't Wailua Falls on the nearby Wailua Stream?) Wailua is best in the morning when the sun shines on it. The flow varies a lot. (There's a photo of it on page 30.) Its water pattern is often exceptionally idyllic, even for Maui. Later in the day vendors sometimes congregate there, selling handmade souvenirs.

You may pass a place called 7 Sacred Smoothies. Good, though expensive

smoothies and banana bread, if the ants don't carry the place away. We must have passed this stand 20 times before we ever found it open. When we mentioned that, they were shocked. They're *always* open during business hours, we were told. OK, fine. They're *always* open. (Except when they're not.)

There's a bridge 9/10 mile past the 44 mile marker. If you pull over in the narrow spot 75 feet past the bridge, your first thought is *there's nothing here.*

WATERFALL ALERT!

Good, that's what every other driver thinks. (You only really see it coming back the other way.) This is one of the better places to get a photo of yourself under a waterfall without worrying too much about getting beaten up by the pounding water and falling rocks—and without walking far. (Sneak over when no cars are coming.) There's a short, sometimes slippery path on the other side of the road (the *downstream* side) that leads to a photo-sized

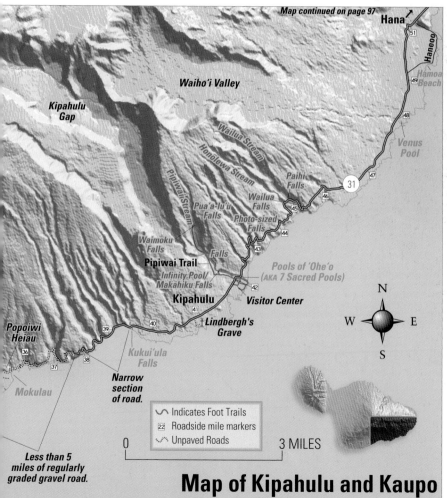

Map continued on page 97

Hana

Waiho'i Valley

Kipahulu Gap

Haneoo

Hamoa Beach

Wailua Stream

Honōlewa Stream

Venus Pool

Paihi Falls

Pua'a-lu'u Falls

Pipiwai Stream

Wailua Falls

Photo-sized Falls

Waimoku Falls

Falls

Pipiwai Trail

Pools of 'Ohe'o
(AKA 7 Sacred Pools)

Infinity Pool/ Makahiku Falls

Kipahulu

Visitor Center

N

Popoiwi Heiau

Lindbergh's Grave

W   E

Kukui'ula Falls

S

Mokulau

Narrow section of road.

⌒ Indicates Foot Trails
22 Roadside mile markers
⋅⋅⋅ Unpaved Roads

0   3 MILES

Less than 5 miles of regularly graded gravel road.

Map of Kipahulu and Kaupo

falls. Not too tall, not too short. A gargantuan tree guards the area. Don't forget your jungle juice.

Are we at the Seven Sacred Pools yet? No, sorry. You'll have to endure yet another falls called **Pua'a-lu'u Falls** just past here. We apologize for the inconvenience. The falls are to the left of the bridge and also fall under it. Driving past these falls, look for a **Blessed Mother Shrine** in a remnant from an old lava tube. It's lovingly maintained by a retired woman in the area. The priest chose this location because Pua'a-lu'u Falls always flows, so there's always water available nearby for blessings and for cleaning the statue.

Those Seven Sacred Pools are just ahead before the 42 mile marker.

'Ohe'o Gulch—AKA 7 Sacred Pools

OK, enough of these serene waterfalls; now it's *playtime*. This series of waterfalls and pools at the shoreline is the most popular attraction in all of east Maui. Why? Because the old name, **Seven Sacred Pools**, sounds so appealing you just gotta check 'em out. Also because the swimming is usually so good and the setting so beautiful. What's not to love? Back when nobody had ever heard of Hana, the owner of the Hotel Hana Maui wanted desperately to attract people here. He had a choice. Tell people they could visit the fabulous *'Ohe'o Gulch* or the wondrous *Seven Sacred Pools* (which he made up). Which do *you* think looked better on a brochure? (For the record, there are not seven of them, and they never were sacred.)

A Real Gem

When a retired airline executive from the mainland named Sam Pryor planned to build a house right near the pools back in 1960, articles began to appear in local papers warning that access to the pools would become a thing of the past. Pryor realized that the pools were so beloved by residents that he contacted the people who sold him the land and insisted that they trade it for land elsewhere, saying the pools should belong to everyone. He later contacted his old friend Laurance Rockefeller and convinced him to buy 52 acres around the pools and eventually donate it to Haleakala National Park. So today, the pools are forever protected.

The pools near the highway are incredibly user-friendly. Falls, pool, falls, pool, falls, pool. It's an ideal playground. The bridge over the first pool is a popular place where daring young dudes (why is it only us males who do this?) jump off the bridge into the pool around 50 or so feet below. Then they jump the waterfall, then the next. It makes for good entertainment. Other, shorter places to jump are also present. By the way, need a new watch? There are rock platforms of various heights where people jump into the water, and the pools beneath them are good places to look for watches, new (loose) wedding rings and other jewelry torn from jumpers during their plunge. (If you see a silver watch with my initials on it, can you send it to me?) Whether you want to jump, swim, hike or just watch, this natural playground is a great place to polish off a day. People *staying* in Hana have it best, because they can get here before the crowds do. When we took the photo on the facing page, we got there at 10 a.m. and had to wait an hour before *anyone* showed up to photograph. In the afternoon, expect a lot of

Playtime!

people to join you in the fun.

Park at the lot past the 42 mile marker. The lot sometimes fills up around peak time (2 p.m.). The loop trail from the lot to the pools and back is just over ½ mile.

We mention leptospirosis on page 34, which can be found in any of nature's freshwater streams or pools. The rangers told us there has never been a confirmed case here due to their control efforts.

Camping is available; see page 177. There are restrooms at the park *but no water*.

The huge valley above the pools, stretching all the way up the mountain to Haleakala Crater, is a wondrous area. Called **Kipahulu Gap**, it has resisted the introduction of most foreign plants brought by man, making it one of the more pristine forests in the state. Endemic birds and plants, found nowhere else in the world, thrive in the waterlogged rain forest above you. It has been designated a biological reserve, and entry past the end of the Pipiwai Trail is closed. Park officials are in a never-ending battle with pigs in this valley. Despite their best efforts, pigs abound here and can wreak havoc with endemic plants.

PIPIWAI TRAIL

Above the pools lies one of the best hikes on the island. You certainly won't have it to yourself, but you get more wowie views and settings per mile on this trail than almost any other. All told it's almost 2 miles each way and you gain 650 feet (not 800, as the park brochure says) from the highway, though the grade is fairly gentle. (The first part is the steepest, and it's not that steep.) Called the **Pipiwai Trail**, it's smashing and takes anywhere from 2½–5 hours, depending on how much of a hurry you're in.

Trails are usually described in HIKING, but we deviate here to make things sim-

The Infinity Pool rests at the top of a 200-foot waterfall. Just make sure you stay at the right end.

pler because there's no chance you woke up, decided you wanted a good hike and drove way over to these-here parts to do it. The trail is down the highway toward the ʻOheʻo Bridge near the 42 mile marker. (See map.)

The trail basically follows the stream. Early into the hike you see a concrete derrick with a pulley on top. Another is on the far side of the bridge. Back when sugar was king, they were used to haul sugar cane across the gorge on its way to the mill down the road. Around ⅔ mile into the hike you come to the Makahiku Falls overlook. Nice, but they often let the vegetation grow, which can cut into your view.

Shortly past this you have an opportunity to deviate onto a well-worn path to the right of the main trail. Take it! If conditions are right, it makes for the kind of photo that you can put on your desk and be assured that people walking by will stop and exclaim, *My God, where is that?!* If you've ever seen an infinity pool at a resort—the kind that have no lip to give the impression while inside that it goes on forever—imagine that very same pool at the top of a 200-foot waterfall! This Infinity Pool has a row of thick rocks to the right that keeps you from going over during normal flows. To the left is where water cascades over during normal flows (so don't go there!). Needless to say, you need to evaluate the setting for yourself. Too much water flow would be ugly, and you always need to be aware in any stream of the potential for flash floods. While in the pool, all you see is the ocean beyond as you hear the water cascading beneath you. We've seen airplanes dip below the field of view—flying below us—and white-tailed tropic birds soar in the valley beyond the

DIVERSION ALERT!

falls. What a scene!

Sometimes the flow grinds to a trickle, making it less dramatic. Behind the pool is a surreal, plant-draped bend in the stream. If you're feeling adventurous, you can scramble over the rockface on the right side, swim across a pool, then scramble over another rockface, and you'll find a large, pretty waterfall that flows even when the Infinity Pool doesn't. (Much of its water percolates under the rocks and gurgles out at the base of the falls below the Infinity Pool.)

Back on the trail, you'll go through a gate and in a few minutes there's a confusing intersection. Confusing coming back, not going up, so remember it. Check out the wise-looking banyan tree with its aerial roots along the way. Without a doubt banyans are the most ancient-looking trees you'll ever see.

After the banyan you can take a side trail to one of the louder waterfalls you'll find. It free falls and smacks onto rocks then runs into a particularly emerald green pool that has undercut the mountain, forming a cave. You can see more of the falls by following the rock steps to the right.

More diversions await, including a pool at least a football field long, then a pair of bridges soon enable you to cross the magnificent stream you've been following. (And yes, foolhardy buggas jump off the first one here, too.) The vantage point from the bridge is tongue-wagging.

What next? Why, a thick, vigorous bamboo forest, of course. (Bamboo, which is a grass, makes an excellent walking stick.) After the boardwalk— constructed to keep you out of the perpetually muddy areas—you eventually come to the end of the line. (Well, you still have to go back, of course.) Slicing 400 feet down the back of a three-way sheer wall of lava, Waimoku Falls marks the instantaneous beginning of this canyon. What a way to end a trail! You could walk under the falls, but remember that any debris falling from above will feel like getting hit by a meteorite. Did you bring your hard hat? Best to view from a little distance. During abnormally dry times in the summer the water flow can diminish somewhat, but it's mostly spring-fed, so its flow is not as rain-dependent.

PAST THE PARK

Back on the highway, about ¹⁄₁₀ mile past the 41 mile marker is an easy-to-miss road that leads to Palapala Hoʻomau Church where the world's greatest aviator, Charles Lindbergh is buried. See box on the facing page. Lindbergh's grave is through the cement post openings, and straight past the older graves on the corner.

At ⁶⁄₁₀ mile past the 40 mile marker there's a small one-car pullout. If you walk across the street, there's an utterly glorious view of the Kipahulu coastline. The road's about to get narrower for a few miles with many blind turns, so be alert for oncoming cars.

At the bottom of this first valley, pull over past the second set of guardrails into the short gravel driveway to the ocean. Looking back the way you came, you'll *usually* see Kukuiʻula Falls plunging into the ocean. (You can't reach the falls by

Towering Waimoku Falls dwarfs a lowly hiker.

Where legends come to die...

Kipahulu will be forever distinguished as the final resting place of aviation great Charles Lindbergh. Most of those from our generation know very little about Lindbergh, and that's a shame. In 1927 the world held its collective breath as this 25-year-old air mail carrier fought weather and fatigue-induced hallucinations for 33 ½ hours to become the first man to cross the Atlantic in an airplane. One of the greatest feats of his time, he did it solo, and it was celebrated as much in its day as the moonshot was years later. He hadn't been able to sleep the night before his flight left New York, so when he landed in Paris he had been awake for nearly 60 hours. Some 150,000 screaming well-wishers met his plane when it landed in France. (More than *4 million* later turned out for him when he returned to New York.) He had no idea when he landed in Paris that he had the world in the palm of his hand. All he wanted was to take a nap.

After the flight, Charles Lindbergh became the century's first media superstar. His life was followed with more interest than any man alive at the time. He represented the very heart and soul of aviation and was a worldwide hero. When his baby was kidnapped a few years later, the ransom demands went on for 2 ½ months, and the baby was eventually found dead just a few miles from his house. (The infant never even made it out of the house alive; he died when the kidnapper's ladder broke on the way out the window.) The Lindbergh baby kidnapping trial was called the trial of the century. (Before anybody had ever heard of O.J.)

In later life, when Lindbergh's old friend Sam Pryor told him, "I have found heaven on earth, and it is at Kipahulu, Maui," Lindbergh visited his friend and was immediately smitten with this part of Maui. He built a home here and spent the last six years of his life in East Maui.

In 1972 Lindbergh was diagnosed with lymphosarcoma. Over time he tried various treatments in New York, but the cancer eventually spread to his lungs. His doctors told him his time was very short. He phoned his physician in Hawai'i and told him, "I have 8–10 days to live, and I want to come back home to die. I would rather spend two days alive on Maui than two months alive here in New York." Against his New York doctors' wishes, he was flown on a stretcher in a commercial 747 (the other passengers had no idea who was behind the curtain in first class) back to his beloved Maui. He spent the next week meticulously planning all facets of his funeral, even designing his coffin and picking the lining. Lindbergh wanted the wild plum tree next to his grave removed, but his grave digger convinced him to let it live there with him. Just over a week later, on August 26, 1974, he died. As the small funeral procession passed the tourists visiting the "seven sacred pools," none had any idea who it was for. Fewer than 15 people were invited to attend, and Lindbergh had asked that his pallbearers wear their work clothes. A Hawaiian hymn was sung as the casket was lowered into the ground and one of his sons said the hymn "just soared out and away with the wind and the crashing of the waves below us."

A short distance from Lindbergh is the grave of Sam Pryor (the friend who lured Lindbergh to Maui) and his wife. Between Pryor's and Lindbergh's graves you'll find six small graves. These were Sam's "children," including Keiki, George, Lani, and his favorite, Kippy. None have last names because his "children" (as he always referred to them) were actually African gibbons. Sam took these apes with him wherever he went. Townsfolk rarely saw him without one of his children.

The inscription on Lindbergh's grave, from the 139th Psalm, reads "If I take the wings of the morning, and dwell in the uttermost parts of the sea." The rest of that passage, not on the stone, is, "Even there would Thy hand lead me. And Thy right hand would hold me."

land, and we have the scars to prove it.) It only occasionally runs dry.

Past the grassy road around the corner, look up the hill in front of you, and you'll see what looks like a rock wall near the top. That's the **Popoiwi Heiau,** a religious structure. What's unusual about it is that it wasn't made by the Hawaiians. It was made by the people who were here *before* them. You see, when the first people arrived here from the Marquesas Islands in about 300 AD, they lived untouched for about 700 years. Then another group came, this time from Tahiti. They killed and subdued the first inhabitants, driving them ever farther northwest. (The first inhabitants were called Menehune by the second arrivals, a derogatory term denoting small in class and stature. The legend was later distorted by westerners who didn't understand, and Menehunes became the Hawaiian equivalent of elves.) The last remnants the Menehunes left behind are some decidedly un-Hawaiian carvings on tiny islands northwest of the main Hawaiian Islands.

Before the 35 mile marker there's a road on your left that angles back toward the ocean and leads to a church and cemetery. It's a dirt road, but 2WD vehicles are usually OK unless it's been raining. Drive to the end and you'll see why it's called **Mokulau,** or "many islets." Dozens of lava outcroppings in the water defying the relentless waves make a dramatic photo op as the water pounds and twists to get past them. Keep an eye out for Hawaiian monk seals that occasionally beach themselves here.

Kaupo Store past the 35 mile marker is your last chance to pick up snacks. (Except possibly Auntie Jane's ahead.) Mostly sodas, chips, ice cream and candy mixed with an interesting collection of antique cameras, clocks and assorted knickknacks. There's also a restroom out back.

We were once at the Kaupo Store when a visitor noted to the woman behind the counter how much Kaupo had *grown* in the 30 years since her last visit. "How has it grown?" asked the woman behind the counter. Lots of new buildings, the visitor replied. The counter woman and I exchanged confused glances, and then she patiently explained to the visitor that the only things that had changed in Kaupo in the last 30 years was that so-and-so had added a new room to his house, and Auntie Jane now has a lunch wagon. That's it! The moral of the story: *Nothing* ever changes in Kaupo.

Past Kaupo Store you'll find **Auntie Jane's Lunch Wagon** on the left. It's a decent place to get burgers or soda, though Auntie Jane has a strange habit of talking you out of burgers because they "take a while to cook; this isn't McDonald's, you know." She sometimes sells coffee beans from wild trees growing up the mountains. It's expensive and fairly weak, but no bitterness is present. They *say* it's stronger than regular coffee; it's not. It's harder for a wild tree to make a go of it than pampered farm coffee trees, and the flavor shows. But it's kind of a cool novelty. You might want to use more beans than you normally would.

Looking around, it's easy to think that nothing important ever happened along here. Actually, this area was subject to a vicious invasion in 1775 by the King of the Big Island. He occupied the area and treated his captives so badly, they called it the war of Kalaehohoa. (Meaning, roughly, *the war where they beat our brains out with clubs.*) When Maui's

DIVERSION ALERT!

king responded, he routed the Big Island king along the shoreline below the 33 mile marker. One of his Big Island lieutenants in this defeat was Kamehameha, who would later become king of all the islands. Kamehameha barely escaped with his life.

Just over ⁴/₁₀ mile past the 32 mile marker is one of our favorite spots to pull over and enjoy the views of Haleakala and the broad expanse of shoreline in the late afternoon. The deep gorges, formed by sporadic but intense rain, show up well in the afternoon. Look to the top of the mountain and you'll see the **Kaupo Gap,** the large, wide opening at the top of the mountain. At one time the gap, caused from erosion, was at least 5,000 feet deep, perhaps deeper, and cut into the very core of the mountain. (There's a similar gap on the other side of the mountain, meaning the volcano was essentially cut into two halves.) Later, lava again poured from the summit, filling the great Kaupo canyon to the shal-

low level you see now. If you look at the left side of the gap, it's not hard to imagine how the lava dammed up against the side of the older mountain and flooded the canyon and the plains below.

Wind is almost always present along here as the trade winds pile up along the flank of the great mountain. We once saw three helicopters struggling to land on a barren, grassy field next to the road. We soon learned that a wedding coordinator had convinced a group of Germans that this would be an ideal place for a wedding reception, so they chartered the expensive helicopters to fly everyone in. We can still picture them standing there, with the wind blowing champagne all over their shirts, as they looked around asking each other, "Whose stupid idea was this?"

Just before the 31 mile marker there's a gate. This leads to **Nu'u Bay,** the only decent ocean swimming area along this entire stretch of coastline. You can open the gate and proceed, but you'll either

Even in the harsh waters off Kaupo, a net fisherman has to eat. This one was knocked down several times before he successfully caught his dinner.

Dry and desolate. Nothing in common with Hana, on the other side of the mountain, except the beauty.

nets. Local fishermen thoughtlessly abandon them when they become entangled on coral heads, which creates a permanent hazard for sea life. We once found a dead reef shark (a normally docile animal) entangled on the bottom here. That's not a sight we'd like to see again.

If the surf is up, the short dirt road just before the 30 mile marker leads to a great place to listen to the surf. The entire Huakini Bay is lined with small- and medium-sized rounded stones. When large waves rake at the shoreline, these stones make a deep rumbling sound that you won't soon forget. The bigger the

DIVERSION ALERT!

need 4WD for the 2/10 mile road or you'll have to walk it. The road terminates at an old cement landing. The snorkeling is fairly good to the left (away from the shore), but don't venture beyond the protected point where the water is rougher and there's a current. The only thing marring the plentiful coral scenery is an unusually large number of fishing

waves, the better. Just don't get too close to the water. The cliffs behind the bay are said to contain ancient Hawaiian petroglyphs, according to a 19th century archeological report we read, but we must confess we haven't been able to find them. Let us know if you're more successful. Be careful of the wicked kiawe (mesquite) thorns.

Modern man is not the first to traverse the island along this route. The ancient Hawaiians built a highway centuries ago, paved with lava stones and wide enough for two. This was how they went from east to west. Keep an eye out on the right side for remnants of it.

Past the 29 mile marker you'll spot the Pokowai Sea Arch, but don't pull over until the road descends to the shoreline. From there you can get out and get a closer look at the arch and shoreline. Though the ocean is almost always whipped and frothed here, we've seen throw-net fishermen braving the water for their catch.

After the 28 mile marker you'll find a brand new two-lane bridge on this one lane road. (As with Hana Highway bridges, federal dollars will only pay for two-lane bridges, even if they are on one-lane roads.) The gulch the bridge spans is beautiful, showing the layers of the different lava flows.

As the road leaves the sea on its way up to the 3,000 foot level, you may wonder what you are missing with all that land and shoreline below. The answer is *nothing!* The land below the highway past here is the most wretched you'll find on Maui. Harsh and unforgiving lava fields, sparse and scrubby brown grass, there is nothing visually pleasing about this area other than some marginally interesting lava rock ruins. (Even paradise has to have an ugly side—this is it.) The shoreline, though rich in fish, is lashed by heavy seas, making it hazardous. Many maps show a trail that goes from south Maui all the way to where the highway started leaving the shoreline. Yeah, the trail's there, but it's sporadic, miserable, ugly and passes by almost nothing of interest.

Surprisingly, this area used to be heavily populated by Hawaiians. Thousands took advantage of the fishing area and the good sweet potato growing conditions in some pockets where there was soil. There was even a forest in those days, before cattle were introduced. Hawaiian ruins are scattered about the rocky fields. Today, native Hawaiians are in the process of trying to repopulate the area. Over 100 families are working as a group to rebuild this part of Maui, called Kahikinui. It won't be easy. Life was always difficult in this land of little rain and ever-present winds. Easier life elsewhere lured their grandfathers for a reason, and they abandoned the land. Even today the homesteaders live with no power or running water, and only time will tell if they are successful.

Past the 15 mile marker you see the Tedeschi Winery. They have a nice wine tasting room and gift shop (albeit with fairly unremarkable wine, some made from pineapple), and it's worth a stop. The grounds are pretty and serene. Across the street is the Ranch Store with a deli/grill if you're hungry.

BEST BETS

Best Hamburger You'll Never See—Auntie Jane's Lunch Wagon, Kaupo

Best Surreal Sunrise—Venus Pool

Best Place to Watch Someone Make a Giant Leap for Mankind—'Ohe'o Bridge

Best Place to Take a Waterfall Shot Without Getting Hammered—Photo-Sized Falls

Best Hike—Pipiwai Trail

Best 'Okole Squeezing View—Infinity Pool

Best Place to Play—Pools at 'Ohe'o (Seven Sacred Pools)

Best Place to Lose a New Wedding Ring—Jumping in the Water at 'Ohe'o

Best Place to *Hear* the Ocean—Huakini Bay if the Surf's Up

Haleakala Crater is unlike any place you've ever seen.

People come to Maui for the ocean, palm trees and balmy weather. So why on earth would you want to use up one of your precious vacation days in the center of the island where you won't find *any* of that? Simple. This part of the island has green, rolling hills, switchback roads, cool mountain air and a *lump-in-your-throat* crater. It may not be typical Hawai'i, but it's definitely worth visiting.

UPCOUNTRY

Upcountry refers to the cluster of towns located 2,000–4,000 feet up the slope of Haleakala. They aren't pointing directly into the trade winds, so rain is less frequent. Drought happens on occasion, sparking water rationing. Since temperatures fall almost 3° with every thousand feet, it's cooler up here than at the shore. It's popular with

people who want to work or play in the tropics, but don't want to *live* there.

Don't tell people who live upcountry this, but in ancient times, Kula residents were considered dim-witted and dense and were the butt of jokes throughout the islands. It stems from the fact that they lived so far from the water that they possessed little sea knowledge, so they were thought of as stupid and backward. Sort of the ancient equivalent of *how many Kulans does it take to pound poi? Five! One to hold the pounder and 4 to raise the bowl over and over. Ha, ha, ha...*

To get upcountry, most people head up the Haleakala Hwy on 37. (The term *Haleakala Highway* and the signs are misleading because it is actually composed of segments from *three different highways,* 37 to 377 to 378.) If it's clear, between the 4 and 5

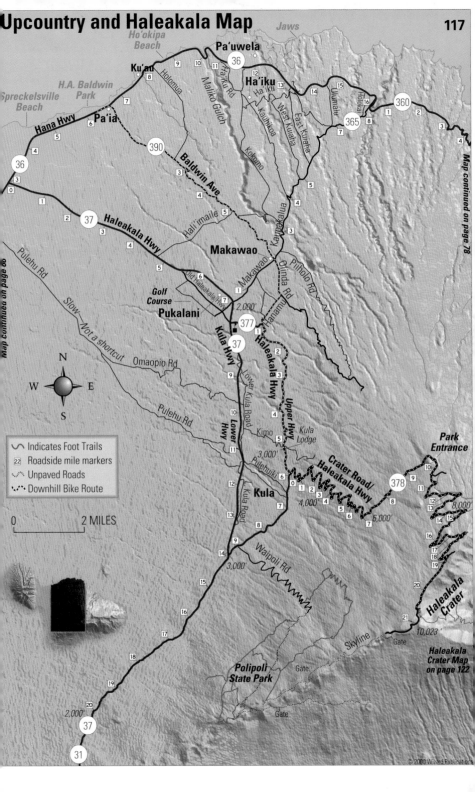

mile markers you get a perspective of just how *big* this mountain really is. It's over 10,000 feet high and from here you can tell by the width that this single mountain hides a monstrous amount of rock.

There are areas mentioned in this chapter that you won't pass by coming up Hwy 37, the most notable being Ha'iku and Makawao.

HA'IKU

Ha'iku is just below the area normally considered upcountry and is probably the least discovered town in Maui. The population is around 10,000, consisting of a mix of old-time locals, hippie-turn-farmers, wealthy mainlanders, Maui business owners and computer commuters. Green, wet and quiet is what they come for, and they're not disappointed. Their higher elevation neighbors sometimes look longingly at Ha'iku's abundance of

water. The roads here tend to be narrow. Twenty feet was considered wide enough in the horse and buggy days, and parts of some roads have maintained that width. There's usually very little traffic on Ha'iku roads during the week. Look at the map on page 117 if you're interested in driving (for no particular reason) some of these pretty roads like Ha'iku or Ulumalu roads. The town is worth visiting if you're in a wandering mood or want a treat from the Ha'iku Marketplace.

MAKAWAO

Makawao is a major upcountry hub. It's supposed to be the island's cowboy town. Most visitor information conveys the impression that you'll see old cowpokes riding horses through town. Not likely. If you see anybody on a horse, it'll probably be a teenage girl wearing a sports bra and pastel pants

The mystic forest along the upper part of Waipoli Road.

Why are the days 24 hours long? Thank Maui.

The Hawaiians believed that in ancient times there was a demigod named Maui. (A demigod is the offspring of a god and a mortal.) Maui noticed that his mother used to complain that the days were too short for her to dry her tapa cloth. So young Maui set his mind to lasso the sun as it streaked across the sky. He went to Hana to watch the sun rise, then tried to catch it at Haleakala but failed. Later, near Kahului, Maui cut down all the coconuts he could find and made a long fiber rope. He climbed Haleakala and hid at a place across the crater called Hanakauhi. When the sun streaked by, he lassoed many of the sun's rays, weakening it. Maui told the sun, "Now I will kill you for hurrying so fast." The sun answered, "Let me live, and I promise that from now on I'll walk instead of run across the sky." Maui agreed and the sun kept his promise. Today the days are 24 hours long as a result of this agreement. (Mondays were apparently exempt from the deal because they seem *much* longer.)

picking up some brie for her mom's get-together. And try to get a good burger in this "cowboy" town, and you'll likely be offered a tofu burger. (Stopwatch has the best *real* burgers.) But it's an interesting place to wander and shop with some unusual finds. For instance, the Rodeo General Store sells "island coconut-flavored gourmet kosher Maui-grown coffee." (You know, it's kind of hard to picture a grizzled old Hawaiian cowboy saying, *Hey, Kimo, pass the gourmet kosher coffee, will ya?)* Around town you'll also find *Titanic*-inspired jewelry, BBQ grills big enough to roast a whole cow, an amazing hot sauce selection at Hi Hearth and Leisure and lots of treats. The absolute best is **Komoda Bakery** on Baldwin Avenue. Unimpressive on the outside, but unreal baked goods at reasonable prices. You can purchase $2 sandwiches at Kitada's at the edge of town on Baldwin Avenue. Makawao is where people with dreadlocks, backpacks and bare feet share the streets with the well-groomed, cell phone-toting business crowd.

Galleries are also common here, though they seem to take themselves pretty seriously. Like the one that claims to be for "peace and the enrichment of humankind with their visions" and they "accept the aloneness in the creative process and celebrate the aloha with their togetherness." Well, damn, that's really good to know. But hey, do you folks sell that velvet painting of the dogs playing poker?

Be aware that mornings can be a zoo in Makawao since the downhill bicycle tours race through town. Also, if you're trying to park and find all those two-hour stalls filled, look across from Ai Street off Makawao Avenue for a free lot.

By the way, no self-respecting Hawaiian cowboy (called paniolo) would ever be caught dead saying, *Get along, little dogie.* Here he would say, *hele makai* (go to the ocean). Other local cowboy phrases are:

Hemo kapuka—open the gate
Pipi—cattle
Lio—horse
Oni—let's move out
Kau ka lio—mount your horses
Waha!—yeehaa!

KULA

Think of Kula as everything past **Pukalani** (which itself offers little other than golfing). Kula has some downright tasty views of the central valley, as well as restaurants and flower farms. Overall, it's not huge on the visitor hit parade, but you may want to consider some of these attractions:

Kula Lodge (878–1535) is the most renowned landmark up here. In addition to its accommodations it has a beautiful (though pricey) restaurant with great views, a pretty garden terrace and a confiscatory gift shop.

On the upper road (377) there's the **Keiki (children's) Zoo** described under TRAVELING WITH CHILDREN on page 36. You need an appointment to visit.

Though there are numerous flower farms, not all are worth stopping for. The best is probably **Sunrise Market and Protea Farm** (876–0200) just up 378. A small but well-tended collection of proteas, gift shop and snack bar.

Polipoli State Park is at the end of that *other* winding road (Waipoli Road) working its way up Haleakala. It's the road few people ever take. (See map.) At the end is an unexpected redwood forest in the middle of this tropical island. The trails are described under HIKING on page 198. It's cool and misty and would seem to belong more to Northern California than the center of Maui.

Kula Botanical Garden (878–1715) is pretty disappointing. We've been there and paid our $4 admission fee, only to see lots of dying plants and 12 birds in their aviary. Avoid unless nature's been real generous with the rain recently.

Past main Kula on your way toward the bottom of the island, the **Sun Yat-sen Park** not far from the 18 mile marker on Hwy 37. History buffs will remember that Sun lived in Hawai'i, attended school here where he learned about democracy, and went back to China to overthrow its last emperor in 1912. If you drive down the road next to the park, you'll (literally) find yourself on EASY STREET.

Past the park the last thing between you and the vast lands of Kaupo is the **Tedeschi Winery,** described on page 115.

HALEAKALA NATIONAL PARK

From Hwy 37 you took 377 then 378, right? (See map on page 117.) You now begin the endless switchbacks necessary to scale the steep slopes of Haleakala. A donut ring of clouds often forms part of the way up, fooling people into thinking the summit's socked in. Most of the time the clouds end before the summit. Watch for mindless wayward cows on this stretch. It's an open ranch, and the witless bovines often wander onto the road. They're occasionally turned into hamburger prematurely by cars traveling too fast in the fog. You will be afforded many outstanding views of West Maui and the valley between the mountains. (Unless you're heading here for the sunrise; then you'll have to see many of the sights mentioned on your way down.)

A Real Gem

If you ever want to *see* what turbulence looks like, take a look at the cloud formations as you drive up and down Haleakala. As a pilot, this is the only place I know of on the island where I can come to and *see* turbulence (as opposed to feeling it) close up as the clouds roll

Sunrise from Haleakala—Is it *really* that good?

Sunrises from atop Haleakala have taken on legendary status. They are said to be comparable to a religious experience, that they will heal your soul, rejuvenate your spirit and perhaps even fix that ingrown toenail you've had lately. In short, they are said to be the best in the world. Sunrises up here are very popular.

The first time we came to watch the sunrise up here, we thought it was the most overrated, over-hyped event we'd seen. Pleasant, yes, but *hardly* worth the effort. Those around us seemed to agree. Also, the first time we were so wretchedly cold that we couldn't have appreciated *winning the lottery,* much less seeing a sunrise. The second time we did it, however, we were blown away by its majesty. Wouldn't have missed it for the world. What's the difference between pleasant and *wow?* Multiple trips have cemented a theory. It's simple—clouds. A sea of clouds *below* you with the sun rising from beneath makes a glorious canvas for the sun to paint. It's like nothing you've seen and when it's good, it's as good as a sunrise can get. Other times, when it's too clear, it's simply…nice…and cold. And for *nice* it's hard to justify the hardship. Fortunately, clouds below you are fairly common.

To get the time of sunrise and a weather forecast, call 871–5054. You'll want to get there *at least* half an hour before sunrise. However, if you don't arrive about an hour before, you run the real risk of not getting a parking spot at the actual summit. You'll have to park at the upper visitor center instead, where all the bike riders stop. If you try to park in the dirt, you may get a monstrous ticket. If you park at the visitor center, consider walking the short distance to the Sliding Sands trailhead. (See map on the next page.) It's less crowded, and you *may* find the wind partially blocked by White Hill next to you. Allow just under two hours from Kihei, a bit over two hours from Ka'anapali. If you don't allow enough time, you'll be one of the poor saps that woke up at 3 a.m. and *still* missed the good stuff. Bring a small flashlight if possible; it's easy to fall down in the dark and numbing cold. If you get here while it's still inky dark, you'll probably see more stars than you've ever seen in your life. No matter how warmly you think you need to dress, dress warmer. Bring every thing you brought from the mainland, if necessary. If you rented an open-air JEEP, here's where you pay the piper. You'll freeze your nuggies off. (In fact, look on the side of the road and you'll see mounds of nuggies frozen off from past visitors.) If the wind's blowing at that high altitude (which is often is), it'll make a penguin scream. We bring our ski clothes, gloves and a wool cap and even still, we sometimes get cold. The temperature rises quickly when the sun does, but few visitors are properly prepared for the morning cold, even in summer. At the summit there's an enclosed viewing area, but it's usually crowded and noisy in there, and the views are more restricted. If properly prepared, consider toughing it outside.

and boil in all directions. While coming down, just past the 8 mile marker is often a good place.

After the 10 mile marker you'll pay your $10 per car entrance fee and enter the park. Try to smile at the poor slob at the entrance gate freezing his/her 'okole off in the booth. Ironically, admittance is often free because (only the government could come up this this kind of logic) they "don't have the budget for someone to collect money all the time." Can you imagine Disneyland making that policy? Anyway, the visitor center and

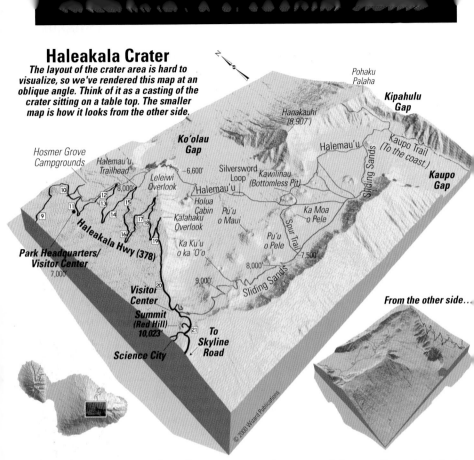

Haleakala Crater

The layout of the crater area is hard to visualize, so we've rendered this map at an oblique angle. Think of it as a casting of the crater sitting on a table top. The smaller map is how it looks from the other side.

Pohaku Palaha

Kipahulu Gap

Kaupo Gap

Kaupo Trail (To the coast.)

Hanakauhi (8,907')

Halemau'u

Sliding Sands

Ko'olau Gap

Hosmer Grove Campgrounds

Halemau'u Trailhead

Leleiwi Overlook

–6,600'

Silversword Loop

Kawilinau (Bottomless Pit)

Halemau'u

8,000'

Holua Cabin

Pu'u o Maui

Ka Moa o Pele

10

12

13

15

14

11

9

Kalahaku Overlook

17

18

16

19

Spur Trail

Pu'u o Pele

7,500'

Ka Ku'u o ka 'O'o

8,000'

9,000'

Sliding Sands

Haleakala Hwy (378)

Park Headquarters/ Visitor Center

7,000'

Visitor Center

20

Summit (Red Hill) 10,023'

21

To Skyline Road

Science City

From the other side...

© 2000 Wizard Publications

campground are the first things you pass. The visitor center has restrooms and the only phone available. This is where you make camping arrangements.

Camping is allowed at several places in the park, including the coveted cabins at the bottom of the crater. See CAMPING on page 177 for more. The campsite at **Hosmer Grove** as you entered the park has a 25-minute **nature loop,** though it seems more neglected than the rest of the park. Consider it dispensable.

As you've ascended the mountain, note how much the vegetation has changed. You're not in Hawai'i anymore, you're in Alaska. Cold, windy and arid conditions favor plants with needles

and very small leaves. One plant that looks like a whisk broom has powder-filled spore casings. Ancient Hawaiians used to come up here and gather the powder to rub into their *da kines* to prevent chaffing on long walks.

The visitor center at 7,000 feet has an average high temperature of 59° and low of 41° in February. In August it averages a high of just 66° and a low of 47°. It's about 10° colder at the summit, and every few years they even get a light dusting of snow or ice. Most of the rain at the summit falls in the winter months, but it's still not nearly as rainy as the lower elevations can be with 54 inches at the 7,000 foot level and much drier at the summit. (If you have computer access, our web site, wizardpub.com has a link to current weather readings on Haleakala, including temperature and wind speed.)

HALEAKALA SUMMIT

After the 17 mile mark you'll see a parking lot for the **Leleiwi Lookout**.

DIVERSION ALERT! Most people blow right by in their frenzy to get to the summit, assuming Leleiwi merely gives them another nice view down the mountain to the coast. Too bad, because Leleiwi is nothing of the sort. Walk five minutes to the end, and the crater itself suddenly explodes into view. What a startling sight! It looks very different than the more traditional view at the top and is well worth the diversion. A small shelter protects you from any wind that may be present.

As you near the summit, keep an eye out for **silverswords** ('ahinahina). You'll know them when you see them. This plant, unique to Hawai'i, first arrived as a California tarweed seed in the feathers of a wayward bird a million years ago and evolved into this striking round silver wonder. They developed their dense covering of silver hairs to live in this difficult environment. It allows them to retain water and ward off the intense sun at this altitude. If you see one

blooming with a large stalk of flowers, pay your respects. Silverswords may live up to 50 years, but, like salmon, they only reproduce once then die. At one time silverswords were endangered when thoughtless people plucked them out of the ground for all sorts of ornamental purposes. Today they are protected and their numbers have rebounded. Be careful walking around them, however, as the fine for damaging them is more than the cost of your whole vacation. For the ancient Hawaiians, there was nothing silver in their universe until they met this plant. Their name for it, 'ahinahina, literally means *gray gray*. That's as close as they could get.

Walking down Sliding Sands Trail will transport you to another world.

There are several trails that are supposed to highlight silverswords, like the one at the **Kalahalu Overlook** up ahead. But you're more likely to see them from the side of the road nearer the summit. While at Kalahalu, take the time to enjoy the view of the crater, which already looks a bit different than at Leleiwi.

There aren't may types of birds that can live up here. Flying in 30 mph winds, which is common, is not a very efficient means of transportation. So they walk most of the time. The three most successful are the native **nene** and the imported **chukar** and **ring-necked pheasant.** A nene is what results when you take wayward geese from Canada and stick them on an island for a few million years. They've left the water and adapted to high, arid lands, losing much of the webbing on their feet in the process. They were almost extinct at the beginning of this century. Today they are protected, but are often accidentally killed because of their laid-back attitude toward cars. They just don't seem impressed with an auto's size, like frogs at night looking into your headlights as they're squashed. People often accidentally back over them. As a result, it's more important than usual not to feed them, or they'll get even cozier with cars. They'll likely come up and beg if they see you, and they're hard to resist, but try. They're often visible at the **Halemau'u Trailhead** between the 14 and 15 mile markers.

Most visitor information refers to Haleakala Crater as the *largest extinct volcanic crater in the world.* Cool! Too bad none of that statement is true. It's not the largest, it's not extinct, and the crater is not volcanic in origin. (In fact, the park now prefers to call this a *basin,*

valley or *wilderness area,* but we refer it as a *crater* because because people will look at you funny if you mention *Haleakala Valley.)*

After Haleakala built itself up, it went to sleep for several hundred thousand years as most Hawaiian volcanoes do. During its snooze, two great valleys formed on either side due to erosion. These valleys cut at least 5,000 feet deep, into the very core of the volcano. They worked their way up the mountain until they met at the summit, back to back. Now the mountain was essentially cracked down the middle, separating the east and west sides, with only a thin ridge between the two great canyons. Then Haleakala awoke for one last series of eruptions before it falls forever silent and eventually sinks under its weight back into the sea. That's what will happen to all of the Hawaiian Islands. (This last series is in its final phase, having last erupted around 1790.)

When it awoke, it did so from the summit, filling the enormous canyons with lava and raising the summit floor you see before you. So, you see, Haleakala Crater is an *erosion* crater that was partially filled with lava and gravel from the crumbling sides, not a volcanic crater like those on the Big Island. When you drive around the bottom of the island, you'll be able to see, from around the 32 mile marker, where and how the lava flowed through the Kaupo Gap and flooded the plains below in an ever-widening flow of molten rock hitting the sea between the 30 and 35 mile markers.

As you approach the top of the mountain, you may find yourself a bit breathless. You've gone from sea level to almost 2 miles high with no time to acclimate. Take it easy and drink plenty of water. You dehydrate very quickly without noticing at this altitude. If you've been SCUBA diving in the last 24 hours and your blood feels a bit carbonated up here, remember—as far as your body's concerned, you may as well be flying. *You got da bends, brah; go back down.*

The upper visitor center after the 20 mile marker has kickin' views, a place to park and restrooms. (Though the latter are inadequate for the number of bikers and tour buses that come up here. Expect lines. There's also a restroom at Kalahaku Overlook.) Early morning bike rides commence from here. They travel 38 miles, downhill virtually the whole way, and end up at the sea. See BIKING on page 174 for more.

The way the clouds race by, clawing at some of the nearby peaks, you could be looking at Mt.

Everest instead of a Hawaiian peak across the crater. The beauty is hard

A Real Gem to describe, but it's unlike any other place we've seen. Adjectives that describe it include desolate, wondrous, arid, majestic, colorful, harsh, peaceful, vast, spiritual, exciting, scary, ancient...all of these and more can be applied to Haleakala Crater. If you were smart enough to dress warmly and can concentrate on things other than the temperature, you'll come up with your own adjectives.

If you're here in late afternoon, you may be treated to something available in only a few places in the world. It happens as you're

standing at the crater's edge, and there's cloud below and in front of you while the sun is low and directly behind you. (Leleiwi is a good place to see it since it's close to the Ko'olau Gap's clouds.) Called **Spectre of the Brocken** or **akaku anuenue** in Hawaiian, it's when you see your own shadow on the clouds with a rainbow surrounding your shadow. It's an *incredible* sight. The Hawaiians felt blessed to experience it because they believed that what they were seeing was their actual soul, and

Though perfectly adapted to live their life above the clouds, the endemic nene is one of the world's most accomplished beggars. Try to resist their charm.

Sharp contrasts, impossibly blue skies, and a myriad of colors; your eyes will be dining on a feast.

the rainbow was a promise from heaven that their souls would be taken care of. If you're lucky, maybe you'll be blessed, too.

The ancient Hawaiians never lived up here, but they did visit for religious purposes and to hunt birds. Many artifacts have been found in the crater. The Hawaiian historian Kamakau says that commoners used to come up here to toss the remains of their loved ones into a pit at the bottom they called Ka'a'awa, now called Bottomless Pit or Kawilinau. (Hawaiians were always fearful that others would desecrate the bones of their ancestors, so this bottomless pit was a perfect place to assure that their remains wouldn't be tampered with.) People who lived at the bottom of the mountain in Kaupo believed that their water came from Haleakala Crater, and they used to bitterly complain that the reason their water tasted so insipid was because of this practice. (Hmm, sort of makes you want *bottled* water while driving through Kaupo.)

Hawaiians also came for the rock. Most lava rock is relatively soft. There are several deposits of harder stone that the Hawaiians used to make adzes (a stone ax) for shaping other tools.

Lastly, Hawaiians came to Haleakala to hide the umbilical cords of their newborns. Hawaiians strongly felt that if rats, notorious thieves, were to steal their baby's umbilical cords, the child would grow up to be a thief. So they hiked to some of the smaller volcanic pits in Haleakala to keep the cords from rats.

At one time imported goats were a huge problem in the crater, eating everything in sight and tearing up the ground with their hooves. You may read that the park has completely eradicated them, though that's not entirely correct. They purposely left a few sterilized males marked with radio transmitters to roam the wilderness. Referred to affectionately as *Judas Goats,* the theory is that lonely males are *far* more effective (and motivated) at locating any unaccounted-for female goats than park personnel could ever hope to be.

Past the upper visitor center parking lot, the road leads to the actual summit itself at 10,023 feet. Winds can be strong up here and can cause windburn if you're exposed to them for an extended period. If it's not windy, as is often the case later in the morning and afternoon, it's tempting to shed your warm clothes. You should know that sunburn happens very quickly up here since the light filters though a thinner atmosphere. (OK, OK, no more nagging.) The peak directly southeast of the summit is called **Magnetic Peak.** Can't find southeast? That's because the iron in Magnetic Peak is messing with your compass.

If you avoid the turnoff up to the summit and instead stay to your left, you're heading to **Science City.** The Air Force and the University of Hawai'i have astronomical observatories up here, but they're not open to the public. The Air Force uses their 12-foot diameter scope to optically sweep space, tracking space junk that could collide with existing satellites. The optics alone for this cost $40 million, and it can spot items the size of golf balls in space. (The shuttle has reportedly lost very few golf balls, but the Air Force *is* tracking a wayward glove.) Astronomers also bounce laser beams off retro-reflectors left on the moon by the Apollo astronauts in the '70s. By timing the reflection they can measure the speed of continental drift. Maui's Pacific plate moves northwest at the same rate that your fingernails grow. (Apparently, their procurement office moves at about the same speed. It wasn't until 2000 that they finally replaced their 70s-era 4mhz computers with newer ones that were only five years out of date. *That's* progress!)

We came up here once in the middle of the night to watch a meteor shower, but the shower was mostly a bust. After dozing for a few minutes in the car, we awoke and thought we were hallucinating. *How can this be?* It looked like thousands of shooting stars in line with each other, like a special effect from a *Star Wars* movie. It took a minute to realize it was a pulsating laser shooting all the way to the horizon from one of the university's many science experiments.

Stay to your left at the road to Science City, and you're on a federal road leading to the FAA's main communicating equipment for the entire state. At press time there was a nasty sign on the federal road telling you that trespassers would be tortured and maimed, or something to that effect. Few people have been to this part of the summit in the past because of the sign. Too bad. We did a little digging and found that the FAA erected the sign to prevent *tour busses* from using the narrow road for (c'mon, everybody, you know the words to this song) *liability reasons.* The FAA doesn't have a problem with smaller vehicles using the road since it's necessary to access **Skyline Road,** a fantastic and lightly used dirt road that meanders down the spine of Haleakala, ending at Polipoli Park. (See BIKING in ADVENTURES or HIKING in ACTIVITIES.)

If you take the federal road (the sign may vanish since the state's considering taking over the road), you'll come to a dirt road on your left with a gate. That's Skyline, and if you walk on it around the corner for a few minutes, you're treated to a magnificent view of most of Kahoʻolawe. Though you're almost 10,000 feet up, the ocean is only 6 miles away. What a sweeping vista! The Big Island—at 4,000 square miles it's almost as big as Connecticut—lives up to its name. It looks positively *huge* from up here.

After all these beautiful sights, it's (literally) all downhill from here. Remember to use a lower gear driving back down, the slope will burn your brakes.

INSIDE THE CRATER

On the other side of the hill next to the upper visitor center is **Sliding Sands Trail.** If you're only going to do one hike at Haleakala, this is the one. The trail descends 2,400 feet fairly evenly over a span of almost 4 miles to the crater floor, but you don't need to go that far to see some of the gorgeous views from your slow but constant descent. Just go as far as you want, and you'll see how much larger and grander the crater looks from the trail. At times it looks big enough to hold another island. The colors inside are amazing. Everything from green, yellow, red, brown, grey and blues are represented. If you don't want to hike it, there's a company that takes people down on horseback, all the way to the bottom. It's an *outstanding* ride, showcasing the crater at its best, and is the coolest horseback ride we've done in Hawaiʻi. See HORSEBACK RIDING on page

A Real Gem

203. The trail leading into the crater is far less windy than up above. The weather is usually sunny, especially in the morning. Clouds will push up from the Koʻolau and Kipahulu gaps as the day progress-es. From inside you'll often see the clouds roiling at the head of the Kipahulu Gap at the far end, like a white waterfall, but passing no farther. Quiet prevails inside the crater, and the ever-eroding walls provide endless gravel. In fact, it's been necessary to dig up the horse hitch at the bottom of the crater three times. Erosion from the sides of the crater keeps raising the basin floor, creating the illusion that the hitch is sinking.

Inside are numerous hiking trails described under HIKING. Though Haleakala's most recent eruption in 1790 was at the coast, the crater is far from dead. Lava flowed in the crater 900 years ago while Hawaiians occupied the island, and perhaps even more recently. And it probably will erupt again.

There are cabins in the crater for the lucky lottery winners. If you get one, enjoy that complimentary firewood. It'll make the most expensive stove fire you've ever had since the park service gets it there by helicopter. Other maintenance is done by rangers on horse and mule.

BEST BETS

Best Tour—Horseback Ride Down Sliding Sands into the Crater
Best Hike—Sliding Sands as Far as Your Heart Takes You
Best *Coup*—Getting a Cabin in the Crater
Best Decadent Treat—Komoda's Bakery in Makawao
Best Sign to Ignore—FAA Sign to Skyline
Best Place to See Someone Shoot at the Klingons—From Science City at Night
Best Way to Freeze Your *Da Kines* Off—Wear Shorts to Watch the Sunrise
Best Place to Get a Glimpse of Your Soul—Leleiwi Overlook

Crystal clear water, luscious beaches like Mokapu, and swanky resorts are why people love South Maui.

Ahh, South Maui. Land of sun and beaches and visions of offshore islands.

Until the mid-1900s, there were few people living in South Maui. Lack of water made it difficult to grow things, and, after all, what else was land good for? Today we know it's good for growing Hawai'i's most important cash crop—*visitors!* South Maui gets so little rain (many years it may only rain three or four times), and its beaches are so extraordinary, that it's a mecca for anyone looking for a dreamy, dependable tropical vacation.

If you look at the map below, the first thing you notice is that the term *South Maui* is not very geographically correct. *South Central Maui* seems more accurate. But South Maui is what the region is historically known as, so who are we to quibble?

We're going to describe it from Ma'alaea at the top of Hwy 31 heading south as far as you can go.

MA'ALAEA

At the intersection of Hwys 30 & 31, Ma'alaea was feared and despised by early airborne visitors. Because it was here, where the Kealia Pond now exists, that clueless aviation officials chose to place Maui's first airport in 1929. (It looked geographically convenient on a map to early planners.) It didn't last long because this is the windiest spot in Hawai'i. The scouring wind ensured that the inbound flight experience would be as terrifying as possible. (So if you think your landing at Kahului was bumpy—*brah, dats nothing!)*

Ma'alaea is still a transportation hub, only now it's for boats. If you take a snorkel or whale watching trip, odds are very good you'll leave from here.

Maui Ocean Center (270–7000) is the other big attraction here and is definitely worth a stop. Opened in 1998, this is a relatively small (compared to some mainland aquariums) but extremely well-done aquarium. The living reef exhibit has a fantastic collection of fish found around the Hawaiian islands, and the sealife seems remarkably well cared for. Turtle Lagoon has lots of turtles roaming around that you can view from above or from a glass wall below the surface. Sting Ray Cove is similarly structured. Elsewhere there is a glass tunnel that passes right through a large tank, complete with sharks. Stop in the tunnel's center, and the sharks pass right beneath the glass floor. The gift shop has a surprisingly fine and vast assortment of gift items, many locally made. It's one of the more impressive gift shops we've seen on the island. The aquarium is more crowded when the weather is bad. The $18 entrance fee may seem excessive due to the small size, but the quality shines.

Ma'alaea's greatest natural asset is its 3-mile long Ma'alaea Beach, stretching all the way to north Kihei. If you're looking for a great walking or jogging beach, this is the one. Early mornings and early evenings are best, as winds punish the area during the day. You won't have it to yourself, but you will have an amazingly peaceful stroll.

While *you* may have come to Maui for the beaches, *birds* visit us for Kealia Pond. This important wetland is home to several species of native birds. There's a turnout and trail between the 1 and 2 mile markers on Hwy 31. (Also labeled as 310 as some signs are marked.) This is a good place to bird watch. During the summer the ponds dry up.

You might want to raise the top on that convertible if you drive Hwy 31/310

Though it may dry up in the summer, the existence of Kealia Pond, a wetland in perennially dry South Maui, is a surprise to everyone except the birds.

at night or morning, especially in the winter and early spring. Clouds of mindless midges (a tiny, irritating, imported bug that often flies up your nose) swarm the area and sound like rain as they pepper your car.

We know we're going to make some enemies saying this, but staying in Ma'alaea is not advised. Though conveniently located, the wind, smoke and dust from sugar operations, a nearby power plant, a landfill upwind, and winter midges—none of which are probably in the brochures you've seen—make Ma'alaea a pretty dicey proposition. They better offer you an outrageous deal; otherwise, consider the offerings farther south.

Those TURTLE XING signs you see refer to hawksbill turtles. In the past they would occasionally cross the road in late spring/early summer to lay eggs in the Kealia Pond. The fence you see now prevents that, and they lay their eggs on the beach. But that's the only time you're likely to see them. They live and feed in deeper waters, far from shore. The turtles you see while snorkeling are usually green sea turtles, which don't nest here, but in French Frigate Shoals, 700 miles from here. (Like restless teenagers, sea creatures rarely want to hang around the place they were born.)

As you're entering Kihei, you have a choice of either taking South Kihei Road along the

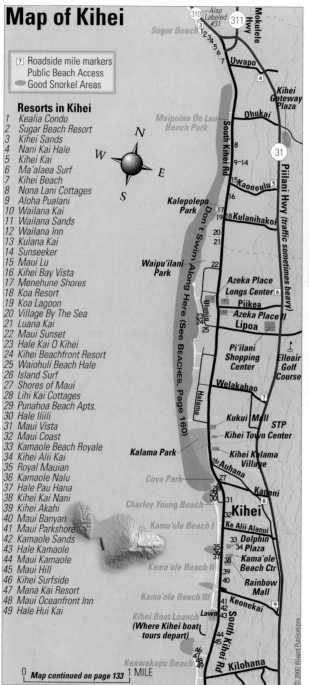

Map of Kihei

☐7 Roadside mile markers
☐ Public Beach Access
● Good Snorkel Areas

Resorts in Kihei

1 Kealia Condo
2 Sugar Beach Resort
3 Kihei Sands
4 Nani Kai Hale
5 Kihei Kai
6 Ma'alaea Surf
7 Kihei Beach
8 Nona Lani Cottages
9 Aloha Pualani
10 Wailana Kai
11 Wailana Sands
12 Wailana Inn
13 Kulana Kai
14 Sunseeker
15 Maui Lu
16 Kihei Bay Vista
17 Menehune Shores
18 Koa Resort
19 Koa Lagoon
20 Village By The Sea
21 Luana Kai
22 Maui Sunset
23 Hale Kai O Kihei
24 Kihei Beachfront Resort
25 Waiohuli Beach Hale
26 Island Surf
27 Shores of Maui
28 Lihi Kai Cottages
29 Punahoa Beach Apts.
30 Hale Iliili
31 Maui Vista
32 Maui Coast
33 Kamaole Beach Royale
34 Kihei Alii Kai
35 Royal Mauian
36 Kamaole Nalu
37 Hale Pau Hana
38 Kihei Kai Nani
39 Kihei Akahi
40 Maui Banyan
41 Maui Parkshore
42 Kamaole Sands
43 Hale Kamaole
44 Maui Kamaole
45 Maui Hill
46 Kihei Surfside
47 Mana Kai Resort
48 Maui Oceanfront Inn
49 Hale Hui Kai

Map continued on page 133

© 2000 Wizard Publications

shore or staying on the highway. The latter you'll use when you're simply interested in getting farther south. Though you won't take it every time, we'll describe South Kihei Road from here because that's where all the goodies are. The map shows all the connecting roads.

KIHEI

Kihei is the unplanned outcome of South Maui's explosion of popularity during the 1970s and '80s. It's a linear collection of condos and strip malls. While it certainly lacks the old world charm of Lahaina, Kihei doesn't try to be anything other than what it is—a beach town—where everything is water-related. As for downtown Kihei, there is no such animal. The closest you could come to defining the town center is the shopping center area near Lipoa and South Kihei Road. And that's a stretch.

Before it was developed, Kihei looked like what you see up the mountain: dry, scrubby and not overly attractive. Water was scarce. With no water to tap from this dry side of Haleakala, planners drilled wells over in water-rich West Maui and piped it in under the central plain. Most people who live here don't even know this, and, when Upcountry experiences its occasional droughts, they look resentfully down the hill at the green of Kihei and Wailea and wonder where *they* seem to get all their water.

South Kihei Road is quite a sight for first-timers. It's so close to the ocean and beaches, you recognize immediately how important the sea is to this town.

When the Big Island's King Kamehameha invaded Maui for the last (and ultimately successful) time, he came ashore in Kihei at one point. The fighting was fierce with Maui warriors employing a novel weapon—*heated* sling-stones.

Kamehameha's forces were a bit intimidated by the hot rocks and contemplated retreating. So Kamehameha ordered all of their canoes destroyed. The message was simple—win or die. With newfound motivation his troops eventually won (with the help of some western cannons) and went on to conquer all the islands.

Since we've already made some residents mad with our Ma'alaea comments, we might as well go for broke. Though South Kihei and Wailea have some of the *best* beaches on the island, North Kihei has some of the *worst*. In short, don't swim in the water from the intersection of South Kihei Road and 311 down to Cove Park, 4 miles south. We explain the gory details under BEACHES on page 160. Simply put, the water is yucky.

As you pass Cove Park, note the color of the water. Brownish, right? Less than 200 feet south the water will get clean and clear again, and the next beach, Kama'ole Beach I, offers fine swimming. From here on it's nothing but great beach after great beach. All are described under BEACHES. Outstanding Keawakapu is the last beach you pass on South Kihei Road Here the road veers away from the shoreline. You'll take a right on Wailea Alanui Road to continue your southward journey.

Breezes usually stiffen into winds in the afternoon in South Maui. (See WEATHER on page 27.) Most beach activity is best in the morning or late afternoon just before sunset.

If you're watching a sunset from South Maui and the sky is clear of clouds, take a look behind you as soon as the sun sets. If Haleakala's free of clouds, too, you'll see that the sun still shines there. It's so tall that the sun sets several minutes later on Haleakala, bathing it in sunlight when it has vanished from your eyes.

WAILEA

The premiere resort area on the island (Kapalua's and Ka'anapali's claims notwithstanding). Expensive resorts line its heavenly beaches. Some, like the Grand Wailea, are so posh and exotic, you'll weep when you final-

A Real Gem ly have to go back to the *real* world. While Kihei was an *every man for himself* development, the Wailea area had a single owner with a single vision: grand, green, groomed and golf. With splendid weather (cooler than Kihei and the afternoon winds aren't as strong), phenomenal beaches, clean water and kickin' views of Molokini and Kaho'olawe, Wailea is a grand success.

There are no mile markers here, and some places don't have signs. If you reset your odometer at the corner of Wailea Iki and Wailea Alanui, we've marked distances on the maps.

Many of the best beaches on the island are found right here. In addition to its beaches, Wailea has a glorious beach-side path. Though not as long or as well known as Ka'anapali's path, it stretches between the Renaissance and Kea Lani resorts (Mokapu and Polo Beaches), and is a perfect way for visitors at one Wailea resort to dine at another without resorting to cars. It also makes a great place for a sunset stroll or a sunrise jogging path. (One place in front of the Outrigger sells coffee for your morning strolls.)

Wailea Alanui becomes Makena Alanui past the Kea Lani. (That's the goofy looking, though very luxurious, resort past the Four Seasons—someone was reading *Arabian Nights* when they designed *that* one.) Segments of the old Makena Road visit less known beaches, such as Palauea and Makena, as well as snorkeling and

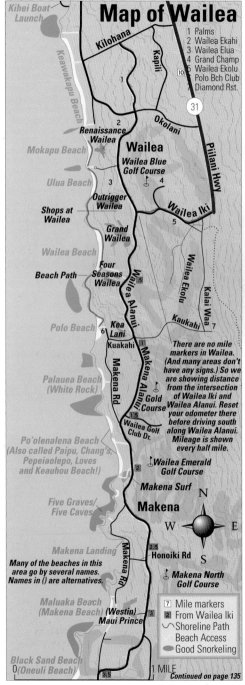

Map of Wailea

1 Palms
2 Wailea Ekahi
3 Wailea Elua
4 Grand Champ
5 Wailea Ekolu
6 Polo Bch Club
7 Diamond Rst.

Kihei Boat Launch
Kilohana
Kapili
Keawakapu Beach
Okolani
Renaissance Wailea
Mokapu Beach
Wailea
Wailea Blue Golf Course
Piilani Hwy
Ulua Beach
Outrigger Wailea
Wailea Iki
Shops at Wailea
Grand Wailea
Wailea Ekolu
Wailea Beach
Four Seasons Wailea
Wailea Alanui
Kalai Waa
Beach Path
Polo Beach
Kea Lani
Kaukahi
Kuakahi
There are no mile markers in Wailea. (And many areas don't have any signs.) So we are showing distance from the intersection of Wailea Iki and Wailea Alanui. Reset your odometer there before driving south along Wailea Alanui. Mileage is shown every half mile.
Palauea Beach (White Rock)
Makena Rd.
Gold Course
Wailea Golf Club Dr.
Po'olenalena Beach (Also called Paipu, Chang's, Pepeiaolepo, Loves and Keauhou Beach!)
Makena Alanui
Wailea Emerald Golf Course
Makena Surf
Makena
Five Graves/ Five Caves
N
W   E
S
Makena Landing
Many of the beaches in this area go by several names. Names in ( ) are alternatives.
Makena Rd.
Honoiki Rd
Makena North Golf Course
Maluaka Beach (Makena Beach) (Westin) Maui Prince
7 Mile markers
2 From Wailea Iki
Shoreline Path
Beach Access
Good Snorkeling
Black Sand Beach (Oneuli Beach)
1 MILE

Continued on page 135

Who would expect an oasis of life in a young lava field, like this one at Cape Kina'u?

diving areas like Five Graves. Kayakers often launch at Makena Landing.

One sound that's becoming increasingly common in South Maui is the call of the gray francolin. This bird starts every morning with a surprisingly vigorous call, which sounds something like a car alarm.

MAKENA

Leaving Wailea and passing the Maui Prince, as you round the corner you'll notice a large hill near the ocean. The drama that created that hill was probably witnessed by the ancient Hawaiians.

Haleakala is in its twilight years as an active volcano. Its time is almost up. The typical life cycle for a Hawaiian volcano is to grow slowly beneath the sea through sporadic eruptions. It then begins vigorous, near-constant growth, building an island. Later it falls asleep for 500,000 to 1 Million years and then awakens for its last hurrah before dying and eventually sinking beneath the sea under its own weight. Oahu's Diamond Head is a prod-

uct of its last gasp 300,000 years ago. Here, on Haleakala's southwestern flank, we see a volcano in its death-throes. Its last eruption was around 1790 at the end of the road ahead. It was a "typical" surface flow; lava squeezed from a vent and flowed downhill. The large hill toward the sea, called Pu'u Ola'i, or Earthquake Hill, was not.

Hawaiian legend states that before the 1790 eruption, this was the last place on the island to erupt. Imagine how it must have looked if there were villagers living here at the time. Lava began quietly pooling beneath the surface in what was supposed to be just another "typical" surface flow. But because it was so close to the shoreline, seawater seeped into the magma pool. This water immediately flashed into steam, building up the pressure in the lava pool. Earthquakes began rumbling as the earth struggled to contain the pressure. Villagers may have begun to notice small amounts of steam coming from the ground. As more lava and seawater combined, something had to give. Suddenly the ground ripped open with a tremendous explosion as fountains of bright orange and red lava shot into the sky. It must have been spectacularly large, because the entire hill you see before you was created as the gas-frothed lava fell to earth and piled up to form the 360-foot Pu'u Ola'i, perhaps in as little as a week. (Looks taller, doesn't it?)

Hiking up Pu'u Ola'i is more difficult than it looks. The trail to the top marches through the cinders (called *tephra* by geologists, in case you just *had* to know) that make up this mass. So, as you take a step up, the tendency is to fall back a few inches, making the climb more tiring. But the view from the top is worth it. You can see Big Beach below on one side and much of Wailea on the other. Directions to the trailhead are on page 202.

You may see signs in the area warning of deer crossing. These aren't a joke. Five axis deer from India were brought here in 1959. They were supposed to have a low reproductive potential. Apparently somebody missed the fine print in their warranty, because in the brief time they've been here, they've multiplied to around 5,000 and are considered a nuisance. Many of them live in this area and are occasionally whacked by passing cars. Golfers at Wailea's courses may find additional hazards on the greens as the deer come down from the mountains during times of drought upcountry and leave souvenirs on the greens.

MOLOKINI

To residents and visitors in the know, the name Molokini conjures up images of crystal clear water and bright, vivid coral. If nature hadn't made this offshore island, the Hawai'i Visitors Bureau

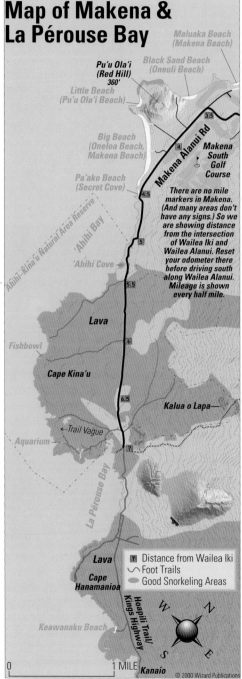

Map of Makena & La Pérouse Bay

Maluaka Beach (Makena Beach)

Pu'u Ola'i (Red Hill) 360'

Black Sand Beach (Oneuli Beach)

Little Beach (Pu'u Ola'i Beach)

Big Beach (Oneloa Beach) Makena Beach

Makena Alanui Rd

Makena South Golf Course

Pa'ako Beach (Secret Cove)

There are no mile markers in Makena. (And many areas don't have any signs.) So we are showing distance from the intersection of Wailea Iki and Wailea Alanui. Reset your odometer there before driving south along Wailea Alanui. Mileage is shown every half mile.

'Āhihi-Kīna'u Natural Area Reserve

'Āhihi Bay

'Āhihi Cove

Lava

Fishbowl

Cape Kīna'u

Kalua o Lapa

Trail Vague

Aquarium

La Pérouse Bay

Lava

Cape Hanamanioa

Distance from Wailea Iki
Foot Trails
Good Snorkeling Areas

Keawanaku Beach

Hoapili Trail/ Kings Highway

0   1 MILE   Kanaio

© 2000 Wizard Publications

would have. This aquatic wonder was created when an undersea vent, held under pressure by the ocean's weight, busted loose with lava and ash, building up what we call a tuff cone (pronounced

A Real Gem

TOOF). The northern half has been eroded away by wave action, creating a semicircular reef far enough offshore to be clear of runoff or sand. So underwater visibility is nearly always 100 feet, sometimes 180.

Visiting Molokini means taking a boat from either Ma'alaea (10 miles away) or Kihei Boat Ramp (6 miles). Though it seems close to Maui, don't try to take a kayak there. Currents and winds between Molokini and Maui are too strong for most kayakers. You *can,* however, rent a power boat (page 238) and visit it on your own.

The crater is a marine and bird sanctuary. You're not allowed to walk on the island. Once inside the crescent, you'll find the water inviting. See page 208 for more on snorkeling and diving Molokini. In the past, the crater has been visited many times by a lonely monk seal who is famous for swimming up to divers. Boat captains have nicknamed him Humpy. The seal is apparently unaware of the law prohibiting human contact with monk seals, for Humpy has been known to get *very* friendly indeed. (I'll leave it to your imagination as to how he got his name.) Just remember that *he* has to initiate contact.

The horizontal notch on the back of the crater is caused by wave cuts. If you were to SCUBA dive down 250 feet, you'd find a similar wave cut, evidence that the ocean was *much* lower during a past ice age.

According to lore, the 19th century King Kalakaua wagered Molokini in a hand of poker with a local rancher. When he lost the hand, he reneged, proclaiming that he hadn't wagered Molokini, but rather *omole kini,* which is a bottle of gin.

Perfect days end with a perfect sunset.

When was the last eruption of Haleakala? 1790...Or is it 1490?

Ask most people on Maui when was the last time there was an eruption here, and you'll be told 1790. It's said so often it's considered an unchallenged fact. The truth is, we don't know *when* it happened. The 1790 date is based on the fact that when George Vancouver visited here in 1794, he drew a map showing the lava flow at Cape Kina'u (at the end of the road in South Maui). But when the French explorer La Pérouse visited in 1786, his map didn't show the cape. This, coupled with the fact that the flow looks very young, allowed people to divided the time and conclude that the eruption occurred "around 1790."

The problem is this: As a mapmaker, La Pérouse was terrible. He didn't get *anything* right. And his map of the shoreline was so crude and inaccurate, you can't use it to use to determine anything—other than the fact that La Pérouse probably flunked out of cartography school. You'd never recognize these islands from his map. Recent carbon 14 dating puts the eruption closer to 500 years ago, give or take a century. And by analyzing crystals in the lava, they can check the direction of the earth's ever-changing magnetic field. The crystals don't match the flows that we *know* happened on the Big Island in 1801.

What about historical accounts? There were people living here and, after all, two centuries isn't *that* long. Didn't they witness it? Sure, they did, but nobody wrote it down. The Hawaiians didn't have a written language until western man invented one in the 1800s. The only known historical accounts come from two sources. One was an American missionary who came to Maui in 1841. He said the native Hawaiians had told him their "grandparents witnessed it." Hmm, pretty slim. The only other account was from a Hawaiian cowboy named Charlie Ako. In 1906 he told a reporter that his father-in-law told him that *his* grandfather had seen the flow when he was "old enough to carry two coconuts from the sea to the upper road," which was 4–5 miles. The reporter plugged in the various ages and dates, assuming 33 years per generation, and came up with around 1750.

So we have map readers saying 1790, historical accounts saying 1750, and some scientific tests saying around 1490. Since we had to use *some* date, we mention the 1790 date in this book. But now you know the full story.

So now if someone tells you that the last eruption took place in 1790, you can look them directly in the eye and tell them with smug certainty...*maybe*.

LA PÉROUSE BAY

As you approach the end of the road, look uphill at the split lava mound. This was where the last eruption took place on Maui. Local legend states that there was a family living there at the time. An old woman came one day and asked for a chicken to eat. The family refused, saying that they first had to sacrifice some to the volcano goddess, Pele. The old woman raged, saying that *she* was Pele and how dare they refuse her. She sent lava flowing their way. The mother and daughter fled toward the mountain, but Pele seized the two and turned them into stone. The hill you see, split in two, is made up of the mother and daughter, forever separated by a vengeful Pele.

La Pérouse Bay is as far as you can go by car in South Maui. It's renowned for two things: dolphins and wind. Dolphins are relatively common early in the morning. A pod patrols the area, and we often see them here around 7 a.m. and at Big Beach by around 10 a.m. But we often go months without seeing them at all. (Maybe dolphins take vacations, too.) Scientists think that, while resting, dolphins are able to turn off much of their brain (including the part that runs their echo-location abilities). They do a sort of snooze-and-cruise at La Pérouse in the early hours, counting on the fact that the shallow water and a light bottom will alert them to predators in the absence of their sonars. This means that, in the morning, dolphins are *literally* operating on half a brain. (Come to think of it, so am I before my coffee.)

It is illegal to chase or harass dolphins or do anything that disrupts their natural behavior. It may be hard to imagine slow, clumsy swimmers harassing sleek, fast dolphins, like a lowly crop duster harassing an F–16 fighter. If you're swimming near them, dolphins can distance themselves from you almost instantly and with very little effort. But when they're resting, they're not in a very fast mood. They don't *want* to work to distance themselves. So if you swim in the same water near them, don't shoot like a shotgun in their direction. You can slowly meander toward their general vicinity, but you shouldn't try to box them in or head them off at the pass. They may initiate the contact, if they are interested. Many times we've been in the water and had dolphins come over to check us out. Most of the time, however, they keep themselves at a cautious distance. If they don't stay away, you can only interpret their actions as curiosity. In short, don't harass or chase them or try to grab them if they come close. If people continually

bug them, they'll simply stop coming to La Pérouse and we'll all lose.

Wind is also a La Pérouse trademark. If you look at the front cover map, you can see that wind coming from the northeast (our usual trade direction) will build up along the bottom of Haleakala and get ejected where the flank ends here at La Pérouse Bay, shooting out toward Kahoʻolawe island. (You can actually *see* the windline in that photo.) The wind-caused chop on the water will usually start at the south end of the bay and work its way north throughout the day. The dividing line between choppy and calm water is often sharp, only 100 or so feet wide.

La Pérouse Bay was well known in ancient times as a place where night marchers could be found. Called Huakaʻi po, it refers to spirits who are still trapped on earth and generally cause mischief at night. To this day, there are places Hawaiians avoid at night because of night marchers. On Kauaʻi there was a night marcher area that had an unusual string of bad car wrecks, which many believed were due to these spirits. (Police, however, blamed the wrecks on the other type of spirits—the kind in a bottle.)

Past La Pérouse there is a hike to a usually deserted black, white and green sand beach called Keawanaku. The snorkeling is great there, but the hiking trail has some obnoxious footing. See HIKING on page 201.

Looking at the map you'll see the upper highway less than 3 miles uphill from Wailea. Access to Haleakala, Upcountry and the Hana Highway is so near and yet so far. There's a very handy dirt road connecting the upper highway to Wailea, but the company that owns it won't let anyone use it. (They blame that old demon, liability.) The county is planning a connecting route for sometime in 2005, but in the meantime, it's a 30-mile detour through Kahului to get up the hill.

SOUTH MAUI SHOPPING

If you're short of time and have a long list of souvenirs to purchase, try the Kihei Kalama Village across from Kalama Park on South Kihei Road. There's parking in the back. You can find everything from fossilized sharks' teeth to fresh leis here. There's also Serendipity for fine ladies clothing.

If you're shopping time is a little more leisurely, start at the Maui Clothing Outlet off Piilani Highway behind the Tesoro Gas Station. Good selection of men's, women's and children's clothing.

On South Kihei Road you'll find Longs Center that has Longs Drugs, a good stop for souvenirs, mac nut candies and coffee. They also have reef shoes and tabis. The T-Shirt Factory next to Longs has good prices on souvenir T-shirts.

Across the street is Azeka Place with Tropical Tantrum for colorful island-style silk clothing, Rainbow Connection for gifts and souvenirs, and Crazy Shirts for quality souvenir sportswear. The sister center Azeka Place II is kitty-cornered. Stop at In's Eelskin and Gifts for…what else? Or try La Pre Shells and Gifts for that $375 golden cowrie shell you wanted to pick up for the folks back home. (Shells from Hawai'i can't be sold here; they're mostly from the Philippines.)

Kama'ole Beach Center has Honolua Surf Co, a good place for excellent surf wear. Those long-sleeved T-shirts are wonderful to don after snorkeling or diving.

At press time, there were three large shopping centers tantalizingly close to opening. The Ma'alaea Harbor Village is near the Maui Ocean Center with lots of new restaurants and shops. Pi'ilani Shopping Center is at the corner of Lipoa and Piilani Highway with a Hilo Hattie, among others, as well as the state's largest Safeway. The new upscale shopping venue will be The Shops at Wailea at Wailea Iki that is replacing the Wailea Shopping Village—literally bulldozed to make way for the new shops. They'll have a selection of pricey designer name shops and restaurants.

If you're not interested in driving around while you shop, there's the South Maui Shopping Express running from the Maui Prince to the Maui Ocean Center (with hotel pickups in between). It's $5 for the one-day pass, and it stops at most centers in South Maui. Continue on the West Maui Shopping Express for a $10 day pass, and you can shop all the way to Kapalua. Call Trans Hawaiian at 877-7308 for additional information about the schedules and fares.

BEST BETS

Best Place for Stroll—Shoreline Path Between Renaissance and Kea Lani
Best Snorkeling—Between Po'olenalena and Palauea, or North end of La Pérouse
Best Place to Toast Your *Da Kines*—Little Beach
Best Place to Chew up Your Hiking Boots—Kalua o Lapa Lava Vent Hike
Best Exotic Resort—Grand Wailea
Best Sunday Brunch—Maui Prince
Best Burger—Maui Onion at Renaissance
Best Place for a Sunset Cocktail—Sunset Terrace at Renaissance
Best Sunset Dinner Without Confiscatory Prices—Jacques on the Beach
Best *Long* Beach Stroll—Ma'alaea Bay
Best Boogie Boarding—Kama'ole III

The desolation of uninhabited Kaho'olawe, its hardpan exposed by unchecked erosion, is a vivid reminder of what both indigenous and modern man can do to the land. Maui is in the background.

One of things that adds to the exotic nature of Maui is the abundance of off-shore islands. Somehow, seeing multiple islands across the water adds mystery to the scene. Islands are never more intriguing than when they are tantalizingly out of reach. Because of the way they are sprinkled about, no other Hawaiian island has such great views of offshore islands. For instance, when you awaken for your first day at Ka'anapali, you are confronted by islands dominating your view. Is that Kaho'olawe? No wait…that's the other part of Maui; the land bridge is below the horizon. Is that Lana'i? No, Moloka'i is where Lana'i should be. Take a look at the fold-out back cover map and the graphic to the right to orient yourself. Moloka'i dominates the view from Kapalua,

Lana'i is offshore of Lahaina, and Kaho'olawe is the closest island to South Maui.

We haven't attempted to make this a complete guide to other nearby islands, but you may want to know a little about your neighbors. Some can even be visited by boat trips listed on page 206 or by air trips on page 188. Since Maui is the gateway to the resorts of Lana'i, we're including some information on them here.

KAHO'OLAWE

If you're staying in Kihei, Kaho'olawe is the impressive island offshore behind the tiny crescent islet of Molokini. Though it looks enticing from afar, Kaho'olawe is an ecological mess.

History revisionists (most of whom have almost certainly never vis-

Moloka'i

Lana'i

Kaho'olawe

ited Kahoʻolawe) attribute Kahoʻolawe's ecological woes to either the military or Western man in general. The truth can be a little more embarrassing. When the ancient Hawaiians discovered these islands, they found on Kahoʻolawe a fragile dryland forest. It was a marginal environment to live in due to its location in the rain shadow of Maui. Dry, thin soil populated by hearty but water-starved trees and shrubs marked the island. In the course of their settlement, the Hawaiians cut down most of the trees on the island to make canoes, firewood, and for other purposes. Without roots to hold the soil together, erosion became the thief that stole the essence of Kahoʻolawe.

In fact, by the time Captain Cook first encountered the islands in the 1770s, Kahoʻolawe was no longer inhabited and was instead used only as a campsite for visiting fishermen. When the king of the Big Island invaded Maui in the 1780s, he made a separate trip over to Kahoʻolawe and was furious when he discovered there was nothing to steal or plunder there and only a few fishermen to terrorize. When Maui children of that era asked their parents why nobody lived on the island across the waters, they were told it was because the island was sacred. Perhaps, but it was also used up.

In the mid 1800s the Hawaiian government used Kahoʻolawe and Lanaʻi as penal colonies. Crimes that got you banished to Kahoʻolawe included rebellion, theft, divorce, breaking marriage vows and murder. Starvation was rampant there, and desperate escape attempts were common.

Later, western man introduced feral animals: goats, pigs and cattle. Their hooves and grazing quickly completed the ecological rampage.

During WWII the military took control of Kahoʻolawe and used it for target practice. It was later seized by direct presidential order for exclusive use by the military. But the damage from their target practice was minimal compared to what the island had already experienced and was mostly limited to a smaller area. (Hitting a stationary island of $44\frac{1}{2}$ square miles is, after all, a pretty poor demonstration of marksmanship. Their goal was to hit a certain *part* of the island.) Often, the military would put an old jeep in an open area and fire at it. Residents of Kihei grew up to the booming sound coming from 7 miles across the water. After a half-century of live fire, President Bush signed an executive order in 1990 halting all target practice on the island. There are a number of unexploded small ordinance scattered about the entire island, enough to make it a dangerous place to wander around.

The result today is an island robbed of her topsoil in many places, leaving nothing but an unforgiving hardpan layer. The areas that still harbor plants feature mostly gray shrubs and grasses. There is no permanent source of water other than wells. But despite that, there is a stark beauty to the place. It looks nothing like the rest of Hawaiʻi. Cleanup of unexploded ordinance is under way, but don't count on booking your Kahoʻolawe vacation anytime soon. The island was transferred to native Hawaiian control in 1994. They are trying to replant the island with native plants and increase the amount of soil. It's a hot, tiring job, but it's hoped that future generations will find a Kahoʻolawe that is much like what the initial Hawaiians found. Going back in time is a rare event in this world, and islands don't often get a second chance. Maybe this time Kahoʻolawe will benefit from our hindsight and our diligence.

Until the 1990s the island of Lana'i was essentially one big pineapple farm. Today, with only 362 hotel rooms, it's an exclusive retreat for those seeking the peace and quiet of Hawai'i's private island.

LANA'I

For most of the 20th century Lana'i was known as the pineapple island. Almost 98% of the island was owned by Dole Pineapple (which was purchased by Castle & Cooke), and pineapple dominated this 140½-square-mile island. In the 1990s Castle & Cooke decided that owning a secluded Hawaiian island was more valuable than owning pineapple fields. So they got out of pineapple and began marketing the island as the "private island," complete with two world class resorts and excellent golfing.

The population is around 2,500 and many work for the company, often paying cheap, subsidized rent. More than once we've seen residents taking the ferry to Lahaina to pick up stacks of pizzas for delivery back to Lana'i City. (Lana'i is a tad out of Domino's delivery range.)

Lying in the rain shadow of West Maui, Lana'i is arid, receiving only 10–20 inches of rain annually in most locations, and it's certainly not the most attractive island you'll visit. Some of its beaches, however, are excellent. Taking the Expeditions Lahaina–Lana'i Ferry (661–3756) for $25 is a good way to get there. (Sit on the right side.) There are also flights into the airport.

Lana'i is an amazingly relaxing place to stay. The second day into our first visit, we were tempted to call the front desk and complain that someone had broken into our room and surgically removed our bones. You can actually *feel* motivation and ambition draining from your body. The downside to the relaxing nature is the lack of options available to you here. The island is dominated by a few players who have more control over you than you may realize. For instance, the company that does most of the boat activities, Trilogy, also owns the island's only Dollar Rent-a-Car

(800 533–7808) and the only gas station, and you may find yourself wondering if they prefer that you take a profitable tour, rather than rent a car. Because renting a car can be difficult—during a visit there were only three dozen vehicles to accommodate all 362 rooms. (Moloka'i has *10 times* that number of cars for a similar visitor count.) And rental car prices will shock you. In fact, *everything* is expensive on Lana'i. (You'll be forgiven if you start to wonder if Lana'i is the Hawaiian word for, "It costs *how* much?") It's easy to let expenses get away from you since nearly every place on the island lets you charge things to your room. (It's called check-out shock, and it can be fatal for those with weak hearts.)

The main beach at the hotel is probably among the top 10 beaches in the state. Called Hulopo'e Beach, it has a huge sand deposit and good swimming coupled with unreal snorkeling on the left (southeast) end of the beach. Venture along the rocky shoreline away from the beach, and you're treated some of the most dramatic underwater scenery we've seen. Not because of the coral (which is sparse) or the fish (which are abundant), but because of the canyon-like lattice structure of the lava and dead coral. Chasms, holes, stacks and arches create a miniature Bryce Canyon with exciting possibilities. Avoid during moderate to high surf, however, or it may get *too* exciting due to surginess.

STAYING ON LANA'I

The island has only three places to stay. Manele Bay Hotel (800 321–4666), which is actually on harder-to-pronounce Hulopo'e Bay, is our favorite. This is where the dream comes true. Check-in doesn't actually occur.

You're greeted in the lobby with a plumeria lei and seated while your credit card is momentarily whisked away to be run through their special NASA-designed hydraulic credit card press, capable of pumping more money out of your credit card than you ever imagined. Then you're shown some of the resort's amenities, and it's off to your room. Service is superb and discreet. There are fishponds and waterfalls scattered around the resort, and the grounds are exotic and flawlessly maintained. Personnel will help arrange your daily activities, such as boating, snorkeling, SCUBA diving or land tours. In the evening, well-dressed patrons glide around the pool after their meal. The restaurants are good, though pricey. (There's a dress code at one of the two restaurants.) Though expensive, the $350 per night resort rate doesn't stick in our craw as much as the fact that the price sheet mentions that they charge 75¢ to call another room—talk about nickel and diming! Rates range from $325–$2,500 per night.

The Lodge at Ko'ele (800 321–4666) is the most expensive lodge you ever saw and certainly the ritziest. Located 1,700 feet up in the misty, cool center of the island, the lodge is for those who want a formal, less Hawaiian experience. (Some Hawai'i residents like it for this very reason. They consider it a getaway.) The place looks more like an English manor than a Hawaiian hotel. Tea time is from 3 p.m. to 5 p.m. We're partial to the black currant tea with scones while sitting next to the fireplace reading from Tennyson or Shelley. (OK, so we don't *really* read from those dudes, but *dang,* the tea sure is good.) Serious-looking attendants in suits (a definite rarity in Hawai'i) attend to the needs and whims of guests. Call us savages, but we prefer the dreamy warmth of the Manele Bay Hotel to the stuffier feel of the Lodge. But if you found this description a bit gauche, you'll probably prefer the Lodge. Tally-ho! (Alas, fox hunting is not offered.) To be fair we're probably overstating it a bit. It's relaxing but feels out of place, and room prices seem excessive for what you get. Even the suites seem spartan for the money. They've won plenty of awards, so maybe we're just full of beans, but it just doesn't seem like the kind of place most people imagine when they decide to come to Hawai'i. Their steak and seafood restaurant is breathtakingly expensive. (You know you're in for a shock when *appetizers* cost you $18.) Expect $45–$65 for dinner. Room rates range from $350–$2,000 per night.

Hotel Lana'i (800 795-7211) is a 10-room hotel that predates the large resorts. It's for the "budget traveler" to Lana'i. (If there is such an animal.) Rates are around $100 per night and up. Their restaurant, Henry Clay's, has fairly tasty and slightly cheaper food than the resorts with rotisserie chicken, fish, rabbit, duck and lobster for $25–$35 for dinner.

Lana'i is the last place you would expect to get worldwide attention. But on New Year's Day 1994, the island became the most exclusive place on earth. The event? A wedding. The groom wanted privacy and could *definitely* afford it. Willie Nelson was hired to perform the night before. The groom rented every hotel room on the island and kept most empty. He also rented every helicopter on nearby Maui and paid them to stay on the ground Then he hired a private security force to patrol the island. No one was allowed on or off Lana'i. (A cameraman who was nabbed by the private security force was later awarded an out-of-court settlement by the groom when it was pointed out that he was in a *public* area.) After all the preparations the groom, whose net worth is nearly half of the entire U.S. defense budget, married his sweetheart on the 12th hole of the island's newest golf course. Only 130 people were allowed to attend the wedding of the richest man in the history of the world, Bill Gates. The man who could marry at (and probably buy) any place on the planet, chose Lana'i to tie the knot. It cost him over $1 million. (But don't worry, he actually made that much *every three minutes* of work one year.) Pretty impressive distinction for little Lana'i, huh?

MOLOKINI is a small, crescent-shaped islet popular for snorkel and SCUBA trips. It's described on page 208.

MOLOKA'I

Moloka'i is a long, skinny island of immense beauty and unimaginable sea cliffs. It's 260 square miles, though it was once much larger. The island owes its shape to the type of cataclysmic event that sometimes occurs with Hawaiian volcanoes. Much of the volcano from east Moloka'i broke off and fell into the sea hundreds of thousands of years ago, where *half-mile-sized* chunks of rock rolled to a stop 100 miles away. The landslide created awesome sea cliffs that are up to 3,000 feet high—the highest in the world—which are continually undercut by the ocean's waves. Think about the mind-boggling forces involved in that event. The entire Pacific rim was affected as tidal waves of skyscraper heights ravaged shorelines thousands of miles away. Moloka'i is not alone in experiencing these kind of apocalyptic

Moloka'i's 3,000 foot sea cliffs are the tallest on the planet. This enormous landslide, from 2,500 feet high, happened the previous day and the map-changing rubble created 15 new acres of land.

residents are on some kind of government assistance. Though the island's nickname is "the friendly island," odds are you'll find just the opposite. Though they are very friendly with each other (the only repetitive motion injury residents are likely to suffer is from drivers constantly waving at each other), many (though by no means all) tend to be pretty reserved with visitors. In fact, more stink eye greets visitors to this island than any other. (It's a favorite of many visitors due to its undeveloped nature, but many complain of feeling unwelcome.) NO TRESPASSING signs are conspicuously few. You either belong somewhere or you don't, and residents don't need signs to tell them that.

Local residents, many of whom are adamantly opposed to more visitors, have a nasty little war going on with the island's largest landowner, Moloka'i Ranch, which owns almost a third of the island (mostly on the drier western half). When the ranch built a pipeline to carry water to another part of the island, vandals destroyed it.

VISITING MOLOKA'I

The two best ways to visit from Maui are either a boat/car trip, or fly over for the mule ride to Kalaupapa.

Maui Princess (667–6165) will take you over on Wednesdays or Saturdays (the former is preferable) and give you a

events. The Big Island had a slide 120,000 years ago, and the resulting wave swept over Kaho'olawe and tossed chunks of coral up to the 1,000 foot elevation level on Lana'i. Kaho'olawe and probably Lana'i and Ni'ihau also experienced monster landslides.

The population of Moloka'i is around 6,700, and there is not a single traffic light on the whole island. Not all is rosy on Moloka'i, however. The island has a perpetually dismal economy. Most of the

car for five hours of exploring, $129 for the first person, $69 for others. They also have van tours, but you'll probably prefer your own car. Once on island, your biggest decision is which way to go. Either turn right (east) if the weather's good, or left if it's not. East wanders along the dry, southern part of the island. Private fishponds line almost the entire shoreline. With no one in front and no one in your rear view mirror, Moloka'i feels like it's all yours. Once 20 miles out of Kaunakakai, the scenery turns dramatic (and the road narrows). The sweet payoff 30 miles from Kaunakakai is the end of the road, and the vista alone is almost worth the trip. Halawa Valley is isolated, quaint and strikingly beautiful. Backed by tall waterfalls, the descent into the valley is marvelous. Once inside, Moloka'i's "friendly" nickname becomes laughable. There's a good dirt road and path leading back to the falls, but makeshift signs tell you not to go. (Unless you pay someone for a guided tour, of course.) Just revel in the bayside scenery. It's as good as the waterfall anyway.

Toward the middle of the island, a 6-mile detour from the highway leads to Moloka'i's biggest must-see. The Kalaupapa Overlook. Moloka'i was notorious in the 1800s as the site of the state's leprosy colony. Leprosy may have been brought back to Hawai'i by a chief who had visited abroad in 1840 or by Chinese laborers a bit later. Located on an isolated peninsula called Kalaupapa, stricken patients were banished to the colony when their condition was discovered. They didn't come here to live with the disease; they came to die. It was a hideous and vile place in those days, completely neglected by a government that only wanted to forget it existed. A 33-year-old priest from Belgium named Father Damien arrived in the 1873 and tended to the unfortunates, living closely with them. Giving no thought to his own safety, he eventually contracted the disease and died there. The method of transmission was baffling to 19th-century doctors. They had no way of knowing that over 95% of the human population is naturally immune to the disease, which means that 19 out of 20 priests sent to Kalaupapa could never have contracted it. Damien was genetically unfortunate to be among the 5% who could.

Though his last 16 years of life were a selfless dedication to the most reviled and abused people among us, he was tormented on his deathbed with the fear that he was unworthy of heaven. According to today's Catholic Church, he had nothing to fear; the church has already beatified him, the second step toward sainthood.

Though the disease has a cure now, there are still former leprosy patients living at Kalaupapa, which is now a national park. (Some Kalaupapa residents prefer the more modern term, Hansen's Disease; others prefer to leave it as leprosy. All hate the term leper.) Mule rides down into the area are the most popular activity on Moloka'i. (See ADVENTURES on page 238.) If you get a chance, rent the 1999 movie, *Moloka'i: The Story of Father Damien*.

From the unbelievably beautiful overlook, you realize why 19th-century Hawaiian officials chose this place. After the volcano collapsed and created the sea cliffs, the apparently cold magma chamber came back to life for one last creation. It erupted at the base of the cliff and created land that is adjacent to, but utterly apart from, the rest of the island. Only a manmade trail, gouged in the side of the cliffs, allows land access.

As you stand at the overlook, with the wind whistling through the trees, the ghosts of misery and pain that were banished there a century ago can seem all too real. It's ironic that a place once so despised is today a visitor attraction. Perhaps that's the only way to completely clear away the haze of despair that once filled the air.

Most of the workers at Kalaupapa live there, but there are a half dozen workers who hike in every day. *Big deal,* you say! Well, yeah, it is. The hike includes going down and then up a 1,700-foot-high mountain—*every day.* They say the biggest hazards are the mules on the trail that don't like to be passed and have a nasty habit of kicking them when they try. Now *that's* a commute!

The other attraction near the overlook is Ka-ule-o-Nanahoa or Phallic Rock. It's a five-minute uphill walk. To the ancient Hawaiians, the 6-foot tall stone in the shape of a gigantic...well, *you* know, represents fertility. It's really quite a remarkable...uh, formation. (It may have had some human help.) Even today, some Hawaiians believe that if you sit or sleep on it, it will make you conceive. Legend states that it's what remains of a husband who should have kept his eye on his work.

The west side of Moloka'i is drier and flatter. Vast beaches line much of the shoreline. You'll have the opportunity to create the only footprints in long stretches of sand. If you're returning your car from either the west or Kalaupapa, don't bother driving back to Kaunakakai to gas up. Save the 20 minutes and eat the extra couple of bucks to have the rental car company gas up.

While in Kaunakakai, the best food is Moloka'i Pizza Café. The pizza is definitely as good as any you'd find on Maui. Very good sauce and fresh, light crust. They also have sandwiches and pasta.

A crowd of one gathers on a Moloka'i beach.

Ideally shaped to provide calm swimming much of the time, Kapalua Beach is a West Maui winner.

Of all the Hawaiian islands, Maui probably has the most user-friendly beaches. Nearly all of the sand beaches on the island are concentrated in the more protected leeward areas of West and South Maui. If you were designing your own island, that's *exactly* where you'd put them, because the other side of the island is exposed to more surf and runoff. The few beaches in Hana are good, but the remaining windward beaches near Kahului won't ring your chimes.

Because of this topographic blessing, Maui is considered by many to be the *Ocean Island.* In fact, so much of the Maui experience is centered around beaches (to a greater degree than any of the other Hawaiian islands) that we've had to endure countless hours assessing the characteristics of each individual beach. Which ones worked best for snorkeling, boogie boarding, swimming or just plain frolicking? Sometimes this research

was as simple as determining if a sunset mai tai worked better at one beach than another. (See, and you thought that writing guidebooks was all fun and games. There's a *serious* worth ethic involved.)

Here, you can snorkel exceptional reefs, boogie board till you're raw, take a 3-mile beach walk, dig your fingers into genuine volcanic black sand, catch rays (all over) on a red sand beach, and sip a cocktail under a palm tree on a golden sand beach. Maui's beaches have earned their legendary status.

The biggest danger you will face at the beach is the **surf.** Though most beaches are on the calmer part of the island, that's a relative term. Most mainlanders are unprepared for the strength of Hawai'i's surf. We're out in the middle of the biggest ocean in the world, and the surf has lots of room to build up. We have our calm days when the water is like glass. We often have days where the surf is moderate, calling for respect and diligence on the part of the swimmer. And we have the high surf days, perfect for sitting on the beach, watching the experienced and the audacious tempt the ocean's patience. To get **current weather forecasts,** call 871–5054. For a **surf forecast,** call 877–3611 or see page 2 of the *Maui News.* Don't make the mistake of underestimating the ocean's power here. Hawai'i is the undisputed drowning capital of the United States, and we don't want you to join the statistics.

Other hazards include rip currents, which can form, cease and form again with no warning. Large "rogue waves" can come ashore with no warning. These usually occur when two or more waves fuse at sea, becoming a larger wave. Even calm seas are no guarantee of safety. Many people have been caught unaware by large waves during ostensibly "calm seas." We have swam and snorkeled the beaches described in this book on at least two occasions (usually more than two). But beaches change. The underwater topography changes throughout the year. Storms can take a very safe beach and rearrange the sand, turning it into a dangerous beach. Just because we describe a beach as being in a certain condition does not mean it will be in that same condition when you visit it.

Consequently, you should take the beach descriptions as a snapshot in calm times. If seas aren't calm, you probably shouldn't go in the water. If you observe a rip current, you probably shouldn't go in the water. If you aren't a comfortable swimmer, you should probably never go in the water, except at those beaches that have lifeguards. There is no way we can tell you that a certain beach will be swimmable on a certain day, and we

claim no such prescience. For instance, a strong storm and accompanying swells in late 1999 swept lots of sand from South Maui beaches and mucked up the water so badly it took months to recover and made beachgoing different than usual during that time. There is no substitution for your own observations and judgment.

A few standard safety tips: Never turn your back on the ocean. Never swim alone. Never swim in the mouth of a river. Never swim in murky water. Never swim when the seas are not calm. Don't walk too close to the shorebreak; a large wave can come and knock you over and pull you in. Observe ocean conditions carefully. Don't let small children play in the water unsupervised. Fins give you far more power and speed and are a good safety device, in addition to being more fun. If you're comfortable in a mask and snorkel, they provide considerable peace of mind in addition to opening up the underwater world. Lastly, don't let Hawai'i's idyllic environment cloud your judgment. Recognize the ocean for what it is—a powerful force that needs to be respected.

This is a good time to repeat that reef shoes, a water-friendly shoe that goes under many brand names, make entering and exiting beaches that aren't 100% sandy *much* easier. Kmart in Kahului, Longs Drugs and lots of other stores sell them. Even if you *think* a beach has a completely sandy bottom, toes have well-known magnetic properties and will often attract that lone jagged rock, ruining an otherwise perfect beach day. While snorkeling, we like to use reef shoes and fins that fit over them. See SNORKELING on page 222 for more.

Theft can be a problem when visiting beaches. Visitors like to lock their cars at all beaches, but piles of glass on the ground usually dissuade island residents from doing that at secluded beaches. We usually remove anything we can't bear to have stolen and leave the car with the windows rolled up but unlocked. That way, we're less likely to get our windows broken by a curious thief. Regardless, don't leave anything of value in your car. (Well...maybe the seats can stay.) While in the water, we use a waterproof fanny pack (available at many outdoor stores) for our wallet, checkbook and keys, and leave everything else on the beach. Sometimes we only bring car keys and tie them to bathing suit drawstrings. We don't take a camera (except disposables) to the beach unless we are willing to stay there on the sand and baby-sit it. This way, when we swim, snorkel or just walk, we don't have to constantly watch our things.

Use **sunblock** early and often. Don't pay any attention to the claims from sunblock makers that their product is waterproof, rubproof, sandblast proof, powerwash proof, etc. Reapply it every couple of hours and after you get out of the ocean. The ocean water will hide sunburn symptoms until after you're toast. Then you can look forward to agony for the rest of your trip. (And yes, you *can* get burned while in the water; that's where most people here get cooked.) Of the sunblocks we've tried, Bullfrog and Neutrogena seem to work the best. Use *gel* (not lotion) based products for better waterproof results.

Water quality around most of Maui can be amazingly clear. (Just look at the photo on page 2–3.) The Pacific Ocean is kind enough to provide a roughly east-to-west current that constantly replaces our water with clean, clear, open ocean water. There are, however, several spots where geography and human action con-

spire to mess up the water, and we don't recommend swimming there. They are: north Kihei, off Lahaina (especially the north part of town), Kahana, Kahului Harbor and around Pa'ia. Waters in these areas can be gross, so avoid them.

Consider using one of those disposable underwater cameras. Even if you don't go in the water, they will withstand the elements. Their quality is better than most people think. Between the Kodak and the Fuji, we give a slight quality edge to the Fuji. The closeup dolphin shot in this book was taken with one.

Always remember that in Hawai'i, all beaches are public beaches. This means that you can park yourself on any stretch of sand you like. The trick, sometimes, is finding the legal public access and finding a parking spot. We'll try to point out a way to all of the island's beaches.

In general, **surf** is higher and stronger during the winter, calmer in the summer, but there are exceptions during all seasons. South Maui is often calm year round. When we mention that a beach has facilities, it usually includes restrooms, showers, picnic tables and drinking water.

Mornings are almost always best. Wind in South Maui and north of Lahaina in West Maui picks up in the late morning and early afternoon.

Beaches with **lifeguards** are **D.T Fleming** and **Hanaka'o'o** in West Maui, the three **Kama'oles** in Kihei, and **H.A. Baldwin** and **Kanaha** near Kahului.

Lastly, remember that just because *you* may be on vacation doesn't mean that residents are. Consequently, beaches are more crowded on weekends.

We're starting our BEACHES section on the upper left side of the island and working our way down the coast in a counter-clockwise direction.

WEST MAUI BEACHES

West Maui doesn't have *as many* good beaches or good snorkeling areas as South Maui, but the best ones here really shine.

❖ **Punalau Beach**—How appropriate that we start the beaches section with a beach that almost nobody's heard of. Also called **Keonehelele'i Beach** and sometimes **Windmill Beach,** it's 1/3 mile long and backed by abundant shade trees. During high surf (usually in the winter) large, well-formed waves break on a lava bench particularly close to shore, making it a perfect place to watch the surf. During calm seas, the beach is fronted by a bouldery tide-pool and clean water, making the snorkeling interesting though shallow. Swimming and snorkeling are only advisable during very calm seas since unusually strong currents can form during higher seas. Access is from a dirt road 7/10 mile past (east of) the 34 mile marker. During the week few visit the beach compared to other beaches in the area. There is a KEEP OUT sign posted at the dirt road, just like at Honolua Bay, but the landowner/company doesn't seem to mind. In fact, camping is even OK there with a *Maui Land and Pineapple* permit.

❖ **Honolua Bay**—This is one of the more awkward areas to describe. That's because water conditions are more variable than most, and there's no sand beach here. It's a popular snorkeling and diving destination. At **A Real Gem** times Honolua has breathtaking underwater scenery, tons of fish, turtles, coral and great visibility. (See photo on pages

OK, OK. So the name Slaughterhouse Beach doesn't exactly look good on a postcard. But the beach sure does.

2–3) Other times, for a variety of reasons, you can't see diddly here. If there's been a lot of rain lately, a stream on the left (west) side of the bay will generally muck up the water. Snorkelers are usually steered to the left side of the bay, but the right side has better coral and visibility, though it's deeper and used often by SCUBA divers. Honolua is a reserve, making fishing and spearing illegal, so fish counts *can* be high here. Unlike most island beaches, mornings aren't *necessarily* best here. Summer is better than winter. If you see lots surfers out around the point to the right, it means snorkeling conditions aren't at their best.

Access is between the 32 & 33 mile markers on Hwy 30. When the road descends to the lowest part, you'll see a dirt road leading to the shore along with outdated KEEP OUT signs. Walk past the gate and enter the water at an old boat ramp. Water is always cloudy at the shoreline, but usually improves as you go farther out.

If you don't mind a slightly longer walk (five minutes instead of three), we like parking at the less-used pullout just before the 33 mile marker. It's a beautiful meandering walk through a draped, jungly forest. Worth the extra walk. Everyone ignores the signs at this bay that say KEEP OUT—PROSECUTORS WILL BE VIOLATED or something to that effect. Access is very much tolerated by the landowner.

Honolua is occasionally canvassed by car break-in maggots, so don't leave anything valuable in your car.

While at your car, you may wonder why so many cars seem to *honk* here. It's because a road sign around the corner tells drivers to to just that. Wouldn't you just *love* to live next to a road sign telling all passing drivers to honk?

❖ **Slaughterhouse Beach**—Ooh, doesn't *that* sound inviting? Hawaiian name **Mokule'ia Bay** (which itself is often misspelled as **Makuleia**), this beach gets its commonly used name from a long-gone slaughterhouse that used to be above the cliffs. This relatively small pocket beach has lots of sand in the summer, which can almost disappear during winter surf. The snorkeling to the right *can* be good, but the beach is subject to water-clouding runoff from an intermittent stream to the left (southwest). There's some shade in the mornings, but none in the afternoon, and the beach is *partially* protected from afternoon winds. The morning views of Moloka'i are stunning; you won't see more detail from anywhere else on Maui. Located north of the 32 mile marker on Hwy 30; access to the beach, 100 feet below the road, is via a concrete stairway.

❖ **D.T. Fleming Beach Park**— Swimming is similar to Oneloa below: good during calm seas, but vulnerable to rip currents when the surf picks up. In fact, these two beaches used to be one, until the West Maui volcano, in its dying days, sent lava to the coast to form Makalua-puna Point, splitting the bay in two. D.T. Fleming is long and wide. There's lots of shade, courtesy of ironwood trees. Picnic tables, BBQs, lifeguards, showers and restrooms all make the beach very popular with locals who come to relax and talk story (shoot the breeze), so weekends can be very crowded. Park facilities aren't as well kept as other area parks. The right side gets occasional runoff, so the ocean isn't as clear as nearby Oneloa. Afternoons can bring an irritating wind, so be sure to bring that old BBQ grill you've been meaning to have sandblasted. (Mornings are calmest.)

Where is everybody? Certainly not at often forgotten Oneloa in West Maui.

❖ **Oneloa Beach**—Not to be confused with the other beach of the same name in South Maui. Despite the huge number of resort dwellings behind this long, luxurious beach, it is surprisingly uncrowded most of the time. Perhaps

A Real Gem

it's because so many of the expensive beach homes nearby are used by people who don't live here and don't rent them out. It's a deceptive beach. The public access deposits you on the eastern (right) ⅓ of the beach and you quickly conclude that this ¼ mile long, wide sandy beach has bad swimming and snorkeling because of a lava bench in the nearshore waters seemingly extending the whole length. Visitors often turn around and leave at this point. What they can't see is that the left ⅓ of the beach usually has a padded sandy bottom, making the swimming delightful when calm.

(Occasionally, the winter surf can temporarily erase some of the sandy bottom.) The snorkeling around the left end can also be very good with lots of fish and some wild rock formations, but don't do it when the surf's up or a washing machine effect will bounce you around. Plus a rip current forms. Take time to climb up the rocks on the left side to poke around the tide-pools and cove. Boogie boarding on the left side can be good for the intermediate *sponger* (local slang). This beach is susceptable to wind. (The GEM designation only applies when the wind and surf are low.) Early mornings are best. The extreme right side is somewhat protected from the wind, but, of course, the swimming and snorkeling aren't very good there. (But we do like hunting for golf balls there lost from the nearby golf course. If you find a club, you know the guy was having an off day.) No shade or facilities except for a powerful faucet and sometimes a hose near the parking lot. From the highway, take Office Road till it dead ends, turn left, then right on Ironwood Lane. If it's too windy for a day here, consider the more protected Napili Bay or perhaps Kapalua Beach.

❖ **Kapalua Beach**—Well known as one of the best swimming beaches on Maui, the bay is usually very protected, making timid swimmers happy. The water isn't necessarily the clearest, so snorkeling is not that hot, and the offshore waters can be rocky. You'll do well to bring your **A Real Gem** reef shoes so you can walk about in the water without fear of stubbing your toe. But Kapalua is a great place to wade into the ocean without worrying about getting beaten up by the surf most of the time, and the palm trees behind the beach are very pic-

turesque. There are two accesses—one from the Kapalua Bay Hotel (which is the longer walk of the two) and the other, which fills up first, near the Sea House Restaurant at Napili Kai condos. The sign says NAPILI LANI.

❖ **Napili Bay**—An excellent beach that seems to generate more fun per square foot than any other beach in the area. It's very recessed into the shoreline, which blocks much **A Real Gem** of the afternoon wind along here. The sand is very steep, so the waves slap the shoreline then recede quickly, creating an impressive undertow during high surf. The offshore waters are quite sandy. This combination creates the best beach on the island for an activity called Monastery Tag (named after a beach in California where we invented it one day after a SCUBA

Grain for grain, Napili Bay seems to invite more fun than any other beach in the area.

dive.) Now bear with me here, it's going to sound strange, but we've shown others how to do this and they *love* it. The three ingredients you need are a steep beach, unchecked (unprotected) waves and a padded, sandy bottom. Basically you lie in the water at the surf's edge and zip up and down the beach up to 40 feet each way on a thin cushion of water, digging feet or hands into the sand to control your ascent and decent. Like a low-to-the-ground sports car, the sensation of speed is greater. Here, you're only inches above the sand and the trick is to go as far up the shore as possible without getting beached. To people on the beach it looks like you're scraping along the sand, but actually you're unscathed as you orient the shape of your body for maximum efficiency. As with all worthwhile and important endeavors, it takes years of practice and dedication. (You see, and you thought we spent all our time doing only *frivolous* stuff.) A mask and snorkel make it easier. On your back, front, head first or feet first, it's important to master them all. You really feel the power of the ocean this way. Best conditions are usually at the center/right portion of the beach.

The beach can get fairly crowded. Access to the middle and south end are from Hui Drive and Napili Place off Lower Honoapiilani Road. See map on page 53.

❖ **Kahana Beach**—Respectably wide white pocket of sand, fairly attractive. Slightly cloudy water, sandy bottom, steep shorebreak. On occasion, lots of seaweed creates marginal water quality. Fronting the Kahana Sunset on Lower Honoapiilani Road. Only public access is from the north along shoreline path.

❖ **Ka'opala Beach**—Nasty, uninviting piece of shoreline beach, which gets its water from a foul creek ½ mile south of here. (Current runs north.) How appropriate that Ka'opala translates to trash. We see uninformed visitors swimming here and can't help wonder if they bring something exotic back from the islands that they didn't count on.

❖ **Pohaku Park**—Pretty little park for picnics or sunsets, but the water is another must-miss. Yucky. Also called S-Turns Park. Located just north of the Noelani condos.

❖ **Honokowai Beach Park**—The swimming and snorkeling is poor, but it's a good place to come with your lunch (Honokowai Okazuya Deli is nearby) and eat to the sound of the surf. On the southern end of Lower Honoapiilani Road.

❖ **Keka'a / North Beach / Airport Beach**—This stretch of sand fronts what used to be the old Ka'anapali Airport and runs to Honokowai Beach Park. In general, it's a somewhat narrow sandy beach and the nearshore waters are rocky, so swimming is only marginal. Reef shoes will help protect your feet. The southern section was accessible at press time from a dirt road across from the Honokowai Marketplace. A large timeshare project was slated to move into that area, so access may change. The northern stretch has access from the resorts across from the Marketplace. Snorkeling is merely adequate and the northern stretch of the beach gets small amounts of the seaweed that is so common (and heavier) farther north. That seaweed is almost constant until you get to Napili Bay, which is clean.

The south end of Kahekili Beach Park has the sandiest bottom—and the dreamiest water.

❖ **Kahekili Beach Park**—A superb park, glorious beach and excellent facilities, including covered tables, a large parking area, restrooms, showers and lawn area. The park accesses a portion **A Real Gem** of Ka'anapali Beach and is sometimes lumped in as **North Beach** or **Airport Beach.** A windbreak running north of here partially protects the ocean from afternoon winds. Kahekili is a popular place for SCUBA diving. Several companies do introductory shore dives here.

Conveniently, the best snorkeling is directly offshore of the pavilion, about 75 or so feet where a nice variety of coral and some fish await. Just plain ol' swimming offshore of the park facilities is not so good, suffering from hidden rocks at the water's edge that you can't see without polarized sunglasses. But if you walk down the concrete path south (left) toward Black Rock, you'll find that when the sidewalk ends, so do the hidden rocks in the water (for the most part), and from there all the way to the end of the beach (¼ mile) is a sandy,

frolicker's delight. (Winter surf sometimes temporarily erases some of the sand, exposing rocks not normally present.) A stream near Black Rock brings colder, fresh water onto the surface a few dozen feet from shore, but doesn't affect things *near* the shore. There's a rumor that an airplane went into the water between the pavilion and Black Rock. (Ka'anapali Airport used to be to your right.) We've spent many hours looking for it and have been unsuccessful. Let us know if you find it. When surf's up there's a current that runs from Black Rock along the shore heading north. Bigger surf can make the water cloudy and difficult to enter. If it's not calm and you choose to swim anyway, better to walk down and let the current aid you coming back to the pavilion.

Kahekili is a magnificent place for an early morning swim, or just bring your cup of coffee and set the day's tone here. Lana'i and Moloka'i are usually bathed in bright light, and the often-tranquil waters create an unusually serene atmosphere.

Access is off Hwy 30 between 25 & 26 mile markers. Take Kai Ala Drive. (Puukoli Sreet is across the street.)

❖ **Black Rock**—This is the large, black lava rock that separates the two halves of Ka'anapali Beach. (It's also where Hawaiian spirits went to meet their ancestors. See page 50 for more.) The snorkel- **A Real Gem** ing around the rock is legendary and mostly lives up to the hype. Lots of fish and a decent amount of coral. Start from the Sheraton side and work your way around the rock; it's mostly a wall of lava-encrusted coral. Only one area around the corner has a lava shelf. Be careful there of surges. Watch for turtles that come to the area as customers of cleaner wrasse fish stations. When returning back to the Sheraton side, if you notice a current around the corner, swim away from the rock along the beach about 75 feet. The current should end and you can swim back to the beach. (That current is from the weak longshore current that bumps up against Black Rock and slithers around it.)

❖ **Ka'anapali Beach**—This beach has a dozen different, often conflicting names. Pick a handful of free magazines around the island and each may have a different name. Some names were appar- **A Real Gem** ently invented out of the blue. Technically, Ka'anapali Beach is everything from Keka'a (North Beach) to Hanake'o'o (Canoe) Beach, but we'll bow to the more common usage and designate it as the sandy beach from Black Rock south to Canoe Beach, including a section known as **Dig Me Beach.** (See map on page 51.) Ka'anapali is one of the finest beaches you'll find on Maui. This portion fronts most of the Ka'anapali resorts and Whalers Village. There's a **concrete path** running the entire length of Ka'anapali Beach, from Black Rock to the Hyatt. It's a *great* place to be at sunset. This beach turns into a kickin', hoppin', happenin' place as all eyes are cast toward the sunset. Dinner cruises ply

It might not be a hidden, untrampled beach, but Ka'anapali never disappoints.

Hanake'o'o/Canoe Beach

validate if you spend $10 (which is *easy* to do).

The waters at Ka'anapali are great when calm. Snorkeling at Black Rock on the north end and near Canoe Beach on the south are good. The middle offers a nice, sandy bottom. When surf's up, waves break on the somewhat steep beach with greater force, and swimming is not advised.

The northern end of the beach is the best. The southern end near the Hyatt has more foot-gouging reef near shore and sometimes seaweed in the water.

❖ **Hanake'o'o/ Canoe Beach**—A major hub of West Maui activity, you have your choice of jet skiing, boogie boarding, body surfing, watching canoe races and...oh yeah, swimming. Snorkeling isn't much to speak of due to poor visibility. There are covered picnic tables and facilities and the beach is popular with locals, especially on weekends. Access is from the parking lot between the 23 and 24 mile marker. Wander north from the lot.

❖ **Wahikuli Wayside Park**—South of Ka'anapali, this long sliver of shoreline is wedged between the highway and the sea. Often nearly empty during the

the waters, beachside restaurants hum, and couples walk the glorious beachside path holding hands and waiting to greet the night. It's busy but not offensively loud. If you're staying in West Maui, you should strongly consider spending one evening doing a stroll along this path, then dining at one of the restaurants along here. Access is from the free garage between the Sheraton and the Ka'anapali Beach Hotel, but it often fills up. You can also park at the Whalers Village Shopping Center. Any shop will

week, there are restrooms and showers, but the restrooms can be pretty scary. (County parks are notorious for their bad restroom maintenance.) The northern end is best, but fairly yucky water and little sand make it a forgettable beach park unless you're just looking for a place to eat your picnic lunch. Between Lahaina and Ka'anapali. Wahikuli means *noisy place,* an appropriate name given how close the beach is to the highway.

❖ **Lahaina**—Lahaina is good for a lot of things, but beach-going ain't one of 'em. The waters off this busy town are usually murky and not suitable for swimming. **Pu'unoa Beach** at the north end is also known as **Baby Beach,** but you probably won't want to spend time there. **Kamehameha Iki Park** (formerly Armory Park) near 505 Front St. is also a place where you could slip into the water, but why would you want to? West Maui has better beaches elsewhere.

❖ **14 Mile Marker**—Many dive shops and free magazines steer snorkelers to a spot on Highway 30 called Mile 14 (referring to the mile marker). To put it bluntly, the snorkeling there usually bites. In fact, we wonder if they have even snorkeled there in the last 10 years. From the highway, it *looks* like it will be wonderful. Driving along, you see lots of reef and contrast, giving the *illusion* of good snorkeling. But once in the water you realize that there's one thing missing—*visibility!* It's often less than 5 feet, even less than 2 feet at times, probably due to a small amount of runoff from the intermittent stream between the 14 and 15 mile markers. It varies with the tides and seasons and is sometimes better, but odds are you're likely to be disappointed. The best snorkeling can be had by swimming 200 yards out to sea *west* of the 14 mile marker; snorkel boats take paying passengers here to a place called **Coral Gardens.** But it's always a bit risky swimming that far away from shore, and the visibility, though improved, can still be topped elsewhere. If you do snorkel this area, do it in the late morning when the sun is brighter but the winds aren't peaking.

❖ **Ukumehame & Papalaua parks**— These are stretches of beach lining Hwy 30 between the 11 and 13 mile markers. Access is easy: Just drive up, open your door and fall out. The only good snorkeling is where the road leaves the shoreline, ascending toward the tunnel heading southeast. The reef and visibility improve markedly. But you'll have to swim from the last stretch of sand at Papalaua, and that can be tiring. Best just to enjoy the beach for what it is—a good place to pull over and revel in the view.

❖ **Scenic Lookout**—Though not a beach, the snorkeling below the scenic lookout between the 8 & 9 mile marker 2 miles southwest of Ma'alaea on Highway 30 is fantastic. Extraordinary fish counts often bless the area. The problem is getting in and out. The trail from the railings is the easy part. At the bottom, entry and especially exit from the water are difficult. Do so only when calm, wear reef shoes into the water, and pick your spot carefully, While exiting, remember the difficult-exit rule: Work with the ocean and let it do the work for you. You can use a surge to bring you up onto a rock if you do it right. While in the water, snorkeling to the right is best. Be careful of surginess. Divers will find deeper waters fairly quickly.

SOUTH MAUI BEACHES

When it comes to good beaches, South Maui has an embarrassment of riches. This is where the tropical beach dream comes true. Perfect stretches of thickly padded sand normally kissed by gentle surf, clear water and palm trees create an instantly pleasing atmosphere. The surf is usually flat in the winter and very small in the summer. The only downside to South Maui beaches is afternoon wind. Shielded by Haleakala during the morning, winds tend to start slithering around the mountain at north Kihei in the late morning and work their way south throughout the afternoon. At the other end, La Pérouse Bay is where the morning wind starts and works its way northward as the day progresses. This means that *morning* almost always offers the best conditions, both for swimming and snorkeling. The last area to get windy and choppy is usually around Wailea, and that's also where the best beaches are, so we're in luck.

❖ **Ma'alaea Bay**—If you're looking for a long beach stroll, have we got a beach for you. Stretching all the way from Ma'alaea Harbor 3 miles down to north Kihei, this beach is a walker's delight. The waters off the Ma'alaea end aren't the friendliest, and winds in the afternoon can be irritat-

ing, but morning and sunset strolls are great here. As you near Kihei, a portion of the beach is known as **Sugar Beach.** Here you can rent windsurfing boards, sailboats and other beach paraphernalia.

❖ **Maipoina Oe Lau Beach Park to Kalama Beach & Cove Park**— One of the dirty little secrets (literally) about Kihei is that you can't—or at least *shouldn't*—swim along the coastline anywhere from the north end of Kihei town to Cove Park. We've shown it on the map as a DON'T SWIM area. We know we're going to make some serious

The 3 Kama'oles: Not a Mexican rock group, just a nice trio of beaches.

enemies with this disclosure, and as far as we know we're the first to let this ugly cat out of the bag, but the water in that whole area is nasty. There is a...waste facility (which we've labeled as STP on the map) that often discharges their treated water right through the center of Kalama Park. Slow but ever-present northward currents take this "reclaimed water" north until it dissipates. (*Reclaimed:* what a great term! Like *pre-owned* cars or referring to leftover turkey sandwiches as *repurposed cuisine.*) Algae flourishes in this water, making the ocean here a bit smelly, murky, full of seaweed and generally unpleasant. (From Kamaʻole I all the way south, the water is *completely* unaffected.) We hate to tell you this, especially if you're renting a wonderful-sounding beachfront place in this area, but it's something you need to know. There are times when the water clears up, such as when storms flush (if you'll pardon the expression) the area. But don't count on it. Avoid Cove Park, Kalama Beach and everything up to and including Maipoina Oe Lau Beach Park. Surfing lessons are common at Cove Park, but we don't recommend the water there except in the winter. Cove Park is not quite as bad in the morning since the ocean current has cleaned the water that has been driven south by afternoon winds, and winter's lighter winds also keep Cove Park cleaner. (Surfers use the whole area, but hardcore surfers will surf in *anything.*)

❖ **Kamaʻole Beach**—Kamaʻole Beach is broken into three parts, cleverly named Kamaʻole Beach I, II and III. **Kamaʻole I** is the biggest and best of

A Real Gem

the three—a long and pretty stretch of fine sand with good swimming much of the time, restrooms, showers and a lifeguard. Access is a snap and your car is very close to the water. Across the street is a convenience store, in case you get hungry or thirsty, and there's a lawn area on the south end of the park. You'll find very good snorkeling around the rocks bracketing each end, especially the north (right) end. (That end is also called **Charley Young Beach.**) **Kamaʻole II** is also a good beach, though not quite as long or as nice at Kamaʻole I. Here, too, good snorkeling exists around the rocky points defining the beach. Of the three Kamaʻoles, **Kamaʻole III** is the most popular with locals. There is a small spot here where waves focus, even during calm seas, which makes the boogie boarding as reliable as you're gonna get in South Maui. There's some decent snorkeling at the north end near the rocks, but beware of a particularly bad surge there if the sea's not calm. There is a *huge* lawn at the south end of Kamaʻole III, which makes a great place to fly a kite or toss a Frisbee or football, and there's a limited playground for the keikis. Unfortunately, Kamaʻole III is also the messiest of the three due to its usage, and the sand beach area is relatively small. All three Kamaʻoles are easily identified from South Kihei Road between Ke Alii Alanui and Keonekai roads. All have showers and restrooms. On S. Kihei Rd. See map on page 131.

❖ **Keawakapu Beach**—One of the most criminally underrated beaches in South Maui. Very long with gobs of fine sand on and offshore. The only resort on the

A Real Gem

Sigh! Lovely Wailea, just another kickin' South Maui beach.

beach is past the north end. The rest is lined with *very* expensive houses. (Some selling for over $10 million!) The area in front of the main public access has a huge, well-padded sandy bottom, perfect for frolicking with minimal fear of stubbing your toe on a rock. (You've never *really* cursed until you've cursed a beach rock that has attacked your foot.) If you walk to the south (left) past the large, glassy two-story house with a blue tile roof, the beach widens and you'll find another large sandy bottom area. This part of the beach is amazingly underused. Farther south is the other Keawakapu entrance. (With the first one and a parking lot at the intersection of South Kihei Road and Kilohana.) Few people other than locals even know about this other entrance (which has a shower) at the unnoticed end of South Kihei Road, and the water offshore is very well sanded. (This is probably a good time to tell you that sunglasses that are *polarized* are amazing at detecting dark rocks on the sandy bottom.) Mornings are best; afternoons can be windy. One caveat about

Keawakapu: Some plants on the backshore attract bees, which usually aren't a problem, but it's sometimes possible to step on an errant bee blown onto the sandy shoreline, especially in the windy afternoon. At the south end of S. Kihei Road. See maps on pages 131 and 133.

❖ **Mokapu & Ulua Beach**—These two beaches are usually spoken of in the same sentence since they share the same parking lot just south of the Renaissance Hotel. When you take the short path down, the beach on your left is Ulua, on the right is Mokapu. The sand at Ulua doesn't extend as far offshore as most of the other beaches in the area. We prefer Mokapu; it's more picturesque, used a bit less and has slightly clearer water. Ulua is a popular dive spot. Though a tad over-dived, it's nice with a lot of coral, albeit crowded, and the visibility is often poor. Night dives have pretty easy access—a big plus. The 36 parking stalls fill up *early* since most slots are snagged by dive companies that take students here for introductory SCUBA lessons. Access to

Mokapu isn't dependent on the parking lot, however. You can park at the southern Keawakapu lot and stroll around the corner along the beach to the left to get to Mokapu. You're at Mokapu when you see a hotel and wooden walkway inland.

❖ **Wailea Beach**—An outstanding beach! Over ⅓ mile long, this classic crescent of sand has been ranked by several beach rankings (yes, there *are* people who do that) as the best beach in America. Terrific clear water, fine-grained sand, picturesque setting, calm waters most of the time, excellent swimming; Wailea should be on your short list of beaches to visit while here. The biggest problem at Wailea is parking. The resort has provided a parking lot, accessed just past the Grand Wailea, but it may fill up if you don't get there early. (However, the Wailea parking lot usually fills up *after* the Ulua/Mokapu Beach parking lot.) Showers and restrooms are provided. As with all South Maui beaches, morning is better than afternoon, though Wailea won't get windy as early as beaches farther north. Snorkeling can be decent at each end when calm. Boogie boarding can be very good for novices at the far south (left) side when there's a little surf. (But remember, small surf is often a South Maui hallmark, so boogie boarding is not always possible.) Waves at Wailea are short, close to shore and easy to catch without fins. Just stand there and jump with them. Stay just far enough away from the rocks at the end of the beach to avoid them. The tiny cove just past the rocks at the south end has a rocky bottom. Good for sunbathing, but not for swimming.

A Real Gem

❖ **Polo Beach**—Easy access and more parking than other Wailea beaches, Polo has restrooms, a shower, picnic tables and BBQ grills on the lawn above the beach. The beach isn't as deep as some other Wailea beaches and there are a few more hidden rocks in the sand, but it's a fine beach nonetheless, and the water is usually clear. Parking is ample and rarely fills up. There are beach chairs lining the beach, though they're *presumably* for guests of the Kea Lani, which backs the beach. Located two miles from the Wailea Iki intersection; see map on page 133.

❖ **Palauea Beach**—Used primarily by local residents who take the short path through the trees to this lesser known beach, it's not usually crowded during the week. Also called **White Rock,** the snorkeling around the rocky point on the left is *very* good. It's also good on the right side, though the water isn't as clear as the left side. The gently sloping shoreline is loaded with sand in the middle and provides excellent swimming much of the time. The bay is recessed, so it doesn't get as windy in the afternoon as other beaches. No facilities, but the easy access and quality of the beach make it a winner. Off Makena Road; see map on page 133.

A Real Gem

❖ **Poʻolenalena Beach**—Probably the least known and certainly least used large beach in the Wailua/Makena area. It's also known locally as Paipu Beach, Chang's Beach, Pepeiaolepo Beach, Love Beach, Keauhou Beach and sometimes Makena Surf Beach. *(How can something so little known have so many names?)* Nearly ½ mile long, there

A Real Gem

have been times when we've found other Wailea beaches crowded and found this beach empty or nearly so during the week. (Weekends are busy here, as all beaches can be.) The water offshore is mostly a broad, flat, gentle, sandy bottom with only occasional outcroppings of rock. The beach is gently sloping, making the water especially good for swimming during the normally calm seas. When there's a little surf, the left (south) side can offer very good boogie boarding. The beach is interrupted toward the right (north) side by lava. Scramble over the lava rocks or around them at low tide, and you may have the northern ⅓ of the beach to yourself.

The beach is bracketed by lava points on each side, and the snorkeling around them is exceptional and little used compared to other snorkel sites. Tons of fish and a very healthy coral community, especially as you venture away from shore along the points, make it a worthy snorkel destination. Usually *lots* of **turtles** at the left and right sides and even the occasional lobster. (By the way, lobsters are sometimes known locally as *bugs*. When you hear someone say, *Hey brah, we go catch bugs,* it means he's going lobster diving.) The right end of the beach is rarely snorkeled and is one of our favorite snorkel sites on the island. So let's see…We have great swimming, great snorkeling, easy access, good boogie boarding when there's surf and a general lack of crowds. *What's not to love?* The two accesses are on either side of our "imaginary" 2 mile marker on the map on page 133. The second one is a bit farther south at the Makena Surf and, though *very* limited, is often unused. It's better since it has showers nearby. Go

Palauea Beach is one of the lesser known South Maui beaches.

Why aren't you wet yet? Maluaka Beach in front of the Maui Prince has lots of shade, good swimming and great snorkeling.

through the unlocked gate and along the walkway. If it's full, use the first access.

One quick nag: The coral and fish in this area haven't been exposed to lots of people. The coral isn't trampled and broken, and the fish haven't been fed much. Please don't start the tradition. Fish feeding completely messes up the balance, leaving only a few aggressive species while driving away the meeker fish. And while snorkeling, be *real* careful not to bump into the coral with your fins, and don't stand on it or grab it. This will keep the reef here pristine and beautiful. (OK, end of nag.)

❖ **5 Graves/5 Caves—**A good SCUBA site and fairly good snorkeling. Turtles are common, and there are several caves. Once in the water divers should head straight out, slightly to the right and look for the caves along the wall. Entry is from a small, semi-protected rocky cove off Makena Road. See map on page 133. You'll walk by a small graveyard (with *seven* graves that we counted, and probably more in the faint lava rock outlines). Sometimes referred to as 5 Caves, sometimes 5 Graves, but neither seems to be accurate. On Makena Road; see map on page 133.

❖ **Makena Landing Beach Park—** This used to be a great place for snorkeling and diving with easy access. Excellent night dives were also available. Notice the past tense. A storm in late 1999 brought an unusual amount of runoff. Since then the bay has become a dead zone often with zero visibility, no fish and dying coral. The turtles that used to live here seem to have relocated to 5 Graves/5 Caves. Sorry to sound so grim, but that's the way it is. A biologist we spoke with said it will take many years to regain its former glory. It's still,

Oneuli Beach/Black Sand Beach is often lost in the shuffle of world-class South Maui beaches.

however, a good, convenient place to launch kayaks.

❖ **Maluaka Beach/Makena**—You'll be forgiven if you get confused as to where Makena Beach is. So is everyone else. Ask a local for directions and **A Real Gem** you could end up in one of *four* places. Oneloa Beach, also called Big Beach, is often called Makena Beach or sometimes Big Makena Beach. (It's also called Makena State Park.) Makena Bay, just north of here, which also contains Makena Landing, is sometimes called Makena Beach. Sometimes Po'olenalena Beach is called Makena Surf Beach. And lastly this beach is sometimes called Makena Beach. It's usually called Maluaka Beach, as the signs often say. Hey, don't blame us, we're just the messengers. For clarification *(ha!)* we'll call this beach Maluaka Beach.

Fronting the Maui Prince Hotel, this wide, pretty beach slopes gently, providing good swimming during calm seas, especially toward the center of the beach where a thick padding of sand awaits. During calm seas keikis (kids) splash about with abandon. There is shade at the south (left) end as well as restrooms, showers and picnic tables. Parking is past the Maui Prince Hotel, where Makena Road backtracks, 3⁶⁄10 miles south of the Wailea Alanui/Wailea Iki intersection. (See map on page 133.) If the lot's full, try using Makena Road just south of Honoiki. There's a drop-off area right at the sand, then you can park your car about 100 yards from the drop-off area, near the Keawala'i Church. Don't walk through the church cemetery.

The snorkeling off to the left (south) is very good with good coral and fish, and usually *lots* of turtles. In fact, this area is one of the famed *turtle towns* that some snorkel boats take people to. Off to the right also offers good snorkeling.

❖ **Oneuli Beach/Black Sand Beach**

A Real Gem

Less known than other beaches in the area since it's not well marked and can't be seen from the road, those who do know about it usually call it simply *Black Sand Beach.* It's on the north (right) side of that large hill in Makena called Pu'u Ola'i, and you access if from the short, well-graded dirt road shown on the map on page 135. Once at the salt and pepper beach it's easy to see how it formed. Pu'u Ola'i is essentially a large mound of lava cinders created from an enormous lava fountain. Wave action has bitten into the cinder cone, causing the loose black cinders to fall into the ocean where they are ground into black sand. Over the years shells have been pulverized into sand and coral has been…well, *processed* by parrotfish, adding salt to the pepper.

The water at Black Sand Beach is usually calm, but the sand gives way to a lava shelf at the water's edge, making the swimming marginal. However, the snorkeling can be great. Visibility is usually cloudy near the shore, so head out and to the left for lots of coral and fish. If it's calm you can snorkel all the way around Pu'u Ola'i and it gets even better. Beware of any currents by occasionally stopping to see if you are drifting. Kayakers sometimes visit the beach, but it's rarely crowded.

❖ **Big Beach/Oneloa/Makena**—Big Beach is what many people think of when they think of a Hawaiian beach. It is considered by many to be *the* beach on Maui. (Not to be confused with another beach in West Maui also called Oneloa Beach.) Almost ⅔

A Real Gem

mile long and over 100 feet wide, this beautiful crescent of golden sand is a dream for swimmers, snorkelers, frolickers and sometimes boogie boarders. When seas are calm, the water is very inviting. You won't find it empty; it's one of the more popular beaches. But you *will* find it enchanting.

During the '60s hippies from the mainland came to Maui looking to get back to nature, and they found their nirvana at what was then an isolated beach. Unable to remember its Hawaiian name, Oneloa (meaning long sands), they referred to is as simply Big Beach, a name that has stuck. (They also called it **Makena Beach,** which is incorrect. Makena Beach is farther north, but that name, too, has stuck.) After several years of hippie occupation, disease outbreaks from a lack of hygiene, lack of proper waste disposal and contaminated water supplies, along with rampant drug use, caused authorities to raid and evict the illegal "campers" in 1972. Today Big Beach is a state park. Porta-potties and picnic tables are available.

The large hill on the north (right) end of the beach is called Pu'u Ola'i, or Earthquake Hill. It was the site of the huge eruption described on page 134.

From the right side of the beach, you can take a short trail to a promontory. (Walk up a little, then turn left rather than continuing up the steeper gravel portion.) On the lava promontory, 20 feet above the water, there are several short trails leading shoreward that end at

Jewel-like waters and endless sand—Big Beach lives up to its name.

nice places to watch the sunset. The views of Big Beach from up here are delicious. On the other side of the promontory is a smaller beach. Let's see. The big beach is known as Big Beach, so what do you think the hippies called the little beach? Hmm, that's a toughie. How about **Little Beach?** (Darned clever, they were.) This ideal pocket of sand tucked away in a nook of Pu'u Ola'i offers great swimming, snorkeling, boogie boarding and bodysurfing. As it's not visible from the road, it is often used by nudists, which, by the way, is illegal in Hawai'i. (We tell you this so that if nudity bothers you, you may want to pass on Little Beach. Hmm. I wonder if there's another reason they call it Little Beach...) Another thing you need to know is that Little Beach is occasionally (but not too often) occupied by squatters in makeshift tents, creating an unfriendly atmosphere. Aside from these caveats, you may want to take a peek at

Little Beach from the trail on the promontory overlooking the sand to see if it's right for you that day. If it is, head on down and stake a claim to some sand. Weekends at Little Beach can be packed. The ocean has a sandy shoreline bottom, excellent for swimming, and the snorkeling around the points at both ends of the beach is good during calm seas. If you swim to Little Beach from Big Beach, the current can make swimming back annoying. Consider walking back if it's a problem that day.

There are two parking lots for Big Beach that you'll see from the road. Actually, if you're not going to Little Beach, consider driving past the second one and park on the road at the south (left) end of the beach where there's shade on the beach and less crowds.

❖ **Pa'ako Beach/Secret Cove**—This beach is *literally* a hole in the wall, or at least access to it is. That impressive rock wall you see just past (south of) Big Beach hides some impressive beachfront

A Real Gem

homes. But across from telephone pole #E2–3 (the first pole you encounter past Big Beach, in case someone steals the marking) is an opening in the wall, a legal public access. Walk through and you find a beautiful little pocket of sand. This is a popular place to get married, and for good reason. In the morning the views of Kahoʻolawe and Molokini from this pocket are outstanding, and the little beach simply looks charming. Since it's small, it doesn't take much to fill up; mornings are best. Off to the left, in front of a beach house, is a smaller pocket of sand. The beach doesn't really have a name, other than Secret Cove.

But the point on your right is called Paʻako, so we'll call it that.

❖ **ʻAhihi Cove**—Located just inside the ʻAhihi–Kinaʻu Natural Area Reserve (where it's illegal to capture or spear fish), the fish life here can be excellent, though visibility is often limited. No sand beach, but the cove is usually protected from wind and surf. South of Wailea; see map on page 135.

❖ **Fishbowl**—First, it's not really much of a beach. Just a sprinkling of sand is all you'll find. But the snorkeling here is excellent. (You probably already figured that out from the name.) This tiny cove out on Cape Kinaʻu (sometimes erroneously identified as Aquarium) offers protected, clear water and lots of fish (though not much coral; the land here is very young). If you venture outside the

Imagine getting married in this spot. Secret Cove is in the hearts and photo albums of couples all across America.

cove, stay to the right where it's at least partially protected. Outside to the left exposes you to much of the ocean's tumult. Kayakers often arrive here around 9:30 a.m. By this time the wind may start blowing, since you're right on the edge of the La Pérouse wind machine. We strongly recommend you come nice and early to possibly have it all to yourself and see it at its best. Access is not easy. It requires a 20–35-minute trek (each way) along a lava trail. It's a good trail but fades from the obvious in one or two spots, then quickly resumes. Some of the lava is encrusted with a green semi-precious gem called olivine, which sparkles in the sunlight. No shade at the cove. The trailhead at the road is not marked, other than some green paint (which hopefully isn't removed) and you may need to walk a few dozen feet until you see the actual trail. The trail is to the left of two reflector stakes 7/10 mile past 'Ahihi Cove after telephone pole #17 but before the next unnumbered pole, which is the second to last pole before they change to the other side of the road. (Something tells me you're gonna need to reread those directions about three times. I'm getting dizzy just writing it.) See map on page 135 for some guidance. Park on the mauka (mountain) side at one of the pullouts.

❖ **La Pérouse Bay**—In South Maui, this is as far as you can go by car. There's no sand beach here except for some small pockets at the south end of the bay, but the fish life is high. La Pérouse Bay is a great example of incomplete information. We won't even guess how many times we've been there and seen visitors carrying their snorkel bag to the shore, only to come out several minutes later dejected, saying they couldn't see anything. All they were told, either in the snorkel shop or from one of the free magazines, is that there is good snorkeling "at La Pérouse Bay." But the visitors saw diddly. That's because the visibility there at the end of the road is *terrible.* The Carter Estate, situated on the bay to the right, is where visibility is the worst. But if you go *past* their little cove, staying along the shoreline on the right, each successive cove gets clearer (though never crystal clear), and the fish life gets better and better. About four coves down, the fish life is some of the best you'll find *anywhere on the island.* The variety is incomparable. (See the great hike/snorkel trip listed on page 230 for more.) The farther out you go, the better the fish life, but the water can get rougher as you go farther, too.

Go *early* in the morning. During normal trade winds, the bay fills in with wind and chop as the morning progresses, and by afternoon it can be cranking. 8 a.m. is better than 9 a.m. To get there, drive to the end of Makena Alanui Road, just past the La Pérouse monument where the road becomes rocky. Enter just to the left of the wire fence that goes to the water. There's a nice lava shelf that works well if the surf's not high. Keep an eye out for pin cushion-like sea urchins. (Or enter from the beach area to the right, though the water is not nice there.) Be cautious of surf and surges along the shoreline past the private cove. Many of the coves past there are protected, but the water outside of them is not.

The area past the end of the road is a popular fishing spot for locals, and more than once we've seen them try to talk visitors out of swimming at La Pérouse. (Assuming we were visitors, we've had fishermen try to convince us that dolphins

Hana doesn't have many beaches, but the few it does have, like Red Sand Beach, are exceptional. The shoreline trail on the left is a little tricky.

were *leaping out of the water*...just down the road at 'Ahihi Cove.)

Past the end of the regular road, 4WD vehicles can proceed to a number of small coves that you can claim for the morning.

La Pérouse is a common place to see dolphins in the early morning. A large pod seems to cruise this area, heading northward as the morning progresses. We often see them here around 7 a.m., then at Big Beach around 10 a.m. Turtles are also relatively common, though more so just north in 'Ahihi Cove.

❖ **Keawanaku**—Any local reading this will say, *where?* That's because this beach really has no name and has been virtually unknown until now. It's past the end of the road in South Maui. You need to hike to it. See ACTIVITIES on page 201 for more.

THE BOTTOM OF MAUI

Past Keawanaku the shoreline is rocky and windy, and the seas are usually harsh. Other than one inaccessible pocket at the base of a cliff and a couple of tiny seasonal sand patches, you could explore the entire 30 miles of shoreline (which we've done), and you won't find *one* sand beach until you get to Hana. The only area frequently accessed (mostly by locals) is **Nu'u Bay**, described on page 113.

HANA BEACHES

Hana has only a few beaches. *Ahh,* but what beaches! A red sand beach, a black sand beach and the best body surfing beach on the island. Since there's no way you'd ever drive all the way to Hana just for a day at the beach, we've deviated from our usually format and listed them under HANA HIGHWAY SIGHTS.

THE NORTH SHORE OF HALEAKALA— FROM HANA TO CENTRAL MAUI

Hana is on the eastern tip of the island, and once you're west of Hana the shoreline turns rocky. There are a few bays that you can visit (listed in the driving tours), but they don't have sand and are exposed to the higher surf normally present all along this windward coast. Not until the towns of Pa'ia and Kahului will you find beaches, and they are *not* in the same league as South and West Maui's beaches.

❖ **Ho'okipa Beach Park**—This is the only beach on this coast that visitors will probably be interested in. Near the 9 mile marker on Hwy 36, it's upcurrent of most of the run off that plagues other area beaches. It's widely recognized as perhaps the best place in the world to windsurf, and boarders from everywhere make their pilgrimage to this spot. If you're not an expert, don't try. If the ocean doesn't get you, the surprisingly snobbish windsurfers will. (Novices use Kanaha Beach.) But this is a *great* place to watch the hordes of windsurfers, as well as the pounding surf that often racks the shore. (Windsurfing is not allowed until 11 a.m.) It's uncommon *not* to have wind here. Car break-ins are a problem, so don't leave any valuables in your car.

❖ **H.A. Baldwin Park**—At the 6 mile marker on Hwy 36, it has a huge lawn, a long crescent of sand, good body surfing (though it's easy to get pounded into the sand here) lifeguard, full facilities, pavilion and nice views of West Maui. The downside is cloudy water from nearby runoff and very crowded conditions on the weekend. During the week it's good for a beach stroll, though you'll find this one of the smellier beaches due to the seaweed thriving off the runoff. Farther east, **Lower Pa'ia** is simply a disgusting beach access 2/10 mile west of the 7 mile marker. 'Nuff said.

❖ **Spreckelsville Beach**—A mixed bag. On the plus side, it's a long, attractive beach with unusually firm sand, deserted most of the time during the week and nice views of the north coast. Several areas have a bench of lithified sand (sandstone) near the water's edge that provides some protection for keikis (kids) and nervous swimmers after you check for safety. On the negative side, current and wind are pretty dependable companions all day long, the water is cloudy, and (this is the clincher) jets departing the island fly over part of the beach, which can rattle your jaw. The best part of the beach (farthest from the airport) is at the 5 mile marker on Hwy 36. Take Nonohe to Keolakai. The other part, off the unmarked road between the 4 and 5 mile marker is more avoidable.

❖ **Kanaha Beach**—This is where most visitors do their **windsurfing** and **kite surfing** lessons. (See page 228 for more on these.) As a beach destination it won't twirl your tassels, but it's perfect for these wind-related activities.

❖ **Waiehu Beach**—This beach, along with nearby **Waihe'e Beach,** are the last beaches on the windward side. Kind of anti-climactic to end it this way after so many great beaches, but these beaches are mostly used by shoreline fishermen and local residents and don't offer much for visitors. The water's a bit murky, the shoreline rocky, and currents can be a problem.

Boat trips are wildly popular on Maui, but we were nervous about publishing this photo. The water is so clean, clear and calm, it makes the photo look like it was retouched. We promise, we don't use tricky photographic filters or computers. This is really how it looks on a good morning.

Pick your fantasy; name your dream. If you had to pick the one thing that keeps people coming back to Maui year after year, this would probably be it. Just about everything you dream of doing in the tropics is available here. This is where it all comes true. But where should you go, and whom should you go with?

Most sources of visitor information, free and not free, tend to steer visitors to the same group of large activity providers, such as boat tours and helicopter companies. Some of these are good companies, but we've found some to be large, arrogant visitor-processing machines that seem to take their status for granted. We've spent countless hours anonymously reviewing smaller companies in addition to the larger ones to give you options that you won't find elsewhere.

Be skeptical when looking at advertisements from different companies. Activity providers in Hawai'i are notorious for using computers to put leaping whales on their ocean tour brochures, or showing kayakers paddling up to waterfalls where it's not possible. Or how about the tour company that advertises that with their jungle tour they'll show you "hidden waterfalls" in Hana. Wow, sounds intriguing. Too bad the "hidden waterfall" photo on their brochure is actually the artificial falls in front of the Grand Wailea Hotel in South Maui. There are shameless attempts to lure your business, and you need to be vigilant in picking who you go with.

The activity industry on Maui is *massive*. You should be *real* skeptical of recommendations from activity desks and activity booths that often only "recommend" companies that give them the biggest commissions. (And those commissions can be *huge*.) Some are contractually bound to certain companies. Even some hotel concierges work this way. Our reviews reflect our personal observations, opinions and experiences. We actually *do* this stuff (anonymously), and this section reflects what we saw. We don't get any money for steering you in a certain direction, a claim that very few can make. While it's true you can *sometimes* get good deals booking though activity companies (or get good deals if you trade some of your precious Maui time for a timeshare presentation), we *strongly* suggest you decide which company you want to go with *before* you see them, and don't let them steer you elsewhere. Also, some companies will give you a discount if you book directly, cutting out the activity brokers.

July, August and Christmas are busy times on Maui, and it may be difficult getting what you want on short notice. In general, if you have your heart set on a particular activity, consider reserving it from the mainland (by phone or Internet), just to make sure there's room for you. For all local phone numbers, the area code is 808.

The biking scene on Maui is certainly more varied than on the other Hawaiian islands. In addition to simply peddling around the neighborhood, there's the famous Haleakala downhill ride and the less-famous Skyline downhill mountain bike ride.

FROM THE SUMMIT TO THE SEA

This is probably the one you've heard about since more than 50,000 people per year do this. You start near the summit of 10,000-foot-high Haleakala and cruise downhill virtually the whole way, ending near sea level. If you opt for the sunrise tours, you'll get to see sunrise from the mountain the Hawaiians called *house of the sun,* which can be glorious. (Unless you don't dress warmly enough.) Though it looks good on your vacation resume and can be lots of fun, we think it may be a bit overrated, especially considering the high cost and safety concerns.

Most people are picked up at their hotels or condos between 2 a.m. and 3 a.m. A quiet or surly stupor fills the van during the 2-hour or so drive up the mountain as thoughts such as "whose stupid idea was this?" or "there better not be any darned sing-alongs on the van" dominate the morning.

Once at the top, 95% of people soon learn that they are seriously underdressed. Temperatures from the low 30s to the upper 40s coupled with 30 mph winds can turn the rarefied air to a symphony of groans and burrs. See page 121 for more on the sunrise and how to prepare for it. When you get cold, you can sit in the van and drink coffee to keep warm.

There are four companies that can start from the summit. (There were rumblings at press time of banning the park portion of the ride.) The three big guys are: **Mountain Riders** (242–9739), **Maui Downhill** (871–2155) and **Maui Cruisers** (871–6014). There are 13 people per trip, with a guide in front setting the pace and a van (called a sag wagon) pulling up the rear. Anyone who gets uncomfortable can get in the van at any time. All three companies use comparable bikes whose wide seats are appreciat-

ed if you haven't been on a bike in a while. It's about $120 for the sunrise trip, and about $10 cheaper if you want to sleep in a few hours later. **Cruiser Phil** (893–2332) is smaller, has similar prices.

A WORD OF WARNING: Because so many people do this, it's tempting to think that the danger must be minimal. It's not. According to the local paper, at least one serious accident per week occurs during these downhill rides. From road rash to broken bones to deaths, this activity has taken its toll on visitors. The first time we did it, we invited visiting relatives to go. Once we got up top, we were told that our nephew was just a tad too short (at 4½ feet), but our 15-year-old niece was able to come. With only 2 miles left on the ride, a bee landed on her (not an uncommon occurrence), and, distracted, she failed to negotiate a turn and took a vicious tumble end-over-end right in front of us, landing on boulders 15 to 20 feet from the road. Even with a motorcycle helmet she had head injuries (a deep gash all the way to the skull) and was hospitalized. A year later she still had lingering problems from the concussion.

Part of the problem is that riders in groups are strongly prodded to ride at least 20 mph, or the tour companies claim they'll be ticketed. And 20 mph (often faster) is pretty fast on some stretches, especially when you're still stiff from the cold. Though the age limit is 12 years old, we don't recommend it to anyone below 16. (Incidentally, those generous souls at Mountain Riders refused to refund her parents' money even though they spent much of the day at the hospital. Also, in case they're reading this, our niece is still waiting for your promised complimentary *I Survived the Haleakala Downhill Ride* T-shirt, which seemed particularly appropriate considering how it ended.)

A FEW THOUGHTS: Mountain Riders tends to get there early; a plus if you want to leave right after sunrise since groups are spaced 10 minutes apart on a first-come basis, a minus if you want to sleep as late as possible. Late arrivals, such as Maui Downhill, may need to wait several hours after sunrise before beginning their descent or travel downhill by van a ways before starting. If you can't stand the thought of getting up so early, you can take a later trip. It won't be as cold, but the chances of riding in rain

The view of clouds, ocean and a cane fire below are tempting, but don't take your eyes off the road.

and clouds are greater the later the day gets. You don't see quite as many views on the way down as you expect simply because you're concentrating on road so much. A small flashlight can be handy at the nearly lightless pre-sunrise summit; many people hurt themselves stumbling around. Sunglasses are recommended on the ride because most helmets don't have eye protection. Contact lens wearers should bring drops. The colder you allow yourself to get before the ride, the stiffer you'll be during the ride. Lastly, if you're going to do the sunrise trip, do it early in your trip, when your body clock is still on the earlier mainland time.

An alternative to the massive downhill companies is to bike it on your own. Companies will take you to the edge of the park (at the 6,600-foot level) and let you ride down on your own, after perhaps first visiting the summit for a sunrise. The increased risk of not having a guide in front of you blocking tackle is balanced by the fact that you get to go *at your own pace.* Also, you can choose a different route if you want. For instance, **Haleakala Bike Company** (575–9575) is located in Haʻiku. So instead of the uninteresting Baldwin Avenue at the end, you can take the more scenic Kokomo Road (first stop sign outside of Makawao) into Haʻiku with just a little uphill riding past Makawao. $49 for the drop-off, add $20 for the sunrise. A pretty decent outfit and location to return the bike.

Upcountry Cycles (573–2888) has similar offerings, but the trip ends sooner at Makawao. $45 for the drop-off, or $65 to include the sunrise. Bike helmets, but no motorcycle helmets. The majority of people who do these rides are really rusty on a bike, so you should hold it against a company that refuses to let you use a full motorcycle-style helmet.

MOUNTAIN BIKE HALEAKALA'S SPINE

One of the most interesting bike rides in Hawaiʻi is down the lesser-known spiny side of Haleakala. See ADVENTURES on page 234 for more.

RENTING A BIKE

If you just want to **rent a bike,** in West Maui try **West Maui Cycles** (661–9005) and in South Maui call **South Maui Bicycles** (874–0068). In Kahului try **Extreme Sports Maui** (871–7954). Most charge around $20–$25 for road bikes, $15–$30 for mountain bikes.

BOATING

See Ocean Tours, page 206.

Boogie boarding (riders are derisively referred to as *spongers* by surfers) is where you ride a wave on what is essentially a sawed-off surfboard. It can be a real blast. You need short, stubby fins to catch bigger waves (which break in deeper water), but you can snare small waves by simply standing in shallow water and lurching forward as the wave is breaking. If you've never done it before, stay away from big waves; they can drill you. Smooth-bottom boards work best. If you're not going to boogie board with boogie fins (which some consider difficult to learn), then you should boogie board with reef shoes or some other kind of water footwear. It allows you to scramble around in the water without fear of tearing your feet up on a rock or urchin. Shirts are very important, especially for men. (Women already have this aspect covered.) Sand and the board itself can rub you so raw your *da kines* will glow in the dark.

In **South Maui,** if the surf is low (as is often the case), your best chance to catch waves is at Kama'ole Beach III. You also stand a good chance at the far south end of Wailea Beach. If there are moderate waves, Kama'ole III is probably too strong. Consider the middle of the beach at Kama'ole I, midway along Wailea Beach, Mokapu Beach, Keawakapu Beach (especially in the middle just south of the two-story house with the blue tile roof) and Big Beach.

In **West Maui,** consider Hanake'o'o/Canoe Beach, Ka'anapali Beach, left side of Oneloa Beach, and Slaughterhouse Beach in the summer. Some shoreline stretches south of Lahaina can be great. Just drive along and look for conditions.

Boards are easy to rent anywhere. It should cost about $5–$8 per day, $15–$20 per week.

CAMPING

Ah, camping in the tropics. The ultimate in low-cost housing. Although Maui isn't loaded with camping opportunities, there are several places worth noting.

Haleakala National Park has some of the best camping on the island. Drive-up campgrounds are at the seashore at Kipahulu (near the pools at 'Ohe'o, but there's no water) and at Hosmer Grove near the crater. Three-night maximum. *Inside* the crater, overnight tent camping at Holua and Paliku require free permits. Apply in person at the park the day of your trip; no advance reservations. If they're booked up, tough toenails. Same

3-night max, (2 nights at a site).

There are three *highly* coveted cabins inside Haleakala Crater, with free wood for the wood burning stove, and *everybody* wants them. We've know people who schedule a trip to Maui simply because they were able to get reservations at a cabin. The cabins hold up to 12, but it's only one party per cabin. The application process is complicated and involves a lottery. You may also have to entertain park officials with juggling or magic tricks and perhaps wash their cars. Call the number below to find out how to apply in writing at least two months in advance. You can call between 1 p.m. and 3 p.m. to check on vacancies, but don't count on it. (And don't count on them answering the phone, either.) Cabins cost $40 per night.

Haleakala National Park
Attention: Cabins
P.O. 369
Makawao, HI 96768
(808) 572–4400

State campgrounds are near Wai'anapanapa Black Sand Beach and at Polipoli Park (high in the mountain). Call **State Parks** at (808) 984–8109 for permits. (Free, but they were thinking of charging $5 per night at press time.) Five-night max. Wai'anapanapa has 12 cabins available for $45, and there's one at Polipoli for $45.

There's only one **county campground** at Kanaha Beach Park (near Kahului Airport. Call 270–7389 for $3 permits. Restrooms, water and shower.

Camp Pecusca (661–4303) has first-come, first-serve camping: tent, A-frame cabins (for large groups), car or whatever. $5 per person, located in Olowalu. Usually dry here.

The **YMCA** in Ke'anae is one of the best deals on the island. For $10 per person you can share a cabin (tent camping is also $10 per person). BBQ grill available (bring food). Spring and summer are the busiest; book in advance by calling 242–9007 and ask for Camp Ke'anae.

Maui Land & Pineapple (669–6201) will let you camp at Punalau Beach north of Kapalua. $5 permits need to be picked up in person near Napili. No facilities.

Quality Motorcycle Tours (242–1015) has multi-day motorcycle camping tours. Call them for details.

You can rent gear at **Base Camp** (573–2267) in Makawao and **Bike Shop** (877–5848) in Kahului. Camp stove gas can usually be found at **Gaspro** (661–1480) in West Maui, **Sports Authority** (871–2558) Kahului, **Base Camp** Upcountry.

Deep sea fishing is synonymous with Hawai'i. Reeling in a massive marlin, tuna or tough fighting ono is a dream of many fishermen. When there's a strike, the adrenaline level of everyone on board shoots through the roof. Most talked about are the marlin (very hard fighters known for multiple runs). These goliaths can tip the scales at over 1,000 pounds. Also in abundance are ono, also called wahoo (one of the fastest fish in the ocean and indescribably delicious), mahimahi (vigorous fighters—excellent on light tackle), ahi (delicious yellowfin tuna) and billfish.

Most big fish like to cruise through deeper waters than what are found off the leeward side of Maui. (The Big Island is blessed with deep water right off the Kona shore.) The shallow water here that the whales love tends to be shunned by large pelagics. On Maui you'll have to take a 30–60 minute boat trip to areas where the undersea topography drops off steeply. But fear not. Once there, large game fish await.

Most boats troll nonstop since the lure darting out of the water simulates a panicky bait fish—the favored meal for large game fish. On some boats, each person is assigned a certain reel. Experienced anglers usually vie for the corner poles with the assumption that strikes coming from the sides are more likely to hit corners first.

You should know in advance that in Hawai'i, the fish belongs to the boat. What happens to the fish is entirely up to the captain, and he usually keeps it. You could catch a 1,000-pound marlin and be told that you can't have as much as a steak from it. If this bothers you, you're out of luck. If the ono or other small fish are striking a lot and there is a glut of them, you might be allowed to keep it— or half of it. You *may* be able to make arrangements in advance to the contrary.

Charters leave from Lahaina and Ma'alaea. Though there are 4-, 6- and 8-hour charters, many won't do 4 hours since half the time is eaten traveling to and from the fishing grounds. We recommend the 6-hour trips. Mornings offer best conditions. Prices are $80–$120 per person for a 4-hour shared charter. You can do a private 6-hour charter for $350–$600. 8-hour private charters go for $600–$900 or more for the big boats. Usually, the bigger the boat, the higher the price since nearly all are licensed to take only 6 passengers. Individual boat rates can change often depending on the season, fishing conditions and whims of the owners. Consequently, we'll forgo listing individual boat rates since this information is so perishable and instead list a few companies that we recommend. Call them directly to get current rates. If you have 4 or more people, make it private so you can exercise more control.

If you're easy-queasy, take an anti-sea-sickness medication. There are people who never get sick regardless of conditions and those who turn green just watching an old episode of *The Love Boat*. Nothing can ruin an ocean outing quicker than being hunched over the stern feeding the fish. Scopolamine patches prescribed by doctors work best. Dramamine II or Bonine taken the night before and the morning of a trip also seems to work well for many, though some drowsiness may occur. Doctors are starting to cozy up to ginger as a preventative. Try powdered ginger, ginger pills or even *real* ginger ale—can't hurt, right?

Tipping: 10–15% split between the captain and deck hand is customary if you are pleased with their performance. If the captain is a jerk and the deck hand throws up on you, you're not obligated to give 'em diddly.

Boats to consider in West Maui are **Absolute Sportfishing** (669–1449), **Aerial Sportfishing** (667–9089), **Finest Kind** (661–0338), **Lucky Strike** (661–4606), and **Marlin Mischief** (662–3474).

In Ma'alaea there's **Makoa Kai** (875–2251), **Piper Sportfishing** (242–8350), and **Rascal** (874–8633). The latter is a typical 6-pack. Their fighting chair looks more like an electric chair, but at least they let you keep most of the fish. $110 per person or $525 for the boat for 6 hours. They'll also tag and release.

The **Excellence** (875–2252) certainly

lives up to its name.—a large, *gorgeous* modern fishing boat. They take only 6 and the boat is *(gulp)* $1,300 per 8-hour day. (Or $250 per person.)

OK, OK, let's be honest. A place that's known as the *windsurfing* capital of the world surely can't have world-class golf, right? So you'd think. But the truth is the golfing on Maui can be outrageous. Granted, it's probably not *quite* as good as some on the Big Island or the Prince Course on Kaua'i, but some courses are pretty close and will blow away most of the courses you've ever played on the mainland. The trick here is to play *early*. Wind can be the instrument of your doom here, and the later you play, the greater the doom.

Overall, South Maui courses offer the best golf and are usually calm in the mornings with winds picking up around 11 a.m. or later. Sunshine is almost guaranteed. West Maui courses at Ka'anapali can offer similar weather with more wind. West Maui's Kapalua courses are *very* windy nearly *all* the time, but best in the morning. Passing showers are common.

At both South and West Maui courses, *greens break toward the ocean,* no matter what your eye tells you. They may even break uphill if it's toward the sea. Also dress codes (collared shirts) are enforced more here. **Carts** are included and mandatory, unless otherwise noted.

SOUTH MAUI COURSES

If you only get a chance to golf once on Maui, we'd recommend South Maui. The exceptional morning weather, views of Kahoʻolawe and Molokini and three of the best Maui courses make the golfing incredible. If you're a great golfer, you'll prefer Makena South. If you're a decent golfer, you'll probably prefer Wailea's Gold or Emerald courses. We'll start at the extreme south and work our way up.

MAKENA RESORT (879–3344)

One of the two Makena courses is among the best on the island, and both Makena courses are ego bruisers. The **SOUTH COURSE** is the most fun of the two. Slower greens than the north, and the hazards are more successfully implemented here. The close ocean proximity is delightful, and the views of Molokini and Kahoʻolawe are tasty. Few adjoining fairways. Hole 3 has a pretty scary view of eight bunkers guarding the green. A relatively short but potentially deadly par 4. Hole 7 is a wonderful 599-yard journey from the champ tees. After the drive, just shoot straight toward Molokini

offshore and stop when you find a flag. Hole 13 has some magnetic water to shoot over. Most seem to underestimate it for some reason. Hole 15 is a dreamy 180 yards from the blues to the ocean. Club down for the steep downhill, but club up for the usual headwind. Hmm, maybe it's a wash. Regardless, it's a classic Hawaiian hole, guaranteed to elicit a contented sigh. Walk to the edge of the green for a beautiful view of the black sand beach. What a day it's been. Can it really almost be over?

The **NORTH COURSE** is nice, but not as fun as the South, and the maintenance wasn't as good at the North Course at press time, especially the front 9. Really good golfers prefer the North, however, with its narrowness and adjoining fairways keeping it tight. But the rest of us mere mortals still like the South. Hole 6 is an odd split fairway. Stay on the left side during your drive to give you a better shot at the green, but not so far left you roll into the gorge. Be sure to look

Course	Par	Yards	Rating	Fees
Makena South	72	6,629	70.7	$140
Makena North	72	6,567	70.4	$140
Wailea Emerald	72	6,407	69.8	$145
Wailea Gold	72	6,653	71.4	$145
Wailea Blue	72	6,758	71.6	$135
Elleair (formerly Silversword)	72	6,522	70.6	$75
Plantation Course, Kapalua	73	7,263	75.2	$200
Village Course, Kapalua	70	6,482	73.3	$175
Bay Course, Kapalua	72	6,600	71.7	$175
Kaʻanapali North	71	6,994	72.8	$140
Kaʻanapali South	71	6,555	70.7	$132
Dunes at Maui Lani	72	6,413	71.6	$75
Sandalwood	72	6,469	70.6	$75
Waiehu Municipal	72	6,330	69.8	$26
Pukalani Country Club	72	6,945	72.8	$55

Carts are included and mandatory at all courses except Waiehu. Metal spikes aren't allowed in South Maui except Elleair. Yards, ratings and slope are from the blue tees.

behind you at the view of Molokini. Some of the greens are as fast as pool tables, so be careful. The back nine is much nicer on this course. At 13 you have a splendid elevated vantage from the blues to the fairway below with scattered bunkers and a nice wide spot to shoot for. Number 14 is an incredible 611-yard romp downhill. Just blast away on your drive, and pat yourself on the back for your distance. 15 is pretty narrow and likely to bite you on the butt.

Both courses are excellent (though both could use better marked paths), but if you can only do one, do the South. No metal spikes.

Rates are $140 with a $15 discount if you wait till two days before you play. $75 twilight, $85 for guests of Maui Prince, $60 kama'aina, and a $35 replay fee. Walkers are allowed on South after 3 p.m. Located just south of Maui Prince, see map on page 133.

WAILEA GOLF CLUB (875–7450) for Gold and Emerald, (875–5155) for Blue.

The Wailea courses are among the most beautifully maintained courses on the island, with fewer hazards and more forgiving play than the Makena courses (though they're still very challenging). The first two are Robert Trent Jones, Jr. layouts, whereas the older Blue Course is an Arthur Jack Snyder affair.

The most popular is the EMERALD COURSE. It's wider than the Gold and starts things off nicely with a gently tapering 354-yard fairway march toward the ocean. Number 4 is another very picturesque hole. Kaho'olawe beckons from offshore. You may see other players on the 10th green, as it's shared with hole 17. Hole 15 is a tough 395 yard uphill par 4. Count yourself among the few who par this bugga. Too soon you

come to the 18th. What a way to polish off a game! Smack toward the 360-foot high Pu'u Ola'i. You're eventually rewarded with a half dozen bunkers surrounding the green. This courses has been named the most "woman-friendly" in golf rankings in the past.

WAILEA GOLD also makes a good first impression as the fairway wanders down 400 yards with striking views of offshore islands. *Oh,* this is going to be a good day. There's only one small water body on the whole course, so live it up. Hole 7 is a long 567 yards with a nicely placed dogleg. Hole 8 is probably the most picturesque. A tough 188-yard par 3 lined up perfectly with offshore Molokini. This hole always reminds you that it's wonderful to be alive. Hole 9 has a pretty intimidating lava embankment in front of you, but it's not as far as it looks. Just give it your usual swing and don't try to kill the ball and you'll make it. It's the well-defended green that you should worry about. At #11 you might as well get your sand wedge ready. More sand around the par 3 green than many South Maui beaches. Both courses are off Wailea Golf Club Dr. See map page 133.

The BLUE COURSE, set among luxury homes off Kaukahi, is older and noticeably duller. When the course director feels the need to brag that the designer is still alive, you know it's one of Maui's older courses. Don't get us wrong. If it were the only course on Maui, you'd tell everyone back home how great the golfing is here. But everything is relative and compared to the Gold and Emerald courses, it's an also-ran. Individual holes don't stand out much, good or bad. They're all nice, but none great. Hole 4, at 562 yards offers a blind par 5, and the second shot may also be blind as well. At 14 slicers will need to drive carefully, lest you hit another driver on Wailea Alanui Road. The Blue is easier on the ego and may lack pizazz, but it's still a fun, relaxing course.

Rates for the Emerald and Gold courses are $145 or $115 if you're staying at a Wailea resort. Blue Course is $10 less, and rates for all drop about $20 during the non-peak season of April 5 to Dec. 20. Blue has discounts for afternoon play. No metal spikes. If you want **lessons,** Wailea has the best facilities and instructors in South Maui for $50 per half hour.

ELLEAIR MAUI GOLF CLUB (formerly SILVERSWORD 874–0777)

Historically, this has been a pretty decent course for the money. Fairly easy play, well-tended greens, and some nice views. Afternoon brings complicated winds; play mornings. At press time the course's new owners were rebuilding the front 9 and upping the par to 72. Consequently, we're not sure if it will stay a decent golf value. **Rates** were $75, off Lipoa Parkway, Kihei.

WEST MAUI COURSES

West Maui offers nice courses in *extremely* windy Kapalua, or lesser courses in somewhat calmer Ka'anapali. We'll describe them from the farthest north heading south.

KAPALUA (669–8044)

Wind, wind, wind. It's important to keep the ball low here, as 30–40 MPH winds *are common.* Kapalua courses are difficult and require concentration and strategy. At Kapalua, seriously consider keeping your scorecard in your pocket or bag because it's easy to lose it to the wind here. (Of course, if you're playing for a few bucks a hole and losing, here's your chance to get out of it.)

KAPALUA PLANTATION COURSE has beautifully maintained fairways and greens. Of the three Kapalua courses, the wind seems strongest here. For what it's worth, it's been our observation that although some tough courses are still fun for higher handicap golfers, this one will eat them up and spit them out. Plantation is a serious course for serious golfers who seem to universally wear serious expressions. None of the dreamy glow of other courses; this is golfing to the death. Hole 3 is your first crack into the wind, and it's here where most learn the need to shoot those line drives. Pop it up, and it'll come right back at ya. At 4 your drive is uphill, into the wind and blind. Hey, nobody said this course would be easy. Hole 5 is 532 yards with a head/cross wind and a deep ravine to your right. At 6 they made wicked use of hills. Lose control near the green, and God knows where it will roll. Hole 8 requires a wonderful lob over a gorge onto the green littered with bunkers. One hazard not on the scorecard is the profusion of pineapple bugs that fly into your face while driving your cart. Don't open your mouth while cruising, or you'll see what I mean. Hole 10 is another blind, uphill, into-the-teeth-of-the-wind hole, with a cleverly located bunker near the green. Par 5 hole 15 has a healthy dogleg ending in a hungry dip well shy of the green. But if you pop it up too high coming out of the dip, no telling where the wind will take the ball. The course ends nicely with an endless 663-yard trek with the wind and elevation helping you. **Rates** are $200 *(hurt me!),* $120 for Kapalua guests, $85 for twilight. It's $25 less for the public April–Nov. Past 31 mile marker on Hwy 30.

KAPALUA VILLAGE is a very pleasant course, probably our favorite of the Kapalua courses. (There was a number reassignment about to take place at press time, so we'll refer to the hole numbers by their presumed new numbers.) Here the wind whistles through trees, giving you a bit of a break compared to the more unobstructed Plantation course. Between holes 3 and 5 you'll gain *800 feet* of elevation, so maybe it's not so bad they require carts. Hole 6 has a lovely setting next to a lake with Cook Island pines clustered on the other side. The view from hole 7 is so beautiful it will make your day. Rolling 367 yards downhill framed with Cook Island pines on both sides, the drive here with the wind at your back is pure joy. Hole 8, too, has

a lump-in-your-throat view down the fairway with bunkers and green in the foreground, ocean and Moloka'i in the background. Make note of the gulch in front of the green. By the way, their somewhat rundown mid-course food stand serves pretty good hot dogs. Take note of the house near the 10th tee. It's the only house on the course—a location perk for being high up in the Kapalua company food chain. You'll notice lots of rain sheds along the course. They get a fair amount of rain here, mostly in the form of numerous passing showers. Winter is wettest, and they don't give weather refunds. **Rates** for both Village and Bay are $175, $110 for Kapalua guests, $80 for twilight. $20 less for the public April–Nov. On Office Road.

KAPALUA BAY is the closest to the ocean of the three Kapalua courses and the easiest to play. There's not an overabundance of sand on this course. The fairways meander amongst several golf course communities. Hole 4 marches right toward the ocean, and glorious #5 actually shoots over the ocean. This 205-yard par 3 is one of our favorites on Maui. You have to hit over the strikingly blue ocean onto the green. Hole 9 shoots over a gentle hill toward the ocean—very picturesque. Note the unseen creek bisecting

Tasty views and tasty fairways—golfing on Maui can be a feast.

the fairway on hole 11. It's a ball stopper. Hole 16 is most unusual. It's a 371-yard par 4 with a pond bisecting it and a creek running *down the center* of the fairway, right where you want to be. Add the wind and an undulating fairway, and you have a very interesting hole. On Kapalua Ave.

Kapalua's GOLF ACADEMY, armed with state-of-the-art teaching equipment, is the best place in West Maui for lessons.

KAʻANAPALI GOLF COURSE (661–3691)

Golf in Kaʻanapali goes back to the '60s, comparatively ancient by Hawaiʻi golf standards. And while the course is fun, it's overpriced for what you get, even for Maui. The course is flatter than the Kapalua courses and the greens certainly less pristine, but it's also a more relaxing play. Wind is far less of a factor (in the morning especially) and rain is uncommon. The North Course is the most popular and difficult, with the South Course having the reputation of being "woman-friendly." Cars and homes are always close by on the north. Kaʻanapali's best asset is its location, so close and convenient to Kaʻanapali resorts. Though not as nice as Kapalua, the diminished wind and rains are refreshing. Both courses have less hazards than Kapalua.

THE NORTH COURSE hole 5 is a pleasant 473 yards, with the second half straddling the beach (a large, but unlikely sand trap). Instead of Kapalua's ironwood and Cook Island pine trees, coconut trees are your floral companions here. (And they're a lot less intrusive, too.) Overall, the holes aren't as distinctive as other courses around the island. **Rates** are $140, it's $120 for Kaʻanapali guests, $70 for twilight.

THE SOUTH COURSE is certainly easier. The hardest thing is crossing Kaʻanapali Parkway in your cart. Things start out with a wide open 490-yard trot to the green. Greens are huge and only slightly undulating. Fewer people make more leisurely play, especially in the afternoon (though that may bring winds). The 4th green is right near the train trestle of the Sugar Cane Train. The 8th fairway is one of the prettier ones on this course. It's 537 yards with short coconut trees most of the way. The South Course seems to receive a bit less maintenance than the north, but it's nice to have fewer houses and cars around. **Rates** are $132, $107 for Kaʻanapali guests, $67 for twilight.

CENTRAL AND UPCOUNTRY COURSES

There's one really good reason to consider golf outside the resort areas—*price!* No $200 greens fees here. Though the quality of the courses may be better elsewhere, if you can't stomach the price, consider some of these courses.

DUNES AT MAUI LANI (873–0422)

Maybe the most underrated course on the island. You get a lot of golfing for your $75. Granted, it's not close to the ocean and winds can be fierce here, but it's not as bad as at Kapalua. Opened in 1999, the course has a delightful layout and lots of character. The designer, Robin Nelson, made splendid use of the natural rolling terrain of this natural sand dune area. With a name like Dunes you shouldn't be surprised to find lots of sand, and you may end up wearing out your sand wedge. Well-placed, numerous and very deep bunkers, along with the wind, create a formidable challenge. Mornings are calmest.

This is an out-and-back design with the wind usually blowing to your left on the first 10 holes (except #6). Hole 4 has smashing views of the West Maui Mountains spiced with its steep, deep, vicious bunkers. Hole 6 is a nice 178-yard over-water par 3. The small but bottomless sand trap in front of the hole is unseen, and if you shoot too far you may soar past the hill behind the green. At 10 you need to listen for the bell from the previous golfers telling you it's clear to shoot. It's a blind, downhill volley par 4, one of the best holes on the course. You end the game with a hideously difficult 558-yard par 5, probably into the wind as the angles have shifted a bit with a narrow strip of land between the lake and the bunkers. You par this one during afternoon winds, and you're my hero.

Rates are $75, $37 for twilight or kama'ainas. No metal spikes. On 380 1⁴⁄10 miles south of Puunene Road.

SANDALWOOD (242–4653)

Ahh, what could have been. This is what happens when bad things happen to fairly good courses. The layout is pleasant with some cleverly designed holes. But financial problems at press time were obvious everywhere. The course was in poor shape, and you should avoid it. Mangy greens, weeds and an overall lack of care made it dreary. Your options are numerous on Maui, and this one should be last on your priority list. Its sister course, the Grand Waikapu, was closed in 1999 for lack of interest. **Rates** are $75, $60 if you're at certain resorts. On Hwy 30 near 4 mile marker.

WAIEHU MUNICIPAL (243–7400)

For a municipal course it's in pretty decent shape. (The groundskeepers at Sandalwood could learn a thing or two from them.) The front 9 are at the ocean. Holes 5–8 are a delight as you hug the shoreline. The course was unmarked at press time, and visitors are constantly asking, "Is this hole such and such?" The course is pretty light on hazards; bunkers are mainly around the greens, so the play is relatively easy and relaxing. In fact, the biggest hazard is its popularity. Weekends are a zoo, but weekdays aren't *too* bad, though certainly busier than resort courses. Winds are steadier here, not as gusty, and usually kick in around 11 a.m. The back nine was built several decades after the first and are up the mountain. Hole 13 is a beautiful elevated drive to the ocean with a dogleg right. Utterly spectacular. This is the only place on Maui you can always walk; you don't have to use the $8 carts. (Pushcarts are $2.) Rates are $26 during the week, $30 on weekends. Residents can play for $8, hence the popularity. North of Kahului on Hwy 340 1¼ miles north of Waiehu Beach Road.

PUKALANI (572–1314)

You realize right off the bat how utterly straight this course is. The designers must have had an unusual fear of curves, but it's great for beginners. No fairway sand at all. Holes are mostly long but pretty straightforward. Even the greens read fairly true. None of this breaking uphill if toward the ocean stuff, and most are pool-table flat. This is a great course to cut loose on. Accuracy and strategy aren't a big deal. Just hit the ball and have fun. Hole 3 is certainly the most interesting. Par 3 over a gulch onto the green. Don't like that option? Fine. Then hit to the *other* green below the hill. (It's nice to have choices.) If no one's behind you, play both and take the better score. (Did I say that?) Bring something warm as it gets chilly up here. Rates are $55, $42 for twilight. No dress code, just relax and golf your heart out. At the end of Pukalani St. off Old Haleakala Highway in Pukalani. (See map on page 117.)

This section actually encompasses several activities. Powered hang gliding (you and your instructor sit in a seat in an ultralight aircraft using a specially designed hang glider wing pushed by a motor), traditional hang gliding (where you lie in a harness and are unpowered) and paragliding (similar to a parachute and is unpowered). I'm a little uncomfortable lumping them all together because they are so radically different, but it seems more logical to organize it this way.

POWERED HANG GLIDING

First I need to get something out of the way. Flying a powered hang glider (known as a trike) is different than any other type of aircraft. When I was growing up, I used to have a recurring dream that I could flap my arms and fly like a bird. My father flew little Cessnas, which, though fun, felt more to me like a car in the air than flying like a bird. I had forgotten my flying dreams until I reviewed a company on Kaua'i that gave lessons in this odd little craft called a trike. As soon as my instructor and I took off, I realized that a person *really could* fly like a bird. *This* was what the flying bug felt like! I was so smitten with the craft that I eventually hired the instructor on Kaua'i to teach me and now I fly trikes myself. So although I have no personal interest in any company teaching trikes in Hawai'i, my perspective isn't as remote as it is for most activities. After all, it's not possible to anonymously review some companies,

like Hang Glide Maui, because I know the pilot. (We're both members of the small ultralight community.)

With that explanation, powered hang gliding is the activity I recommend, for several reasons. One, it's the safest of all three flying methods, *by far*. You have an engine, the craft is bigger and more stable, and it even has a powered parachute attached to the craft...just in case. (Even my dad's Cessna can't make that claim.) Trikes take off and land on regular runways (in this case at lovely Hana), and the ease and grace of the craft is glorious. (Rent the movie *Fly Away Home* if you want to see what they're like.) It's as close to flying like a bird as any form of flight I know. Trikes are what I have come to love so much and, in my opinion, are the safest form of ultralight flight available. (I'm not a daredevil and wouldn't fly them myself if I felt unsafe in them, though any time you're in the air you're potentially at risk, even on the airlines.) I grin like a fool every time I fly and have never reviewed an activity that generates more enthusiastic responses from other participants. It seems that whenever I see people coming off a trike (since I use the same airports that the trike companies do), passengers are frothing at the mouth with excitement, proclaiming that it's the best thing they've ever done on vacation.

The local company is **Hang Glide Maui** (572–6557). The pilot, Armin Engert, is certified as a Basic Flight Instructor and is well known and respected in the ultralight and hang gliding communities. Since I can't review him anonymously, I *can* tell you that his skill as a pilot is something I aspire to. Armin has a camera mounted on the wing to take a photo of you during your lesson— just in case no one back home believes

Taking a lesson in a powered hang glider along the Hana coast—what could be cooler?

you. There's a 240-pound weight limit. The cost of a half hour in-air lesson is $95. It's $165 for a hour. Expensive? Perhaps. But it's so unspeakably cool that the memories will stay with you for a lifetime.

HANG GLIDING

Traditional hang gliding, on the other hand, is where you and your instructor leap off Haleakala in a tandem harness. Quite a bit more daring, huh? You have no motor and are more vulnerable to the winds. (But it's very quiet.) Weather cancelations are much more common and it's not unusual to drive all the way up the mountain only to get skunked by clouds or wind. **Haleakala Hang Gliding** (876–1510) has this available for $250. They'll start on Haleakala and glide down to around the 2,400 foot level in 30–40 minutes. There's a 220-pound weight limit.

PARAGLIDING

Paragliding is, in my opinion, the least safe of the three. You are very susceptible to gusts of wind and to landing where you *don't* want to land. **Proflight** (874–5433) jumps off Haleakala hanging below what is essentially a gliding parachute. When I asked about passenger safety, I was told it was "relatively safe" except for the occasional "skinned knees on landing." When I pointed out my knowledge of their industry and their record, they 'fessed up to a bit more. Though they're nice folks and it's probably thrilling, personally, I am too uncomfortable to fly with them. If you choose to, it's $175 for a half-hour 4,000-foot descent.

To see Maui from the sky is to explore areas you can't reach by land. Paradise in the tropics is a breathtaking experience from the air. There are radically different reasons on each of the outer islands to take a helicopter tour. We've never been shy in our strong advocacy for helicopter tours of Kaua'i and even the Big Island. Kaua'i, aside from being astoundingly beautiful, has three jaw-droppingly compelling reasons to take a helicopter tour: the Na Pali coast, Waimea Canyon and Wai'ale'ale Crater. The Big Island, too, has an aerial objective worth flying to: the active Kilauea volcano, which is awesome from the air. Maui has...some *very* pretty scenery. But is it worth the big bucks you'll have to shell out for a helicopter flight? It depends. As a pilot myself with hundreds of hours in the skies over Hawai'i, I can tell you that flying along the Hana coast and through the West Maui Mountains is fantastic, especially when it's been wet. It's incredible, but I don't get the same lump in my throat as when I fly over Kaua'i or the Big Island's Kilauea volcano. If a flight over Kaua'i doesn't move someone, then they can't be moved by anything. If a flight over the Big Island's volcano doesn't excite, then check your pulse. But a flight over Maui isn't like that. It's very nice, very pretty, but it's probably not an emotional event. It's simply cool. Maui has much to experience, but helicopters aren't as vital here as they are elsewhere.

Then there's the fact that helicopter flights are more expensive on Maui than the other islands. Even companies with outlets on Big Island or Kaua'i charge more for air time on Maui. It might be because of the confiscatory commissions paid to activity booths on Maui, but maybe also because that's what the mar-

Early morning helicopter flights sometimes show the top of West Maui—before the clouds roll in.

ket will bear here.

The difference between Maui companies isn't as pronounced. They fly similar routes, charge similar prices, and mostly fly 6-passenger A-Stars. They have 4 main flights, listed with the best ones first.

#1 WEST MAUI/MOLOKA'I SEA CLIFFS

This is the best of the flights to take. After seeing West Maui and the beautiful and inaccessible Honokohau Falls, you fly across the channel and look at the stunning 3,000-foot sea cliffs of Moloka'i—an awesome sight, never to be forgotten. Then slip through the middle of Moloka'i, along the fringing reefs, then back to Maui. After going up Olowalu Valley, into the center of West Maui, you'll come out 'Iao Valley to end the hour-long flight for about $200.

#2 CIRCLE MAUI

You won't actually circle the island, and some see more of West Maui than others. For our Air Maui "complete island" flight, the West Maui portion only went into one valley before reversing back to the airport. The benefit over the Moloka'i flight is that you get to see East Maui, which, hopefully, includes a peek into Haleakala Crater (clouds permitting—they aren't allowed to fly *into* it but instead look over the rim) and the Hana coastline. An hour for about $200.

#3 WEST MAUI

West Maui's 'Iao Valley, another valley with beautiful waterfalls called the Wall of Tears, and the pretty northeast coastline. It's 30 minutes of flight for a little over $100.

#4 EAST MAUI

Similar to the circle island without West Maui. 45 minutes for about $150.

A FEW TIPS

These prices are list prices. Many companies will give some kind of discount if you ask them. Ask them about coupons, Internet discounts, or tell them you'll book through an activity booth if they don't discount it some. Sometimes they'll deeply discount if you book at the last minute, especially single passengers. In the late afternoon, call around and ask if they have room the next morning, and you may get a better rate.

If you decide to take a flight, consider doing it early in your trip. It'll help orient you to the island.

Morning is almost always best. Be done by 10:30 a.m. for best viewing conditions. Wind and clouds increase as the morning and afternoon progress, and conditions get bumpier.

For photos, use a fast film, such as ASA 400. Don't let the camera touch the vibrating window. Glare from the window can be a problem while filming. A circular polarizer can cut through almost all of it. Few point-and-shoot cameras will accommodate polarizers, but all SLR cameras will. Dark clothing also reduces glare.

Only one company, Alexair, has a microphone so you can talk to the pilot. This is very nice because often you'll have a question about something you see. Others may say they don't have mikes for safety reasons, but that's laughable. For instance, one company has you hand notes to the pilot if you have questions. Which do *you* think is safer—the pilot *hearing* your questions, or *reading* your note while flying? Most probably don't have mikes for money reasons, plain and simple.

For some reason, helicopter pilots are notoriously bad with their facts during narrations. Our Air Maui and Sunshine Helicopter flights had such bad "facts" that we bought the tapes of the flights to see how much conveyed was correct. The results were pretty poor, especially Air Maui's.

The state charges extra to park at the Kahului heliport, and the lot often fills up.

Don't wear earrings; they interfere with the headsets.

Here's the deal on seating: The best seats are up front—period. They may tell you otherwise in order to console you with your backseat position, but the front seat offers better visibility and allows the island to rush at you. But seating, especially up front, is dictated by weight, and lighter people usually go up front. Also, single riders often get placed up there since companies don't like to break up couples.

If you are sitting in the back, you want to be on the side where all the action is. On the West Maui/Moloka'i trip, the left seats are the best because of the route. On the circle, East or West Maui trips it depends on the direction they go. If they visit the south part of Haleakala and the crater first, then head up then along the Hana coast, the left side is best. If they head straight for the Hana coastline, the right side is best. Talk to them on the phone and ask which route they're taking, then request a seat where the main action will be on *your* side. If they are hesitant to guarantee seats, make sure they know that you'll consider them weasels if you don't get the seat you're looking for. Most of the time you'll be accommodated, even while they claim that "the computer assigns seats" or "the weather dictates our route." If they don't sound accommodating, go elsewhere.

Many companies now video the trip and will sell you the tape afterward. That's kind of cool, and you can hear your pilot on the tape, but the quality of these tapes won't match what you can buy from a pre-recorded tape, where sights were captured in their best light. It's your call as to which, if any, you want.

AIRPLANE TOURS

Without as many narrow valleys as Kaua'i or the Big Island's Hamakua Coast, hovering isn't as important here, so airplane tours are a good alternative to more expensive helicopter flights.

Volcano Air Tours (877–5500) can leave from either Kahului or West Maui Airport and tours East Maui before heading to the Big Island to show you the active volcano. It's 2 hours in the air for a little more than the cost of a 1-hour helicopter flight, $220. A good product. The only ding is it's a low-wing 9-passenger aircraft, so the view is partially blocked, but the windows are very large

Company	Phone #	Tours	Aircraft Type	2-Way*
Alexair Helicopters	877–4354	2, 3 & 4	6-Pass. A-Star Heli	Yes
Blue Hawaiian	871–8844	1, 2, 3 & 4	6-Pass. A-Star Heli	No
Air Maui	877–7005	1, 2, 3 & 4	6-Pass. A-Star Heli	No
Hawai'i Helicopters	877–5922	1†, 2, 3 & 4	Twin Engine Heli	No
Sunshine	871–0722	1, 2, 3 & 4	A-Star & 4-Pass. Heli	No
Volcano Air Tours	877–5500	E. Maui, Big Island Kilauea	Low Wing Plane	No
Paragon Air	244–3356	4 Island, Maui & Moloka'i	High Wing Plane	No
Pacific Wings	873–0877	Maui & Big Island	Low Wing Plane	No

* Indicates whether craft contains a microphone for you to talk to the pilot
† Includes Lana'i and a landing at Kalaupapa on Moloka'i for $240.

and everyone gets a window seat.

Paragon Air (244–3356) does tours of Moloka'i and Maui. Their 4-island tour covers Maui, Lana'i, Moloka'i and Kaho'olawe in a somewhat rushed 75 minutes for $145. Make sure you get their high-wing plane.

Pacific Wings (873–0877) has a Maui and Big Island tour in their low-wing 8-passenger plane for $200.

IMPORTANT NOTE: If this section seems shorter than you would expect, it's because we put *lots* of shorter hikes in the HANA HWY SIGHTS section and elsewhere. There are many 10–30 minute hikes sprinkled in those sections since we felt that you were more likely to hike

them on a driving tour than head out there for that purpose alone. Also, one of the tastiest trails on the island, at **'Ohe'o Gulch** (AKA **7 Sacred Pools**) is under SOUTHEAST MAUI SIGHTS. See page 199 for more on hikes listed elshwhere.

You can get highly detailed government **topographic maps** at **Base Camp** (573–2267). It takes 17 to cover Maui, and they are $5.25 each.

If you're going to do much stream hiking or wet rock hopping, pick up tabis (a fuzzy mitten for your feet), which cling well. You'll find them at the various Longs Drugs or at Kmart in Kahului.

WEST MAUI HIKES
Acid War Zone to the Blowhole

There's a quicker way to reach the Nakalele Blowhole mentioned on page 57, but hiking to it along this route is definitely more fascinating. There is a small parking lot near the 38 mile marker past

Remember, there are lots of short hikes listed in HANA HIGHWAY SIGHTS, like this one at Pua'a Ka'a, and a longer, delightful hike listed under SOUTHEAST MAUI SIGHTS.

Kapalua near the northernmost point on the island on Hwy 30. Despite what you may be told by a vendor selling wares in the area and a misleading sign, you *are* allowed to hike on the old jeep road and past the light beacon that leads to the blowhole. This is according to county personnel we spoke to. This is not a long hike—at most 30 minutes each way without side trips—but the terrain is excellent.

See map on page 58. From the parking lot, make your way toward, then along, the sea cliffs. The trail is vague and spotty, but you shouldn't have trouble making your way as you first walk through a gulch toward your right before reaching the cliff. (Other paths are more inland but less interesting.) Keep going right. The cliffs are pockmarked with crags and caves, and the bouldery landscape around you is awesome. About 10–15 minutes into the walk, just before a light beacon, you'll notice some small pools below the cliffs. From down there you can see how big the sea arch you saw from the cliffs really is. Down at the pools there's decent swimming and a crack in the rock toward the sea that snorts air during high surf. The scenery is pretty down there, but access is tricky. You need to hop along boulders then scale a questionable ladder with a questionable rope tied to a questionable metal stake. These pools might not be worth it. Infinitely better pools are available at the Olivine Pools on page 60.

Back on the trail, you descend past the lighthouse and here the trail snags the uninformed. A small blowhole shooting from the notch of a lava shelf and wall fools most hikers. Probably 90% turn around here. But wait: This *ain't* the blowhole! Continue along the shoreline and soon you come to an alien landscape. It looks like a war zone fought

with acid. Billions of tons of sea spray, blown by the wind, has carved up the soft rock here. The land is literally being eaten in front of you. Take your time to examine some of the lava formations up close. This part of the island is like no other. The surroundings are so surreal that we're amazed that no one has used this area in a movie yet.

About 20–30 minutes into the hike you come to the **Nakalele Blowhole.** There's a nice vantage point above and slightly upwind of the hole. (But you can still get wet when the ocean behind you occasionally explodes sea spray.) You can make your way around the lava to the bottom. Stay upwind to remain dry. See page 57 for more on the blowhole itself. Return the way you came.

Though not overly strenuous, this hike can be a windy affair, sometimes too windy. (Nakalele means *the leaning* because the wind is sometimes strong enough, especially during the summer, to lean into it.) If the wind is blowing you away and you still want to see the blowhole, see page 58 for a more direct (though less interesting) route. Wear good shoes; flip-flops are a bit too casual for this terrain.

Mushroom Rock Shore Hike

This is one of those *you're-on-your-own* hikes. Explore a wild, gorgeous shoreline, go as long as your desire takes you, then take the easy way back. The hiking is makeshift much of the way. Not much trail, just make your way, and be careful of the wind and crumbly soil and rock. It's not strenuous unless you want it to be. Like the blowhole hike, wind can sometimes be a problem here.

In West Maui 9/10 mile past the 41 mile marker on Hwy 30 there's a turnout on the ocean side. (See map on page 62.)

From here walk toward the ocean, then toward your left to a bluff overlooking the shoreline. The cliffs in front of you are striking, even for Maui. After overlooking a small islet, you'll see several discontiguous cow paths (and sometimes no paths) to your right. If you amble the right way, you'll quickly come to a cove with a shallow reef and a rusty old pole holder driven into the rock. The little rock sticking out is an enviable place to ponder the shoreline if you're not too afraid of heights. All is presided over by a mushroom-shaped rock to your right. By the way, the snorkeling on the downwind side of the reef below is exciting, but only when calm (which is not too often). Experts only. From here either make your way back the way you came, or trudge up a gully-looking feature in the crumbly soil. Then make your way back to the shoreline to your right. Perhaps you'll stop at the mushroom-shaped rock before making your way around and then along the shoreline.

From here there's no real trail most of the time. You're exploring. Sometimes you're along the shore, sometimes you'll have to make your way inland around the large lava hills. The scenery is wild, raw, striking and, quite often, it's all yours. You can't really get lost since you're following the ocean, and the highway is not too far inland. You can spend from 30 minutes to several hours, depending on how far along the shore you want to go and how fast you go. But you won't soon forget this piece of shoreline. This is a delicious, secluded Maui ocean hike. The wind and spray have carved and chewed the landscape with unequaled artistry, and, with no crowds or trails, sometimes you feel like you're the only person in the world.

If you hike a mile along the shoreline (less as the crow flies), you'll come to the **Olivine Pools** described on page 60. Keep an eye out for yellow/orange stripes in the lava. These are deposits of ash from when the island was young and restless. Gigantic volcanic explosions caused the ash layers that were covered with later lava flows. Erosion now reveals what a violent volcano this was in its youth. Not far past here you'll have to ascend from the ocean and walk along the sea cliffs. Southeast of here there are areas where residents of Kahakuloa have dumped some of their garbage, the only mood spoiler. Continue as long as you want, then make your way inland to the highway and walk back to your car.

Waiheʻe Valley Trail

This one's a 2-mile (each way) pretty valley hike that wanders along a dirt road, then a trail through forest, ending at a pleasing man-modified waterfall. It takes about 1½ hours each way. It's moderately strenuous with your only climbing at the beginning. Then it's fairly flat for the rest of the hike. Along the way you'll need to cross the stream twice on old swinging bridges, then cross twice without them.

To get there, you head north of Kahului on Hwy 340. Before the 5 mile marker is Waiheʻe Valley Road. (See map on page 195.) Turn mauka. After ½ mile the road becomes unpaved. Either park there, or drive another ¼ mile and park at the rocky intersection. Turn right onto the road/trail.

After your initial climbing (around 300 feet) the road levels and becomes prettier. This trail parallels two ditches built in the 1880s and 1905. Some of the tunnels bore through *blue rock,* a hard lava that required much more effort. Mostly Chinese immigrants worked on the ditches and tunnels, and

Indiana Jones? No, he's from Australia. (And he's holding the hand guide in a nervous death grip.) The Waihe'e Valley hike crosses the stream on two swinging bridges.

they did it with dynamite, picks, compressed air and percussion drills.

At one point a sign says No TRESPASSING. Technically you're supposed to get a permit from Wailuku Agribusiness to hike this trail. But it's one of the more popular on the island, and we've never heard of anyone actually getting a permit. (We've asked lots of people hiking it, and none even knew a permit was needed.)

The trail soon becomes notched deep in the mountain, and the river's below you. Then you come to your first swinging bridge. (You may have to cross a small stream first if the water diverter is overflowing.) Use the guide wires and walk with your knees bent to absorb your footfalls to minimize the swinging. If you're uncomfortable, the stream's probably dry here, and you can cross on its bed if you want. In a few minutes, the next bridge crosses the stream before it's

diverted. A trail bypasses the bridge, but you'd have to boulder-hop.

Two more crossings (without bridges) require boulder-hopping a short distance. The beauty of the valley here is incredible. Mosquitoes are more numerous—did you bring your bug juice?

Just before the trail ends, an opening in the vegetation exposes the back of the valley with the gorgeous 2,000-foot **Mana-nole Falls** a mile away. (It looks farther.) An abandoned portion of the ditch leads you to the **'Ali'ele Falls,** modified as an abandoned diverter. (Also labeled as 'Ele'ele on some maps.) A rope swing awaits if you have the nerve. The roar of the falls can be delightfully loud. Local kids often come here on weekends or during the week in the summer. According to Hawaiian legend, you were supposed to throw a ti leaf in the water here. If it swirled around and around, you were permitted to jump. If it made a circle then went under, then you shouldn't jump because a lizard god (called a mo'o) would seize and kill you.

Waihe'e Ridge Trail

A very pretty trail with smashing valley views and a vigorous forest to gawk at. You'll gain about 1,500 feet over the 2½ miles to the end (then return).

You'll want to do this hike early as clouds moving in later in the morning diminish the view. We like to be hiking this trail by 8 a.m. to maximize our weather chances.

From Kahului, get on Hwy 340 heading north. (See map on page 195.) At ⁹⁄₁₀ past the 6 mile marker is the road to Maluhia Boy Scout Camp. Another ⁹⁄₁₀ mile up that road is the trailhead.

The trail gets your heart pumping right away, as a cement road climbs 200 feet in short order, then the dirt path to the left ascends through a forest of guava, kukui, swamp mahogany and Cook Island pines. By ½ mile you've gained 400 feet. Shortly after, a switchback corner reveals a pretty gulch. Look to the left and you see **Makamaka'ole Falls.** Ahead is a peak and the trail switchbacking up. Clouds often come up the gulch and down from the ridge, colliding right in front of you. (And sometimes *into* you.)

Soon you get your first incredible view of Waihe'e Valley. It's beautiful! Some paths through the grass

afford closer looks. Look down and you may see the Waihe'e Valley Trail. Now the trail is along the ridge, and you're blessed with numerous commanding views (clouds permitting).

Several switchbacks and flat areas later you'll eventually reach the end of the line—a hill called **Lani-lili** at 2,563 feet. If the clouds haven't moved in yet, the views are grand. If you've got your head in the clouds, enjoy the aural and visual silence.

13 Crossings

What do you call an unnamed trail that crosses the Makamaka'ole'ole Stream 13 times, ending at an unnamed falls on an unnamed branch? We call it 13 Crossings. You're never out of earshot of the stream, so it's pretty hard to get lost.

You start just over ⁸⁄₁₀ mile past (west of) the 7 mile marker on Hwy 340. (See map on page 195.) There's a small turnout, maybe a gate, maybe not. It was unmarked and had a broken gate at press time. This area was designated Hawaiian Homelands by Congress, so

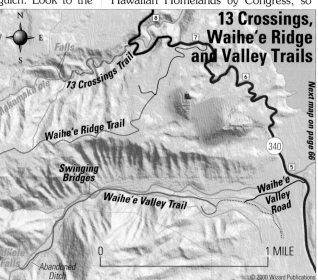

13 Crossings, Waihe'e Ridge and Valley Trails

Falls

13 Crossings Trail

Makamaka'ole

Waihe'e Ridge Trail

Swinging Bridges

Waihe'e Valley Trail

Waihe'e Valley Road

340

Next map on page 66

'Aī'Kele Falls

Abandoned Ditch

0   1 MILE

© 2000 Wizard Publications

please be respectful and don't leave anything behind.

You soon begin your crossings. Most of the year the stream flow allows you to boulder-hop and keep your feet dry.

After six crossings you go through a beautiful bamboo grove littered with Hawaiian ruins. Needless to say, don't move any of the stones here.

Nearby, at a place called **Kukuipuka,** there was a place of great importance. In ancient times, commoners' lives were governed by the kapu system. There were a dizzying number of laws to observe. Those of lower classes weren't allowed to look at or even walk on the same trails as upper classes. Men and women were forbidden to eat together; citizens were not allowed to get close to a chief or allow their shadows to fall across him, etc. All manner of laws kept the order. The penalty for breaking any of the laws was usually the same—death by club, strangulation, fire or spear. (It's nice to have choices, huh?) If the offense

was severe enough, the offender's entire family might be executed. It was believed that the gods retaliated against lawbreakers by sending tidal waves, lava flows, droughts and earthquakes, so communities had a great incentive to dispatch lawbreakers with haste. If a lawbreaker could elude his club or spear-wielding pursuers, however, he had one way out of his mess—the area's Pu'uhonua (place of refuge). **Kukuipuka** was such a place.

This predesignated area offered asylum. If a lawbreaker could make it here, he could perform certain rituals mandated by the kahuna pule (priest). After that, all was forgiven and he could return home as if nothing had happened, regardless of the violation. Defeated warriors could also come here to await the victor of a battle. They could then pledge their allegiance to whoever won and live out their lives in peace.

At one of the crossings (you're perpetually going upstream) the stream seems to split with the trail heading

Some hikes require luscious treks through bamboo forests.

between the two sides. Take it, then take the right fork shortly thereafter. The falls are just ahead around the corner.

A pretty waterfall backed by steep walls is your reward after 30–60 minutes of hiking. (It depends on how quickly you do the crossings. Some people hop right across, others struggle.) Look up and you'll probably see a short rope assisting you to the second, far prettier falls. Going up the rope isn't too bad, but coming down is certainly an 'okole squeezer. It's your call. At the second falls you see a long, skinny rope leading 35-40 feet up the almost vertical wall. It leads up to...well, we don't know. It required too much faith in an unknown rope, and frankly, we didn't have the stones to try. If you do, let us know. (By the way, we are totally baffled as to how someone strung that upper rope in the first place.)

Lahaina Pali

This is a trail that slips up over part of the West Maui Mountain, peaking at almost 1,600 feet. Along the way you get excellent elevated views. Unfortunately, this is a shuttle hike, with trailheads 6 miles apart (by car), a bit less by foot. Either hike to the top and return, or go one way if you've arranged transportation at the other end.

The biggest tip is to start from the Ma'alaea side in the morning. See map on page 45. You're already 200 feet up, and the sun will be at your back. The hike starts at the 5 mile marker on Hwy 30, heads toward the mountain, to the left about 500 feet, then inland on a shaded trail. Enjoy the shade here because there won't be much more. As the trail gets progressively steeper, you'll start to get expansive views of Maui.

After climbing to the top, your vantage point changes as you descend to the other trailhead at Hwy 30's 11 mile marker. The ocean and offshore island views create an exotic landscape. Bring lots of water because you'll be exposed to the sun most of the time.

UPCOUNTRY AND HALEAKALA HIKES
Haleakala Crater

There are 27 miles of trails inside Haleakala Crater, and the views from inside are incredible. The catch is that you need to descend 2,400 feet (and, of course ascend on your return) down **Sliding Sands Trail** over a $3\frac{8}{10}$ mile span (each way) to get to the bottom. You can get to the bottom via **Halemau'u Trail** (which is only 1,400 feet down and 4 miles each way), but that trail, though beautiful, is more vulnerable to bad weather. If you want to hike many of the trails at the bottom, you'll need to camp inside. (See CAMPING.) Sliding Sands itself is incredibly scenic, even if you choose not to go all the way to the bottom. Consider just wandering down until just before you start to worry about the ascent. If you want a longer Haleakala hike, one of the best hikes on the island, see ADVENTURES on page 241.

At the far end of the crater is the **Kaupo Trail,** which descends all the way down the mountain. You'll only access it if you're camping. Though it's easy to look at a map and think that an all-downhill trail might be easy, don't be fooled. The footing in many places is slippery with soft dirt and loose rocks, and it can be steep. The constant downhill can put enormous strains on knees and other things you didn't think of—like your toenails. If your shoes don't fit right, you may find that the unrelenting tapping will cause you to lose them. (Trust me. Been there. Done that.)

Polipoli State Park

An example of the varied nature of the island, this is a hike through a redwood forest. Here? On Maui? Yup. Back in the 1920s and '30s the state and the Civilian Conservation Corps undertook a reforestation program in this area that had been destroyed by cattle. They planted redwood, sugi, cedar and many other types of trees (though these are not native to Hawai'i). The trees have since flourished.

Getting there is part of the fun—if you like narrow, winding roads. See map on page 117. From Kahului on Hwy 36, take 37 to the second 37/377 intersection (near the 14 mile marker on 37), and take 377 north for ⅓ mile or so and turn right on Waipoli Road. From here you'll have 6 miles of a winding paved road that offers smashing views of

A forest of redwoods is the last thing you expect to find in the tropics, but Upcountry's Polipoli Park is one of Maui's surprises.

all of West Maui and the valley between the two great volcanoes. Believe the signs that tell you to watch for mindless cattle on the road. After 6 miles, the road becomes unpaved. This last 4 miles is bumpy but usually driveable in regular cars.

Once at the parking lot (you took the right fork near the end) you'll want to walk back up the road for 100 feet or so to the start of the **Redwood Trail**. After a couple of minutes you'll pass to the right of a cabin and begin your descent into forest. The area looks much more like Northern California than Hawai'i, and the coolness of the air at 6,000 feet is a refreshing change. The descent is fairly gentle and constant. Be aware of tree roots in the trail that may try to trip you. About 25 minutes into the hike you come to the large redwoods. Some of the redwood trees are around 100 feet tall and dead-on straight with trunks up to 6 feet in diameter. Pretty impressive growth in so short a time. When the Redwood Trail ends at 1⁷⁄₁₀ mile, either retrace your steps or take the **Plum Trail** and make it a 5-mile loop hike. (This is preferred.) A trail map to Polipoli is on page 234.

Assuming you make it a loop, the Plum Trail somewhat gently regains most of the 1,000 feet you lost on the Redwood Trail. When Plum Trail meets **Haleakala Ridge Trail,** take the left turn. (Plum is not well defined after it meets Haleakala, so don't follow it.) A ½ mile into Haleakala Ridge there's a sign saying, POLIPOLI PARK 1 MILE. Look for the short spur trail there, and then take the right fork. It leads to a smashing and very expansive view all the way down the mountain to the shoreline. Weather permitting, you'll see three of the Big Island's volcanoes—Mauna Kea (nearly 14,000 feet high), Kohala in front of it and Mauna Loa to the right. Up till now you probably haven't had any wind on this hike, protected by the ridge from the normal trade winds. But here on the ridge the wind can be howling. Back on the spur trail, the other fork leads to a cave.

Back on the Haleakala Ridge Trail, in another half mile is a confusing intersection. Take the left fork to go back to your car.

This trail is very nice when the weather is good, but dark when it gets really cloudy. Go early in the morning for the best conditions. It takes most people 3–4 hours to complete the loop and it's moderately strenuous. Despite what you might hear, this trail is not open to mountain bikes.

HIKES DESCRIBED ELSEWHERE

Short and not-so-short trails are described in other parts of the book for several reasons, either because of their remoteness, adventurousness or short-

ness. They include **Punalau Falls** on page 82, the marvelous **Wailuaiki** and the **Upper Pua'a Ka'a Falls,** both on page 87, **Blue Pool** on page 91, the **Red Sand Beach** on page 97, **Venus Pool** on page 103, and the **Pipiwai Trail** with the waterfalls including the **Infinity Pool** on page 108. The ADVENTURES section starting on page 230 has the **La Pérouse Bay Lava/Snorkel/Hike,** the **Four Falls of Na'ili'ili-haele, Mountain Bike Haleakala's Spine** (which you can also hike), a **hike to the heart of an eruption,** a **hike in a lava tube,** and the **Haleakala Crater Grand Loop.** And West Maui has the **Olivine Pools** on page 60 and **'Iao Valley** on page 67. There's also the short trail around **Kealia Pond** on page 130.

OTHER EAST MAUI HIKES

In addition to the hikes mentioned above, there are a few other East Maui hikes worth noting.

Wai'anapanapa Coast Hike

One of the nicer coastal lava hikes you'll find. It displays the raw coastline, backed first by palm and hala trees, then showcases the most recent lava flow in the Hana area that created the black sand beach. Though there's no big climbing, the second portion of the trail is somewhat undulating, so you have lots of little climbs, and the footing later is awkward. This hike can last anywhere from 30 minutes to 4 hours, depending on your thirst for scenery.

You start at Wai'anapanapa State Park near Hana (see page 93 for directions). Park to the right of the main beach, walk to the shoreline and head right along the shore. Soon a low-hanging sea arch and a blowhole (that only

Lava arches are common along the coast of the Wai'anapanapa hike.

on bushes, not trees.)

Angry seas can make this hike even more dramatic. The water is so clean and clear, and it's exhilarating to see large waves punish the shoreline here. At one point, the trail passes a natural split in the land. The lava bridge keeps you from falling in. A little farther the trail has a big step down; it's preferable to a vague trail going around.

In about 30 or so minutes you come to meager remains of a small heiau (temple). Nobody knows what it was used for. The trail gets vague for a minute, but should become clearer shortly after. Ahus (small piles of rock) help mark the trail. The footing has been pretty good up till now, but from here it becomes harsher and clumsier. Hiking shoes or boots can be helpful, as can a walking stick. You'll be walking on young (500-year-old) lava which created the black sand beach as lava shattered on contact with the sea and the new sand drifted into the bay.

Watch for columnar lava. These (usually) six-sided lava columns are at the shoreline in several places. They form when a lava pond cools, shrinks and cracks. The cracks work their way lower and lower as the rock cools, so the lava literally pulls itself apart. When you pass a community fishing shack (everyone pitches in to keep it up), it's 2 miles to Hana Bay. The prettiest part of the trail is behind you. Large red ants seem to be making a good living off the stark lava here. Keep walking until you're halfway

blows during monster surf) indicate the kind of scenery you'll see. (Don't get too close to the tapered blowhole; it's a one-way trip down.)

About 10 minutes into the hike, at an area marked by some offshore rocks and a couple of arches, stop and listen for a hissing sound. The ocean's waves are undercutting the lava here in some places, and when the tide is right waves will force air up through a tiny hole and you can actually hear and feel the ocean breathing. (Get too close, and you'll feel it spitting, too.)

The colors are very vivid as you walk along. The raw, black coastline smashed by white frothing water next to impossibly blue ocean all backed by lush, green palm trees makes a delicious meal for your camera. Soon you'll pass an enormous grove of hala trees, noted for their cage-like roots. Some locals cynically call them tourist pineapples, as their fruit does look similar. (Real pineapples grow

to being tired, or you get to Hana Bay, whichever comes first, then turn around. It's about 7 miles (round trip) to Hana Bay, if you go that far. Make sure you bring water; lava fields make you thirsty.

Waikamoi Nature Trail

Between the 9 and 10 mile markers on the Hana Highway. Two nature loops, one about 10 minutes, the other about 30 minutes make a pleasant diversion on the Hana Highway drive if you need to stretch your legs a bit, but it's not worth driving out there just for this. This hike is good for families, and you gain, at most, 200 feet.

If you start from the left-most trail and work your way up the gradual incline, there are a few concrete benches scattered along the way. Sometimes there are nice views of the highway beneath you and the valley beyond. Patches of bamboo interrupt the mostly eucalyptus, hala and strawberry guava forest. At the intersection, either take a right (back to your car for the 10 minute hike) or left for the longer one. The latter eventually leads to a picnic area with BBQ. The sign there says END OF TRAIL, though, in fact, the path continues. When it forks, take a left and walk a few minutes, and it leads down to a stream and dam.

Back at the picnic area, on your way down to your car on a jeep road, if you veer to the left, it leads to a small reservoir. Otherwise, continue back to your car.

Wahinepe'e

This hike takes you up a hunters' road, through a bamboo forest and then links up with a road paralleling one of EMI's diversion ditches. During the first part you'll be climbing constantly, gaining about 250 feet. Note the density of

the bamboo around you.

You start at the dirt road $^2/_{10}$ mile past the 10 mile marker on Hwy 360 (Hana Hwy). Once at the top (about $^1/_4$ mile), take a left and the road will pass 2 small waterfalls. The payoff for this hike isn't a single tongue-wagging view or falls, but rather a nice trek through a healthy forest of eucalyptus, koa and many other species, many draped with vines. About $^1/_2$ mile into the ditch road, you come to an intersection. If you go right at this and every other intersection, it will bring you to the upper road. Straddling the upper road, the forest is even healthier and prettier up here at 1,200 feet. Take the road as long as your interest holds out, then retrace your steps by taking lefts at the intersections. Make mental notes where the intersections were; there's more than the map shows. We had a tough time mapping this area, even from the air. This hike is anywhere from 20 minutes to 6 hours, depending on how far you go. If you go all the way to the upper road, you gain 1,000 feet. It's a nice forest trek. As for access, this is a reserve, but EMI has the water rights. See page 76 for more on that.

SOUTH MAUI

Certainly not a hotbed of good hiking, but there are two that stand out.

Keawanaku Beach

How about a hike along a lava trail that leads to a black and white sand beach that is usually deserted and was unnamed until this publication? From the end of the road in south Maui, where most cars park at La Pérouse Bay, a 4WD road leads southeast for almost a mile, passing numerous small coves. When the road opens up to a relatively new lava flow (approximately 500 years old), you turn to the left, through a wire fence, and the trail (now called the Hoapili Trail or Kings Highway) shortcuts inland for a while, crossing Cape Hana-manioa. See map on page 135. This part of the 6-foot wide trail was made in the early 1800s and probably used to transport cattle across the harsh lava. As you walk this part of the trail, keep this in mind: The ancient Hawaiians crossed these types of trails barefoot. In fact, they often had to run through the sharp lava during battle, where there were no trails at all. But for the rest of us tenderfoots, we recommend hiking boots to protect the ankles. The footing on the Hoapili Trail is made of mostly fist-sized chunks of lava and is obnoxious. An ancient phrase associated with this area is "the cloudless rain of Honuaula." Many a time we've hiked in this area and felt rain, though no cloud was even remotely nearby (due to the strong winds along the flank and the rain clouds up the mountain).

Just less than a mile into the lava field trail you'll see lots of vegetation at the shoreline (700 feet away) and a spur trail leading there, which starts at a small lava rock wall. The main part of the spur trail leads to Keawanaku Beach. (Other vague trails leading off the spur trail are avoidable.) This area has several structures, including the remains of a Hawaiian heiau (religious site).

Normal trade winds build up along the southern flank of Haleakala and often howl along this part of the island. The beach itself is normally protected from these trade winds. We've hiked to this beach during unusually strong trade winds, when gusts exceeded 50 mph and the ocean was an ugly mess of white-caps, only to find the bay at Keawanaku calm, windless and protected. (During less common Kona winds from the south, it would be a different story.) The

snorkeling off to the left (east) of the bay is exceptional along the 10–20 foot wall, covered with coral and loaded with fish. The bay is usually (but not always) protected from much of the surf and the water is beautiful and clear. The natural protective wall extends farther than it looks from the shore, bending around to the left and extending farther. The right side has several caves that you can explore if there's no surge or surf. (Surge would bounce you around in there.)

This beach is a jewel set amongst the unforgiving lava, mostly black sand with white and a touch of green sand. (The latter comes from a semi-precious gem called olivine.) There are some beach boulders near the shoreline, but a generous repository of sand offshore usually keeps the shoreline relatively sandy except after severe storms, which can temporarily move the sand offshore, usually during the summer. The area (and a nearby point) was called Keawanaku and some old-time Hawaiians used the name for the beach, but it is not listed in any of the old literature as having that name. (Perhaps because the flow is relatively recent and the beach so new, the Hawaiians never named it.) Nonetheless, we have deferred to the old-timers and called it Keawanaku Beach.

Ten minutes farther along the Hoapili Trail is tiny Wawaloa Cove. Snorkeling there is not as good, and the currents are tricky. Just past Wawaloa are some excellent ruins, worth taking a look.

Pu'u Ola'i (Red Hill)

Short, but a bit more tiring than it looks. It's the 360-foot-high cinder cone in South Maui described on page 134. Walking up the cinder trail is similar to walking up a sand dune. One step up, half a step down. But at the top you have a commanding view of Makena and Big Beach. Sunsets from up here can be unusually grand. It's also a great place to spot whales in season.

To get there, take Piilani Hwy (31) till it ends at Wailea Iki. (See map on page 133. Turn right, then left onto Wailea Alanui. When you see the entrance to the Maui Prince Resort, the dirt road is ⁸/₁₀ mile past the resort on your right. The trailhead is a little hard to see, less than ²/₁₀ from the paved road, but if you wander through the forest 100 or so feet, you should see the trail slicing up the back side of the mountain (away from the ocean).

Horseback Riding

If you want to see the countryside but don't want to walk it yourself, you need your very own beast of burden. (I always loved that phrase.) Maui has lots of horseback rides, from forest to plains to lava fields to the inside of a crater. Some are awesome; some are a snore. Picking one depends on what you want to see.

Pony Express (667–2200) is our hand's-down favorite. They go down Sliding Sands Trail to the bottom of Haleakala Crater. The views are unlike anything you've ever seen and positively drop-dead gorgeous. This is a *great* trip. They only take 8 people per day, so it's a good idea to book as far in advance as possible, 3 weeks during busy times, 2 weeks during slow times. Call even earlier from the mainland to ensure your spot.

Since they want you near the summit of Haleakala at 9:30 a.m. (though they leave later), you might want to come up for the sunrise, then check out some of the short trails and overlooks before meeting them.

The ride is a single file, nose-to-tail affair, and you'll probably only trot a little coming up. But the way the unspeakably beautiful crater changes and unfolds effortlessly as you descend the trail will stay with you for a lifetime. Distances look huge as you descend the 3⁸/₁₀ miles to the floor 2,400 feet below. The air is usually crystal clear inside, almost like there's no air at all. Once at the bottom, you have lunch at a trail junction. Croissant sandwiches never tasted so delicious than when you've had them in the crater. There are some bees around, attracted to the horse droppings, but few people seemed to mind. On the way back up, you see the crater from the other direction. How is it that it can still enrapture someone after several hours?

The trail can be a bit dusty, and the sun is strong up here. Expect to pass envious hikers on the way back up. Wear a long sleeve shirt, a jacket and a hat. Cheap gloves are also advisable since you can burn the back of your hands while holding the reins. Weather is usually good in the crater and winds far less than up above. Most of the rain here comes in the winter. There's no restroom at the bottom. At $140 for the 4-hour trip it may sound pricey, but the quality of the trip is unmatched. We've reviewed lots of horseback rides throughout the state, and we'd be hard-pressed to think of one we enjoyed more. They offer a longer crater ride, all the way back to Kapalaoa cabin and explore more of the crater floor for $175. At 12 miles, it's for those with toughened 'okoles. They also have cheaper rides at their ranch, but the views can't compare.

At press time Pony Express was the

The first time we ever climbed 2,400 feet back up out of Haleakala Crater we didn't even break a sweat. Of course, we had help.

only ones doing horseback trips into the crater. Another company, **Maui Mule Ride,** had ceased operations "for now," so we couldn't review them. If another company starts up and does trips down the other crater trail, Halemau'u, beware that the weather in that part of the crater is usually more iffy.

OTHER BUCKAROOS

The next best ride is past **Hana** at **'Ohe'o Stables** (667–2222). They take people along 'Ohe'o Gulch (where the so-called 7 Sacred Pools are). Breakfast trip is about 4 hours (2½ in the saddle) for $119. Add $20 for the lunch ride. 225 lb. weight limit. If you don't want to hike the wonderful Pipiwai Trail, this is a nice alternative. (The horseback views of the falls and valley are a bit more remote, however.)

Mendes Ranch (871–5222) has a pretty nice ride on their beautiful ranch in West Maui. It's about 2½ hours of riding followed by a BBQ lunch back at the stables. They ride up to a spectacular overlook of Waihe'e Valley, then head to the

ocean for more good views. It's a nose-to-tail ride with only two *very* short runs allowed. Guides range from helpful and friendly to decidedly less so. In all, a good trip for $135. Cheaper rides available. Our only complaint is that they make outrageous and false claims to get you in, and it's really not necessary. For instance, their brochure says you'll "gaze down into Eki Crater to view some of Maui's largest waterfalls." Well, *Eke* Crater is at 4,400 feet elevation, near the center of West Maui. Wow, what a view that would be! On the phone they say you'll ride up to 3,000 feet. Hmm, still pretty awesome. The guide says you'll make it to 2,000 feet. The reality? You go to *1,000* feet. C'mon, guys, just be accurate. The ride is good enough without the inflated claims. On Hwy 340 at 7 mile marker.

Heading toward Hana, **Adventures on Horseback** (242–7445) takes you on a 4–5 hour ride (they call it 6) to Twin Falls. They describe it as a "rain forest ride," which is being pretty generous. There's a small part through forest, but most of it is on a dirt road. Nonetheless, it's a nice excursion, they serve lunch, and the guides do a pretty good job. It's pretty expensive at $175. 225 lb. limit.

Makena Stables (879-0244) in South Maui takes people to Kalua o Lapa, the last active volcanic vent on Maui, mentioned under ADVENTURES. Though the destination is interesting, the journey is a bit less so.

Kayaks are a fun way to see the coastline. None of Maui's rivers are fit for kayaking, but the shoreline offers lots to explore. The best areas are those that you can't reach by land without difficulty. One of the best trips is to the heretofore unnamed **Keawanaku Beach,** but it's a little tricky and described in ADVENTURES on page 243.

Other areas to kayak are south of Olowalu in West Maui starting at Papalaua Wayside Park between the 11 and 12 mile markers. Paddle southeast along the pretty shoreline below the highway, staying close to land to keep winds from making your life more difficult. Most put in at the 14 mile marker, but it's much less interesting there.

If you can arrange it, in the afternoon it's nice to put in at Kihei and let the wind help you go down the coast, then come out at Makena Landing. Kihei winds tend to be from north to south along the coast; West Maui winds tend to go from nothing to blowing offshore, which is more dangerous.

Also consider the coastline south of Big Beach at 'Ahihi Cove heading south. You can go around Cape Kina'u to Fishbowl, Aquarium and on into La Pérouse Bay, but be watchful of winds,

especially in the afternoon.

Lots of companies put in at Makena Landing because it's so easy to launch. The kayaking from there is fairly good, though not great.

Winds will be your biggest factor. Don't let a breeze help you down a shoreline if you have to paddle back against it. Unless you've arranged for pickup, better to paddle in less breezy areas. The ocean can go from calm and light winds to wavy with strong winds over a span of about 100 feet. White caps on the water are caused by wind, and it's easy to drift from a protected area to an exposed area. Stay alert.

Many of the big resorts rent kayaks by the hour for confiscatory amounts. If you want to strap one to your car and have it for the day, in West Maui **Rainbow** (661-1970) rents kayaks. In South Maui the best is **South Pacific Kayaks** (875-4848). Also consider **Maui Eco-Tours** (891-2223)

Kayaks can be rented for around $40-45 for two-person kayaks, $25 for singles. **Maui Eco-Tours** will deliver for $10 or $15 per kayak to some locations, as will **Tradewind Kayaks** (879-2247).

Kayaks with rudders are *much* easier to paddle. You'd be surprised at how much effort goes into keeping one straight otherwise. Wind causes kayaks to weathercock—turn into the wind—and rudders help a lot. **South Pacific** has singles and doubles with rudders, though they're about $55. **Maui Eco Tours** has singles with rudders for $25.

For guided tours consider **South Pacific, Maui Eco Tours** and **Tradewind.**

In Hana, **Maui Snorkel and Kayak Tours** (248-7711 or 264-9566) has short, kayak/snorkel trips at Hana Bay for $59.

Call them Jet Skis, Wave Runners (which are brand names) or personal watercraft—whatever your name for them, these motorcycles of the sea can be rented only in Ka'anapali from **Pacific Jet Sports** (667–2066) from mid-May to mid-December. (They have to close during whale season.) Their attitude is kind of snotty (perhaps because they're the only game in town), but you don't care much while you're riding. They use pretty powerful craft (mostly 700 Wave Runners) and pretty much give you free rein in their circular course. That's good because it gives you more freedom...but it also leaves you free to hurt yourself. If you've never ridden before, these animals are a scream. (Literally for many riders.)

Early morning is usually very smooth, late afternoon choppy. Late morning seems a good balance to give the water some texture. They offer ½ hour for $47, full hour $68. The half hour will tucker out most people, especially if you're like me and you drive it like it's stolen. Spend the extra few bucks for the goggles and experiment with different ways to hold your feet while you sit. Despite their brochure's claims, you're actually given little instruction, so be careful. Go fast enough during bumpy seas and turns will be like a controlled crash, so don't turn too fast unless you know what you're doing. Extra riders are allowed for $10, but we recommend one person per craft. Doubling up seems to increase the risk of the passenger falling off, from what we observed. Some people seem to feel that these craft are hazardous to the ocean,

others say modern jet skis are no different than regular boats. We honestly don't know which is the case, we're just saying what it's like to rent one. They meet off Canoe (Hanaka'o'o) Beach.

There are several companies that provide various types of land tours. Some are better than others. They include **Temptation Tours** (877–8888). They do van tours of the Hana Coast for around $125. Though we recommend that you drive this yourself, if the winding road bothers you, this tour is better than not seeing the Hana Highway. **Sugar Cane Train** (661–0080) is listed as one of the "must dos" in much of the free literature strewn about the island, but we can't help wonder if they've actually done it. Picture a slow-moving train that chugs through abandoned sugar cane fields, along a golf course and through a residential area. Dull, pointless and overpriced. Perhaps some kids will like it, but adults should blow their money elsewhere. In Lahaina. $15 for adults, $8.50 for kids.

Hidden Aventures (665–0559) has guided JEEP tours. **Quality Motorcycle Tours** (242–1015) has various motorcycle tours of the island. Pretty flexible folks.

This is probably the single biggest activity that people pay to do on Maui, and for good reason. The calm, clear waters make it a boater's heaven. Maui's boating conditions are superb due to the shape of its coastline, and it has close island neighbors to visit.

In some ways, this is one of the most difficult sections to write about. The section's length is a testament of your varied options. *So* many choices and fleeting characteristics make it dizzying. We may take a boat tour and rave about it, but the day after we go to press, the boating company may sell their 50-foot sailing yacht and begin taking passengers out on an inflatable raft from Wal-Mart. It's hard to keep up.

Most of the boats leave from Lahaina or Ma'alaea (close to Kihei). A few small boats leave from the Kihei Boat Ramp.

Boating trips can generally be broken down into four types:

SNORKEL TRIPS

PURE SAILING TRIPS

WHALE WATCHING *mid-Dec.–mid-May*

DINNER CRUISES

Many of the snorkel trips *claim* they also whale watch, but that is mainly composed of making a beeline to their snorkeling spot and hoping to spot one of the buggers. That's like calling them fishing boats because they drag a lure behind them on their way to Molokini.

We need to clarify something up front. Taking a boat trip on Maui is like making a dessert with chocolate, ice cream and peanut butter. No matter how you combine the ingredients, you're gonna end up with something sweet and tasty. (See, *that's* what I get for writing while hungry.) The boater's ingredients are the boat, sun, water and fish. Unless the weather is horrible, even if you're boating with complete idiots, odds are you're still going to have a fun, relaxing time, because boating Maui's often placid waters can't be beat. Since not all boating companies are created equal,

our job is to steer you to the ones who seem to do the best job (and away from the idiots). We've anonymously ridden scads of boats off Maui, and the difference is striking. But remember as you read these critiques: Even bad boat trips are usually fun.

We've noticed that there seem to be two types of crews: Those composed of cocky guys and gals who spend all their time and energy showing their crew mates and you how impossibly cool they are. (The old *don't you wish you were as cool as me* syndrome.) Then there are crews who channel more of their effort to help ensure *you* have a good time. We obviously lean toward the latter.

SNORKEL TRIPS
Where They Go

Most boats go to two locations. Ma'alaea departures usually do their first stop at Molokini and the second at **Turtle Town.** *Where is Turtle Town,* you may ask. The answer seems to be, *wherever they say it is.* Different companies take people to different "Turtle Towns" and it seems to be more of a marketing gimmick. (After all, doesn't the name *sound* intriguing?) For instance, Wailea Kai (through Ocean Activity Center) calls the area off Keawakapu Turtle Town. Well, the snorkeling there is pretty boring, and you're not likely to see many turtles. Another "Turtle Town" is off the Maui Prince. One is even near Ma'alaea. There are two near Po'olenalena, etc. Despite the picture the salesmen paint of water swarming with turtles, the odds are probably 50-50 that you'll actually see one. Don't go with the *expectation* that you'll swim with turtles. If you do, great. Otherwise, just enjoy the water, coral and fish. Visibility will seem merely fair, but that's only because you probably just got spoiled for life at Molokini on the first stop. People who would have been thrilled with 80-foot visibility before, suddenly sniff indignantly because it's not 180 feet like Molokini on a good day.

Molokini is 3 miles off Maui's coast and 10 miles from Ma'alaea Harbor. It's one of the most widely known snorkel and diving spots in Hawai'i. (See photo on page 208.) It's a sunken crater that is now a marine sanctuary. The floor is well coated with colorful coral. It's illegal to feed the fish here, though you'll quickly realize by their behavior that these little beggars *are* hand fed. (We've even seen boat personnel feeding them after telling passengers not to.) There's no need for you to do it; fish *assume* you will. The fish count inside isn't as great as other places on Maui, but it's still high, and with the incredibly clear visibility (usually 120–180 feet) it's a good place to snorkel. The bottom topography isn't

overly interesting, just a gently sloping floor. We've repeatedly snorkeled the entire crater, and the best snorkeling is usually on the inside left (from the outside looking in—the side closest to Maui). Boats that park elsewhere usually tell you *they* park in the best spot, but they're wrong. (SCUBA diving is a different matter.) The inside right is second best, with the center the least interesting. (That's relative; the center still has lots of coral and fish.) Don't stay in one place; swim over near the shore for more coral, then to deeper water for more fish. When the water's calm, the center/left (where the Prince Kuhio usually moors) is where currents may deposit any fine floating debris, so it's best to avoid that part. It's *usually,* though not always, calm inside.

Molokini's biggest problem is its popularity. On a given day over 1,000 snorkelers may visit the crater, sometimes twice that many. Each boat moors in a certain spot, and you are asked to

Molokini is where you'll find the best water visibility in all Maui. These early boats have the very best spots. Dive boats at the submerged corner, snorkel boats at the inside edges.

stay close to your boat. If you're in a less interesting part of the crater, you may need to swim through a sea of other snorkelers and violate the boat rules to get to a better part. But stay inside the crater and away from the far edges, especially the far right side (as you're looking inside) where the crater wall is submerged. Currents there can be bad.

Probably the best advice we can give about Molokini is to discard any preconceptions. So much has been written and said, so many exaggerated paintings exist, so many doctored photos, that people get a certain picture in their mind of what to expect. Best to go in with a blank slate, and you'll probably leave full of wonder.

If you take a boat from Lahaina, you usually stop at **Coral Gardens.** There's more than one, but one is offshore of the 14 mile marker. It offers lots of beautiful coral and decent, though not stellar, visibility. (But better visibility than shore-bound snorkelers will find.) Another Coral Gardens is below the Hwy 30 tunnel.

A few tips

Many of the companies, like Pacific Whale Foundation, are real stingy with the food. After your first snorkel you're apt to be pretty hungry and may not be offered any food. Consider bringing your own stash of snacks with you. You may be able to sell them to other hungry customers at prices confiscatory enough to pay for your trip. *(I have a bid of $8 for a chocolate chip cookie. Do I hear $9?)*

Another consideration is warmth. Though the water temps range from 75° to 80°, you may want to consider renting a thin wet suit from a dive shop to keep you snug. The second snorkel site tends to chill people, especially in the winter. (February has the coldest water.)

Of course, boats that rent wet suits tend to *under*-report the temperature about 5° to convince you to rent.

Catamarans are twin-hulled and slice through the water much more cleanly than single-hull boats and, if wide enough, are more stable (less rocking) on the water.

If you're uncomfortable using the boat's snorkel gear (either for sanitary or fitting reasons), consider renting it elsewhere and bringing it along. Most boats have only one size mask. Also, when you defog your mask (using either dedicated goo or your own spit), rub it hard into the inside glass then rinse quickly.

If you want a towel, you'll probably have to bring your own.

Small, white tip reef sharks, which are essentially harmless, are often seen at Molokini. *Don't worry* about them. Worry about getting sunburned.

Below deck is a bad place to be if you're worried about getting seasick. Without a reference point, you're much more likely to let 'er rip down there. If you *tied one on* the night before, do yourself a favor and take Dramamine, Bonine or apply Scopolime patches *before* you go. Ginger is also a very good preventative and treatment for seasickness.

People come off these trips *toasted,* especially in the summer. Make *sure* you slather on the sunscreen, or you'll be sorry for the rest of your trip.

Morning snorkel trips nearly always offer better snorkeling and calmer seas. The only upside for **afternoon snorkel trips** is price. The only time we recommend windier afternoon trips is when you only want to sail.

Allow enough time to find a **parking** spot. At Ma'alaea they can fill up if your boat isn't one of the first to leave, and you'll have to park at the aquarium.

where most boats use buses to drive you back to the harbor. In Lahaina, the Mala Ramp can also tax parkers' patience. For Lahaina Harbor, consider the lot near Prison Street.

Don't take any inflatable raft trips out of Ma'alaea. Too much bumpy travel time across windy Ma'alaea Bay. Only go from the Kihei Boat Ramp and Lahaina. Inflatables from Lahaina to Lana'i are bumpy, too.

SNUBA (page 224) is often available. Inside Molokini Crater it's harder to justify the extra $45 or so as you really won't see much more than the snorkelers see a few feet above, but it's kind of fun. (Other locations make more sense for SNUBA.)

Best Snorkel Boats of the Bunch

Probably the best of the *big* boats is **Four Winds II** (879–8188). This is a 55-foot power catamaran that makes morn-ing treks to Molokini. Though they take up to 130 people, the boat is nicely designed to accommodate many without feeling as crowded as some of the others. There's a good mix of sun and shade, and the upper deck perimeter bench seats allow you to spin around and face the water while resting on the railing—a nice touch. Their usual mooring spot at Molokini is the best of any of the boats. Their food setup is also the best of the lot. All the BBQ burgers, chicken, fish, hot dogs and veggie burgers you want are waiting for you when you get out of the water. (They're not as generous with the cookies, however.) Open bar longer than any of the others. One negative aspect—they don't go to a second site—can be a positive in that they spend more time at the crater, making it feel more leisurely. (Their second "turtle town stop" is where they stop just outside the harbor on the

Boat	Phone	Max. Passengers	Type of Boat	Departs	Wet Suits	Snorkel Stops	Rest Rooms	Food
Four Winds II	879–8188	130	55' Sailing Cat	Ma'alaea	Yes	1	Yes	BBQ
Paragon	244–2087	36/24	47' Sailing Cat	Ma' & Lah	Yes	2	Yes	Deli
Pacific Whale Foundation								
Ocean Spirit	879–8811	100	65' Power Cat	Ma'alaea	No	2	Yes	Deli
Manute'a	879–8811	48	50' Sailing Cat	Lahaina	No	1	Yes	BBQ
Navatek II	873–3475	149	82' Power Cat	Ma'alaea	Yes	1	Yes	BBQ
Maka Kai	879–4485	100	65' Power Cat	Ma'alaea	Yes	2	Yes	Deli
Trilogy I-V	661–4743	Lots	Sailing Cats	Everywhere	No	2	Yes	Deli/BBQ
Alii Nui	875–9259	36	60' Sailing Cat	Ma'alaea	Yes	1	Yes	BBQ
Lani Kai	244–1979	70	53' Power Cat	Ma'alaea	Yes	2	Yes	Deli
Prince Kuhio	242–8777	149	92' Power Boat	Ma'alaea	Yes	2	Yes	Deli
Mahana Na'ia	871–8636	68	58' Sailing Cat	Ma'alaea	Yes	2	Yes	BBQ
Pride of Maui	242–0955	140	65' Power Cat	Ma'alaea	Yes	2	Yes	BBQ
Seafire	879–2201	18	25' Raft-like	Kihei	No	2	No	Barely
Blue Water	879–7238	24	19' & 30' Raft-like	Kihei	No	1–3	No	Deli
Kai Kanani	879–7218	42	46' Sailing Cat	Maui Prince	No	1	Yes	Deli
America II	667–2195	24	40' Racing Yacht	Lahaina	Sailing Trip			
Scotch Mist	661–0386	24	50' Sailing Sloop	Lahaina	Sailing Trip			
Cinderella	244–0009	6	50' Sailing Sloop	Ma'alaea	Sailing Trip			
Maui Princess	667–6165	149	118' Power Boat	Lahaina				
Lahaina Princess	667–6165	100	65' Power Boat	Lahaina	No	2	Yes	BBQ
Island Princess	667–6165	24	38' Sailing Cat	Lahaina	No	1	Yes	Barely
Flexible Flyer	244–6655	6	54' Sailing Sloop	Ma'alaea	No	1	Yes	Deli

way back and point out turtles. In fairness, it *is* a good place to spot them, you just won't swim with them.) Our only real gripe is that they advertise themselves as a *sailing* catamaran, and their brochures show billowing sails. Their definition of "sailing" is raising one sail *while motoring* downwind on the way to Molokini. *C'mon, guys,* either sail for real or stop pretending you do. All in all, however, Four Winds is a winner. Morning Molokini is $72, afternoon trip to Coral Gardens or occasionally Molokini is $39. SNUBA, Rx masks, underwater camera and wet suits available for extra. Their hefty see-through sea-boards are *very* nice for timid kids and adults. The "glass bottom" on the boat itself works well for kids, but adults might not be too impressed. Freshwater hose shower on board, and there's a slide into the water.

The best of the medium-sized boats is **Paragon** (244–2087). They use 47-foot sailing catamarans and have good snorkel gear and crew. These guys *really* like sailing and are much quicker to raise and maintain their sails than most companies, often sailing both ways, not part of one way. The boats hold 36, and there's shade for ⅓ of the passengers plus what the sails provide. Riding the net (lying on the front trampolines) is a hoot on the way back. Soothing and dry if it's calm, thrilling and wet if seas are up. The outside of the trampolines are the wettest. At Molokini they moor at a pretty good spot and they let you roam the crater—no short leashes. The deli lunch isn't as nice as others' BBQ, and their ladder into the water is poor, but overall this is a very good product. Since it's smaller, expect a slightly bumpier ride than Four Winds II. Wet suits and Rx masks available for extra. Ma'alaea to Molokini trips are $72, no second snorkel spot. For their Lana'i

trip they snorkel outside Manele Bay and then give you a picnic lunch to take ashore. $136 for the Lana'i trip, which only takes 24.

Four Winds II and Paragon don't snorkel at two spots. If that's a priority, **Pacific Whale Foundation** (879–8811) leaves from Ma'alaea. Their biggest boat, **Ocean Spirit,** is a nice, 65-foot power catamaran. (It's skinny, so it rocks more than most cats do.) There's plenty of shade and a sunny top. The snorkel gear is a mix of ultra-cheap and decent. The crew attitude is good, though some of their narrations are appallingly inaccurate. Like when they tell you that "Lana'i stopped growing pineapple in 1990 because they only had enough water for either pineapple or people. So they stopped growing pineapple and let the people come back to the island." Good story, but totally bogus. Our biggest complaint with PWF is that they are remarkably stingy with food. Nothing awaits you after your first snorkel. You wait till they go to the next place, then after the second snorkel it's a deli lunch. And expect to get your hand slapped (figuratively) if you go back for seconds. But their price is good, so perhaps that's the reason. All profits go to whale research and education. $58 for the Molokini trip. They take a 100 people, which is tight.

From Lahaina, **Pacific Whale Foundation's** 50-foot **Manute'a** is a sailing catamaran to Lana'i. Power out and *maybe* sail back. They hunt for dolphins, which are often outside the harbor at Manele Bay, and snorkel there. $74, up to 48 people (which is tight). BBQ lunch and open bar.

Another good product, for totally different reasons, is **Ocean Activity Center** (879–4485). They use the **Maka Kai** and **Wailea Kai. Maka Kai** is a 65-foot, two-deck power catamaran. The price is *very* cheap, $55, and they take up to 100 people. Wet suits and Rx masks are available to rent, and you can claim one of their fishing lines while trolling to the spots for $10. *(That's* cheap!) If you want one, nab a corner pole. Overall, it's a good experience. On the negative side, the boat is pretty tired-looking and it's a bit crowded on board, though not as bad as others. Their mooring spot at Molokini is not at a good part of the crater, and they keep you on a pretty tight leash so you can't swim to the better parts. No SNUBA or SCUBA offered, and they won't let you ride the bow. On the positive side, in addition to the price, their second spot is better than the other guys'. They are more generous with the food (with the deli waiting for you after the first snorkel), and there's an open bar after the second snorkel (with surprisingly good mai tais). The crew is very good and seems to work hard to ensure you have a good time. Shower on board. In all, they are more than worth the money if you don't mind 99 fellow passengers. Our biggest gripe is their "live marine show," where they capture sea critters and "gently" display them for you on the boat before tossing them back. We've talked with marine biologists who tell us that this kind of "show" has a very high mortality rate with the eels, octopus and other unfortunate specimens. Their other boat, single-deck **Wailea Kai,** is mainly used for Japanese visitors and for those who need pick-up at their hotel, so it costs more. Also, Wailea Kai goes to a terrible second spot. Avoid Wailea Kai in favor of Maka Kai.

There are two good small boats. **Flexible Flyer** (244–6655) is a 54-foot sailing sloop that takes only 6 people. $129 for their Molokini trip. They do a lot of private charters, which runs $600 for five hours. It's nice having a boat like this virtually to yourself if you have a small group to share the cost. Book in advance. **Cinderella** (244–0009) is a 50-foot sailing sloop that provides similar services.

Blue Water Rafting (879–7238) is a rigid-hull inflatable (a V-shaped hull surrounded by a rubber pontoon). They do things different. From Kihei Boat Ramp you head down the coast, past La Pérouse to a lava flow at Kanaio (which literally means *the bastard sandalwood tree*). After exploring the unusual lava formations, you head back, usually to La Pérouse Bay to a rather dull snorkeling area, then stop at another, better site for snorkeling and a deli lunch. The boat does a scorching 40 knots, and the ride is a blast (though less comfortable than a cushier boat and certainly wetter). Little shade. Consider a light, waterproof jacket for the morning trip out and wet riding later. $75 for 4 hours. They also have a 5-hour trip for $99 that includes Molokini, but we recommend the shorter trip. Best seats are on the back, left side. Wind past La Pérouse can be fierce, hence their early start.

Others To Consider

Navatek II (873–3475) out of Ma'alaea is an 82-foot long, very wide, stunningly smooth two-deck power catamaran. It uses a cool technology called SWATH (small waterplain area twin hull), which keeps the boat above the water except for two torpedo-like projections that propel the craft. The only water that it doesn't handle well is when waves are overtaking it from behind (which few craft handle well). It holds up to 149 people, which would be a bit too tight, but we've never been on it when it was full.

Their snorkel trips to Lana'i include

meals, open (free) bar (and a good one at that) and snorkel gear (Rx available). They usually take you to Lighthouse (Shark Fin Cove) on Lanaʻi, good for beginner snorkelers but somewhat dull for the more advanced. No second stop; SNUBA available. They keep you on a tight leash—too tight—so you can't wander too far from the boat. Crew is top notch except the shaky Hawaiiana information, and the boat very comfortable. Pancake and waffle breakfast, BBQ burgers and chicken for lunch. Great for families, easy entry into the water. No towels (except to buy). You also might want to bring a sweatshirt for the morning. $115.

The biggest operator, by far, is **Trilogy** (661–4743). They have lots of boats (five at last count with another on the way) and leave from Lahaina, Maʻalaea and even Lanaʻi. They can generally be summed up with four words: *nice boats, mediocre crews.* The company feels like a visitor processing machine, and you are their raw ingredients. They take over 50,000 people a year. That's not to say you won't have a good time, but the crews seem over-represented by snippy smart-alecs like those mentioned on page 207. Their snorkel gear is cheap—how much fun are you going to have if your cheap-o mask keeps leaking?—and we're not sure it's rinsed between charters based on the amount of sand we've seen in the masks. No wet suits available. On the positive side, they serve a decent lunch, and the boats, when they sail, are fun. We like lying on the trampolines while sailing. At best they'll probably only sail part of one way, so keep that in mind. On Lanaʻi all the Trilogy boats usually visit a "secret spot" (which they call Shark Fin Cove) which usually has calm, though somewhat dull, snorkeling. Overall, Trilogy strikes us as a company that has gotten so caught up in marketing (at which they excel) that they've forgotten the reason people take boat trips—*to have fun!*

Trilogy has many charters, ranging from Lahaina to Lanaʻi snorkel trips for $159 to whale watching trips December through April to Maʻalaea to Molokini snorkel trips. Call for complicated rates.

Snorkeling, BBQ and thou. What else is there?

Other Snorkel Trips From Ma'alaea

Alii Nui (875–9259) is a 60-foot sailing catamaran. It's pretty pricey since you only go around the corner to "turtle town" (at Olowalu) for one snorkeling location for $89. A lousy deal, but at least they feed you fairly well.

Mahana Na'ia (871–8636) has a 58-foot sailing cat. $70 for Molokini and "turtle town." Kind of crowded since it's one deck for up to 68 passengers.

Pride Charters (242–0955) uses a 50-foot, single-hull, dreary-looking boat called **Leilani** and a 65-foot catamaran called **Pride of Maui.** The latter has a *very* crowded feel with 140 people packed on board; the quintessential cattle boat. Even with smaller crowds it feels like a life boat on the *Titanic.* Uncomfortable backless benches on top with no shade. On the plus side, they park in a good spot at Molokini. Their second spot, "turtle town," is at 5 Graves/5 Caves. They have a slide and SCUBA and SNUBA available and a small number of wet suit rentals for snorkeling. For their BBQ lunch they precook burgers, chicken, hot dogs and veggie burgers, wait till they're cold, then line you up and reheat them. Get in line early as it can take *forever.* Open bar after second stop. At $82, the trip is not a good deal.

Lani Kai through **Friendly Charters** (244–1979) has a 53-foot power cat with 70 people. Interior shade. $75 for Molokini and turtle town, you can do better.

Prince Kuhio (242–8777) is Maui's 92-foot, 149-passenger cattle boat. Molokini/Turtle Town (Maui Prince). Their mooring spot is perhaps the worst of any of the boats. Right near the potentially junky area mentioned on page 208. Only positive is that the boat's real easy to get around on.

Other Snorkel Trips From Lahaina

Lahaina Princess (667–6165) is a 65-foot, single-hull boat that does morning trips to Molokini from Lahaina for $69. It's twice as far as a trip from Ma'alaea and their second stop is near Olowalu. Going to Molokini from Lahaina in this type of boat isn't a great way to go. Plus it really rocks when moored. Consider driving to Ma'alaea for your Molokini trips.

Maui Princess (667–6165) is a huge, 118-foot boat that does dinner cruises described on page 278. They also have boat/drive tours of Moloka'i for $129 for the first person, $69 for additional people, Wednesdays and Saturdays. You get a boat ride plus a rental car for 5 hours. A cool way to see Moloka'i for the day. See page 144 for more. They also have trips to Lana'i and a snorkel trip.

Their **Island Princess** is a 38-foot

sailing cat that mostly motors. Only 2-hour trips, which are unimpressive but dirt cheap. Starts at $19. Only consider if you are itching to get on the water, have kids or are running low on cash.

Sea View (661–5550) is proof that a slick brochure can make *anything* look good. A tired, old glass-bottom boat holding 64. Two-hour trip includes snorkeling for $44. You can do *much* better.

Ocean Riders (661–3586) uses a 30-foot rigid hull inflatable to circumnavigate Lana'i for $115. These are rougher and wetter than more traditional craft, and shade is not too ample. But they snorkel three spots, and it's nice to see Lana'i's more interesting windward side. They even visit Lana'i's large shipwreck. Their most intriguing product is when they circumnavigate Moloka'i. Seeing the sea cliffs from the ocean is awesome. Unfortunately, they rarely do this because of winds. Even when calm, they seem reluctant to book the trip. Too bad. If you get lucky, you'll see quite a sight. Bring something to keep warm or dry.

Other Snorkel Trips From Kihei

If you just want to take a quick snorkel trip out to Molokini and don't want all the frills, **Maui Dive Shop** (879–3388) takes their 33-foot, single-hull boat from Kihei Boat Ramp to Molokini (only 4 miles) then "turtle town" for a 3-hour tour. (Just like Gilligan's Island.) Up to 24 people (which makes it *crowded*), continental breakfast and juices and sodas. No frills, but for $39 you ain't paying for frills. Snorkelers can accompany divers on their boat dive charter, but that costs $75 since you're taking up a diver's spot.

Kai Kanani (879–7218) is a 46-foot sailing cat (that usually motors, not sails despite the brochure photo). Since they leave from the Maui Prince in Makena,

it's an easy 20-minute trip to Molokini. They spend 3 hours there then bring you back to shore at Maui Prince's "turtle town." $65 for up to 42 people, deli lunch included. A pretty good product.

Seafire (879–2201) is a small, unimpressive, raft-looking rigid hull craft that goes to Molokini and turtle town for $50. Cheap, no frills, 3 hours, 2 stops. Only if price is paramount.

PURE SAILING TRIPS

You're not really heading for anywhere and you aren't really interested in *doing* anything—you just want to sail. Most are schooners (single hull with little or no shade other than what the sail provides). If you're up front, schooners require you to move more often than the twin-hulled catamarans (cats). When it's too windy to go on a snorkel trip, it's probably great for sailing.

America II (667–2195) is the real deal—a genuine 12-meter racing yacht that participated in America's Cup. It's a fast, sleek schooner that takes 24 people (which is crowded). Price is cheap at $30 for the 2½-hour morning sail and $33 for the afternoon 2-hour sail (more winds). Sunset sail is $33. Boat is usually full; snacks and drinks provided.

Scotch Mist (661–0386) is a 50-foot sailboat that accommodates 25 (which would be too crowded for comfort since it's not a wider catamaran), but they usually take about a dozen. They'll go out with as few as 4 passengers, which makes for a relaxing time. Their 2-hour afternoon sail is just right to whet your nautical appetite. No shade except for the sail. Below deck is a bit dreary, but on top it's a nice, clean boat, and the experience is fun. Sodas and beer provided. Out of Lahaina; 2-hour afternoon or sunset sails are $35 and $38, 4-hour morning snorkel sail is $55.

Cinderella (244–0009) is a nice-looking sailing yacht. Comfortable in back, less so up front, it holds 6. Pricey; call for ever-changing rates. Snorkel available.

Flexible Flyer on page 212 can be chartered as pure sailing boat.

RENT YOUR OWN BOAT

If you want to rent your own power boat and go where you want, when you want, see page 238. To rent a sailboat see page 240.

WHALE WATCHING is seasonal and described on page 227. **DINNER CRUISES** are under NIGHTLIFE on page 278.

Parasailing is where you become a human kite, attached to a parachute and pulled by a boat via a long rope. It's a 7–10-minute ride though that includes reeling in and reeling out. It's been our experience that parasailing *looks* more fun and thrilling than it really is and doesn't seem worth the money. Think of it as a $40+ amusement ride. (People afraid of heights, however, will no doubt be properly terrified.) Off Lahaina, at least the view of town is grand. Tip: Don't wear slippery shorts; you'll cinch forward in your harness. (Especially important with guys…if you know what I mean.) At press time, the companies all left from West Maui and only from mid-May to mid-December. (They have to close during whale season.) They are **Parasail Ka'anapali** (669–6555), which is probably best deal with their 1,200-foot line for $40 (extra person is $10). **Lahaina**

Parasail (661–4887) has 400- and 800-foot lines for $45 & $52, and **UFO Parasailing** (661–7836) has a 7-minute 400-foot ride for $45 and a 10-minute 800-foot ride for $55. The latter two give no discounts for the second person.

OK, here's where Maui's often placid waters pays off. The diving here can be incredible. The usually calm morning waters off South and West Maui make boat rides short and sweet. In addition to its nearshore dives, Maui has two great offshore dives. West Maui has the awesome **Lana'i Cathedrals II** to journey to, and South Maui has the humbling **back wall of Molokini.**

We've noticed that, overall, the dive operations on Maui seem to be of a slightly higher caliber than on Kaua'i or the Big Island, perhaps because there's so much competition. Prices are lower, too. (It's good to see that *some* things are actually cheaper on Maui!) They're usually more professional here with less of the *dive shop attitude.* (You know the attitude—when you go into a shop, and the guy behind the counter never gets off his stool or takes off his sunglasses, doing everything he can to convey the impression: *I'm so stylin', don't you wish you were just like me?*)

However, many of the dive companies have provocative brochures showing divers cavorting with all sorts of critters, including the holy grail of SCUBA encounters, the whale shark. We're not saying it doesn't happen, just don't *expect* it. People have been known to experience spontaneous human combustion, but we've never seen *that* happen either. We only know one friend who claims to have swam with a whale shark here. (And he lies a lot.)

So you'll know our perspective when we review companies, we should tell you what we do and don't like when we go on a dive. On a bad dive, the dive master takes the group on a non-stop excursion that keeps you kicking the whole time. No time to stop and explore the nooks and crannies. Good outfits will give you a briefing, tell you about some of the endemic species here, what to look for and will point out various things on the dives, keeping it moving but not too fast. Bad outfits kick a lot. Good outfits explain the unique qualities of Hawai'i's environment. Bad dive masters may tell you what *they* saw (but you missed). Good companies work around your needs, wishes and desires. Bad companies keep everyone on a short leash. Good dive masters know their stuff and share it with you. Bad dive masters don't know squat but imply they know it all in order to impress you. As divers, we tend to like companies that wander toward the boat for the latter part of the dive and allow you to go up when you are near the end of your tank, as opposed to everyone going up when the heaviest breather has burned up his/her bottle.

During times when we feel the diving conditions are bad (poor vis or big swells), we like to call around and ask about conditions. We appreciate the companies who admit it's bad and we hold it against those who tell us how wonderful conditions are. (Companies that have failed this test miserably include SCUBA Shack, Boss Frog's, Makena Coast, Tropical Divers Maui, Dive Maui, and Maui Diamond Sea Sports.) Maui Dive Shop has always been dead-on in honesty about conditions.

THE TOPS ON MAUI

The best companies we've found have been in South Maui. Regardless of the profession, it seems that the cream sooner or later rises to the top. So it is with the dive industry on Maui. Without question, the best dive outfits on the island are **Prodiver Maui** (875–4004) and **Mike Severns** (879–6596). **Prodiver** takes only 6 or 7 on their ample boat, so you never feel crowded. They have a good boat, good crew, good pace and a good attitude. They treat you well, handle the dives just right, and have plenty of snacks and beverages. You can tell that the joy of diving hasn't left them. It's $109 per 2-tank, gear or not. They also do boat scooter dives for $149. *Lots* of fun. If they're full **Mike Severns** is also a quality outfit top to bottom. Everyone gets a computer, good gear and plenty of snacks. With excellent briefings, perfectly led dives, a good 13-passenger boat (2 groups) and the right attitude, this is a great company to go with. With so many years of experience, they are very adept at finding critters and showing them to you, and their knowledge is phenomenal. Since they know the sites so well, they key in on what to brief you on before the dives. Many companies do this, but nobody does it as well. $100 for a 2-tank, $15 extra for gear. Book both in advance.

Ed Robinson (879–3584) is also a very well-run company and is a very acceptable alternative choice. Good ascent policy, good briefing, they go nice and slow during the dives, and their divemasters seem pretty knowledgeable. Most (though not all) do a good job. They have two 12-passenger boats (groups of 6). Normally, dive companies don't handle growth well. (They tend to turn into diver processing machines.) So far Ed

Robinson has managed to keep up the quality. Their boats, like most single-hull boats, rock pretty bad in heavy swells, but that's usually only relevant when they go to Lana'i. The Wednesday Lana'i trip from South Maui is, however, wonderful, though the trip is long. An easy company to recommend. $105 for 2-tank, but they usually won't do the Molokini back wall except on the $145 3-tank.

Maui Dreams (874–5332) does good shore dives along South Maui. Their enthusiasm is evident and welcome. It's like you're diving with friends. They'll go out with only one person if necessary, even for a night dive. That's unusual for a dive company. (They could use a better briefing and maybe some food.) $59 for one tank, $79 for two.

Maui Dive Shop has several locations on the island, including the largest and best shop, which is in Kihei (879–3388) and another large shop in Lahaina (661–5388). Their larger shops seem very well run and the personnel are professional; their smaller shops are so-so. Their rental gear is pretty good, though we've noticed that they adjust their regs real loose and we've occasionally had problems with free-flow, even when the adjustment was backed off. Though you certainly won't find many steals, the Kihei shop is so complete it's hard to beat.

As for diving, they do a pretty decent job, though it's a bit of a processing machine. Not bad, but not in the same league as the others mentioned above. They have boat, shore, night and scooter dives. They claim to be the only ones who will *guarantee* a Molokini back wall dive. Sure enough, we've seen them go when no one else would dare to go. Good or bad? You decide.

In **West Maui,** the best boat dive company is **Extended Horizons** (667–0611). They often go to Lana'i and do a pretty good job. The best shore dive company in West Maui is **Pacific Dive** (667–5331).

WHERE TO DIVE

Though most boat captains will poll their customers asking where they want to go, they'll try to steer you to places they think are good that day. Two places stand out as some of the best diving in Hawai'i.

One of the coolest is **Cathedrals II** off Lana'i. Most boats leave from Lahaina, but some, like Ed Robinson, do some trips from South Maui. Not only is the

Sometimes swimming in a crowd isn't so bad.

large lava room with several entrances here dramatic, the sealife can be great. On a 2-tank dive here we saw, among other things, four reef sharks, two *huge* octopuses, a frogfish *(very cool)*, harlequin shrimp, ghost shrimp, pipefish, a titan scorpionfish, lots of black coral, slipper lobster, and—oh, yes—*a pod of dolphins!* (This was one of the single greatest day dives we've ever done.) Obviously Cathedrals won't always deliver dives like that, but it *can* be awesome. Not necessarily an advanced dive. You need to book this trip specifically. Boats leaving from Lahaina offer shorter treks. Dive lights are helpful. **Cathedrals I** is also great, but not as good as II.

The other standout location is the **back wall of Molokini.** This is *outside* the crater. It's not necessarily the fish life that makes this a good dive, though the fish are numerous. Rather, it's the dramatic way the wall plunges into the abyss. Its presence is never far from your mind. And as you round the corner from Molokini's shadow to the sunlight (penetrating to an incredible depth), it forms an awesome spectacle. Later, you may look down a see a black tip reef shark cruising the neighborhood 90 feet below you—and another one 90 feet above you. This is an easy dive to go deep, and most companies will screen to make sure you're up to the task. Since there's nothing much to stop you from going all the way, it's important that you be comfortable regulating your buoyancy. Don't want you setting any new depth records in your state of rapture of the deep. Bring a light for the shadow side.

The *inside* of Molokini isn't nearly as dramatic to dive as the outside, but it's easier. Either way, trips to Molokini are very short. It's only 7 miles from the Kihei Boat Ramp.

GOOD SHORE DIVE LOCATIONS

From South Maui to West Maui, all are described in greater detail under BEACHES.

Black Sand Beach (Pu'u Ola'i) has good coral and fish life, but you'll have to swim along the hill's shoreline over 800 feet to get to the areas deep enough to justify SCUBA. Around the point, before Little Beach, there are some excellent caves. Ocean entry is over a lava shelf, try only during calm seas. Visibility is poor until you leave the shoreline area. Just follow the hill around as far as your will takes you.

Ulua is where intros usually take place in South Maui. There's lots of good reef, though visibility tends to be poor.

Makena Landing used to be great. A freak rain storm in late 1999 washed so much stuff in the water, it choked off the reef, killing much of it. It never recovered. Fish life was wiped out and hadn't returned at press time.

5 Graves/5 Caves described on page 165 can be excellent.

Scenic Lookout described on page 159 can be exciting, though the gear-hauling and entry is a bit annoying.

Black Rock is fun, and there are dive companies at nearby resorts.

Kahekili Beach Park is a popular intro spot because of the easy entry. Kick straight out for best conditions.

Honolua Bay *can* be incredible. Though depths rarely exceed 40 feet, the right side of the bay has an extensive reef area and lots of fish. (The opening photo on page 2–3 is Honolua Bay.) Eels are common. Head out 100–200 feet before dropping.

IF YOU'VE NEVER DIVED BEFORE

Intro dives are how nearly all of us certified divers started. You'll get instruction, and a dive instructor will be nearby during the dive. Most do it as a shore dive. Though certified, we still do intros with companies to see how they do. Most intros take place at Ulua Beach in South Maui or Kahekili Beach in West Maui. If you have any asthma, heart disease, high blood pressure, ear problems or are on medication, call the dive company before you arrive. They may need a signoff from your doctor for some things.

Maui Dreams in South Maui has very reasonably priced intros—$59—and does the best good job we've seen on Maui. **South Pacific Dive School** is the cheapest on the island, working South and West Maui, for only $40 at press time. *(That's cheap!)* Good if price is your major issue, but they use smaller tanks. **Mobile Scuba Schools of Maui** does South Maui intros for $50, also with small tanks.

The two things that annoy us with companies doing intros is patronizing attitudes, and the use of 63-cubic foot tanks. Most new divers suck a lot of air and 80s, though heavier, are the way to go, not the smaller 63s. (Perhaps this is cynical, but maybe some use 63s so that they can get you in and out faster since your air won't last as long.)

OTHER DIVE COMPANIES

There are tons of them out there. We haven't been impressed with **Maui Dive Shop's** intros or **Octopus Reef**. There's absolutely nothing about **Boss Frog** that we like. Pushy, rude and abrupt. **Makena Coast** is adequate. **Beach Activities** (662–8207) has painless shore dives at Black Rock. **Lahaina Divers** (667–7496) is a big company, with fairly big boats and *very* big crowds. Up to 30 people per boat seems to meet the definition of a cattle boat. Consider smaller operations unless you *like* crowded dives.

A FEW TIPS

Despite assurances that the gear has been checked out, if you rent gear to dive on your own, it's a good idea to hook the regulator to the tank before you drive away from the shop. Though we have our own gear, we often rent from shops and boats to evaluate the gear, and we've had problems with leaking regulators and tanks not filled completely with some shops. Anyone can have it happen once, but if it happens twice at a shop we'll dump on them.

Dives, like snorkeling, are usually best in the morning. Afternoon winds can lower visibility and raise surf.

Some companies try to put you in 63-cubic foot tanks. If you don't want to be rushed, tell them you want 80s. Many will comply.

I'd like to pass on a tip that has helped my diving more than any other. I used to be a less-than-stellar breather. Never the last one out. I tried skip breathing—holding your breath while not ascending, which, of course, you're *not* supposed to do—but only got marginally better results at the cost of headaches caused by a buildup of CO_2. Then I learned the secret to make a tank last a long time. Breath *continuously,* never stop, but do so slowly. A long, slow inhalation followed immediately by a drawn out exhalation keeps CO_2 from building up and keeps your body from thinking it's low on air. (I use my tongue at the top of my mouth to spray the air out slowly.) You never feel deprived and the tank lasts *oh so long.* The only downside is less silence during your dive. Now, I'm almost always the last one out and only the tables tell me when to come up, not my gauge. See your dive instructor. (That's the diving disclaimer equivalent of *see your doctor*.)

Hawaiian Reefs—Why is it that...?

What is that crackling sound, like bacon frying, I always hear while snorkeling or diving?
For years this baffled people. In the early days of submarines, the sound interfered with sonar operations. Finally we know the answer. It's hidden snapping shrimp defining their territory. One variety is even responsible for all the dark cracks and channels you see in smooth lobe coral. A pair creates the channels then "farm" algae inside.

Why are there so few shellfish in Hawai'i?
It's too warm for some of the more familiar shellfish (which tend to be filter-feeders and Hawai'i waters don't have as much stuff to filter). But Hawai'i has more shellfish than most people are aware of. They hide well under rocks and in sand. Also, people tend to collect shells, which depletes the numbers.

Why do coral cuts take so long to heal?
Coral contains a live animal. When you scrape coral, it leaves proteinaceous matter in your body, which takes much longer for your body to dispatch.

How did the early fish get here over the vast open ocean?
Often in the form of larvae, which could travel in the ocean's current for long periods of time without the need to feed in the inhospitable open ocean.

What is the state fish?
Well, it used to be the humuhumunukunukuapua'a, but today we don't have a state fish. When the law expired it was not renewed because they "didn't want to revisit this partisan issue." (How can a state fish be partisan?)

What do turtles eat?
Dolphins. (Just teasing.) They primarily eat plants growing on rocks, as well as jellyfish when they are lucky enough to encounter them. Unfortunately for turtles and lucky for us, jellyfish aren't numerous here.

Is it harmful when people play with an octopus?
Yes, if the octopus is harmed while trying to get it out of its hole. Best to leave them alone.

Why does the ocean rarely smell fishy here in Hawai'i?
Two reasons. We have relatively small tide changes, so the ocean doesn't strand large amounts of smelly seaweed at low tide. Also, the water is fairly sterile compared to mainland water, which owes much of its smell to algae and seaweed that thrives in the bacteria-rich runoff from industrial sources.

Why is the water so clear here?
Because relatively little junk is poured into our water compared to the mainland. Also, natural currents tend to flush the water with a continuous supply of fresh, clean ocean water.

Why do my ears hurt when I dive down and how are SCUBA divers able to get over it?
Because the increasing weight of the ocean is pressing on your ears the farther down you go. Divers alleviate this by equalizing their ears. Sounds high tech, but that simply means holding your nose while trying to blow out of it. This forces air into their eustachian tubes, creating equal pressures with the outside ocean. (It doesn't work if your sinuses are clogged.) Anything with air gets compressed. (The ancient Hawaiians, who loved Kulan jokes, probably would have said that's why people from Kula get headaches when they dive.)

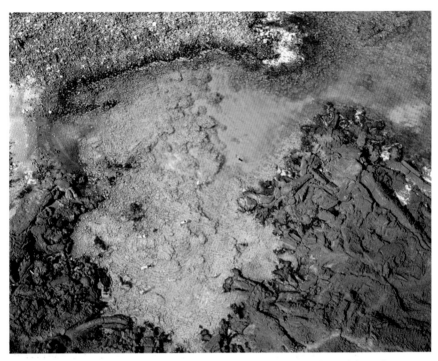

Fishbowl makes for good, easy, protected snorkeling, if you don't mind the walk.

Here we go again, frothing at the mouth about the water. But give us the benefit of the doubt here. The truth is snorkeling on Maui can be outrageous. Clean, clear water in many locations, calm surf much of the time, and gobs of fish and coral. The trick is knowing where to go. We've literally snorkeled miles and miles of coastline, from the top of West Maui to the bottom of South Maui, looking for good spots. If you look at our various maps, the areas shaded in darker blue represent our best finds. In general, the best snorkeling is in South Maui, though the West does have a few gems.

We'll admit that we're snorkeling junkies and never tire of experiencing the water here. If you snorkel often, you can go right to our list below of recommended areas. But if you're completely or relatively inexperienced, you should read on.

For identifying ocean critters, the best books we've seen are *Shore Fishes of Hawai'i* by John Randall and *Hawaiian Reef Fish* by Casey Mahaney. They're what we use. You should see plenty of butterflyfish, wrasse, convict tang, achilles tang, parrotfish, angelfish, damselfish, Moorish idol, pufferfish, trumpetfish, moray eel, and humuhumu-nukunukuapua'a or Picasso triggerfish—a beautiful but very skittish fish. (It's as if they somehow *know* how good they look in aquariums.)

We know people who have a fear of putting on a mask and snorkel. Gives 'em the willies. For them, we recommend boogie boards with clear windows on them to observe the life below.

A Few Tips:

♦ Feeding the fish is generally not recommended because it introduces unnatural behavior to the reef.

♦ Use *Sea Drops* or another brand of anti-fog goop. Spread it *thinly* on the inside of a dry mask, then do a quick rinse.

♦ Most damage to coral comes when people grab it or stand on it. Even touching the coral lightly can transfer your oils to the polyps, killing them. If your mask starts to leak or you get water in your snorkel, be careful not to stand on the coral to clear them. Find a spot where you won't damage coral or drift into it. Fish and future snorkelers (not to mention the coral) will thank you.

♦ Don't use your arms much or you will spook the fish. Just gentle fin motion. Any rapid motion can cause the little critters to scatter.

♦ Water temps range from 75° in February to 80° in September. The lower end may seem chilly; consider renting a short, thin wet suit.

♦ We prefer using divers' fins (the kind that slip over reef shoes) so that we can walk easily into and out of the water without tearing up our feet. (If you wear socks or nylons under the shoes, it'll keep you from rubbing the tops of your toes raw.)

♦ If you have a mustache and have trouble with a leaking mask, try a little Vaseline. Don't get any on the glass—it can get *really* ugly.

THE BEST AREAS TO SNORKEL

See the writeups in BEACHES for info on each specific area. Some snorkeling sites have specifics you need to know.

South Maui Snorkeling

We recommend Fishbowl, Aquarium and the excellent coves along the north side of La Pérouse Bay (see page 230). Don't bother with the part of La Pérouse nearest your car. The entire point separating Po'olenalena Beach from Palauea Beach is great, especially from the Po'olenalena side. Also, the south end of Po'olenalena is good. Between Maluaka and Black Sand Beach there's some good snorkeling. The point separating Kama'ole I and II is pretty decent. North of Keawakapu works pretty well. as does south of Wailea Beach, though you'll have to go out farther there.

West Maui Snorkeling

The scenic lookout between the 8 and 9 mile marker is good if you can deal with the entry and exit. Honolua Bay offers excellent snorkeling about ⅔ of the time. Black Rock at Ka'anapali Beach can be superb. The south end of Oneloa in Kapalua is good much of the time. The 14 Mile Marker on Hwy 30 is ridiculously overrated, but the area below the cliffs southeast of the 11 mile marker is great if you can deal with the long swim.

ODDS AND ENDS

Renting gear is easy. Maui is littered with rental places, and you won't have any trouble finding them. We probably lean toward **Maui Dive Shop's** many locations (879–3388). They also have divers' fins available for extra that will fit over your reef shoes and wet suits. Most places charge about $2–$4 per day, $10–$20 per week for gear. Many shops have low prices in hopes of luring you in and then selling you other activities or timeshares. Also keep in mind that at some shops, the employee gets a commission for selling you more expensive gear. Get what *you* want, not what *they* want you to get. Make sure the mask fits without having to suck in too hard through your nose. Snorkels with drain valves and dry snorkels work better than ordinary tubes.

The most common way that visitors get bad **sunburns** is while snorkeling. You don't feel it coming because of the cool water. Do yourself a favor and consider wearing a T-shirt.

Don't judge a snorkeling site by the first 20 feet. Shorelines are often cloudy. You'll usually have to venture farther out for good quality.

It's a good idea to check on the **snorkeling conditions** the day before you plan to snorkel. Call 871–5054 for a weather forecast. For a surf forecast, call 877–3611 or check page 2 of the *Maui News* newspaper.

GUIDED SNORKEL TOURS

If you're intrigued but nervous about snorkeling, **Ann Fielding's Snorkel Maui** (572–8437) has a very patient and methodical lesson/tour. For $75 she'll spend several hours with you, getting you used to the gear and water, then lead you along a South Maui tour. Lunch included. Ann is a real life marine biologist with great knowledge, so you'll learn much about our marine environment.

If you're a little hesitant about trying SCUBA, consider SNUBA. That's where you swim below a raft with tanks and a 20-foot hose, regulator in mouth and an instructor by your side. Anyone 8 and older can SNUBA. (You need to be 12—10 through PADI—to SCUBA.) **SNUBA Tours of Maui** (879–8410) takes you on a shore dive in North Kihei (just north of the nasty area) or 14 mile marker in West Maui. Neither are stellar locations. It's $59. Some of the boat trips listed under OCEAN TOURS, have SNUBA available. Groups of 4–6 per trip; expect about 45 minutes of bottom time on the shore dives, a bit less on boat dives.

You won't *Run Silent, Run Deep.* You won't hear the sound of sonar pinging away in the background. And it's rare that anyone shoots torpedoes at you. But if you want to see the undersea world and *refuse* to get wet, *dis is da buggah.* **Atlantis Submarine** (667–2224) uses a 48-passenger sub out of Lahaina that ambles about over a reef, which is, to be honest, is a bit plainer than the type you'd choose to snorkel or SCUBA, but it's still cool. This is the opposite of an aquarium—this world belongs to the fish and *you* are the oddity. This $79, 40-minute ride is a kick. Most kids like it if they are old enough to appreciate the sights. We took friends on this trip once, and a huge manta ray cruised by the window. Of

SNUBA is sort of like SCUBA lite. Good for those nervous about taking the plunge. This is at Molokini.

course, their 2½-year-old son was *far* more impressed with the plastic fish card tied to the inside hull than the 14-foot ray just outside the window. But adults like it, and even certified divers like us get a kick out of it. Claustrophobics will probably be too busy staring through the windows to be nervous. Photographers will want to use fast (at least 400 speed) film and turn off the flash. Mornings are usually best. Wear a bright red shirt, and watch what happens to its color on the way down.

Ho, da shreddin's da kine, brah. (Just trying to get you in the mood.) Surfing is synonymous with Hawai'i. And why not? Hawaiians invented da bugga. Lessons aren't as hard as you may think. They put you on a large soft board the size of a garage door (well...almost), so it's fairly easy to master, at least at this level. Surf is usually very small in South Maui, often too small even for beginners, and the wind that arrives late morning and in the afternoon complicates the learning process. Lahaina is a *much* better place to learn. Plus, the South Maui area where they teach—Cove Park because of its fairly reliable surf—has yucky water. (See page 160 for more on that.)

In Lahaina try **Goofy Foot Surf School** (244–9283). They're very good teachers and guarantee that you'll ride a wave or it's free. Two-hour lessons are $55 per person for groups of 5, $125 for a private lesson, $200 for a couple. By the way, a goofy footer is a person (in this case the owner) who surfs with his *right* foot forward instead of the usual left. Pretty goofy, huh? Also consider **Surf Dog Maui** (250–7873). Smaller groups; they, too, do a good job.

A Punalau goofy foot grommet shreds one cherry bugga with Moloka'i behind 'im—dude.

If you're in Kihei and don't want to drive to Lahaina, try **Big Kahuna** (875–6395). $55 for two hours.

If you're experienced, West Maui has easily accessible water, so you may want to simply drive along and look for the kind of waves that work best for you since it's very swell-direction dependent. Launiupoko State Park south of the 18 mile marker often has a good break, kind of far out. The area south of the 19 mile marker can also be good.

Lahaina Harbor has a very dependable break, even in fairly low surf.

Honolua Bay is one of the best sites—if you know what you're doing.

One site that's received national attention in the last few years is **Jaws**. An unusual formation below the surface kicks in when the surf gets bigger than 15 feet (which happens about a dozen times a year in the winter). Then the waves become magnified and form a curved shape. They have been known to reach 70 feet here. Only a handful of experts can surf Jaws (using Jet Skis to tow them out and save their bacon when needed). Less than 15-foot surf means zippo is happening. (We're assuming you only want to *watch* at Jaws.) If the surf is pounding, the most direct route from Hwy 36 is Hahana Road (between the 13 and 14 mile markers). Go to the left on Hahana after the fork, and take the dirt road at the end of Hahana. It's along a gulch (there will be trees and such along your right). If it's real dry, a regular car *may* make it, but probably only 4WDs should try. If wet, consider one of the other roads amongst the pineapple fields. (See map on page 117.) It's private land, so ML&P may opt to close the road.

The best surf shops are in Kahului. They include **Second Wind** (877–7467), **Hi-Tech** (877–2111) and **Extreme Sports** (871–7954). In Lahaina, try **Honolua Surf Co.** (661–8848) or their Kihei shop (874–0999).

By the way, a collection of surfers is known in surfing lingo here as a *quiver.*

And a little kid surfer who doesn't have a job or car yet is called a *grommet*. Just thought you'd like to know.

Lest you think of yourself as da best island surfer consider this: Hawaiian legend states that Chief Kihapiilani once surfed a wave from Maui to Moloka'i. He was said to have been adorned with leis, and that no surf spray was found on the flowers. *(Hey, we don't make up the legends, we just report them.)*

Maui is the undisputed whale watching capital of Hawai'i. The shallow waters between islands here is the whales' preferred birthing area. Few industries in Hawai'i bring as much shameless phony advertising as whale watching. Computers allow fake scenes with relative ease. (For the record, we don't use computers to doctor our photos.) Some show whales leaping so close to boats you think they're going to get swamped. Just so you know, boats are forbidden by federal law from getting closer than 100 yards. The fine for violating a whale's personal space is obscene. Whales are allowed to initiate closer contact (and they're rarely fined), but in general, count on staying a football field away. That's OK, because these oversized buggas are so big that at that distance they're still incredibly impressive.

Though they're not the only whales here, humpbacks are the stars of whale watching. They work in Alaska in the summer, building up fat, then vacation here from December to March or April where the females bear their young and the males sing the blues. More than 1,000 whales come to the islands each year, and the mothers and calves stay close to shore. Only the males sing, and they all sing the same song, usually with their head pointed down. No air bubbles come out while singing, and scientists aren't sure how they do it. Humpbacks don't eat while they're here and may lose ⅓ of their body weight during their stay in Hawai'i. (I doubt that very many *human* visitors can make that claim.)

There's no question that the whale watching varies from year to year. Some years the humpbacks are boisterous and raising hell, constantly breaching, blowing and generally having a good time. Other years they seem strangely subdued, as if hung over from their Alaska trip. What's really going on is that some years Maui's whales visit other Hawaiian islands. Perhaps whales, too, want to avoid getting into a rut.

See OCEAN TOURS on page 206 for a description of the different boats. The best whale watching company, not surprising, is **Pacific Whale Foundation** (879–8811). After all, this is their passion. It's $21 or $31 for a 2-hour trip. Their knowledge is phenomenal, and the trips are fun. They even have hydrophones to listen to the beasts. Of their different boats, the Ocean Spirit is better than the Pacific Whale.

Others to consider are **Maka Kai, Blue Water** (bumpy but fast) or **Maui Princess** (big and slow but stable).

Most whale watching trips are 2 hours and most charge around $30. Bring binoculars if you have them.

From land, good places to spot whales are from the top of Pu'u Ola'i in South Maui (see HIKING), the Scenic Lookout between the 8 and 9 mile markers or the light station at McGregor Point between the 7 and 8 mile markers, both on Hwy 30 past Ma'alaea.

Hard-core windsurfers, you have arrived. You've reached the promised land at Hoʻokipa.

#

Windsurfing is the result of taking a surfboard and attaching a sail to it. When properly instructed, you can zip along faster than the wind. It's a first class adrenaline charge.

No matter where you go in the world, if you ask people where the best windsurfing on the planet is, Maui is nearly always rated as the best. That's because of an accident of geography. Our amazingly consistant trade winds from the northeast are speeded up near Kahului by the venturi effect between the two mountains, so it's always windier there than the general trade speed. The shoreline orientation means the wind is usually along the shore to slightly onshore and parallel to the wave direction. Perfect!

By common agreement, no shortboard windsurfing (meaning everyone who's not a beginner) can windsurf before 11 a.m. (Surfers get to use the waves up till then.) This is strictly enforced by local residents. Also, if you're interested in advanced lessons or simply renting your gear, local regs state that companies aren't allowed to deliver. You'll have to bring the gear yourself. (Beginners on longboards are exempt from the delivery rule and the 11 a.m. rule because winds after 11 are considered to difficult for learners.) Unless you're advanced, don't try to windsurf at Hoʻokipa, the Mecca of windsurf spots. Local users won't allow beginners at the sacred spot, and there is no shortage of young toughs there to enforce the ban on novices. Beginners, instead, will find Kanaha Beach near Kahului Airport the best place to learn.

A 2½ hour lesson is about $70 per person with 3 people per class. During that time you'll actually windsurf, though tacking and jibing (changing directions by heading into or away from the wind) may elude you. In general, it's a hard sport to master at the beginning, and you should expect to fall in the water 70 or so times during your lesson, so don't be discouraged if you're not streaking like the wind gods you see around the island. (Falling's not so bad; in fact, you'll probably get real good at it.) Shorter and slimmer people seem to learn their board balance more quickly. During your lesson, don't be shy about telling your instructor to show you *exactly* what you're doing wrong.

The companies we've had good luck with are HST (871–5423) and **Action Sports** (283–7913). Also giving lessons is **Second Wind** (877–7467) and **Extreme Sports** (871–7954). All meet at Kahaha at 9 a.m., but you'll have to go to their nearby offices to pay. (No exchanging money at the beach.)

Maui Ocean Activities (667–1964) has locations at the Grand Wailea in South Maui (mornings only), and the Hyatt and Whalers Village in Ka'anapali. Though conditions aren't as good as Kanaha, if the the surf is high on north facing shores (as happens often in the winter), you're probably better off on the south or west. They give lessons of up to 4 people every hour. For 2½ hours it's $59, a 1½-hour is $49. For the Ka'anapali locations, pick early afternoon.

Wear a T-shirt to keep the mandatory life jacket from rubbing you, and wear reef shoes while boarding. (Most provide.)

KITEBOARDING

Also called kitesurfing, you may not have heard of this. It's a fairly new sport, so we're putting it here. Imagine a modified surfboard, shorter and boxier than a normal board, with fins at both ends and straps for your feet. Then let a special, controllable two-line kite drag you along.

Like windsurfing, you don't have to go the direction the wind takes you, you have control. Despite what some instructors tell you when they want to sign you up, it's harder to learn than windsurfing. But *oh,* what fun it is! More fun than windsurfing, if you can get over the steeper learning curve. One way you can prepare before you get here is to buy a two-string kite and master it so that you can instinctively maneuver the kite. It's not that hard, but it helps if you can steer the kite without thinking.

The best place to learn is **Kiteboarding School of Maui** (873–0015) in Kahului. Each 2-hour lesson is $75, and you probably won't be boarding until the third lesson. They also have 3-hour private lessons for $80 per hour, which is overpriced. The first 2-hour lesson is learning to operate the kite (which is a hoot). Lesson two is called body dragging. Though it sounds like something they do to you if your credit card is declined, it's actually when you let the kite drag you through the ocean while you manipulate it. Next comes the good part—*riding the board.*

Action Sports Maui (283–7913) also gives lessons, though we don't recommend them. Our problem with them is that when we asked them if kiteboarding is easier to learn than windsurfing, they soothingly assured us it is and that most will be boarding at the end of the 3-hour lesson. (Which is laughable.) Perhaps that's to help justify their breathtakingly expensive rates of $180 for 3 hours (which we predict will come down soon).

In fact, because it's so new, we expect many changes, including more people giving lessons, and maybe cheaper prices.

If you want to *watch* kiteboarding, head over to Kanaha in Kahului. Kiteboarders use the west (left) end.

One of many coves hidden along the north shore of La Pérouse Bay.

Some of the activities described below are for the serious adventurer. They can be experiences of a lifetime. We are assuming that if you consider any of them that you are a person of sound judgment, capable of assessing risks. All adventures carry risks of one kind or another. Our descriptions below do not attempt to convey all risks associated with an activity. These activities are not for everyone. Good preparation is essential. In the end, it comes down to your own good judgment.

LA PÉROUSE BAY LAVA/SNORKEL/HIKE

La Pérouse is known around the island as the end of the road. This is as far south as you can go by car in South Maui. Some people also know that La Pérouse is where they stand a good chance of seeing dolphins in the morning. But the one thing people *don't* know about La Pérouse is that the north end of the bay has some of the best hiking in South Maui, as well as some of the

best snorkeling on Maui. (Granted South Maui is not renowned for its hiking. It's like being the best hockey player in all of Peru.) The snorkeling spots that most people use at La Pérouse are terrible. You need to know *where* to go.

The catch is that you have to hike to it, and the trail is on lava (which is sharp). Also, if you want to make a loop hike out of it (not come back the same way), you'll have to make your own way through about 400 yards of *raw* lava. (You don't *have* to make it a loop.) But the exploration possibilities along this forgotten part of the coast are exciting.

La Pérouse Bay was formed when lava erupted from a vent just up the mountain around 1790, creating Cape Kina'u. All of the land around the cape is young. The shoreline here is starkly beautiful. The protected coves, the windblown bay, the views up the mountain, the lack of crowds, the odds of seeing dolphins dancing in the bay and the waters bursting with fish make this one of our favorite areas in South Maui.

See map on page 135. You start just before the end of Makena Alanui Road, 2/10 mile before the road's end you'll see a turnout on the mauka (mountain) side and a trail on the ocean side marked by a sign facing south. It passes through sand along a barbed wire fence at first, behind the enviously located Carter Estate. This sand *used* to be the shoreline beach...before the 1790 lava flow cut it off and pushed the shoreline further out. The lava drooled down the mountain, ebbed up against the hill on the mauka side of the highway and flowed around it, creating the pointed shape of old land that you're now passing through. (The kiawe trees—mesquite— were brought in during the 1800s.) Once the sand ends, you have two options. You can continue straight ahead a little more than 1/2 mile through the lava field to the shoreline where snorkeling awaits, or veer to the left and take the less worn trail along the shoreline for some truly *great* snorkeling and magnificent views.

Assuming you opt for the shoreline trail, it comes to the bay backed by the estate, then wanders southwest along the shore, becoming somewhat vague in spots. The fish in the cove near the estate seem to love jumping out of the water, watch for them. You may see a few wasps in the area, but we've never had any problem with them. Lest you be confused by the PRIVATE PROPERTY signs, the trail at the estate's cove is on public land; it's only toward the estate that the the land is private. The next cove has somewhat cloudy water, but views from there are good. Look up the mountain and notice all those hills. Those are volcanic vents sprinkled up the hill that you probably never noticed from other perspectives. Each hill is from a separate eruption.

Staying along the shoreline, the next cove sometimes has some of the densest fish counts we've seen on Maui. You'll know you're at the right cove because there's a sign driven into the lava out on the left point of the bay aimed at kayakers. The sheer variety of fish here is dizzying and their numbers sometimes unrivaled. The quantity varies with the tides, seasons and how often some local residents come out to illegally fish in this reserve. But when conditions are right, we'd be hard pressed to think of another place in all Maui that's as fish-rich as this cove. One reason for the high fish count is that there isn't a tradition of fish-feeding here. So please, please don't start the precedent. Fish-feeding results in a few more aggressive species multiplying and driving out the meeker fish, dwindling the variety to a few audacious species. There's not much coral here—the land is too young. If you're coming out here early, as we recommend, wait to put on your sunscreen until after you've been in the water.

After this cove, more delightful coves present themselves, protected from the white, choppy water of La Pérouse Bay. A pair of inland ponds (cut off from the ocean) are lined with a white substance that looks like sand...but that ain't no sand. It's a phenomenon we call lava field quicksand, which doesn't occur too often, but we can tell you from experience that you don't want to go swimming in it. In fact, any inland pool that is completely cut off from the ocean is off-limits to swimming. They are fed from water seeping through the porous lava rock and are too fragile to accommodate recreational swimmers.

Farther along, past the golden pool, is another snorkel area open to the ocean. Here, too, you'll find a dazzling array of fish. Though not quite as dense as the last cove, the undulating underwater topography is even more beautiful than the first cove. The waters outside the cove and in the finger of water on the left side, are also loaded with fish, but currents there can be tricky. Best to stay in the cove on the right unless it's real calm.

The trail fades for a hundred feet or so past this cove. Regain it up the small lava hill just past the last small clear pool. The next cove is the largest yet. Among the few locals who are aware of it, it's known as the **Aquarium,** and it doesn't disappoint. It's a fairly large area to roam, and the cove and surrounding shoreline is usually protected from the wind by a lava embankment. Fish, eels and octopus are common here. Access is a little awkward since the trail doesn't quite go all the way to the shoreline. You'll have to scramble over raw lava for a few dozen feet. Once you've snorkeled, either turn around here, or, if you want to make a loop, you'll have to go in a direction parallel to the shoreline for 400 or so yards. It's tough terrain, and you'll probably take the occasion to curse us once or twice. Take your time and be careful on the sharp lava. See map on page 135 for orientation.

After your trek through raw lava hell, you'll come to two large ponds—one by the shoreline, the other inland. The ocean off the shoreline pond offers good snorkeling, but not as good as what you've seen so far. The trail back to your car is on the far side of the inland pond and will seem like a highway compared to the last 400 yards. The inland pond is golden-coated and surrounded by vegetation and a smattering of seabirds trolling for grubs in the gooey bottom. It's hard to believe that this oasis of life has erupted from the sterile lava over the span of

a mere two centuries. Footprints near the shoreline can last for years, so don't venture beyond the surrounding rock.

Some Basics

Like everything at or near La Pérouse, the earlier you do this hike/snorkel the better. We like to start hiking at 7:30 a.m. or 8 a.m. That way we avoid the winds that kick up in the late morning and afternoon, and we avoid the hot sun on this dark lava field. Afternoons can be blustery, possibly even knocking you over on the rocks.

You'll also want to bring hiking shoes or boots; lava is murder on footwear. If you tend to be skittish while hiking, not as confident in your footing, some cheap garden gloves for grabbing the lava might come in handy. All told, you can spend anywhere from from 1 hour to 4 hours on this hike, depending on how long and often you snorkel, and if you make a loop of it. Though we usually use hiking sticks, we don't use them here as the lava tends to chew up the tips.

THE FOUR FALLS OF NA'ILI'ILI-HAELE

Quite a mouthful. But imagine *four* waterfalls, one right after another, in a beautiful setting, and all relatively near the high- way. It's the kind of scene most people dream of.

First things first. The trail is on EMI land. (See page 76 for more on that.) Unlike most land EMI uses, this parcel

Na'ili'ili-haele Falls Map

Vague

Main Trail

0 Feet   1,000

Falls

© 2000 Wizard Publications

This hiker (pictured at the bottom of the falls) reached the forth, and best, falls at Na'ili'ili-haele. It's not too far, but it does include overcoming a hurdle. (Literally.)

boulder-hop across—IMPORTANT!—follow the trail as it hugs the bank upstream to the left. Don't take one of the false trails heading up the hill. A downed tree fools you into thinking the trail doesn't hug the stream bank, but it opens up afterward. Go *through* the tree.

Fairly soon an *apparent* spur trail leads to the first waterfall (which you'll hear). Take the spur, as the main trail will only peter out and lead you to impenetrably hau bush. The 15-foot falls are nice but a bit too small. Oh, my, we're getting spoiled. Cross the stream (boulder hop again) and the trail continues on the other (east) side. Up through the bamboo (with a few awkward spots) and you'll soon come to waterfall #2. This is as far as many will go. Falls #2 has most of the ingredients people want. Very pretty with a nice swimming pool, rounded pebble shore with sun and shade. You may find yourself falling asleep to the sound of the water.

One of the things that separates a hike from an adventure is uncertainty of outcome. So it is here. On the left side of the falls, a trail leads up to...a dilemma. A fairly sheer 12-foot rock face is in your way. There are two more falls ahead. At press time there was a thick rope (which we don't vouch for) to assist your climb, but it's not easy. And coming back down isn't much fun either.

they actually own. (Most of the rest is leased from the state.) Locals have simply been using the trail for years without a problem, but we'll leave it up to you to secure permission from them. The trailhead is 6/10 mile past the 6 mile marker on Hwy 360 across from some tall Cook Island pines. There's a dirt turnout on the right and a gate.

At first the trail can be slippery and awkward as it goes down through bamboo, across a ditch, through more bamboo, then right to the stream. After you

Most will probably settle for the first two falls. If you don't, here's what to expect.

It has probably taken you 30 minutes to get to falls #2. After overcoming the rock, you'll soon come to a long pool. A trail on the right side through the wild ginger helps, but eventually you'll have to get in the water and swim 100 or so feet up the pool. (Have I lost you yet?) Then you'll scale a man-high waterfall (#3), walk around the bend, and claim your prize: a gorgeous waterfall, at least 35 feet high (maybe more) in a drop-dead gorgeous scene. It's official. You have now arrived at paradise.

Now, that's a lot to go through to get to a waterfall, even a beautiful one. Why do it? Because it's a lot to go through, and it rewards you with a beautiful waterfall. That's it. Nothing deeper than that. Just an adventure you never would have had back home.

In case you're wondering, *yes,* there are more waterfalls past #4. And *no,* you'll never see them. It would be crazy to scale falls #4. Don't even think about it.

Reef shoes or tabis are a big help for the last part of the journey. If you want to take a photo of falls #4, either get a waterproof bag, waterproof camera, or hold your camera high while swimming the length of the natural pool. (Hard to do.) Also, if you don't want to start the hike at the gate mentioned previously, you can start at the pullout ³⁄₁₀ mile after the 6 mile marker and follow the stream. But this is much more difficult, and the first part of that trail is harder to follow.

MOUNTAIN BIKE HALEAKALA'S SPINE

OK, so everyone's heard of the Haleakala Downhill bike ride mentioned on page 174. But few are aware of this—There's a road called Skyline that meanders down the *other* side of the volcano, and it makes an incredible downhill *mountain bike* ride. After Skyline's downhill trek you have 2 miles of relatively flat dirt road, then almost 6 miles of paved downhill yee-haw riding. Best of all, there are no commercial operators clogging the roads.

Map labels:

21

Summit 10,023'

Science City

Gate

N E W S

Skyline Trail (Closed 4WD Road)

7,800'

9,000'

8,000'

Waipoli Rd

Waiakoa Trail (1.2)

Gate

8,000'

Kahua Road

Gate

6,800'

Mamane (1.1)

Gate

0   1 MILE

Boundary (4)

5,600'   Waiohuli

7,200'

∿ Foot Trails
∴ Unpaved Roads
∿ Contour Lines = 40 ft

Redwood (1.7)

Polipoli Trail (.6)—*Lengths are in miles*

Tie

Parking (6,160')

Haleakala Ridge Trail (1.6)

5,300'   Plum Trail (1.7)

5,900'

© 2000 Wizard Publications

Here's the deal. To do this you'll probably need two cars—one to leave at the end of Waipoli Road, the other to take you and your bikes to the summit of Haleakala. You'll probably find that renting a cheap-o car for a day is about the same price as renting a mountain bike. Leave the car and a bike rack (which you get when you rent the mountain bikes) at Waipoli and Hwy 377 (the upper highway—see map on page 117), then head to the summit (not the upper visitor center).

Once at the top, ride your bikes down the short road, hang a right (the 21 mile marker is there) and at the next intersection stay to the left to get to Skyline Road. (If the nasty government sign bothers you, see page 127 for an explanation.) Skyline is just over a mile downhill from the summit.

The spine of Haleakala with its chain of craters makes a glorious mountain bike ride. All downhill without the crowds.

Once on Skyline (marked by a gate) you'll hate what you see. The first mile is a pretty ugly surface of loose lava rocks, and you'll be forgiven if you want to walk your bike on parts of it. It's an easy walk and the views are awesome. After a mile the road gets smoother, though it's always on a loose surface, so don't get too crazy. Avoid locking your front tire, or it will wash out. The road continues to improve the lower you get, and the riding gets more fun since you're a bit less worried about your traction. A gate at 3½

miles into the trail is easy to ride around.

Watch for the **Mamane Trailhead** at almost 4½ miles into Skyline; it's on the right and easy to miss. This is perhaps the best part of the ride. It's just over a mile on a smooth, but narrow trail with killer views, and it seems tailor-made for mountain biking. The intersection of Mamane and Waiohuli is marked by a large lava pit crater. This was an eruption vent, where lava gurgled down the mountain. Stop and poke around for a minute. Also, it makes an ideal shelter if it starts raining.

The short trail segment from the

Mamane/Waiohuli intersection to Waipoli Road is the steepest, and you may want to walk the bike over part of it.

Once on Waipoli Road, the free ride is over. It's 2 miles, mostly flat but with a little uphill, to the paved part of Waipoli Road. Raise the seat and take it slow. Once on the pavement, the 1½-lane road is a delightful, extremely winding downhill joyride. Keep the speed down, and watch for cars on this sparsely driven road. All told you rode almost 16 miles and lost nearly 7,000 feet!

Some tips...

You'll probably want to lower your seat *a lot* for the downhill part for more comfort, stability and a lower center of gravity. It also allows you to use your legs more to keep some weight off your 'okole on the bumpy parts. Rent a bike with front shocks (for about $30). Rear shocks, too, if your tush is tender.

Some may not like the narrow Mamane section. They (and those who miss it) can continue on Skyline where it will wrap around to Waipoli. Add 2 miles of pedaling if you do it this way.

This adventure will take most of the day if you include the shuttling. A good time frame is to pick up the car in Kahului, pick up the bikes at around 9 a.m. (we use **Haleakala Bike** 575-9575 in Ha'iku because they are a good shop and conveniently located for this). Then head to Waipoli to leave the car.

If you feel guilty about all that downhill riding, you can always take the Waiakoa Trail after Mamane for a 1,200-foot climb before rejoining Waipoli Road. (But you're probably not feeling *that* guilty.)

If you've never mountain biked before, yes, you probably can do this. We've taken a novice and she loved it, but she rode *nice and slow* and walked when she

felt uncomfortable. Wear long pants and a jacket and bring a tire patch kit. Sure, the riding surface is harder than the traditional downhill ride, but you go at your own pace, which is a big deal for safety.

HIKE TO THE HEART OF AN ERUPTION

Here's another example of uncertainty of outcome. You're either going to love this hike or hate it badly.

Maui's last eruption was around 1790 and the vent where most of the lava came from, called Kalua o Lapa, can actually be visited. The problem is that, although there is a trail most of the way, at some point you'll have to make your way through the lava field on your own. Though the lava near the vent isn't nearly as difficult to walk through as the lava near the highway, it's still a difficult surface to trek through.

Rather than make a traditional map of the hike, we are including a marked aerial photo to use in navigating your way. Use it to orient yourself relative to hills, various patches of vegetation in the lava field and the vent itself.

You'll start near a telephone pole on the mauka (mountain) side of the Makena Alanui Road. It's ¹⁄₁₀–²⁄₁₀ mile before the La Pérouse Monument at the end of the road, almost as far south as you can go in south Maui. (See map on page 135.) Walk through the forest for a few dozen feet and on a faint lava trail directly toward the forest-covered hill in front of you. The trail vaguely skirts the boundary between the vegetated hill and the lava field, around to the left for a few minutes, until a break in a lava wall on the left signals the start of the actual trail.

The trail is made up of smaller pieces of lava. Your destination, the lava vent, is easily discernable as a charred-looking hill with a deep gash down the center.

It's simply the most recent of many similar vents that are studded along the spine of Haleakala, marking the final stage of a dying volcano.

About ⅓ of the way up you come to a fork in the trail; stay on the main one to the right. At another junction, with a quasi-rock wall, take the left fork. At this point, if you turn around you'll notice that this is a four-way junction, with another trail coming up that you didn't see. If you return this way, make sure you take the correct one. (The aerial photo will help clarify this.) Looking back at the sea in the early morning, the normal trade winds should be roughing up the waters in front of and to the left of Kahoʻolawe, leaving the little sliver of Molokini in the calm. As the morning progresses, the choppy water will work its way toward Molokini.

Where a 100-foot long rock wall ends, you should see a trail off to your right; take it. You're heading toward the forest. Once at the forest the difficulty begins. You want to skirt the edge of the forest, veering constantly to your right until you see the vent in front of you. Trail segments disappear in spots and are strong in others. Then you'll come to a series of ribbons of smooth pahoehoe lava meandering through the harsh aʻa lava like natural sidewalks. The pahoehoe starts and stops abruptly, and it's up to you to discover as many segments of it as possible as you make your way through the raw lava field toward the vent above you. Some people wear gloves here to help balance in the lava field. The lava here is hell on shoes. Hiking shoes or boots are *strongly* recommended, as sneakers will get chewed up in no time.

At the base of the hill is a large lava tube

Since part of this hike requires navigating through the lava field, use this photo to orient yourself relative to hills and vegetation patches.

with its ceiling caved in. Don't get too close to the edge. This tube was the volcano's aorta, where most of the vent's lava blood flowed to feed the rest of the flow. If you want to get to the top, walk around to the right of the hill rather than up and over from the bottom. Around the right is a road in the lava that a horseback company uses to bring riders to the vent. (They don't get to see the bottom of the vent the way you did.) The lava flow is conservation area, not private property. The horseback company owns the forest around you, not the flow you're walking through. Even the road on the side of the vent is conservation land, so you're allowed to be there.

Go around back and the short walk from road to the summit is suddenly very windy. You're exposed to the winds that have piling up along the bottom of the island, often venting off right here. The view from the top is striking; just don't get knocked over. Notice the colors of the spatters of lava on top that blobbed out of the vent back in 1790.

Either return the way you came, or, as you return down the short stretch of road, look for a straight-shot trail of grass leading back toward the ocean. It's an old, abandoned 4WD road. It's easier coming back this way than going through the raw lava field again. The trail passes to the right of a rock wall part of the way with occasional vague spots. Small shoots of kiawe trees tend to claw at your legs at times. At this point you'll be amazed at how much better you walk through the lava; your feet have learned what to do. Use the aerial photo to go around to the right of the vegetated hill and back to your car.

Hazards include sharp lava that may shred your shoes, or your 'okole if you fall on it. Winds rock 'n' roll after the early morning burns off, so do this hike early. Navigation can be difficult. The trails are easy to follow, it's just that there are too many at times, and then there are none. The lava is surprising hard on shoes. We've hiked through hundreds of miles of lava on the Big Island but never had our shoes worn as quickly as we did here. All told you're hiking less than 3 miles, but it may seem like more. Your altitude gain to the top of the vent is about 500 feet, gentle most of the way.

DAY TRIP TO MOLOKA'I'S KALAUPAPA

Moloka'i's formerly notorious Kalaupapa leprosy settlement (see page 146 for more) is an isolated peninsula on the island's spectacular north side. Surrounded by sea cliffs thousands of feet high, the views from here, not to mention the incredible history, are available as day trips from Maui. The most popular way is Moloka'i Mule Rides (567–6088) which takes you down a 1,700-foot cliff to the settlement below. Book in advance.

Once at the bottom, Damien Tours (567–6171) are led by the settlement's septuagenarian sheriff who's also a patient, Richard Marks. Marks is a colorful character who will keep you entertained for the 4-hour tour. Bring a lunch. It's $32, which is quite a deal.

Paragon Air (244–3356) has a package from Maui that includes flight, aerial tour of the sea cliffs, lunch and the ground tour for $199. A bit pricey. No one under 16 allowed. Same deal with Air Links (871–7529).

TAKE YOUR OWN BOAT TO MOLOKINI

There are lots of charter boats you can take to Molokini. But what if you want to do things your own way? At press time,

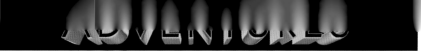

only one company, located in South Maui, rented power boats. Sea Escape (879-3721) at 1979 South Kihei Rd. rents various sized craft. They'll meet you at the Kihei Boat Ramp and set you adrift. Take it virtually any place you want. And with speeds of almost 50 MPH, you can go to a lot of places. The catch? Price. They charge a $325 for the 20-foot boat, $475 for the much nicer 24-foot power cat, plus $20 for gas. That gets you 4 hours. It's an extra $50 per hour after that. That's a *big* chunk of money. If you have 4 to 6 people, it's not quite as painful when you split it. Seeing the area this way is a real hoot. But nobody ever said hoots were cheap. For liability reasons you need to have driven a power boat before.

HIKE IN A LAVA TUBE

Maui Cave Adventures (248-7308) has an interesting tour. Their land has access to Ka'eleku Cave, a lava tube from Hana's past. They take up to 12 about a mile (each way) in the cave. Along the way they explain various geologic features. The cave has some nice formations. This isn't like mainland mineral caves. Lava tubes aren't as colorful. But it's a fascinating journey through a volcanic pipeline. Their enthusiasm and love of the cave is evident throughout. There is an area toward the beginning that requires a radical stoop, but the rest of the 2-hour trip is pretty open. During this time you'll steadily gain around 350 feet. (Humidity is high and the temp is around 69°.) It's a bit more physical than many think, but certainly not a strenuous hike.

Our only quibble is that some of their geology is pretty suspect, and a geology narration is a big part of the trip. Examples: Lava bombs are *not* made of solid iron. The last eruption in the Hana area was 500 years ago, not 10,000. And the Big Island's caves are not too small to explore. Some are taller than this cave and one, near the Volcano Village Post Office, goes for over 30

A skylight interrupts the pitch black darkness of Ka'eleku Cave.

miles. They have clearly had some geologists help them with their narrations but it could use a bit more polishing. This minor criticism aside, the quality of the tour and the company is great. We recommend the $50 2-hour tour over the $100 6-hour tour.

By the way, if you ever wanted to see what utter blackness looks like, the kind where you can't tell whether your eyes are open or closed, ask them to let everyone turn off their lights. That's darkness like you've never seen. Then ask about the time the owner, by himself, had to grope his way back to his pack when his flashlight failed.

COME SAIL AWAY

You want to sail your own boat, but only one thing stops you—*you don't know how to sail!* Well, here's your chance. Maui Sailing Center (879–0178) has a small trimaran (the sailing equivalent of training wheels) that's easy

to sail. Only about 10 minutes of instruction and two can sail away, or at least a couple of miles away. Sailing is gobs of fun. The clean sound of the boat cutting through the water is oh, so memorable. It's $35 per hour or $100 for 4 hours. The second person sits behind and on the hull with their hand on the boom. We've tried to rent the boat in marginal conditions, and they've talked us out of it. That's good; they seem to take safety seriously. They also have Hobie Cats and other sailboats if you have a little experience. North of Kihei at Sugar Beach on the beach behind Margarita's Restaurant. In West Maui, The Hyatt (661–1234 ext. 3290) also rents Hobie Cats for $45 per hour.

TRY A NIGHT OR SCOOTER DIVE

Some people say SCUBA diving is no longer considered an adventure *in and of itself.* Too mainstream, too common. Hmm, fair enough. But these dives are

Cruising in style.

another matter entirely. Night dives are inherently exciting and unpredictable, as your eye follows the powerful light, wondering what it will reveal. You don't see anything that's beyond your beam, and that adds to the fun. You may come across parrotfish wrapped in their natural transparent sleeping bags, moray eels out free swimming, lobsters (known here as bugs) trying to avoid being tomorrow night's special, needlefish strangely attracted to your light, Spanish dancers shaking their maracas, perhaps even a manta ray. You never know what a night dive will bring. Maybe little, maybe the motherload, but a whole different crew works the reef's night shift. The same reef you may have seen yesterday suddenly seems so much more mysterious and thrilling in your light.

See the SCUBA section for recommended dive companies. Most (though not all) do night dives. An example is Maui Dreams (874–5332), which does 1-tank shore dives for $69. Mike Severns (879–6596), Ed Robinson (879–3584) and Extended Horizons (667–0611) have good boat night dives, though not every night. A boat night dive example is Maui Dive Shop (879–3388), which does 2-tank night dives to Molokini and another South Maui spot on Wednesdays for $110.

Scooter Dives aren't your usual cerebral exploration. These dives are an unabashed thrill ride, like an underwater roller coaster. Forget finding exotic fish or colorful reefs. Here, the object is to cruise like you belong here. It wasn't until my first scooter dive that I realized that humans can be incredibly graceful in the water. Usually we look clumsy and awkward. But scooters allow you to maneuver like a sea lion. They are amazingly precise and easy to learn. After just a few minutes

practice, it's easy to skim the bottom, do loops and corkscrews and soar like an underwater eagle. In short, they're a blast!

Keep in mind that having a scooter doesn't eliminate the laws of biology. You're still not supposed to rise faster than a foot a second. And the scooter makes depth changes so effortless and subtle, you'll often find yourself with some pretty ferocious mask squeeze if you're not careful. Here's where the breathing tip mentioned on page 220 really pays off. Because you're almost always exhaling, it provides a safety cushion for the depth changes. But be cautious and aware of what you're doing. If you're doing a loop, don't do it too shallow where the relative differences in depth are more pronounced. Also, you don't burn much air, but should still ask for an 80 tank. And make sure your BC is nice and snug. Things tend to come loose more easily with the increased speed.

Maui Dive Shop (879–3388 in Kihei and 661–5388 in Lahaina) uses scooters that allow an hour dive, same with Ultra Dive (891–1442) at the Renaissance in South Maui. The latter will also take you to 5 Caves/5 Graves, a cool spot. Island Scuba (667–4608) in West Maui at the Marriott and Beach Activities of Maui (662–8207) at the Sheraton also do this. 5-Star has several resort locations. They like to stop often and explore the reef by fin, which isn't as much fun as a nonstop ride. Tell them if you don't want to stop. Expect to pay around $100. Prodiver Maui (875–4004) does scooter dives from a boat for $149. They only take 4 people even though it's a good sized boat. A great company to go with.

HALEAKALA CRATER GRAND LOOP

One of most incredible hikes on the island. It takes you down into glorious

This is one long and winding trail that you don't have to go back up. At least, not this way.

Haleakala Crater, across the floor, then back up via another trail. The views are unspeakably good, and the colors are amazingly varied. All told it's a 13-mile hike. Though you start at 9,800 feet and eventually drop to 6,600 feet, you'll only climb back up 1,400 feet to the 8,000 foot level. Granted, climbing 1,400 feet isn't a picnic, but it's much easier than recapturing the 3,200 feet you lost coming down. See map on page 122.

Doing this hike necessitates leaving a vehicle at the Halemau'u Trailhead between the 14 and 15 mile marker and then starting at the Sliding Sands Trailhead past the 20 mile marker. You can either leave your car at Halemau'u and try to get a ride up or rent an extra cheap-o car for the day. The latter is a sure thing, whereas getting a ride isn't.

Park at the Visitor Center and start at the Sliding Sands Trailhead around the corner. It's downhill virtually the entire way—until you pay the piper during the last 2½ miles. More on that later. On the way down, you may want to take the side trip to **Ka Ku'u o ka 'O'o**. The crater reveals its character only as you continue changing elevations and angles. After the trail levels, descends, then levels out again, you'll take the spur trail (there's a horse hitch at the intersection) to the left, heading north. Looking at the map, you'll want to veer right, then left at the next intersections to visit Kawilinau, formerly the Bottomless Pit. (The map makes this simpler.) See page 126 for more on this pit. Turn left and about 100 yards past the pit is an area called Pele's Paint Pot. Minerals in the rock created this colorful rock canvas.

After the Silversword Loop, our old friend green will start to return as the vegetation increases as you get closer to the mountain and the Ko'olau Gap. Stop and rest at Holua Cabin if you wish, envying the lucky buggers who literally won the lottery for the right to stay there.

In another mile, it will be time to pay your dues. In terms of elevation, you've had it pretty easy for these last 10 miles. Now it's time to sweat. Fortunately, the trail switchbacks are only moderately steep. One of the switchbacks wanders over to the other side of the mountain, giving you a magnificent view (clouds permitting) of the Koʻolau Gap. Make sure to stop many times on the way up to enjoy the incredible views.

A few basics...

Bring *gobs* of water with you. You lose water at a ferocious clip at this altitude. Since the only real climbing is at the end, it's no big a deal to drag more water than you *think* you'll need, *suck 'em up* all day, and pour out the excess before starting the climb. Also, bring a hat and sunblock. You fry fast up here. Rain is possible, especially at the end as you're climbing back up. A light rain jacket is a good idea, especially in the winter. Dress warm for the top and cool for the bottom. You never know what kind of weather you'll encounter on this hike. Hiking sticks can help with all the elevation changes, but the surface will be pretty brutal on the tips.

KAYAK TO AN UNNAMED BEACH

Until this publication, Keawanaku was unnamed and virtually unknown. We discovered this beach while hiking (described on page 201) and quickly realized that it would be a great beach to kayak to.

The key to this adventure is to start *early*. When the winds kick up in the late morning and early afternoon, it becomes one of the windiest places on the island. Fortunately, mornings are usually fairly calm, and once the winds start, they help you somewhat on the way back, with an along the shore then offshore alignment. We put this in ADVENTURES because the winds need to be respected and anticipated. If you don't start early, they could cause problems for you. See KAYAKS on page 205 for more on renting a kayak.

Two kayakers discover Keawanaku, a hidden oasis in a sea of harsh lava.

By their very nature, restaurant reviews are the most subjective part of any guidebook. Nothing strains the credibility of a guidebook more. No matter what we say, if you eat at enough restaurants here, you will eventually have a dining experience directly in conflict with what this book leads you to believe. All it takes is one person to wreck what is usually a good meal. Many of us have had the experience when a friend referred us to a restaurant using reverent terms indicating that they were about to experience dining ecstasy. And, of course, when you go there, the food is awful and the waiter is a jerk. There are many variables involved in getting a good or bad meal. Is the chef new? Was the place sold last month? Was the waitress just released from prison for mauling a customer? We truly hope that our reviews match your experience. If they don't, please let us know.

This DINING section was pretty overwhelming for us. A huge number of choices made it difficult to select which ones to include. (And hey, we can only *eat* so much!) Restaurants come and go, but if there's a place that you *really* loved (and don't forget the ones you *really* hated), please drop us a line at the address or e-mail on page 4.

Unlike some travel writers who announce themselves to restaurants (to cop a free meal, if the truth be told), we always review anonymously and only expose ourselves after a meal (not literally, of course) if we need additional information. By their reviews, many guidebooks lead you to believe that every meal you eat in Hawai'i will be a feast, the best food in the free world. Frankly, that's not our style. Like anywhere else, there's ample opportunity to have lousy food served with a rotten ambiance by uncaring waiters. In the interest of space,

RESTAURANT INDEX

we've left out *some* of the dives. We did, however, leave in enough of these turkeys just to demonstrate that we know we live the real world. Restaurants that stand out from the others in some way are highlighted with our ONO symbol.

For each restaurant, we list the price *per person* you can expect to pay. It ranges from the least expensive entrées alone to the most expensive plus a beverage and usually appetizers. You can spend more if you try, but this is a good guideline. *The price excludes alcoholic beverages since this component of a meal can be so variable.* Obviously, everyone's ordering pattern is different, but we thought that it would be easier to compare various restaurants using dollar amounts than if we used different numbers of dollar signs or drawings of forks or whatever to differentiate prices between various restaurants. All restaurants take credit cards unless otherwise noted. When we mention that prices are reasonable, please take it in context. We mean reasonable *for Hawai'i.* (We *know* you pay less back home.) Food in Hawai'i is expensive, even if it's grown here. (You probably pay less for our fruit on the mainland than *we* do here.)

When we give directions to a restaurant, *mauka side* of highway means "toward the mountain" (or away from the ocean). The shopping centers we mention are on the maps to that area.

The difference between local and Hawaiian food can be difficult to classify. Basically, local food combines Hawaiian, American, Japanese, Chinese, Filipino and several other types and is (not surprisingly) eaten mainly by locals.

Pacific Rim is sort of a fusion of American and various countries around the Pacific, including Asian and Hawaiian. It's a fine (and subjective) line between American and Pacific Rim. We don't have a separate **Seafood** section because nearly every restaurant on Maui serves fish.

Lu'aus, those giant outdoor Hawaiian parties, are described at the end.

When a restaurant requires **resort wear,** that means collared shirts for men (though nice shorts are *usually* OK) and dressy sportswear or dresses for women.

Some restaurants have the annoying and presumptuous habit of including the tip in the bill automatically. Be on the alert for it or you may double-tip. And what if you get horrible service and don't *want* to tip. Then you're left in the awkward position of making them remove it.

Dining at the resorts is expensive, but you probably aren't being gouged as much as you think because their costs are exorbitant. One resort GM we know confided that they had over $7 million in revenue for their food and beverage department in a recent year, but only made $100,000 in profit. (And this was the first year they had ever made *any* profit on food.)

Below are descriptions of various island foods. Not all are Hawaiian, but this might be of assistance if you encounter unfamiliar dishes.

ISLAND FISH

Ahi–Yellowfin tuna; excellent eaten raw as sashimi. (A friend taught us how to paint ahi steaks with mayonnaise, which *completely* burns off when BBQ'd but seals in the moisture. You end up tasting only the moist ocean steak.)

Ahu–Skipjack tuna, heavier than ahi.

A'u–A billfish such as marlin or swordfish; steaks are usually broiled or barbecued; meat is firm and white.

Kumu–Goatfish; firm, white meat. Steamed kumu is an island specialty.

Mahimahi–Dolphinfish (not the mammal!), white, delicate, moist, firm.

Mano–Shark; firm, white meat.

Moonfish/Opah–Mild, firm, pink flesh.

Ono/Wahoo–Moderately coarse, white meat that's very moist and delicious.

Snappers–White, firm, yet tender with a mild flavor. 'Opakapaka, Kalekale, and Onaga are the best.
- **Ehu**–Red snapper
- **Kalekale**–Pink snapper
- **Onaga**–Red snapper
- **'Opakapaka**–Pink snapper; especially good to eat.

Ulua and Papio–Jack fish with white, firm, flaky meat.

Lu'au Foods

Chicken lu'au–Chicken cooked in coconut milk and taro leaves.

Haupia–Coconut milk custard.

Hawaiian sweet potatoes–Purple inside; not as sweet as mainland sweet potatoes but very flavorful.

Kalua pig–Pig cooked in an underground oven called an imu, shredded and mixed with Hawaiian sea salt (outstanding!).

Lomi salmon–Chilled salad consisting of raw, salted salmon, tomatoes and two kinds of onions.

Poi–Steamed taro root pounded into a paste. It's a starch that will take on the taste of other foods mixed with it. Best eaten with kalua pig or fish. Visitors are encouraged to try it at least once so they can badmouth it with authority.

Poke–Raw fish marinated and mixed with seaweed.

Other Island Foods

Apple bananas–A smaller, denser, smoother texture than regular (Williams) bananas.

Barbecue sticks–Teriyaki marinated pork, chicken or beef pieces barbecued and served on bamboo sticks.

Bento–Japanese box lunch.

Breadfruit–Melon-sized starchy fruit; served baked, deep fried, steamed or boiled. Definitely an acquired taste.

Crackseed–Chinese-style spicy preserved fruits and seeds.

Giri giri–Home-made sherbert.

Guava–About the size of an apricot or plum. The inside is full of seeds, so it is rarely eaten raw. Used primarily for juice, jelly or jam.

Hawaiian supersweet corn–The finest corn you ever had, even raw. We'll lie, cheat, steal or maim to get it fresh. Grown in Kula.

Huli huli chicken–Hawaiian BBQ style.

Ka'u oranges–Big Island oranges. Usually, the uglier the orange, the better it tastes.

Kim chee–A Korean relish consisting of pickled cabbage, onions, radishes, garlic and chilies.

Kona coffee–Grown on the Kona coast of the Big Island. Smooth, mild flavor; available everywhere.

Kulolo–Steamed taro pudding.

Laulau–Pork, beef or fish wrapped in taro and ti leaves, then steamed. (You don't eat the ti leaf wrapping.)

Liliko'i–Passion fruit.

Loco moco–Rice, meat patty, egg and gravy.

Lychee–A reddish, woody peel that is discarded for the sweet, white fruit inside. Be careful of the pit. Good, small seed (or chicken-tongue) lychees are so good, they should be illegal.

Macadamia nut–A large, round nut.

Malasada–Portuguese donut dipped in sugar.

Manapua–Steamed or baked bun filled with meat.

Mango–Bright orange fruit with yellow pink skin. Distinct, tasty flavor.

Manju–Cookie filled with a sweet center.

Maui onions–Grown in Kula, some people eat them like apples.

Musubi–Cold steamed rice, sliced Spam rolled in black seaweed wrappers.

'Opihi–Limpets found on ocean rocks. Eaten raw mixed with salt. Texture is similar to clams or mussels.

Papaya–Melon-like, pear-shaped fruit with yellow skin best eaten chilled. Good at breakfast.

Pipi Kaula–Hawaiian-style beef jerky. Excellent when dipped in poi. (Even if you don't like poi, this combo works.)

Plate lunch–An island favorite as an inexpensive, filling lunch. Consists of "two-scoop rice," a scoop of macaroni salad and some type of meat, either beef, chicken or fish. Sometimes called a box lunch. Great for picnics.

Portuguese sausage–Pork sausage, highly seasoned with red pepper.

Pupu–Appetizer, finger foods or snacks.

Saimin–Noodles cooked in either chicken, pork or fish broth. Word is peculiar to Hawai'i. Local Japanese say the dish comes from China. Local Chinese say it comes from Japan.

Shave ice–A block of ice is "shaved" into a ball with flavored syrup poured over the top. Best served with ice cream on the bottom. Very delicious.

Smoothie–Usually papaya, mango, frozen passion fruit and frozen banana, but almost any fruit can be used to make this milkshake-like drink. Add milk for creaminess.

Taro chips–Sliced and deep-fried taro; resembles potato chips.

WEST MAUI AMERICAN (INCLUDES SEAFOOD)

BEACH WALK MARKET & PANTRY 667–1200

Here's the deal. You're out frolicking on Ka'anapali Beach and you get hungry. What's a person to do? You don't want to leave. At the Marriott they have a little place along the shoreline path (they were converting it from a Pizza Hut Express at press time) serving pizza, sandwiches and the like. It wasn't complete when we went to press. **$5–$10.**

BUBBA GUMP SHRIMP CO. 661–3111

ONO Remember the movie *Forrest Gump*, when Bubba describes all the ways you can fix shrimp? Well, the owners of this small chain apparently didn't see it because most of the recipes mentioned in the movie aren't on the menu. But that's OK because this is a really easy place to like. The whole restaurant is based on the movie, and the dishes are named after its characters. Very friendly service (so friendly the waiter may come and sit at your table as he takes your order), fun, loud and over the water. (Waves actually splash under the window tables, if you're lucky enough to get one.) The friendly service can seem a bit unresponsive until you realize that the ping-pong paddle on the table that says, "Stop Forrest Stop" is meant as a signal to the waiter that you want him. (Beats the heck out of the old eye-contact method.) The food is mostly fairly good (certainly not great) with lots of shrimp dishes (obviously!), fish, some steak, burgers and salads. The peel-and-eat shrimpers' net catch makes a good appetizer, and they have some very good fresh fish. Their Medal of Honor Margarita is smokin' good, and the portion is hefty. We only have two complaints: They won't take reservations (and long waits are not uncommon), and they obviously want to turn tables over fast. Don't let them rush you. Eat at *your* pace, not theirs. Overall, a fun atmosphere and acceptable food make a good experience. On Front Street in Lahaina between Lahainaluna and Papalaua. **$15–$25** for dinner. Large gift shop available in case you're worried about not spending enough money there.

Buns of Maui 661–4877

This small shop has utterly delicious cinnamon rolls. The flavor permeates every part of the roll, not just the surface. (Calm down, now.) They also have other effective baked goods and some pretty good breakfast sandwiches. (They need better bagels, though.) Overall, a good place to start the day in Lahaina. In Old Lahaina Center between Papalaua and Lahainaluna. Access from Papalaua. **$2–$5.**

Cheeseburger in Paradise 661–4855

A legendary place in Lahaina, it's fun to try at least once. Sharing a name with a song by Jimmy Buffet (who promptly sued them when he discovered the restaurant), the decor has plenty to keep your eyes busy during your stay. An eclectic assortment of items strewn about, rang-

ing from a shark eating a cheeseburger to odd Hawaiian memorabilia. The food is reasonably good (ironically, the cheeseburgers are merely fine). Try the chili cheese fries (hold the onions) for an appetizer. The Polynesian coconut shrimp are tasty but come with only six shrimp along with a large mound of their delicious fries. Some of their drinks, like the Black Sand Beach, are memorable. All in all, this is the sort of place that will please you a lot the first time and become less pleasant on repeat visits. Service, surprisingly, seems *better* when they are busy (which is often) and diminishes with the crowds. **$5–$10** for breakfast, **$7–$15** for lunch and dinner. Good vegetarian burger selection. On the water on Front Street and Lahainaluna. No reservations.

Coffee Store 669–4170

An acceptable, though not compelling, place to go for your morning coffee. Mediocre baked goods and coffee, often understaffed when busy. In Napili Plaza near 29 mile marker on Hwy 30. Also in Azeka II and Ka'ahumanu Mall.

Dollies Pub and Cafe 669–0266

Average pizza and beer with sandwiches and some pasta. They're too generous with the vast amount of pizza cheese; consider asking them to tone it down. Wish we could say more, but the price isn't too bad. (Well, I guess their bottled beer selection is pretty good.) **$7–$15** for lunch and dinner. In Kahana Manor Shops on Lower Honoapiilani Road just south of Hoohui Street. (See bottom of map on page 53.)

Erik's Seafood Grotto 669–4806

Very pleasing and restful ambiance,

especially the tables near the aquariums. (The railing tables at sunset can be very bright and hot.) Wonderful and eclectic seafood menu with some beef and lamb. Their BBQ shrimp is a death-defying combination of shrimp wrapped in bacon, topped with mozzarella, dipped in BBQ sauce and broiled. (Hey, we never said it was cholesterol-friendly.) Good upstairs views overlooking Moloka'i (you'll have to ignore the powerlines). Salads are pretty plain-Jane, so go for the soups, especially the red clam chowder. We almost gave them an ONO, but all their love and attention seems to go into the entrées, because their accompanying items aren't stellar. **$20–$35.** On Lower Honoapiilani Road north of the road to West Maui Airport (Akahele).

FISH AND GAME BREW AND ROTISSERIE 669-3474

All too often brewpubs suffer from mediocre food, but not here. The food is delicious and well presented. Portions are generous, as well. Service is friendly and fun. The egg rolls are a great appetizer. Good ribs, great black tea duckling. We haven't had a bad meal here yet. They make some pretty good beers—try the sampler. We like the Hefeweizen with a little lemon. Meals are expensive in this area, but given the location and quality, it's not unreasonable (for West Maui, that is). **$5–$8** for breakfast, **$8–$14** for lunch, **$15–$30** (or more) for dinner. Reservations recommended. They seem strangely ill-equipped for breakfast, almost like it was an afterthought. In Kahana Gateway, 27–28 mile marker, Hwy 30.

GARDENIA COURT 669-5656

Located in the Kapalua Bay Hotel, they have breathtaking views with a lawn, palm trees and the shoreline with Moloka'i as the backdrop. Breakfast is OK, but avoid the buffet. Not real good, expensive (almost $20), and their cozy relationship with the birds is a problem. Too many times we've seen birds eating from the buffet table. Seeing mynah birds stealing scrambled eggs from the serving spoon that you just used can definitely ruin your appetite. They also have have birds perched over your table doing…well, what birds tend to do. So pick your table carefully. **$8–$20** for breakfast.

GAZEBO 669-5621

Gazebo benefits greatly from its location. Without it, they probably wouldn't get an ONO. Eating near the shore with wicked ocean, Napili Bay and Moloka'i views for relatively little money (for this area) makes the food and service seem better. They've got a good selection of omelettes, and their signature mac nut pancakes are pretty good. Lunch is burgers, sandwiches and salads. Both are served simultaneously from 7:30–2 p.m., which is handy. They only have 15 tables and fill up easily (they don't take reservations), so you may have to wait. **$5–$10** for breakfast, **$8–$12** for lunch. Park at Napili Shores and walk through the resort.

HARD ROCK CAFÉ 667-7400

Similar to the Hard Rock Cafes on the mainland but with tasty views of the ocean and Lana'i. Rock 'n' roll memorabilia line the walls as music fills the air and music videos provide the eye candy. (The music is sometimes too loud—outdoor tables are quieter but have less ambiance.) The food ranges from pretty good to slightly below average, and the ONO we give applies only if you're in a rockin' mood. They'd never get an ONO based on the food alone. Burgers, salads, sandwiches and smokehouse items, such as ribs (which aren't very good), pig sandwich (which *is* good) and chicken. Most portions are large. Appetizers, such as chicken tenders, sometimes miss their mark by being too tough. Desserts are large and delicious. **$8–$16** for lunch and dinner. In Lahaina Center on Front and Papalaua streets.

HONOLUA STORE 669–6128

Ever wonder where employees in an ultra-expensive resort area eat? Well, for many, it's right here. They get an ONO because of the price alone. Inexpensive food is as scarce in Kapalua as RV parks. Simple, cheap breakfasts. Lunch is burgers, fish and chips, and sandwiches. Service is pretty blank and uncaring; repeat your order several times to be sure you get what you want. But it's the only place in the area where two can eat for $10–$15. On Office Rd near the Ritz. (Quite a contrast.) **$3–$5** for breakfast, **$5–$8** for lunch.

HULA GRILL 667–6636

It's with nervous trepidation that we give them an ono. Food can be good. It can also be awful. For instance, their chicken should be banned from the island. But many other items can be excellent. Their lobster and scallop pot stickers are outrageous, as are their desserts. The ambiance is very nice—next to Ka'anapali Beach with nice water views and great sunsets.

Sandwiches, lots of salads and pizzas for lunch, steak, seafood and pasta for dinner. In Whalers Village in Ka'anapali. **$9–15** for lunch, **$20–$35** for dinner.

HULA HULA CAFE 661–9771

Some good breakfast choices, and they open early (6 a.m.) and serve breakfast till 2 p.m. Good breakfast specials. They mostly have protected outdoor tables. Lunch is sandwiches and burgers (no fries). They tend toward light seasoning in most items, so keep those salt and pepper shakers nearby. Portions are ample. In Wharf Cinema Center south of Dickenson on Front Street. You can park at the lot on Luakini and enter from the back. **$5–$8** for breakfast, **$6–$9** for lunch. Free delivery in Lahaina.

KIMO'S 661–4811

Dreamy location along the water's edge for lunch. Dinner is upstairs and slightly away from the water. (Some of the otherwise excellent dinner views are cut off by the roofline.) Lunch items are hit or miss, but mostly pretty good. Good burgers and bratwurst (need better fries, though). Their Hula Pie for dessert is worth the accolades. At dinner you can eat downstairs (which at night is designated the bar) where some cheaper items are available. Otherwise, dinner is steak and seafood, usually with good results. Kimo's has a good atmosphere and usually good food. **$7–$14** for lunch. **$20–$30** for dinner (except the cheaper burgers). Good place for a sunset cocktail. Try the Mickey Goon. 845 Front St. between Lahainaluna and Papalaua. Reservations recommended for dinner.

LEILANI'S 661–4495

ONO Two totally different menus and two totally different experiences. Downstairs, the Beachside Grill menu is a bargain considering the location and setting vs. the price. Stir fry chicken cashew, BBQ ribs or chicken pizzas are **$10** at the beachside setting. (Killer Hula Pie dessert.) You can order this menu at lunch or dinner. For the regular dinner menu upstairs, it's mostly steak and seafood for **$16–$25**. *Usually* good service and fairly good food, but with a *tasty* view, hence the ONO. In Ka'anapali at Whalers Village.

MOOSE MCGILLYCUDDY'S 667–7758

This is a hopping place at night. Dinner is mostly steak (cow, not moose) and some seafood and is popular with singles looking for…well, what singles are always looking for. Entertainment and dancing at night. Lunch is mostly burgers. Avoid breakfast here unless you have *a lot* of time. Because if it takes 10 minutes for them to acknowledge your existence, 20 minutes to get a table and 25 minutes to get your food, you've donated almost an hour of your morning to the Moose before you even get a chance to eat. And for some reason, people are less willing to wait for breakfast than lunch or dinner. **$5–$10** for breakfast, **$8–$13** for lunch, **$14–$30** for dinner.

PLANTATION HOUSE 669–6299

ONO Tongue-wagging views all the way down the golf course to the ocean and Moloka'i, along with a rich, spacious feel, create an effective ambiance. Service at breakfast and lunch can be a bit pretentious and not as good as at dinner. Breakfast has items such as crabcakes benedict (good) and potato pancakes (avoid). The small lunch menu ranges from ½-pound burgers to vegetable and goat cheese wraps, as well as pasta, and lunch can be excellent. Dinner is mostly steak and seafood. Quality is hit or miss; unusual for a restaurant of this caliber. **$8–$13** for breakfast, **$9–$18** for lunch, **$25–$35** for dinner. Hard to find. Take Hwy 30 north, 1 mile past the Kapalua exit, turn right at the Plantation Golf Course, then left to the clubhouse.

REILLEY'S 667–7477

Relatively good (though dinner is overpriced) steak and seafood overlooking the Ka'anapali Golf Course and the highway. Our first time there the waiter strongly recommended *against* the crab and scallop-stuffed chicken—that's novel. Consider the vegetarian pasta, the prime rib or the seafood fettuccine. Spicy crab cakes are a good appetizer. Their generous and minty Leprechaun Pie makes a good dessert. **$13–$20** for lunch, **$20–$45** for dinner. Located on Ka'anapali Parkway near Hwy 30.

SMOKEHOUSE BBQ 667–7005

It's a little different than you may think. From the outside it looks like one of those places that has been here forever so it *must* have good BBQ. Unfortunately, the food tastes like the building looks. Flavors are subtle to a fault. It's not Texan, but rather a blend of Texan and Asian and doesn't work well for us. But at least they have an excellent location—some tables are only 10 feet from the water—and the outdoor tables are relaxing. (Indoor table ambiance is sort of ocean-side watering hole.) It's at 1307 Front St., north of busy downtown Lahaina. Ribs, BBQ turkey (which doesn't have a BBQ taste to us), steak, fish, sausage and burgers. A rack of ribs is a pricey $20 at dinner. $7–$10 for lunch, $15–$30 for dinner.

SWISS CAFÉ 661-6776

Basically a sandwich shop with some pizza (so we put them under American). The sandwiches are pretty good. Cold sandwiches, such as roast beef or turkey, hot sandwiches, such as Italian Boboli or turkey broccoli melt, and veggie sandwiches, such as the Mexican garden or the avocado. The pizzas are cheap tasting and don't meet the standard the sandwiches do. Breakfast is mostly bagels, muffins or the egg croissant. $6–$10 for lunch and early dinner. $2–$6 for breakfast. At 640 Front St. in Lahaina between Dickenson and Prison next to the Burger King and across from the Banyan Tree Park.

TERRACE RESTAURANT 669-5399

Overlooking the pool and ocean, the price is cheaper because you can only get to the place by slithering by the cage containing the wild timeshare salesmen. Be careful—they're hungry and persuasive. The food is adequate, nothing more, but it won't hurt your wallet as much as others in the area. Typical breakfast items, burgers, sandwiches and salads for lunch, as well as a small dinner menu with fish and steak. Service is not so hot, but then neither were the eggs. $5–$10 for breakfast and lunch, $8–$20 for dinner. In the Sands of Kahana resort on Lower Honoapiilani Road just south of Hoohui Road south of Kapalua.

WHALERS VILLAGE FOOD COURT

ONO We certainly didn't give them an ONO because of the food. Five stalls with average food court options. (Though the Pizza Paradiso is better here than their full restaurant in Honokowai.) Our happiness stems from the fact that the court offers some of the few cheap meals in Ka'anapali, and food always tastes better when you've just walked in off the beach. Even McDonald's tastes good when there's sand stuck to your feet. In Whalers Village Shopping Center next to Ka'anapali Beach.

WOODY'S OCEANFRONT GRILL 661-8788

Great over-water location. Burgers, sandwiches, ribs, fish and salads for lunch; steak, chicken and seafood for dinner. Fairly good food, average service. An acceptable place for a meal, especially at the outdoor tables near the railing. $8–$20 for lunch, $20–$30 for dinner On Front Street in Lahaina between Lahainaluna and Papalaua.

WEST MAUI CHINESE

CHINA BOAT 669-5089

ONO Food quality is good enough to merit an ONO, but the service needs to improve as they are not attentive enough, so the ONO is marginal. Tell them to spice up your food and they will *fully* comply. $8–$15 for lunch, $12–$25 for dinner. Full bar. Instead of Chinese music, you're more likely to hear Pavarotti. From Honoapiilani Hwy (30) take the road from the West Maui Airport (Akahele) to the shore, then turn right. It will eventually be on the mauka (mountain) side.

Orient Express 669-8077

A mix of Thai and Chinese dishes, plus Harry's Sushi Bar inside. With all that, odds are something will please the Asian food lover. At Napili Shores Resort on Lower Honoapiilani Road north of Napilihau Road. (See map on page 53.) Dinner only; it's *roughly* $15–$30 (hard to predict here).

West Maui Local

Honokowai Okazuya Deli 665-0512

How refreshing! A place in northern West Maui that serves good food but doesn't feel the need to soak you. Ambiance is...well, none, actually. Best to get it to go. The owner is a former executive chef for Mama's Fish House and the Kea Lani, so they know how to cook here. But instead of opening another highbrow (and high cost) restaurant, they've channeled their energies toward the lower-end market. The menu is diverse enough to eat here repeatedly. Teriyaki steak, spaghetti and sausage, fresh fish, kung pao chicken, steamed tofu—the menu is all over the place and we weren't sure how to classify them. We like to take food over to nearby Honokowai Beach Park if it's not too windy. (There are a few stools inside, but it's hot.) $6–$10 for lunch and dinner. Located on Lower Honoapiilani Road just north of Honokowai Beach in the AAAAA Rent-A-Space Mall.

Noodle Cafe 661-1661

A decent selection of sushi, ramen, saimin, teriyaki beef sandwiches and other Asian/local dishes. It's not that the food is great, but it's pretty good and the price is more than reasonable for Lahaina. In Lahaina Center on Front Street and Papalaua. $6–$10 per person.

West Maui French

Chez Paul 661-3843

This small and quaint restaurant (just over a dozen tables) is out in remote Olowalu. (In fact, this pretty much *is* the town.) So how is it they have survived this seemingly poor location since the '60s? Good food that's beautifully presented and good service. Though portions are small quality of their French entrées is outrageous. Check your credit card limit before you arrive, because you can either spend *a lot* or *a fortune*. $30–$50 *perhaps,* but the beluga caviar hors d'oeuvre by itself is *$66.* Are you getting the picture? At the 15 mile marker on Hwy 30. Reservations strongly recommended.

West Maui Italian

BJ's Chicago Pizzeria 661-0700

Good views overlooking the harbor if you get a table on the ocean side. Chicago-style deep dish pizzas have super-thick crusts that are surprisingly light. They also have some pastas and sandwiches. Pizzas take a while and when they come, you're first comment to the waiter is, "I didn't order it with tomatoes." They know. All pizzas come with very light sauce and stewed tomatoes. (They don't usually tell you.) They'll serve it without the tomatoes and with more substantial sauce (which is better) if you request. For some reason decent pizza is hard to find on Maui, and BJ's is probably as good as it gets here.

Nice selection of beers and some wines. Their menu has some bizarre statements on it, such as that Captain Cook discovered Lahaina in 1792. (He never visited Lahaina, and he had been dead for 13 years by 1792.) It also says that today, Lahaina is "much the same as Cook found it." (Yeah, and parking was a bugga back then, too.) **$9–$18** for lunch and dinner. At 730 Front St.

GABBY'S PIZZERIA & DELI 661–8112

Located in the 505 Front Street shopping center, they have acceptable pizza, pasta and some sandwiches. It'll do in a pinch, but you probably won't go out of your way for them. **$5–$15** for lunch and dinner.

LONGHI'S 667–2288

ono Longhi's is an institution in Lahaina. Opened in 1976, the upscale Italian/seafood food is almost always excellent and is a favorite with many locals and visitors. We could have put them in either the American or Italian category (they call it Mediterranean). Their seafood is consistently great. They do wonderful things with lobster, shrimp and fresh fish. Try the ahi torino; it's marinated in olive oil, garlic and basil, rolled in bread crumbs and sprinkled with mac nuts, then sautéed. Their steak Longhi is lightly marinated, grilled, sliced and then surrounded with basil sautéed in butter. *Very* good. The pasta is also excellent. Our only real gripe about Longhi's is that they don't give you a menu. They ask you what you are interested in and tell you what they have in that category. (And they don't always volunteer the price.) Maybe we're just more visual people, but we like to see things in in front of us before we decide. (They post a menu downstairs that you may want to look at before you're seated.) Parking can be difficult there at night, but they have free valet parking for dinner. Extensive wine list. Dinner is expensive (and everything is a la carte) at **$20–$60** per person, **$10–$20** for lunch. On 888 Front St. at Papalaua. Reservations recommended.

LUIGI'S 661–3160

Pizza, pasta, veal, seafood, scampi and steak. Mediocre quality. Not horrible, but you probably won't return. The outdoor tables on most days are very windy—bring a staple gun to keep your personal items from blowing away. **$15–$25** for dinner, some decent early bird specials. **$6-12** for breakfast. Watch for the automatic tip in your bill and be prepared for some stink eye if the waiter thinks you're staying too long. On Ka'anapali Parkway near Hwy 30.

PIZZA PARADISO 669–2929 IN HONOKOWAI 667–0333 IN WHALERS VILLAGE

As pizza lovers, we are sad to report that we haven't found any truly great pizza on Maui. The hype is pretty big at Pizza Paradiso. Signs and ads proclaim they are were voted "best pizza on Maui" and reviews from a guidebook saying it was the "best pizza I ever had." After repeatedly eating here, we can't help but wonder—were they eating in the same place? In fairness, the crust is fairly good and unusual: spongy but effective. But the pizza is lifeless and tasteless, as well as overpriced. It's on par with a really good frozen pizza, but does that impress you? Even if you order by the slice, four slices and two sodas for $17 is *steep.* (The zucchini crostini, by the way, is *ter-*

rible.) Desserts are either the tasty but expensive home-made tiramisu, mediocre Roselani ice cream or old Costco bakery items. **$5–$13**. Two locations, Honokowai Marketplace (between 25 and 26 mile marker on Hwy 30) or Whalers Village on Ka'anapali Parkway in Ka'anapali. The Whalers Village location, though only a stand, is better, and the pizza is greatly enhanced by the fact that you could have walked there from Ka'anapali Beach.

WEST MAUI MEXICAN

COMPADRES 661–7189
Pretty good food, though a tad pricey. Good chips and salsa. Six different kinds of enchiladas. Usually reasonable specials Tue. and Wed., ample portion sizes. Tasty (though expensive) margaritas. Try the Banana Chingalinga dessert—big enough for two. Almost gave them an ONO. In Lahaina Cannery, Front Street and Kapunakea (north of where the Lahaina map ends). **$6–$9** for breakfast, **$7–$20** for lunch, **$10–$20** for dinner.

NACHOS GRANDE 662–0890
It's a bit disheveled inside. Food is like a slightly elevated Taco Bell with a bar. Cheap ingredients sometimes combined reasonably well, sometimes not. But price isn't bad. In Honokowai Marketplace south of the 26 mile marker on Hwy 30. **$5–$10** for lunch and dinner.

WEST MAUI PACIFIC RIM (INCLUDES SEAFOOD)

A PACIFIC CAFE
667–2800 IN HONOKOWAI, 879–0069 IN KIHEI
 The presentation at this upscale restaurant is excellent, and most (but definitely not all) of the entrées are delicious. For appetizers, the ahi–mahi mahi nachos are like nothing you've ever had. Delicious! They also make very good mussels. Entrées such as mahi mahi with garlic-sesame crust and lime ginger sauce are outrageous. But sometimes entrées such as swordfish or chicken fall short. Owner Jean-Marie Josselin has numerous restaurants around the state with mixed results. The Kihei location will *probably* please, but we're leaving ourselves some wiggle room in case they disappoint you. Honokowai works a little better. **$30–$45**. Located in Kihei in Azeka Place II on South Kihei Road between Lipoa and Kulanihakoi. West Maui's is in Honokowai Market-place north of Ka'anapali.

BAY CLUB 669–5656
 With gorgeous views, a soothing piano player and a romantic atmosphere, this is a great place for a relaxing, albeit expensive, seafood dinner. Sunsets here are outrageous. The food is very well prepared, though portions are small, so you'll want to consider those appetizers. (This confirms Einstein's Theory of Dining Relativity, where he concluded that at expensive restaurants, portions are inversely proportional to price.) We've never had a bad entrée here. Their chocolate Jack Daniels torte is profoundly evil. Dinner is **$35–$50**. At the Kapalua Bay Hotel; see map on page 53. Resort wear required.

JAMESON'S
669–5653 IN KAPALUA, 891–8860 IN KIHEI
Located on Kapalua Drive in Kapalua, they have excellent views of the golf

course below, but they inexplicably close those tables except during dinner, so your views will probably be overlooking a tennis court. The food is generally, but not uniformly, fairly good but rarely stellar. Dinner works best. Ingredients don't seem to be as high quality as you'd expect. Lunch is a hodgepodge of fish tacos, sandwiches, calamari spinach salad (which doesn't work), crab cakes, burgers, etc. The ahi and salmon firecracker rolls work well as an appetizer. Dinner is mostly steak, seafood and lamb. Their wine list is vast and well chosen, including many verticals (a series of annual vintages). Overall, Jameson's is capable of a good meal, but you can't depend on it. **$6–$15** for breakfast, **$10–$15** for lunch, **$25–$35** for dinner. In Kapalua Bay Golf Course and the Maui Coast Hotel, South Kihei Road.

SEA HOUSE 669-1500

Spectacular location right next to the beach at Napili Bay. Try to reserve a window table. They thoughtfully leave sun screens down during the brightest part of the late afternoon, then raise them for sunsets, which are awesome from here. *Yeah, but what about the food?* Well, it's good too. For an appetizer (which are expensive, but large), we love the Royal Hawaiian—crab stuffed prawns with killer wontons and Thai chicken skewers. Also consider the olapa ahi. Dinner is fresh fish (which they occasionally overcook), filet mignon or chicken. Quality is usually very good and service is fair. Lunch is sandwiches (such as crab and croissant) and some sushi and salads. **$6–$12** for breakfast, **$10–$15** for lunch, **$20–$40** for dinner. 5900

Lower Honoapiilani Road at Napili Kai Beach Resort. The south parking lot is small and fills up, so consider the northern lot. Both require you to grope through the resort to the restaurant.

WEST MAUI VIETNAMESE

LEMONGRASS 667-6888

Small, simple but pleasant interior, great quality ingredients and tasty food make this a winner. Vietnamese and other Asian dishes, such as shrimp pops, curry chicken with rice (could be a bit hotter), stir fry tofu with veggies (excellent), spring rolls (also great), etc. **$10–$20** for lunch or dinner. Behind Lahaina Center at 930 Wainee St.

WEST MAUI TREATS

ASHLEY'S YOGURT & ICE CREAM 669-0949

Best shave ice we've found in West Maui. Lest you be confused, shave ice is *not* a snow cone. Snow cones are made from crushed ice with a little fruit syrup sprinkled on. True shave ice (that's *shave,* not *shaved*) uses a sharp blade to literally "shave" a large block of ice, creating an infinitely fine powder. Add to this copious amounts of exotic fruit flavors, put it all on top of a big scoop of ice cream, and you have an island delight that is truly *broke da mouf.* Ashley's also has a "heavenly espresso nut sundae" that is awesome. The small and pricey sundae uses their incredibly effective espresso sauce (a little goes a long way) with killer results. They won't win many awards for friendly, gushy service, but the treats are ono. In Kahana Gateway, 27–28 mile marker, Hwy 30.

The Bakery 667-9062

ono Hidden away in an industrial area, their baked goods are very good, reasonably priced (for Lahaina) and popular with locals. Strudel, croissants, bagels, macaroons, fresh bread, etc. Most items are quite tasty. From Hwy 30 between Papalaua and Kenui, take Hinau mauka (toward the mountain), turn right at the end. It'll be on the right side and isn't much to look at. **$2–$5.**

South Maui American (Includes Seafood)

Alexander's Fish, Chicken & Ribs 874-0788

Fairly reasonable prices but the portions are on the small side. For most items you get a choice of fried or broiled. Otherwise, everything else (including the mixed veggies) is fried. Their combos of two (fish, chicken, shrimp, ribs or veggies) are probably their best deal. The food is tasty but a bit greasy. Order at the counter, then wait for your number and eat at the outside tables. On the mauka side of South Kihei Road across the street from the fake whale at Kalama Park. **$7–$11** for lunch and dinner.

Annie's Deli and Catering 875-8647

We hope they make most of their money on the catering part. Tiny deli on South Kihei Road behind KKO across the street from Kamaʻole II Beach Park. Small breakfast selection; eat outside on a few hopelessly rocking tables with chairs that need a good cleaning. The $5 Aloha breakfast is the best bet here, but the food is only mediocre and overpriced given the cheap-o surroundings. Crowds seem to confuse the otherwise friendly service. Sandwiches for lunch. **$3–$6** for breakfast, **$4–$8** for lunch.

Bubba's Burgers 891-2600

The food isn't great, though many items are pretty good, such as the fish sandwich. Bubba's is mostly a burger joint, and the servings are too small. But Bubba's has sort of a contrived atmosphere that works—funky and irreverent—and the burgers *can be* tasty. Grab a lanai table after a day at the beach. Across from Kalama Park at 1945 S. Kihei Rd. **$4–$8.** They have free internet access.

Buzz's Wharf 244-5426

Great views of the boats coming in and out of Maʻalaea Harbor. Food is usually fairly good with definite exceptions. Their prawns are great—they seem to use an excellent grade of Tahitian prawn. Other items are hit or miss. Burgers, fish and teri chicken for lunch, steak and seafood for dinner. Overall, it's a good place to try after your boat trip, though it's pricey and service is often disorganized or unresponsive since they tend to be busy. At Maʻalaea Harbor off Hwy 30 south of the 6 mile marker. **$10–$25** for lunch, **$20–$40** for dinner.

Dina's Sand Witch 879-3262

ono Part sandwich shop, part pub. A good selection of sandwiches, ¼-pound hot dogs, and saimin (which is good). Healthy portions and good ingredients. The walls are literally wallpapered with money. Over the past 20 years customers have given them currency, mostly ones, with their signatures and comments. Thousands of them cover the walls, creating a unique ambiance. **$6–$9** for lunch and dinner. On *North* Kihei Road, just north of Kihei town past Margarita's Restaurant on the ocean side of Hwy 310 next to the Sugar Beach Resort.

GRAND WAILEA–DINING ROOM 875–1234

Bright and open, the restaurant overlooks the resort and ocean. Their breakfast buffet for $19 is good, but you'll be forgiven if you expected a bigger selection. Want eggs? Then it's either scrambled or nothing. The quiche is good. Lots of fruit, some breads and meats. Bad bagels. Don't leave your plate without posting a guard...the birds are watching. At Grand Wailea Resort.

HAWAIIAN MOONS 875–4356

A health food store with some good sandwiches, hot bar and smoothies. Sandwiches are large and tasty. Pretty good baked goods.

JACQUES ON THE BEACH 875–7791

It's rare to be able to eat with a dynamite ocean view and not get soaked by the prices. That's what makes Jacques so refreshing. Very expansive oceanside views. West Maui looks like another island from here. Sunsets are very nice. (From here it sets earlier than the newspaper indicates in the summer—over West Maui.) The air is filled with an eclectic assortment of music, from old jazz to Latin to New Age, creating a relaxing atmosphere. The service is fairly good and the food usually well prepared. Mostly generous portions (so don't fill up on the tasty herb rolls). We called it American, but its menu is an assortment from lots of countries. Potstickers with spicy dipping sauce is a good appetizer; entrées include pasta,

lamb lasagna (perhaps a bit too meaty), spicy peanut chicken, steak and fresh fish. Meats are sometimes a bit overcooked, but overall Jacques is a good bargain for the money. Their only hardship is that the fishpond offshore occasionally clogs up with seaweed, creating an unpleasant smell. (But not too often.) **$13–$30,** dinner only. In North Kihei at Menehune Shores north of Kulanihakoi Road on South Kihei Road.

KEAWAKAPU GENERAL STORE 879–8997

Only mentioned because if you're lounging around on Keawakapu Beach and get hungry, at the north end of the beach this store at the Mauna Kai sells fairly decent hot dogs. **$3–$5.**

KIHEI CAFFE 879–2230

Some tasty food if you can overlook their shortcomings. Breakfast is best (they open at 5 a.m. on weekdays) with good omelettes, breakfast burritos and some truly kickin' raspberry twisties. Service is not much to speak of, and we prefer the plastic forks over the seemingly less-than-sterile metal cutlery. Some of the outdoor tables are almost penned in, making it popular with parents trying to corral their keikis. (Kids seem to like the teddy bear pancakes.) Lunch is mostly sandwiches and salads. They have box lunches that you can grab for later in the day. Kihei Caffe makes mostly good food, but we wouldn't mind if it was a bit cleaner and the staff a bit warmer. On South Kihei Road across from Kalama Park. **$5–$9** for breakfast, **$7–$10** for lunch.

KKO 875–1007

Nice views across the street from the ocean, but the food is a bit more disappointing. Blueberry pancakes are good but pricey ($5 *for one*), and the tofu scramble is decidedly lacking in flavor. Lunch includes sandwiches, fish and chips, and burgers. Quality is a bit better. Dinner is steak, seafood and ribs. Overall, the quality is average, nothing more, nothing less. On S. Kihei Rd. across from Kama'ole II Beach. **$5–$10** for breakfast, **$8–$15** for lunch, **$15–$20** for dinner.

LIFE'S A BEACH 891–8010

Average burgers, chicken sandwich, burritos, hot dogs, and fish and chips for lunch and dinner. A local watering hole. Good 4–7 happy hour with cheap mai tais and beer. **$7–$10** for lunch and dinner. S. Kihei Road across from Kalama Park.

MA'ALAEA WATERFRONT 244–9028

American: The food here is superb and the flavor combinations well-conceived. They have many different kinds of fish prepared 9 different ways. Cajun spice, broiled with Hawaiian salsa, baked in parchment paper, stuffed with Alaskan king crab, etc. They use good quality fish. (Some restaurants sometimes mask bad fish with overpowering sauces, but not here.) Their crab cake appetizers, when they have them, are great. Service can be good, but sometimes clumsy, and the parking situation is terrible. Just a few spots; you'll probably have to park out on the street and walk to the place. But the food makes it worth it. The outdoor (smoking) tables have beautiful views, but the indoor tables don't take much advantage of the location. Extraordinary wine list with over 150 wines. Avoid the booth behind the hostess stand. Take

Hwy 30 to Ma'alaea, then turn on Hau'oli Road. Only potential bad side is the possibility of midges at the outdoor tables during bad swarms. See 131 for more. **$20–$50** for dinner.

MACK & JACK'S LOBSTER SHACK & DELI 875–9231

Decent variety of generally underwhelming sandwiches and soups. Poor service. Check to make sure they get the order right before you leave. Deliveries available, so why not spend the day waiting for them? **$7–$12** for lunch and dinner. In Dolphin Plaza, 2395 S. Kihei Rd.

MAUI ONION 879–4900

Located next to the pool at the Renaissance in Wailea, with nice views of the ocean. With a name like Maui Onion, they better have outrageous onion rings—and they do. They use a secret recipe, so we better not tell you that they dip the onion in pancake batter, roll them in Japanese panko flour (like bread crumbs) then fry. Maui Onion also has the very best burgers on the island. Since it's a resort they're pricey—over $10 for the 1/2-pounders, an extra $1 for fries. But it's a great burger treat. Their wraps are good, too. Try the excellent home-made ice cream sandwiches for dessert. Lunch only, till sunset. **$12–$20.**

NICK'S FISHMARKET 879–7224

One of the finest restaurants in South Maui. Exceptional seafood in an elegant setting. The menu changes often, but we've never had or even *heard* of a bad meal here. Try the calamari for an appetizer. Their Hawaiian lobster is fantastic. So is everything else. Try the chocolate "deca-dense" for dessert. World class wine list. The service is unbelievable. Order a drink and see if it takes more than a minute. (And their drinks are *well*-concocted.) It's the closest thing we've seen to saying, "Tea, Earl Grey, hot." (You either get that one or you don't.) It's like a contest to see how excellent they can make the service. Though attentive, they *don't* come around every five minutes, when your mouth is full, asking, "How is everything?" They just keep a watchful eye on you. We've never seen a water glass go empty. So what's the catch? *Exactly what you think.* Nick's isn't cheap. But if you need a good pampering, Nick's is the place to go. **$30–$50** for dinner. In the Kea Lani Resort in Wailea. Reservations recommended. Resort wear required.

PALM COURT 879-4900

First, the menu changes seasonally, so it's hard to steer you toward (or away from) a certain dish. They call it "Mediterranean with a Hawaiian twist." Well, we don't have a category for that, so we'll call it American. Dinner is available either off the menu or as a buffet, and service seems somewhere in between the two types. Spartan, but not too lacking. Food quality is very good, and the buffet is a reasonable deal for the quality and for Wailea. Mostly steak and seafood. The view overlooks the ocean filtered through trees. Might want to avoid the lanai seats. People can and do walk through from the outside. Desserts are masterful and will wound your mouth. In Renaissance Hotel on Wailea Alanui. **$8–$15** for breakfast (buffet is $17) **$20–$40** for dinner (buffet, offered most nights, is around $35).

PEGGY SUE'S 875-8944

Small but effective 1950s style diner serving generous-sized burgers (second 6-oz patty is less than $1.50 extra), ribs, salads, hot dogs and some sandwiches, such as steak, chicken and fish. Their burgers are second only to Maui Onion's. Baked fries could use some seasoning. Portions are fairly generous for the price, and they have a good keiki (kid) selection with PB&J and grilled cheese sandwiches. Service can be slow because they are often busy, especially at lunch, and the waitresses seem overworked. Getting a table can be hard at peak eating times. Real milkshakes are tasty (love the peanut butter) and the jukebox playing old 45s adds to the flavor. In Azeka Place II shopping center on S. Kihei Road near Lipoa. **$8–$12** for lunch and dinner.

PIZAZZ CAFÉ 891-2123

Southern cooking with a pleasing jazz ambiance. Items include Southern favorites such as fried okra for appetizer (very tasty with a good batter) or sweet potato chips (very ono), catfish and fried shrimp, po'boy sandwiches along with non-Southern items such as burgers, taro burgers and wraps. Portions are good on some (like the wraps) and small on others (only eight small shrimp; come on, you can do better than that!). Quality is usually good, but occasionally disappointing. Sometimes understaffed at night. Often there are live jazz performers at dinner. (Sometimes big names.) **$8–$15** for lunch, **$15–$25** for dinner. On South Kihei Road, mauka side between near Piikea Road in the Azeka Place II Shopping Center. Often busy at dinner, reservations recommended.

PRINCE COURT 874–1111

ono Located at the Maui Prince hotel, they have a Sunday brunch that is legendary. It's pricey ($40) and the buffet service is surprisingly slipshod for a restaurant of this caliber, but the food is awesome and the variety stunning. Choose from the many breakfast items, the omelette station or try Chinese food or roast beef. The desserts are exceptionally evil. It books up most of the time, so reserve as early as possible. They also have a Friday seafood and prime rib buffet for $38. Other nights are off-the-menu, such as steak, seafood, venison (deer) and lamb. Quality is usually top notch. The ocean views are pretty good and the atmosphere relaxing. **$25–$50.** South of Wailea off Makena Alanui Road.

SPORTS PAGE 879–0602

A smoky sports bar with decent ½-pound burgers and sandwiches for $7 or $8 (but pitiful salads). Good pupu (appetizer) selection and (not surprisingly) a big beer selection. **$7–$13** for lunch and dinner. 2411 S. Kihei Rd at Kama'ole Beach Ctr.

STELLA BLUES 874–3779

Having heard that this was the "best" breakfast on the island, we are surprised at how bad the food tastes. Someone needs to alert the cooks about a radical new concept—*seasonings!* Take the delicious-sounding French toast as an example. How are they able to combine vanilla, cinnamon, eggs and bread to produce something so utterly tasteless? (Years of practice?) For lunch it's sandwiches and burgers, mostly Italian items, such as pasta and veggie lasagna for lunch and dinner. Service can be friendly but appallingly unresponsive. **$5–$10** for breakfast, **$8–$11** for lunch, **$13–$20** for dinner. Located on South Kihei Road in Longs Center north of Lipoa Road.

SUNSET TERRACE 879–4900

ono Not really a restaurant, but rather the lounge at the Renaissance in Wailea. You're four stories above the ground with lush landscaping and coconut trees below you. An excellent place for a sunset cocktail. Pupus and fairly decent pizzas available. After sunset they light the torches around the resort. In all, a very relaxing place.

TONY ROMA'S 875–1104

Part of a mainland chain serving ribs, chicken cooked lots of ways, etc. Dependable food at slightly elevated prices, ribs have a pretty decent sauce, the sausage sandwich is tasty, and the salads are average. They have a wicked skillet brownie sundae, rich and big enough for several people. It's hard to get real excited by Tony Roma's, but you're also not likely to be let down either. On South Kihei Road at Kukui Mall across from Kalama Park. **$7–$17** for lunch, **$8–$25** for dinner.

VOLCANO GRILL & BAR 875–1234

At the pool at the Grand Wailea, it's a good place to enjoy a cocktail and light food for a sunset in the winter. (Their 6 p.m. closing is too early in the summer.) Yeah, they have the usual resort $8 hot dogs and $10 sandwiches, but you can grab something to drink and head over to the beach for a relaxing late afternoon.

South Maui Greek

PITA PARADISE 875-7679

(ono) We've never seen people who could do so much with pitas. Here they're freshly made and topped (not actually filled—it's more like a wrap) with all manner of ingredients. Chicken, veggies, fish, meat balls and greens in clever combinations. Kabobs, too. Their ziziki bread makes a good appetizer. **$7–$15.** 1913M South Kihei Road in Kihei Kalama Village across from Kalama Park. Closed Sunday.

South Maui Italian

ANTONIO'S 875-8800

(ono) Southern (Sicilian) style Italian, nice ambiance, spotlessly clean. The food is great here. Many varieties of pasta, lots of veggie items, good lasagna, and the veal osso buco is delicious, as are the raviolis. The flavor combinations here are wonderful. The home-made tiramisu is a good way to end it. Decent wine list, and the service is attentive. But don't try to mess with the recipes. We were there once with someone who asked them to hold the onions. The chef personally came out and indignantly proclaimed that *everything* he makes has onions, so...deal with it. In Longs Center on South Kihei Road. **$12–$25** for dinner.

AROMA D'ITALIA 879-0133

Pleasing ambiance, southern Italian style cooking (red sauces). Traditional menu with few surprises. Their best bet is the spinach or sausage lasagna. Pass on the pastas with marinara, which are bland. Grilled shrimp tastes...wrong. And the focaccia bread is too light. Overall quality ranges from average to below average. You can do better. **$8–$18** for dinner. On South Kihei Road in Kihei Town Center near Foodland.

CAFE CIAO 875-4100

(ono) A good selection of Italian items. Lunch is pizza (with limited but unusual toppings), Italian sandwiches and pasta. Dinner features some excellent pastas, such as risotto ai gamberoni (arborio rice sautéed with tiger prawns in a lobster sauce) and other similarly compiled plates. Also lobster, veal and lamb, plus dinner pizzas. Seating is outdoors. Pricey but good results. Service is usually (but not always) good. In the Kea Lani Resort in Wailea. **$13–$25** for lunch, **$20–$40** for dinner.

SHAKA PIZZA 874-0331

It's disappointing that good pizza is so hard to find on Maui. Other islands have places that stand out, but not so on Maui. Shaka is ordinary, nothing more. Their regular pizza has extremely thin and fairly tasty crust, but unremarkable sauce and toppings. It's so thin that you'll be surprised at how much pizza surface area you can dispose of, so order larger than you normally would. They also have gourmet pizzas, such as spinach pizza, clam and garlic, and white pies that are fine, but not great. Cheese steaks and other sandwiches also available. To be honest, their sandwiches are their best asset (love the sausage sandwich), though pricey. A 14-inch sandwich is almost $10! They deliver. **$3–$10.** By-the-slice pizza reasonably priced. On South Kihei Road, mauka side, just north of Lipoa Road.

South Maui Japanese

Hakone 874-1111

 Very good Japanese food. Most items are very well prepared. Excellent shabu shabu. Many non-traditional items like lobster, pineapple steak and even ostrich. Good service. Try the taro ice cream for dessert. Buffets on Monday nights. $20-$50 *and up.* In the Maui Prince Hotel south of Wailea.

Hana Gion 879-4900

 An exceptionally vast menu with selections ranging from traditional entrées, teppan-yaki, shabu shabu and a wonderful sushi menu. The upscale Japanese setting is restful and serene. Prices at Japanese restaurants are hard to predict, but figure at least **$25-$45** to do dinner right. In the Renaissance Wailea Beach Resort. Reservations recommended.

Harry's Sushi Bar/Lobster Cove 879-7677

 It's really two restaurants in one, and *the ono only applies to Harry's.* There, you'll find well prepared sushi and a good selection. Price, which varies greatly depending on your appetite, is probably **$10-$25.** Lobster Cove is their seafood restaurant portion. Though the food is fairly good, it's obscenely overpriced. Like lobster tail served with four shrimp for $40. *Waaay* too much. Fresh fish starting at $30 is about 25% too high. Their views overlooking the Wailea Blue golf course are particularly serene, but unless you've got money burning a hole in your pocket, only eat at the sushi bar. **$25-$55** for Lobster Cove. On Wailea

Iki between the end of Hwy 31 and Wailea Alanui.

South Maui Local

Azeka's Ribs and Sushi 879-0611

Their marinated beef ribs have taken on legendary status, but frankly they're a bit overrated. People rave about them, and with the sweet, soy, sugar and garlic taste, the flavor's good, but they're *very* greasy and fatty. For less than $6 you get the ribs and any side you want—as long as it's rice and mac salad. (Ironically, they only serve ribs on Wed, Sat and Sun—the rest of the time you get them cold for $6 a pound and cook 'em yourself.) Other items, such as the teri burger, also seem excessively fatty, even for local food. The sushi's pretty good for the money, however. Whatever you get, take it to go. Flies at the cement tables can be real pesky. In Azeka Place Shopping Center, Kihei, next to Ace Hardware. **$3-$7.**

Da Kitchen 875-7782

 Good selection of local items, such as loco moco, teriyaki chicken, chicken katsu. The saimin could use a little work but the teri chicken sandwich is good. If you're presently wanted by the Cholesterol Police, don't come here, they may raid the place. But if you're looking for generous portions of not-so-healthy local food at cheap prices, you could do a lot worse than Da Kitchen. **$4-$9.** In Rainbow Mall, next to Denny's on South Kihei Rd.

South Shore Grinds 875-8472

 A real find. They have outstanding salads (excellent

lemon lime power salad), chicken (love the curry chicken) and burgers such as pesto burgers, Thai ahi burgers and veggie taro burgers. The food is distinctive and hard to classify. (So we chickened out and put them under Local.) Pupus include Moloka'i chips, which are thinly sliced sweet potatoes with a Cajun powder and banana curry for dipping. Excellent when they slice it thin enough, but sometimes they don't. Plate lunches include chicken katsu with a sweet and sour plum sauce. We know we're jumping all over, but so does their menu. The food is good, creative and reasonably priced. **$6–$10** for lunch and dinner. On Huku Lii Place, behind the gas station, in Kihei Gateway Plaza between the 4 and 5 mile markers of Hwy 31.

Suda's Snack Shop 879-0139
Nothing higher than $5. Cheap burgers, hot dogs, saimin and other local dishes. Taste isn't much to speak of, but it's cheap. On South Kihei Road at Uwapo Road. **$3–$6.**

South Maui Mexican

Cafe Navaca 879-0717
You start out with their fresh tortilla chips made from red peppers, white corn and blue corn—nice touch. But then the salsa is sort of lifeless. Then your food comes. Everything (except the beverages) is heavily laden with onions. Flavors are only average, and aggressive flies can really irritate you during lunch at the outdoor tables. (There are a few indoor tables.) Dinner is indoors in another, nicer room and often there's live music. (Usually a guitar player or a

salsa band.) The price is too high given the mediocre food. They have 13 kinds of tequilas and some innovative and well-crafted adult beverages. **$5–$10** for breakfast, **$9–$18** for lunch and dinner. On South Kihei Road across from Kalama Park.

El Restaurante Pasatiempo 879-1089
Well, now we know what food in a Mexican hospital must taste like. It's as if seasonings have been banned from the kitchen. An example are the enchiladas. Picture unseasoned shredded beef in a saltless tortilla, covered with tomato water, next to yellow steamed rice and flavorless refried beans. All yours for only $9. What a deal! You may find yourself looking longingly at the *comparatively* gourmet Mexican food at Taco Bell across the street. In Azeka Place II on South Kihei Road north of Lipoa. **$8–$15** for lunch and dinner.

Maui Taco
879-5005 in Kihei, 871-7726 in Kahului, 665-0222 in Napili, 661-8883 in Lahaina

This small, local chain is a good place to go for tacos and burritos. Nothing fancy, but it's not overly expensive (though it's not cheap). They have a good selection and the protions are large. Their various locations are pretty different. The Kihei location (Kama'ole Beach Center) is their best, followed by the Kahului location (Ka'ahumanu Center), then Napili (Napili Plaza), followed by the disappointing Lahaina location (Lahaina Square). Sometimes their food is warm instead of hot, and don't forget the condiments bar if you find you need more seasoning. **$5–$10.**

SOUTH MAUI PACIFIC RIM (INCLUDES SEAFOOD)

A PACIFIC CAFE 879-0069
See review on page 256.

FIVE PALMS 879-2607
Let's start with the positive. They have one of the tastiest views of any restaurant. As soon as we walked in the first time, we knew we wanted to use their view for our dining section photo (page 244). It's right on the water and looks right down Keawakapu Beach. They close off the upwind windows and open the downwind windows, allowing them to feel open-air without the normal afternoon winds messing things up. So if we liked it so much and used it for our chapter opening, why no ONO? Look, with their view, a serving of *Alpo* would almost taste passable. And though it's very nicely presented, the flavors and service are mediocre. Entrées include teriyaki ahi sandwich, salmon fettuccini and chicken stir fry for lunch, and prime rib, whole opakapaka (head and all) and lobster for dinner. For the money, transgressions like cheap, stale bread and server forgetfulness along with the bland flavors are too much to swallow to give them an ONO. Or how about spending $40 for lobster and receiving it at nearly room temperature? Clean up the service and flavors, guys, and we're all yours. **$8–$15** for breakfast, **$12–$17** for lunch, **$25–$50** for dinner. 2960 South Kihei Road in the Mauna Kai Resort.

HUMUHUMUNUKUNUKUAPUA'A 875-1234
ONO Often called simply Humu (for obvious reasons), this is a truly memorable place to eat, good enough to save for your last night on the island, and one of our favorites on the island. Exceptional ambiance: You're surrounded by and actually *over* a huge fishpond. Some of the fish and lobster swimming around are actually the main course. (But don't tell them.) Waterfalls and thatched roofs add to the exotic Polynesian feel. It's very expensive, but the food and service are excellent. Consider the outrageous sea scallops, lau lau or fresh fish. They also have a wonderful filet mignon. We haven't had a bad meal yet, but we continue to dutifully review them just to be sure. (Isn't that selfless of us?) They sometimes interrupt you while you're eating to ask if you want their chocolate soufflé, which takes 20 minutes to cook. It's wicked! We took a vegetarian here who, when he told them his proclivities, received a szechwan stir-fry (not on the menu) that he raved about. (His 2½-year-old loved petting the lobster—the staff is very accommodating to keikis.) In the Grand Wailea Resort; allow an extra 10 minutes to walk through the fabulous grounds or save time parking at Wailea Beach access lot. **$30–$55** for dinner.

SEAWATCH 875-8080
Located at the Wailea Gold Golf Course on Wailea Golf Club Drive, the views of Molokini and Kaho'olawe from the outside tables are excellent, and it's a good place for a late breakfast as it and lunch are both served from 8 a.m. to 3 p.m. The kalua pork and Swiss is pretty good (though it's not the same kalua pork you get at lu'aus), and most of the sandwiches work pretty well. Their banana lumpia (sort of a banana eggroll-like dessert) is a good way to top things off. Service is good. **$5–$12** for breakfast, **$7–$15**

for lunch, or a pretty pricey $25–$40 for dinner.

South Maui Thai

Royal Thai Cuisine 874–0813

Vast selection of Asian items, very tasty food, good vegetarian selection and excellent flavor combinations. They also have good desserts. In Azeka Place Shopping Center on South Kihei Road just north of Lipoa. $8–$15 for lunch and dinner. (No lunch on weekends.)

South Maui Treats

Cinnamon Roll Fair 879–5177

Pretty decent cinnamon rolls (they're good about putting more goo on top if you want) and gigantic 10-inch cookies for $1.50. They're not exactly the greatest cookies in the world, but, hey, what do you want for a buck and a half? At Kama'ole Shopping Center, Kihei downstairs from Denny's.

Coconut's Bakery & Cafe 879–0261

Probably the best bakery we've found so far in Kihei. Items such as apple bread pudding and the strudels are excellent. (Avoid the seven-layer bars, however.) Good for a quick breakfast. In the Kukui Mall, South Kihei Road. $2–$4.

Jabooka Jooce 879–5662

Good smoothies and lots of choices. Examples are Pacific Blues with orange pineapple juice, bananas, raspberries and blueberries, or try the Blackberry Blast with apple, banana and blackberries. On South Kihei Road across from Kalama Park. $4–$6.

South Beach Smoothies 875–0594

Good selection of well-concocted smoothies, fairly reasonably priced, and with tasty results. Most are $3 or $4. Only wish some of the thicker smoothies came with larger diameter straws. (Pick, pick, pick.) Ah, well, you can't have it all. In front of Maui Dive Shop, 1455 S. Kihei Road just south of Lipoa Road.

Sweet Spot
879–8611 in Kihei, 871–0875 in Kahului

Located in Kukui Mall on South Kihei Road and Maui Mall in Kahului, they serve locally made but fairly dull Roselani ice cream. (Only the butter brickle stands out.)

Central Maui American

Aloha Grill 893–0263

A surprising find in the Kau Kau Food Court in the Maui Marketplace in Kahului. Good food, friendly folks and innovative fast food menu. Examples are taro burgers (in fact, lots of veggie burgers), mahi burgers, chik nuggets (no meat), chili dogs (called "classical gas") and pretty good plain old beef burgers. Be sure to look around; there are usually lots of specials and food experiments shown. Their bone jar shakes have real peanut butter and chocolate ice cream with milk—small but *extremely ono!* $5–$9 breakfast, lunch and dinner, but doesn't open till 8 a.m.

Koho Grill & Bar 877–5588

Good family feel, the service is very responsive and friendly. Food is a good value for

Maui. Typical breakfast items (their otherwise tasty potatoes could use a tad less cheese). Lunch is usually very busy and includes ½ pound burgers, plate lunches (an example is teriyaki beef with rice and macaroni salad), sandwiches, fajitas and several salads. Dinner is chicken, some stir fries, steak and fish. Quality is good for most items. This place is popular with local residents. In Kaahumanu Shopping Center (on the outside of the mall) on Hwy 32 in Kahului. **$4–$8** for breakfast, **$5–$9** for lunch, **$10–$17** for dinner. Price is very reasonable for this area. The build-your-own fajitas are good—if you build them right—and will fill up anybody for under $10. Service here is uneven. (Or as Momma used to say, fair to middlin'.)

DOWN TO EARTH 877-2661

ONO A health food store, cafe, deli and bakery. It's ironic that health food stores often have such bad food, but this one is an exception. Limited selection but outstanding quality. The hot bar sells food by the pound, including veggie lasagna, enchiladas, potatoes with herbs, steamed veggies, black bean soup, teriyaki tofu, etc. A few of the items are left without seasoning, which you can sprinkle on yourself. Also consider the veggie wraps. Every item shows all the ingredients. The bakery is excellent, and the goods aren't dry as is often the case in health food stores. (Try the mac nut bar.) Good salad bar. There are some easy-to-miss tables upstairs. In Kahului on Dairy Road across from Maui Marketplace. (The store itself is also very nice.) **$3–$8.**

SIMPLE PLEASURES CAFÉ 249-0697

We had no idea how to classify them, so we just dumped it in American. Menu is essentially a relatively small selection of vegetarian soups and quiche prepared in Swedish, Indian and other themes. Creamy carrot, mung bean, spinach with rosemary, broccoli. Most are quite tasty, and they're good at letting you sample them. Some yummy desserts (love the strudel and the chocolate truffle), and they're friendly folks. Though the lack of heartier dishes may deter some, it's an interesting place to try. You'll probably either love it or hate it. Vineyard and Church in Wailuku. **$5–$8,** lunch only at press time but hours are squirrely, so call.

WOODY'S HOT DOGS

Sometimes you don't want anything fancy, just a hot dog on the run. Woody's is a stand in front of the hardware store in Maui Marketplace on Dairy Road with simple hot dogs and polish dogs. **$3–$5.**

CENTRAL MAUI ITALIAN

MARCO'S GRILL AND DELI 877-4446

Pasta, pizza, hot and deli sandwiches and some steak. The food is not bad—the home-made sausage and linguini is quite good—but the price seems a bit high for Kahului. They don't even bring bread, which they really should for the money. Appetizers and breakfasts are overpriced. It's a pleasing, jazzy/Italian atmosphere, and their bar is well stocked. (With an admirable selection of single malt scotch.) **$8–$14** for breakfast, **$10–$30** for lunch and dinner. On the corner of

Dairy Road and Hana Highway in Kahului.

PIZZA IN PARADISE 871-8188

Formerly called Two Fat Guys from Boston Pizza (who sold it because their "crane business was too good"), the pizza is average at best, soggy at its worst. The price is reasonable and the portions are generous (by the slice is a very good deal), but you'll be underwhelmed by the taste. **$3–$10**. At 60 E. Wakea Street between Puunene (Hwy 311) and Hukilike Street.

CENTRAL MAUI LOCAL

BA-LE 877-2400

ONO You can forget classifying this place. They call themselves a French Sandwich and Bakery, but serve mostly Asian dishes, huge portions, flavorful results, very cheaply. Vietnamese plate lunches, French sandwiches, local entrées—and you'll probably spend about **$5**. Located in the Kau Kau Food Court in Maui Marketplace on Dairy Road **$3–$7**.

TASTY CRUST 244-0845

ONO Let's start by saying the place is kind of dumpy. And it's not as...kempt as we'd like. But if you're looking for very cheap and very hearty, this is the place. Their pancakes are known island-wide. Light, soft and large with a good texture, they even serve peanut butter with them, if you want. (I know how it sounds, but you'd be surprised how well the flavor combination works.) Portions are large, but the plate is too small to negotiate the syrup transfer. (That's pancake

tech-talk.) They also have limited omelettes, loco moco (a local style cholesterol lover's best friend, described on page 247) and eggs. In the traditional local way, spam or vienna sausage available with breakfast. (Locals *love* Spam.) Lunch is saimin, pork chops, spare ribs and burgers. This place is a long-time local restaurant that lasts because they serve large portions at a good price, and they do what they do well. *That's* why we gave them an ONO. **$3–$6** for breakfast, **$5–$9** for lunch. No credit cards. In Wailuku on Mill Street near Central. From 32 go right on Central to the end. Turn right on Mill. Opens at 5:30 a.m.

TIN YING 242-4371

Hideous local and Chinese dishes. 'Nuff said. 1088 Lower Main in Wailuku. **$5–$10**.

WEI WEI BBQ & NOODLE SHOP 242-7928

Greasy but cheap Asian and local food. Some good, some bad. **$5–$10**. Wailuku on Imi Kala off Mill St.

CENTRAL MAUI MEXICAN

LAS PIÑATAS 877-8707

ONO This is the place to go for a quick bite but you still want to sit down and eat reasonable quality, relatively inexpensive Mexican food in acceptable surroundings. (If that sounds less than glowing, it's because *you aren't paying* for a glow at this place.) Burritos are very large and around **$5–$6**. Chicken enchiladas are pretty tasty. On Dairy Road in Kahului between Hana Hwy and Maui Marketplace next to Kinko's. And yes, they do have lots of piñatas hanging from the ceiling. **$5–$9** for lunch and dinner.

CENTRAL MAUI VIETNAMESE

A SAIGON CAFÉ 243–9560

One of the more exciting restaurants on Maui, their food is outstanding. The menu is vast and contains an enviable array of foods, many from other Asian countries. Their garden delight summer rolls with roasted pork, garlic, toasted rice, sprouts, lettuce and cucumber rolled in rice paper with a sweet and sour garlic sauce is a *great* way to start it off. Their shrimp pops (ground shrimp pasted on a stick of sugar cane, steamed and grilled) are also a novel appetizer. We've eaten here more times than we can count and have never had a bad meal. Consider the garden party shrimp (with or without a shell), tofu with curry and lemongrass, Vietnamese burritos...it all works. Service is very competent and accommodating. **$8–$20** for lunch and dinner. It's tricky to find. Coming down Hwy 32 into Wailuku (like you're going toward the Iao Needle), turn right onto Central, quick right onto Nani, right onto Kaniela, then it will be on your left side at Kaniela and Main. At press time there was no sign out front because the owner, who has the signs, is "waiting for the right day to put them up" and has been "too busy." This is a popular place with locals; reservations recommended.

CENTRAL MAUI TREATS

HOME MAID BAKERY
244–7015 IN WAILUKU, 874–6035 IN KIHEI
Decent selection of baked goods, some

breads and tasty hot malasadas (a Portuguese donut) all served with icy service—like you're in line for prison food. If you don't need a warm hug to start the day, you may like the baked goods here. 1005 Lower (east) Main between Hookahi and Waena in Wailuku. Their Kihei location has a much poorer selection and doesn't seem as flavorful.

MAUI BAKE SHOP 242–0064

Good baked goods, some small pizzas, soups, and prepared salads and sandwiches. Try the raspberry lunette. They have some real cute baked items for keikis and they're cheap. On Vineyard and N. Church in Wailuku. **$2–$5.**

ROCKY MOUNTAIN CHOCOLATE FACTORY 873–7773

This chocolate chain serves pretty tasty chocolates and other treats. They have some very imaginative combinations and seem to constantly introduce new items. That's the only reason—*we swear*—that we have to keep regularly reviewing them: to try the new items. They also serve an ice cream made on the Big Island, called Tropical Dreams, which is outstanding. **$2–$5.** Next to the Kau Kau Food Court, Dairy Road in Maui Marketplace in Kahului. Pricey but tasty.

STILLWELL'S BAKERY & CAFÉ 243–2243
Lots of salads, smallish number of sandwiches and a few specials, along with numerous baked goods. Most entrées are **$5** or **$6.** Some of the sandwiches, like the ham and cheese, go well with their fruit glaze. (Mac salad needs work, though.) If you're there around Christmas, check out their home-made

gingerbread houses, everything edible. Most of the baked goods are good, but not great. On Hwy 32 on the right side just before you enter Wailuku.

ELSEWHERE

This is a scattering of restaurants outside of the main dining area. Their classification is in the review. Hana is handled separately in HANA HIGHWAY SIGHTS.

CASANOVA 572-0220

ONO Italian: When you first walk in there's a dance floor in front of you, then they take you to the actual dining area, which is more upscale. Dinners work pretty well here, but some portions are too small. For instance, raviolis are good but there are only five of them. The Rigatoni Beverly Hills is an unusual but effective flavor combination with its odd creamy red sauce. Their thin 12-inch pizzas make good appetizers if you can split them with others. It's relatively reasonably priced, given the food. **$15–$25** for dinner. On Makawao Avenue in Makawao. It was for sale at press time, so things may change. They also have a deli next door with pasties, sandwiches and pizza by the slice.

CHARLEY'S 579-9453

ONO American: Good breakfast menu with the usual items plus breakfast burritos, tacos and veggie entrées. Lunch is good burgers, sandwiches, some fish and stir fry. Dinner is mostly Italian. Pasta, pizza and ribs. Good food, good service. Known locally as an occasional hangout for celebrities who have homes on the north shore of Haleakala. So does Charley himself do the cooking? Hope not. Charley was a dog. He lives on as the restaurant's logo. **$5–$11** for breakfast, **$7–$12** for lunch, **$12–$23** for dinner. On Hwy 36 in Pa'ia.

COLLEEN'S PIZZA AND BAKESHOP 575-9211

American: Located in Ha'iku on Ha'iku Road, the baked goods are very tasty. Definitely worth the stop. A bit less sweet than most bakeries. Breakfasts are fairly decent as are lunches which offer sandwiches. The pizza, however, is marginal. Served only at night, they have decent crust but the toppings are bland and pizzas are too cheesy. (But they sure do stay hot a long time. The Earth's core cools faster than their pizzas.) **$3–$10.**

HALIIMAILE GENERAL STORE 572-2666

ONO Pacific Rim: The location for this somewhat upscale restaurant is unexpected. You have nowhere, then you have Hali'imaile, which is 3 miles south of nowhere. The food is very good, if a bit overpriced given the location. Small lunch menu with items such as the blackened ahi wrap (very tasty but pricey at $16—after all, it's just fish, greens and mashed potatoes in a tortilla!), seafood coconut curry and a few sandwiches. Lunch during the week only, and they tend to rush you. Dinner brings items such as Jawaiian blackened chicken, duck and Indonesian stir-fry. Desserts are rich enough to make you sweat. We almost withheld our ONO because everything feels about 25% overpriced. Keep that in mind. **$10–$22** for lunch, **$20–$35** for dinner. On Hali'imaile Road between Baldwin Avenue and Haleakala Hwy (37). See map on page 117.

JACQUES BISTRO PA'IA 579-6255

(ono) Pacific Rim: Tasty seafood, linguini, roast duck, steak and seafood curry in a nice ambiance. Creative appetizers include Tahitian ceviche, poki and sashimi. Easy to like. **$12–$25.** Dinner only. On Hwy in Pa'ia.

KOMODA STORE AND BAKERY 572-7261

(ono) Treats: Who would expect that in this uninspiring, little semi-dumpy building would reside some of the best bakers on Maui? Their cream puffs are legendary around the island (more like eclairs). Stick donuts, malasadas (Portuguese donuts) chocolate croissants; we've liked almost everything we've tried here. (And we're quite diligent in reviewing them every time we're in the neighborhood.) They've been here since the island rose from the sea. (OK, OK, since 1916.) Service is friendly and the price is very reasonable. As at most bakeries, before noon is best. On Baldwin Avenue in Makawao just off Makawao Avenue. **$2–$4.** Closed Sun. and Wed.

KULA LODGE 878-1535

(ono) American/Pacific Rim: This is an easy place to like. The views and ambiance are glorious. With sweeping views down the mountain, you can see South Maui, West Maui mountains and Kahului. An all-glass wall takes full advantage of the views. During spring and summer, some outdoor tables near an incredible stone and brick oven are available. The food is usually excellent. Steak and seafood; try the Asian spiced fish (seared with Moloka'i sweet potato mash and soy ginger beurre blanc). Prices are high, even for lunch, but it's a treat worth splurging for, at least once. Early dinners are best, and you get some pretty unbelievable sunsets from up here. Desserts can be rich and decadent. (Though sometimes, surprisingly, they can be stale. When we've pointed it out, they've refused to charge us for it.) Breakfasts are sometimes too busy, as they fill up with bicyclists. **$10–$20** for lunch, **$20–$35** for dinner. On Upper Highway (377) before 378.

MAMA'S FISH HOUSE 579-8488

(ono) Pacific Rim: This is where we come when we want to treat ourselves, so let's cut to the chase. Nearly always delicious food, extremely pleasing ambiance and usually great service. They are right next to a beach and tide-pool; the only thing between you and the sand are picturesque palm trees. If you opt for lunch or an early dinner, you may see windsurfers plying the waters offshore. We like early dinners best. (They start dinner at 5 p.m.) It's usually less crowded, and the views are as tasty as the food. Ask for a covered outdoor table. You know as soon as you walk up the gecko walkway and through the banyan tree root archway (which got that shape when it crushed a building) that this will be special. The mostly seafood recipes are very imaginative and change daily, so it doesn't make much sense to mention specific ones. But we've never had a bad meal here. They even give credit on the menu to the fishing boat that caught each particular fish. The only negatives are that it is a poorly kept secret (so expect company and maybe a difficult time getting a reservation), and the price is expensive. **$25–$35** for lunch, **$30–$50** for dinner. But you won't mind paying top dollar if you get a top quality experience, and you probably will. Located northeast of Pa'ia on Hwy 36 just past the 8 mile marker. Reservations strongly recommended.

POLLI'S MEXICAN RESTAURANT 572–7808

Mexican: Fairly good selection of standard Mexican items, plus ribs and BBQ chicken. Service is nothing special, often snippy. Most of the items are pretty flavorful. Not too pleasing inside, but a decent place for lunch. If the service and surroundings were better, we may have given them an ono. **$8–$16** for lunch, **$11–$21** for dinner. Located on Makawao Avenue in Makawao. Their motto is, "Come on in, or we'll both starve."

PUKALANI COUNTRY CLUB 572–1325

ONO Local: At the golf course in Pukalani (end of Pukalani Street off Old Haleakala Hwy—see map on page 117), they have some pretty tasty local dishes such as kalua pig, lau lau, tripe stew, lomi salmon and teriyaki steak. A good place to try local style, and the views are awesome. Decent price. **$7–$15** for lunch and dinner.

SANDY'S ISLAND

Treats: Good shave ice, nice and finely shaved, but they are actually too generous with the syrup. Have 'em go easy, and make sure you get it with ice cream

on the bottom. On Hwy 36 in Pa'ia, ocean side.

STOPWATCH BAR & GRILL 572–1380

ONO American: In a town that prides itself on its cowboy heritage, it's surprisingly hard to get a decent burger here in Makawao. That's why we gave an ONO to Stopwatch. The burgers are pretty decent (though they may cook them more than the medium-well they claim—consider telling them medium or med-rare), and they have some great specials at lunch. Often a 1/3-pound burger and a beer are around $7, add a buck for fries. They also serve fish and chips, fresh fish, fried chicken and sandwiches. Not much healthy stuff; head down the road for that. **$6–$11** for lunch and dinner. As a small sports bar, it's sometimes a bit smoky inside. Good views. Our biggest complaint applies to all Makawao restaurants. After prolonged rains, they are sometimes invaded by irritating gnats, which can make things miserable. On Makawao Avenue southwest of Baldwin Avenue.

THE VEGAN RESTAURANT 579–9144

ONO Vegetarian: We're not vegetarians, but we really enjoy the splendidly flavorful food here. Great selection, hearty portions and quality ingredients. The garlic noodles, vegan wraps, tacos—we've liked every item we've tried other than the mediocre veggie burgers. Small, unimpressive interior is not as—shall we say, sparkling—as we'd like. Located in Paia 2/10 mile up Baldwin Avenue from Hwy 36.

NIGHTLIFE

The sun has set and the scenery faded, but you don't want the day to end. If you're a night owl, you'll find that Maui probably has enough to keep you happy, but don't expect Las Vegas. This is still a relatively quiet island, expecially in South Maui.

Nightlife is something that's ever-changing. Many restaurants are constantly bringing in new musicians and trying new things. We hate to pass the buck, but by definition, nightlife is something that changes all the time. Different establishments do different things, sometimes every week. No one covers this week's action as well as an insert in Thursday's *Maui News* newspaper called *Maui Scene.* Pick up a copy to see what's shaking this week. It includes special events, concerts, movies, stage plays, resort entertainment, galleries, and it has coupons.

For **movies,** the best theatres are in Kahului. (West and South Maui's theatres are small and unimpressive.) Call 244–8934, ext 2004 or 1609 to get all the theatres' movies.

West Maui Nightlife

Lahaina is the center of West Maui nightlife. One of the most effective ways to feel out the nightlife in Lahaina is to walk along Front Street and see what strikes your fancy. Popular places include **Moose McGillycuddy's** (667–7758) on Front Street, which is usually a pretty happen' place with music every night. Expecially popular with the 21–25 crowd. **Maui Brews** (667–7794) in Lahaina Center can also be a rockin' place, and they have an impressive 16 beers on tap.

In **Ka'anapali,** watching the cliff diver mentioned on page 50 is a good way to start things off. Several of the beachside path restaurants there often have live music. Most of the resorts also have goings on.

South Maui Nightlife

Nightlife isn't as good in South Maui. That said, **Hapa's Restaurant & Night Club** (879–9001) is South Maui's hottest night club and is off Lipoa in Lipoa Center. The place usually starts jumping after 9 p.m., and they often have some excellent musicians. If you're looking for action, this is the place. The restaurant serves decent food. It's broken up into the "Haole Kine (burgers etc), Local Kine (poke, Korean chicken wings, Port-a-gee soup), and From Da Oven (pizza)." Entertainment nightly; call to see which night sounds right for you. At press time, Willie K rocked the place every Monday and was great. **Pizazz** (891–2123) sometimes has good jazz musicians performing at night. And **Tsunami** (875–1234) at the Grand Wailea is a resort night club that is sometimes fun.

Nightlife Elsewhere

In **Hana,** find a bright light and watch the geckos eat night bugs—you crazy party animal, you. Actually, the **Hotel Hana Maui** often has some pretty good local musicians at their restaurant.

Upcountry isn't a nightlife mecca either. Might want to wander around Makawao and see what's shakin'. **Casanovas** has a dance floor and lively music on weekends. Sometimes **Stopwatch** has live performers.

In Pa'ia, **Charley's** has music on the weekends with occasional drop-ins from local celebs like Willie Nelson.

In **Kahului** the **MAUI ARTS AND CULTURAL CENTER** is on Kahului Beach Road. Call 242-7469 to see what's happening there. Their Castle Theatre is a great place for a movie or play. The two rows of balconies provide excellent vantages.

LU'AUS

We've all seen them in movies. People sit at a table with a mai tai in one hand and a plate of kalua pig in another. There's always a show where hula dancers bend and sway to the beat of the music, and sometimes a fire-knife dancer twirls a torch lit at both ends. To be honest, that's not far from the truth. Lu'aus can be a blast, and, if your time allows, they are highly recommended. The pig is baked in the ground all day, creating succulent results when prepared right. Shows are usually exciting and fast paced. Maui's lu'aus have all you can eat and drink (including alcohol) for a set fee. If the mai tais they are serving don't satisfy you, they have an open bar to fill your needs. Remember that piece of info when you pick up your first complimentary (and sometimes watery) mai tail. The bartender will season it for you or serve you whatever you want. Since they are usually held outdoors at night, you might want to consider spraying mosquito repellent on your legs before the show or wear slacks.

Lu'aus will usually cost you **$62–$70**, and the better ones are at the higher end. The best two are in West Maui. Book them in advance. If you want to know what lu'au foods are like, see page 247.

Different resorts hold their lu'aus on different nights. These change with the whims of the managers, so verify the days listed here before making plans. Here's how they stack up.

West Maui's OLD LAHAINA LU'AU (667-1998) is your best bet. We've reviewed virtually all the neighbor island lu'aus, and we can say that Old Lahaina has the most professional crew we've yet encountered. Competent, friendly and always up, they make you feel very welcome. The organization is quality top to bottom. The grounds, next to but not *on* the shore, have an assortment of thatched hales. Free drinks, served almost all night, come from their accommodating bar. The food is standard lu'au food and quite tasty.

The show strives for a more authentic Hawaiian feel than the others, achieving good results most of the time. No lounge lizard MC singing *Tiny Bubbles* or *Hukilau,* no shiny foil shirts. Other things missing from the more typical shows, however, include fire-knife dancers (because that's Samoan, not Hawaiian) and the Maoris wandering through the audience threatening you. Also missing is the part where they haul people from your table up onstage to embarrass them. (Which, truth be told, can be a hoot to watch when done right.) All of these are omitted since they are considered unauthentic. We *really* miss the fire dancers and Maoris (they can be lots of fun to watch), but that's the price you pay for authenticity. Perhaps the stage could be a bit higher so all of the 400 visitors can see better, but this is minor quibbling. They fill up often, so book in advance if you can. On Front Street across from Lahaina Cannery.

Also in West Maui, the **HYATT LU'AU** (667-4420) in K'anapali is a good nightly lu'au. If you can't make it to the Old Lahaina Lu'au or are looking for a bit more flash in the show, this is the second best lu'au on the island. The food is pretty good and the show is unusually good. Very disciplined and well choreographed without as much Hawaiian lounge lizard presence as some other shows. It's located next to the beach, but you can't see the ocean from your table. Actually, our only complaint is that they make you stand in line for up to half an hour in the hot sun before bringing you in. But once you're inside, the Hyatt does an admirable job. As with most lu'aus, you might want to pass on the watered-down mai tais and consider the free open bar, if you're libation-inclined.

West Maui's other lu'aus are at the **MARRIOTT** (661–5828) and the **ROYAL LAHAINA RESORT** (661–9119). The Marriott was in too much flux at press time, so we avoided reviewing them. The nightly Royal Lahaina is our distant third choice.

Also in West Maui is Lahaina's **FEAST AT LELE** (667–5353). It's not a normal lu'au (no buffet; it's a five-course Polynesian dinner with show). The price is much higher than the lu'aus ($89), but the food's better. Book in advance. They seat 135 max.

In **South Maui** at press time there were only two lu'aus consistently held, both in Wailea, and they were not held nightly. The **RENAISSANCE** (879–4900) is definitely the best. Though the show is a tad Vegasy, the MC doesn't spend too much time on stage. The stage is a little too small and the dancers seem a bit constrained, but the setting is nice and the food is pretty good. Near but removed from the beach. (Good desserts, too.)

The **OUTRIGGER LU'AU** (879–1922) is on a small lawn next to the ocean on picnic tables and folding chairs. Their proximity to the water is good (and they have a pretty good fire dancer), but overall, the quality is average.

DINNER SHOWS

Well, *technically* there are no dinner shows on the island. Lahaina, however, has two night-time attractions that you should consider. Think of them as dinner shows without the dinner. The best is **WARREN & ANNABELLE'S** (667–6244), probably the single most amazing show in all Hawai'i. Put simply, our jaws never stop dropping the whole time. After the first time we saw it, we were so impressed we told everyone we knew on Maui, "You gotta go see this." Most said, "Oh, I don't really like magic shows." Doesn't matter. It's not the kind of magic show you're thinking of. It might sound corny, but the whole evening's magic. Every person we've ever sent to this show has come back a raving fool. (Now the island is populated with raving fools. We're sorry to be the ones responsible.) You enter the theater in a most unique way. (We won't give it away.) Then you're in an incredibly beautiful parlor, elegant in every way. You spend some time inside having *very* tasty pupus and desserts or cocktails while their resident ghost (Annabelle) plays at the piano. You call out a song and she probably knows it. (Hey, wait a minute. If the ghost has been dead for 150 years, how come she knows the theme to *Cheers*?) Then it's into the cozy 78-seat magic theater for—

we promise you—the most amazing show you'll ever see. No smoke and mirrors, no elaborate props. Don't think David Copperfield or anything like that. Just a close-up view of a very engaging (and hilarious) man doing the absolute impossible. And we mean that literally. In fact, the first time we saw the show, we were so blown away that we were convinced that some of the audience members had to be plants. After the 1+ hour show, we told Warren our suspicions. One of us told him, "I've seen great magicians, but *nobody's* that good." He proceeded to do some of the same things with us. (We didn't tell him who we were that night—just viewers.) We don't want to give anything away, but we can tell you that Warren does things that have literally kept us awake at night. It's simply not possible, and we've come to the awkward conclusion that Warren is simply not of this world. We've seen lots of magicians and even taken one to see Warren. But none of us has ever seen anything like it and we've since seen the show several times. After the show nobody wants to leave. They just want to discuss what they saw. If you only see one show on Maui, this is it. $38 per person, plus whatever you eat and drink before the show.

The other show, **'ULALENA** (661–9913), is the biggest, most elaborate show ever to take place on Maui. It's also known as **Maui Myth & Magic,** which is awkwardly named because it has nothing to do with magic. This 700-seat theater was specially created for musical shows. Over time they may add other shows to the roster, but at press time 'Ulalena was the only show. The show is a Hawaiian opera about life in Hawaii before and after western contact, and about the gods and their deeds. The theater is state of the art with booming sound and excellent lighting. The show is sung entirely in Hawaiian; there is no dialogue and no narration. Carefully read the handout they give so you'll get an idea of what's going on. Nonetheless, much of the action will be lost on most visitors who aren't aware of Hawaiian legends and history. The percussion throughout is effective and the dancers disciplined. The show was actually written by Canadians, and, as a result, the story shows a pretty shallow view of Hawaiian life. There are also some glaring historical gaffs. Like the introduction that contends the first settlers were from Tahiti. Actually, the first settlers came here from the Marquesas Islands in 300 A.D. The Tahitians arrived 700 years later and killed or subdued the first settlers. And the Hawaiians are shown to be happily toiling away in peace, harmony and innocence until the evil westerners arrive. Actually, the 200 years preceding western contact were the bloodiest in Hawai'i's history. And Captain Cook is portrayed as the Prince of Darkness, complete with black hat and mask, who literally walks on the backs of the trusting natives. (See page 17 for the real skinny on Cook, who they fail to mention was killed by the Hawaiians.) In this story, westerners bring only guns, sickness and sadness. But this is mostly forgotten by some very creative scenes. Like the dazzling waterfall scene where the actress/spirit dangles from the falls. And the last three scenes are beautiful and uplifting; hopefully, you'll leave smiling. 'Ulalena is a mixed bag but fairly fun and entertaining. It's certainly not the best show on Maui (we much prefer Warren & Annabelle's). Looking around at the audience, some (mostly men) seem to get restless during the show; others seem to find it pretty entertaining. Cost is $35. They don't serve dinner, but you can get packages that include meals at nearly restaurants.

DINNER CRUISES

Not all the Hawaiian islands offer these, but Maui's often placid evening waters make dinner cruises a delight here. The best on the island is **NAVATEK II** (873–3475). See page 212 for more on this very smooth boat. Leaving from Ma'alaea for a two-hour cruise down South Maui, the boat takes up to 80 people inside the enclosed lower deck. The food is good for a dinner cruise—prime rib and a small lobster tail—and the presentation is on white linen. The tables are a mix of sizes and the windowside two-person tables are the best. (And seated first.) Open bar included; it's a pricey $87 per person. Our only complaint is their poor dessert presence.

In West Maui the **MAUI PRINCESS** (667–6165) is a huge 118-foot yacht, up to 149 passengers at dinner. $78 per person includes filet mignon and chicken, open bar, live entertainment and dancing. While the brochure may show a cozy table for two, there are, in fact, four people seated at each table; just so you know. Half the tables are along the open, topside railing, the other half are in the middle. If the anemic mai tais are too tame for you,

don't hesitate to take them to the bar and have them *seasoned* for you; it's all free. The crew is good and, while you may expect glorified airline food for such a large crowd, the food (chicken and steak) is better than we expected. Even the desserts are good. The slow cruise during the sun's golden hour creates pretty views of Lahaina and Ka'anapali. After dinner there's dancing below decks. The boat is very smooth, and they stay out longer than the other dinner cruises. From 5:15–8 p.m. leaving from Lahaina Harbor.

The **WINDJAMMER** lives up to its name. $69 for the buffet with 93 people *jammed* onto a 70-foot schooner. If you're fortunate enough to get a table on the bow, count yourself lucky. Otherwise, look for an experience that's too crowded. One good thing is that they sometimes sail, if there's enough wind for it. (But you're in the lee and it's the evening, so don't count on it.)

DINNER ON A BEACH

This is one of the more romantic treats you can give your honey. Just the two of you and your own personal chef on a beach or grassy perch overlooking the ocean. (It will make up for the time you forgot her birthday.) We've done it and it's quite impressive. **TABLESIDE CHEFS** (875–8980) takes people to one of several locations in South or West Maui (we chose north Maluaka Beach) and serves 3-, 4- or 5-course meals for $235–$275 per couple. Arrange in advance to be sure they have an opening.

That's it…we're not leaving…ever!

Your selection of where to stay can be one of the more important decisions you'll make in planning your visit. To some, it's just a place to sleep and rather meaningless. To others, it's the difference between a good vacation and a bad one.

There are four main types of lodgings on the island: hotels, condominium resorts, bed and breakfasts, and single-family homes. The overwhelming majority of visitors stay in one of the first two types. Hotels offer more service but lack kitchens. Condos usually have full kitchens and more living area but usually lack daily maid service. Many condos have minimum stays—usually three to seven nights. This varies between different rental companies. If your group or family is large, you should strongly consider renting a house for privacy, roominess, and plain ol' value. There is a list of **rental agents** on page 297 who represent most of the condos and many of the vacation homes on the island.

Condos

When describing condos **(shown in this color)**, three-bedroom/two-bath units are described as 3/2, two-bedroom/one-bath units are described as 2/1, etc. Differentiation between half baths and full baths is not made. The price spreads for rooms of a given size are due to different views, different locations within the resort and sometimes seasonal fluctuations. So when you see that a 2/2 unit rents for $110–$140, you should figure that $140 units have a better view or are closer to the water. The terms Ocean Front, Ocean View, and Garden View are used rather capriciously in Hawai'i, so we often avoid them. Unless otherwise noted, all condos come with telephones, complete kitchens, coffee makers, lanais (verandas), cable TV, ceiling fans and have cribs available upon request. None have a/c, and maid service is usually every few days or less unless otherwise noted.

Condos are in blue, hotels are in green.

In many ways, condos are more comfortable, though less plush. Some people want to get up and have their coffee before leaving their rooms. The important thing to remember about renting condos is the fragmented nature of the market. Each unit usually has a different owner, they all use different rental agencies to manage them, and it changes all the time. (Spreadsheets, blinding headaches and blurred vision are all necessary to figure it out.) Therefore, when we review them, we may look at 10 units and get 10 winners. You may rent one and get a dump because the owner is using furniture from a landfill and carpet from the finish line at the Maui Marathon. An individual owner may opt not to participate in the community hot water, instead giving you a tiny, underpowered hot water heater while all the other units bask in hot water. Or a resort may be scrupulously maintained, but an individual unit (yours) may have a recurring problem with marauding ants. The owner may use a different cleaning service, leaving you in a squalid mess. You truly never know what you're going to get. There's no way to take into account the individuality of units, so to a certain extent, you are playing the odds with many condos.

HOTELS

As for hotels (shown in this color), unless otherwise noted, all *do* have a/c, telephones, small refrigerators, lanais, cable TV and cribs available. None have room service unless we mention it. But if they *do* have room service, watch for built-in tips. It's easy to double tip, and you can bet that no one will point it out to you. Rooms are smaller than condos since they don't have kitchens and usually don't have a separate bedroom.

All prices given are RACK rates, meaning without any discounts. Tour packages and travel agents can sometimes get better rates. Many places offer discounts for stays of a week or more, and some will negotiate price with you. Some won't budge at all; others told us *no one* pays RACK rate. Also, be aware that these prices are subject to taxes of 11½%.

The gold bar indicates that the property is exceptionally well priced for what you get.

Solid Gold Value

The gem means that this accommodation offers something *particularly* special, not *necessarily* related to the price.

A Real Gem

WHERE ARE THE REST?

We ran into a *big problem* when we tried to do this section. What worked on Kaua'i and the Big Island—printing in-depth reviews of nearly every place to stay other than B&Bs—was *impossible* here. There are almost 150 hotels and condo complexes on the island. Our book would have been as heavy as a phone book if we tried. We had two choices: Give the bare bones info on all of them or do detailed reviews on a small fraction. Neither choice seemed palatable.

So we came up with a third way: List minimal info on all, print detailed reviews on some, and post full reviews of the rest on our web site, **www.wizardpub.com** After all, most people use this section *before* they come to the islands. And with the web (which has infinite space available), we could do more, like post larger aerial photos of the resorts with specific buildings labeled when appropriate, constant updates when necessary and put links to the various rental agents or hotels right in the review, allowing you to go to their sites and get more photos of the rooms. You should remember, however, that resorts post photos to lure you in, and some aren't above posting modified or overly flattering shots when they were new and sparkling. Our aerials don't lie and are designed to give you a feel for their ocean proximity (does oceanfront *really* mean oceanfront?), so you'll know what kind of view to expect from a given location within the resort. Resorts whose review is posted on our web site are identified with **WEB REVIEW**

Though most of our web site is available to all, we thought that these extra reviews should only be available to readers. So when you get to the page with the reviews, you'll have to enter the following number:

mr1101

You'll only have to enter this once and from then on, you can look at all of them.

Please remember that all these reviews are *relative to each other.* We'll repeat that later because it's so important. Even staying at a dump right on the ocean is still a *Golly!* experience. In other words, *Hey, you're on the ocean in Maui!* So if we sound whiny or picky in critiquing a resort, it's only because their next door neighbor might be such a better experience. It doesn't mean you'll be miserable, it just means that *compared to another resort,* you can do better.

Also be aware that we don't review long-term condos or apartments or resorts that are all or nearly all timeshare. Unfortunately, we also don't review **B&Bs.** Reviewing the B&Bs in depth just isn't practical, though we recognize how nice it is to stay in some. And while in our Kaua'i and Big Island books we were able to list a B&B service that could link you up with one, we haven't found anyone on Maui that we're comfortable recommending. (There are off-island services, but, again, we're not comfortable

recommending someone who's not on-island.) So we're going to have to pass the buck and suggest that you use the Internet and hope for the best.

We're describing the resorts geographically from the top of West Maui to the bottom of South Maui with others, including Hana, at the end. All resorts (except Ma'alaea) are shown on the various maps. If you have trouble seeing some things on the aerial photos, go to the web site where the photos are larger. An alphabetized list is on page 280.

Kapalua Accommodations

Kapalua resorts are few and in the extreme far north of West Maui. Weather is poorer here than any other resort area, featuring strong winds much of the time and more passing drizzly showers. It's a long drive to off-site attractions, but many people like the relative seclusion.

RITZ-CARLTON KAPALUA
(800) 241-3333 OR (808) 669-6200
WEB REVIEW

VILLAS AT KAPALUA (BAY, GOLF & RIDGE)
(800) 326-6284 OR (808) 669-9696
(800) 545-0018 OR (808) 669-8088
WEB REVIEW

KAPALUA BAY HOTEL
(800) 325-3589 OR (808) 669-5656

196 rooms, 2 pools, spa, 24-hour room service, valet parking, 3 restaurants. You could describe this hotel in two words—understated

A Real Gem

elegance. Kapalua Bay Hotel is a low key, low stress, relaxing resort without lots of razzle-dazzle. We've heard some refer to it as a vanilla resort, but they miss the point. It's *supposed* to be vanilla—high quality vanilla without a lot of spices, just superb ingredients. It's like French vanilla ice cream after an expensive meal, not a flaming souffle. If it's the souffle you want, try the Grand Wailea. (Wow, that analogy is *really* deep.)

Rooms are nicely furnished, bright and open with a wide layout and wide glass doors overlooking the grounds or ocean. They're 500 sq. ft., including the lanai. Their category selection is more fair than some others, so ocean view really means ocean view. (None of this *stick your head out the lanai and look for something blue* business.) Sunsets from here are excellent, and except for a few weeks around the winter solstice (December 21), the sun sets between Lana'i and Moloka'i. Service is excellent and professional. There's almost two employees for *every* guest room. Grounds are quiet and serene. Their beach, Kapalua Beach, is one of the best swimming beaches on the island, usually calm and fairly protected. Things are a tad more formal here, so they'll thank you to wear proper attire in the lobby. (Hint: No bathing suits unless you have a cover-up.) They have that annoying "resort fee," which is a mandatory $7 per day to include things that probably should be free anyway at these rates—things like local calls and room safes—but at least that includes valet parking.

The resort offers deep discounts for the Kapalua golf courses.

One problem here is the weather. Kapalua is usually windy, and they get a fair amount of passing drizzly showers. Not all the time, but no one will argue that Kapalua's weather is as good as Ka'anapali's. When it's nice here, this is a fantastic place to stay. But sometimes the weather will dampen things. One other consideration is that you're on the fringes of civilization. Great for calm and quiet, a bit less great for enjoying activities outside the resort.

Rates are $320–$570, suites are $1,100 and up. Lots of good packages available for RACK rate payers, including some incredible golf packages.

Napili Accommodations

Napili accommodations are mostly mid-'60s buildings and are clustered around wonderful Napili Bay.

NAPILI KAI BEACH RESORT
(800) 367–5030 OR (808) 669–6271
WEB REVIEW 🔹

MAUIAN ON NAPILI BAY
(800) 367–5034 OR (808) 669–6205
WEB REVIEW 🛁

NAPILI VILLAGE
(800) 336–2185 OR (808) 669–6228
WEB REVIEW 🛁

HALE NAPILI
(800) 245–2266 OR (808) 669–6184
18 units, daily maid service. A dreamy location on Napili Beach, clean, comfortable rooms, and an extremely warm staff make you feel like visiting ohana (family). Like many Napili resorts,

A Real Gem

most visitors are long-time repeats. Layouts and furnishings are amazingly

Hale Napili

variable, but most are quite nice and most face the ocean. It was built in 1965 and is certainly not plush, but Hale Napili is an easy place to like—and an easy place to return to. Rates are $95–$165.

NAPILI SUNSET
(800) 447–9229 OR (808) 669–8083
WEB REVIEW

THE NAPILI BAY RESORT
(800) 661–7200 OR (808) 661–3500
WEB REVIEW

NAPILI SURF BEACH RESORT
(888) 627–4547 OR (808) 669–8002
WEB REVIEW

NAPILI SHORES
(800) 688–7444 OR (808) 669–8061
WEB REVIEW

NAPILI POINT
(800) 669–6252 OR (808) 669–9222
WEB REVIEW

HONOKEANA COVE
(800) 237–4948 OR (808) 669–6441
WEB REVIEW

Kahana Accommodations

This area, from Kahana down to (but not including) Honokowai, includes the strip of condos and hotels that line the shoreline. Most built in the '70s. Some are good values. The biggest problem is that, with few exceptions, most have no beach or the water has seaweed. We don't want to overstate the seaweed problem. It's just that you probably won't find the crystal clear water available in other parts of the island, and we don't want you to be surprised when you find yourself swimming in it.

KAHANA SUNSET
(800) 669–1488 OR (808) 669–8011
WEB REVIEW

KAHANA VILLAGE
(800) 824–3065 OR (808) 669–5111

42 units, pool, spa. Wonderfully spacious rooms, high-grade appliances and a

A Real Gem

great oceanfront location. Though you're not on a sandy beach, the proximity to the ocean is stellar. Units have lots of glass and an open feel, but are still private if you want. The ground floors are massive 1,600 sq. ft. 3/2s with sunken tubs, wet bars, nice kitchens, and the additional bedrooms are equally large. The shoreline from the ocean front units seems delectably close.

The ocean view building with units 37–42 would probably be classified as ocean*front* at most resorts, which makes it a particularly good bargain. Upstairs units are 1,200 sq. ft. 2/2 townhouse-type units with the second bedroom a loft-type—not quite as desirable as the lower units. All units have nice, large lanais. Kahana Village is a good value for the price. 2/2s are $185–$260, 3/2s are $240–$355.

KAHANA OUTRIGGER
(800) 367–6092 OR **(808) 667–7088**
WEB REVIEW

KAHANA REEF
(800) 822-4409 OR **(808) 669-6491**
WEB REVIEW

HOLOLANI
(800) 367–5032 OR **(808) 669–8021**
WEB REVIEW

ROYAL KAHANA
(800) 688-7444 OR **(808) 669–5911**
WEB REVIEW

VALLEY ISLE RESORT
(800) 367–6092 OR **(808) 667–7088**
WEB REVIEW

SANDS OF KAHANA
(888) 669–0400 OR **(808) 669–0423**
WEB REVIEW

KAHANA BEACH RESORT CONDO HOTEL
(800) 922-7866 OR **(808) 669–8611**
84 units, pool, daily maid service. So which are they, a condo or a hotel? A condo. A tired, dumpy building with dreary, overpriced rooms and cheap furnishings. They're on Kahana Beach. Formerly owned by the same folks who own Pleasant Hawaiian Holiday (at press time new owners contemplated convert-

ing it to timeshare), odds are you won't be paying the RACK rate we list. As part of a package where you're just looking for a place to lay your head for little

money, it'll do fine. Just don't expect much, and you won't be disappointed. Studios are $170–$230, 2/2 "suites" are a ridiculously priced $250-$285. Hope you did *much* better than those RACK rates.

KAHANA VILLA
(888) 661–7200 OR **(808) 669–5613**
WEB REVIEW

NOELANI
(800) 367–6030 OR **(808) 669–8374**
WEB REVIEW

MAHINA SURF
(800) 367–6086 OR **(808) 669–6068**
WEB REVIEW

POLYNESIAN SHORES
(800) 433–6284 OR **(808) 669–6065**
WEB REVIEW

KULEANA
(800) 367–5633 OR **(808) 669–8080**
WEB REVIEW

HOYOCHI NIKKO
(800) 487–6002 OR (808) 669–8343
WEB REVIEW

HALE MAHINA BEACH RESORT
(800) 367–6092 OR (808) 667–7088
WEB REVIEW

LOKELANI
(800) 367–2976 OR (808) 669–8110
WEB REVIEW

HALE ONO LOA
(800) 487–6002 OR (808) 669–2531
WEB REVIEW

KALEIALOHA
(800) 222–8688 OR (808) 669–8197
WEB REVIEW

MAKANI SANDS
(800) 227–8223 OR (808) 669–8223
WEB REVIEW

KULAKANE
(800) 367–6088 OR (808) 669–6119
WEB REVIEW

NOHONANI
(800) 822–7368 OR (808) 669–8208
WEB REVIEW

HALE MAUI
(808) 669–6312
WEB REVIEW

PIKAKE
(800) 446–3054 OR (808) 669–6086
WEB REVIEW

HALE KAI
(800) 446–7307 OR (808) 669–6333
WEB REVIEW

PAKI MAUI
(800) 922–7866 OR (808) 669–8235
WEB REVIEW

MAUI SANDS
(800) 367–5037 OR (808) 669–1902
WEB REVIEW

(ASTON AT) PAPAKEA RESORT
(800) 922–7866 OR (808) 669–4848
WEB REVIEW

Honokowai Accommodations

Resorts in this area are in a different category than the ones directly north of here. The condos have hotel services and hotel prices. The sandy beach here is the northern part of North Beach, not the beach traditionally known as Ka'anapali. It's cleaner (not much seaweed) than the beach patches north of here, but the nearshore waters are a bit rocky. The beach is not anywhere near the caliber of Ka'anapali Beach. There's a grocery store nearby for condo users.

(ASTON) KA'ANAPALI SHORES
(800) 922–7866 OR (808) 667–2211
WEB REVIEW

EMBASSY VACATION RESORT
(800) 535–0085 OR (808) 661–2000
WEB REVIEW

MAUI KAI
(800) 367–5635 OR (808) 667–3500
WEB REVIEW

(ASTON) MAHANA AT KA'ANAPALI
(800) 922–7866 OR (808) 661–8751
WEB REVIEW

(ASTON) MAUI KA'ANAPALI VILLAS
(800) 922–7866 OR (808) 667–7791
WEB REVIEW

Ka'anapali Accommodations

Royal Lahaina Resort
(800) 222–5642 or (808) 661–3611
WEB REVIEW

Maui Eldorado
(800) 688–7444 or (808) 661–0021
WEB REVIEW

Sheraton Maui
(800) 782–9488 or (808) 661–0031
WEB REVIEW ◆

Ka'anapali Beach Hotel
(800) 262–8450 or (808) 661–0011
WEB REVIEW

Ka'anapali Royal
(800) 676–4112 or (808) 661–3484
WEB REVIEW

The Whaler
(800) 367–7052 or (808) 661–4861

360 units, pool, spa, 5 tennis courts, BBQs, a/c, fitness center, massage room, daily maid service. What a steal! This 1975-built property consists of two 12-story towers on delicious Ka'anapali Beach. The rooms and

Solid Gold Value

resort are immaculate, and the services for a condo resort are admirable. The daily maid will even do your dishes if you want. We debated which ocean views were best but lean toward north facing views because Moloka'i looks better than Lana'i from your lanai. Oceanfront has the best views, of course, but the extra $100 is kind of painful. Regardless, consider the 1/2s instead of the 1/1s. The extra full bathroom is welcome for $10 or $15. The resort is well-run and friendly. Rooms have a great layout with a bedroom and common room sharing the view. You have signing privileges at many other Ka'anapali properties. RACK rates are reasonable already, but you get a free car if you book direct and ask for it. Unquestionably the best deal in Ka'anapali. Studios are relatively spacious at 640 sq. ft. (and some have pull-down beds offering more usable room) at $195–$240. 1,114 sq. ft. 1/1s are $255–$330. At 1,118 sq. ft. the 1/2s are $265–$450, and 1,952 sq.ft. 2/2s are $430–$645.

Westin Maui
(888) 625–4949 or (808) 667–2525
WEB REVIEW

Ka'anapali Ali'i
(800) 642–6284 or (808) 667–1400
WEB REVIEW ◆

Maui Marriott
(800) 763–1333 or (808) 667–1200
WEB REVIEW

Hyatt Regency Maui
(800) 233–1234 or (808) 661–1234
815 rooms, 2 pools, spa, 6 lighted tennis courts, room service, 10 conference rooms, 19 shops, fitness center

A Real Gem

and spa, lu'au nightly, valet parking, child care program. Wow, where do we start? This is the biggest resort on Maui consisting of three 8- and 9-story building among 40 acres of spacious and exotic grounds. The two outstanding pools are large with waterfalls, and one has a fast 150-foot waterslide and a swinging bridge. Between the two is a poolside bar filled with the roar of the artificial waterfalls. The lobby is next to the huge atrium which, in the mornings, is filled with the sound of wild birds there to steal some food.

Best part of beach

There are plenty of extras available to guests. For instance, there are free guided rooftop astronomy demonstrations with their 16-inch scope, tours of the wildlife strewn about the grounds (like warm weather penguins, swans and parrots), and a nice oceanside fitness center and spa with all the bone-melting fixin's. There are four restaurants, including the Cascade Grill & Sushi Bar and the Swan Court, both have dreamy atmospheres though they're not cheap. Speaking of which, downstairs near the pool is the cheaper food court-style eatings called the Pavilion. Feel free to wear your bathing suit there. Watch the thieving birds who'll rob you blind if you turn your back.

The Hyatt has a good lu'au (the oceanfront rooms in the Lahaina Tower are exposed to the sound until 8–8:30 p.m.). The only ding with the Hyatt is that their part of Ka'anapali Beach sometimes gets seaweed blooms, especially in front of the Napili Wing. There's

also more reef in the nearshore waters, so you can't frolic in the shallow waters without reef shoes or you may tear up your feet. Valet parking is $10, but you can self-park for free. They have ocean activity booths where you can rent water toys like boogie boards and snorkel gear at normal resort prices (meaning expensive—boogie boards are $5 *per hour*) as well as Hobie Cat sailboats. But what some resorts charge for—items like coffee in your room and room safes—Hyatt gives you for free.

Hyatt's keiki program (called Camp Hyatt) is $50 per day, plus they'll watch your little one at night for $10 per hour. Weddings are popular here and they have a good wedding infrastructure. There are "couples only" activities available as well.

In all, the Hyatt does a very good job. It radiates the dreamy warmth that you want from a fantasy resort. It's especially pretty at night. And the Hyatt feels less crowded when full than some other Ka'anapali resorts. Rooms are nicely furnished and are a respectable 451 sq. ft. costing $300–$500, Regency rooms (which are marginally nicer but have more amenities—namely free continental breakfast in a private lounge) are $525–$575. Suites are $600–$3,000.

Lahaina Accommodations

When visiting West Maui, people usually speak of staying in Lahaina. The irony is that relatively few people actually *stay* in Lahaina. Nearly all West Maui accommodations are north of Lahaina, in Ka'anapali, Honokowai, Kahana, Napili and Kapalua.

MAKAI INN
(808) 662–3200
WEB REVIEW

LAHAINA ROADS
(800) 669–6284 OR **(808) 667–2712**
WEB REVIEW

LAHAINA INN
(800) 669–3444 OR **(808) 661–0577**
WEB REVIEW

PLANTATION INN
(800) 433–6815 OR **(808) 667–9225**
WEB REVIEW ◆

MAUI ISLANDER
(800) 688–7444 OR **(808) 667–9766**
WEB REVIEW

PIONEER INN (BEST WESTERN)
(800) 457–5457 OR **(808) 661–3636**
WEB REVIEW

LAHAINA SHORES
(800) 628–6699 OR **(808) 661–4835**
WEB REVIEW ◆

Ma'alaea Accommodations

As mentioned on page 131, we don't particularly recommend staying in Ma'alaea unless you're simply looking for a place to lay your head at night. It's the windiest place to stay on Maui and possibly in the whole state. Dust from sugar operations, smell from the landfill upwind, sometimes annoying flying midges from the nearby silt pond and other reasons make it a questionable place to choose to stay. Many people come back year after year; others grumble of Ma'alaea's shortcomings. In this case we have to side with the grumblers. Price is the only thing that should lure you here, and prices range from $85–$215. Some pluses, however, include the central location (between West and South Maui), the awesome winds do tend to keep things cooler (which is good because they charge $10 per day extra for a/c), they all have pretty nice views with three located on a sandy beach, and units here tend to be fairly well maintained. **Ma'alaea Bay Rentals** (800) 367–6084 or (808) 244–5627 has the most units here. Call them if you're set on staying in Ma'alaea.

We're choosing to devote the space we'd normally use to describe the nine resorts here to what we consider more viable accommodations elsewhere. That may anger some, but we only have so much space and it doesn't make sense to use so much for Ma'alaea when you can do so much better at other locations. We will mention that your best bet is probably **Island Sands** (800) 367–5242 or (808) 879–2778. A nice, clean 84-unit building with rates for 1/1 units at $110–$120. 2/2 are $125–$175. Summer is cheaper and windier. It's not on the sandy beach area but it's a short walk.

Other vacation rentals are at **Makani a Kai, Hono Kai, Kana'i a Nalu** and **Ma'alaea Kai**. The other condos are mostly long term.

North Kihei Accommodations

We're separating Kihei into North and South for a simple reason. The ocean and beaches in part of North Kihei suffer from the quality problems we mention on page 160. South of Cove Park, however, Kihei's beaches are lovely. Also, the extreme northern part of Kihei (Sugar Beach area) often has wind, dust, and sometimes bug and smell problems (mentioned in the reviews). We're not trying to portray North Kihei properties as bad places. In fact, some are wonderful places to stay. But remember, our job is to review accommodations *relative to each other.*

Web address for all accommodation reviews is www.wizardpub.com

KEALIA CONDOMINIUM
(800) 265-0686 OR (808) 879-0952

Kealia Condo

50 units, pool. A dreary, sterile institutional building, but it's fairly clean. They suffer from the curse of the midges (page 131), which breed by the billions in the pond across the street. It's really windy here. In all, you can do much better for the money. 1/1s (which are a small 556 sq. ft.) are $100–$150, 2/1s are $165–$195 and they, too, are small at 730 sq. ft.

SUGAR BEACH RESORT
(800) 367-5242 OR (808) 879-2778
WEB REVIEW

KIHEI SANDS
(800) 882-6284 OR (808) 879-2624
WEB REVIEW

NANI KAI HALE
(800) 367-6032 OR (808) 875-0630
WEB REVIEW

KIHEI KAI
(800) 735-2357 OR (808) 879-2357
WEB REVIEW

MA'ALAEA SURF
(800) 423-7953 OR (808) 879-1267
WEB REVIEW ♦

KIHEI BEACH RESORT
(800) 367-6034 OR (808) 879-2744
WEB REVIEW

NONA LANI COTTAGES
(800) 733-2688 OR (808) 879-2497
WEB REVIEW ♦

ALOHA PUALANI
(800) 782-5264 OR (808) 874-9265
WEB REVIEW

WAILANA KAI
(866) 891-1626 OR (808) 891-1626
WEB REVIEW

WAILANA SANDS
(800) 882-8550 OR (808) 879-8550
WEB REVIEW

WAILANA INN
(800) 399-3885 OR (808) 874-3131
WEB REVIEW

KULANA KAI
(808) 879-2806
WEB REVIEW

SUNSEEKER RESORT
(800) 532-6284 OR (808) 879-1261
WEB REVIEW

MAUI LU
(800) 922-7866 OR (808) 879-5881
WEB REVIEW

KIHEI BAY VISTA
(800) 535-0085 OR (808) 879-8866
WEB REVIEW

MENEHUNE SHORES
(800) 558-9117 OR (808) 879-5828
WEB REVIEW

Koa Resort
(800) 541–3060 or (808) 879-3328
WEB REVIEW

Koa Lagoon
(800) 367–8030 or (808) 879–3002

Koa Lagoon

42 units, pool, planned spa, BBQ, VCR and stereo, a/c, answering machine. What a steal! Though the building isn't overly impressive from the outside, the mid '70s concrete walls hide an incredible find (and block the sound, as well). Exceptionally stunning oceanfront views, with West Maui as part of the backdrop. Rooms are impeccably clean, comfortable, and large at 867 sq. ft for the 1/1, 1,000 sq. ft. for the 2/2 (lanai included). Six floors; the upper floors have some palm tree crowns in the view. The beach isn't a good swim-

Solid Gold Value

ming beach, but it's pretty. This is one of the best deals in Kihei with one big caveat: The area has a seaweed problem, especially bad next door at Menehune Shores, who tend to scrape the seaweed off the beach and pile it up. When it's at its worst, especially in late fall, the smell from the seaweed is a prob-

lem. When the problem's bad, we don't recommend Koa Lagoons. Other times it's not a factor, and rooms have a/c so you don't need to keep the windows open to stay cool. 1/1s are $90–$120, 2/2s are $120–$140.

Village By The Sea (aka Kauhale Makai)
(800) 822–4409 or (808) 879-5445
WEB REVIEW

Luana Kai
(800) 669–1127 or (808) 879–1268
WEB REVIEW

Maui Sunset
(800) 367–2954 or (808) 879-9272
WEB - REVIEW

Hale Kai o Kihei
(800) 457–7014 or (808) 879-2757
WEB REVIEW

Kihei Beachfront Resort
(800) 822–4409 or (808) 879-5445
WEB REVIEW

Waiohuli Beach Hale
(888) 249–9917 or (808) 875–9917
WEB REVIEW

Island Surf
(800) 367–2954 or (808) 879–9272
WEB REVIEW

Shores of Maui
(800) 367–8002 or (808) 879-9140
WEB REVIEW

South Kihei Accommodations

The beaches are nice from here south. Enjoy the water.

Lihi Kai Cottages
(808) 879-2335
WEB REVIEW

PUNAHOA
(800) 564–4380 OR (808) 879–2720
WEB REVIEW

HALE ILIILI
(800) 488–6004 OR (808) 879–7288
WEB REVIEW

MAUI VISTA
(800) 535–0085 OR (808) 879–7966
WEB REVIEW

MAUI COAST
(800) 895–6284 OR (808) 874-6284
WEB REVIEW

KAMA'OLE BEACH ROYALE
(800) 421–3661 OR (808) 879–3131
WEB REVIEW

KIHEI ALI'I KAI
(800) 888–6284 OR (808) 879–6770
WEB REVIEW

ROYAL MAUIAN
(800) 367–8009 OR (808) 879–1263
WEB REVIEW

KAMA'OLE NALU
(800) 767-1497 OR (808) 879-1006
WEB REVIEW

HALE PAU HANA
(800) 367–6036 OR (808) 879–2715
WEB REVIEW

KIHEI KAI NANI
(800) 473–1493 OR (808) 879–9088
WEB REVIEW

KIHEI AKAHI
(800) 367–5242 OR (808) 879–2778
WEB REVIEW

MAUI BANYAN
(800) 922–7866 OR (808) 875-0004
WEB REVIEW

MAUI PARKSHORE
(800) 822–4409 OR (808) 879–5445
WEB REVIEW

KAMA'OLE SANDS
(800) 367-5004 OR (808) 874-8700
WEB REVIEW

HALE KAMA'OLE
(800) 367–2970 OR (808) 879–1221
WEB REVIEW

MAUI KAMA'OLE
(800) 367–5242 OR (808) 879–2778
WEB REVIEW

MAUI HILL
(800) 922–7866 OR (808) 879–6321
WEB REVIEW

KIHEI SURFSIDE
(800) 822–4409 OR (808) 879-5445

Kihei Surfside   Mana Kai

84 units, pool, gas BBQs. A semi-circular building with nice views north down the coast, especially rooms ending with 01.

Solid Gold Value

Though built in 1974, it's clean, tidy and they have nice extras like a good front office, large lawn area, putting green, games like croquet and horseshoes, video rentals and a free extra data line in each room. It's a short walk to Keawakapu Beach. Lanais are walled on the side for privacy. There are three room layouts; 1/1 D units (500 sq. ft) 1/2 B & C units (680 sq. ft.), and 2/2 A units (830 sq. ft.). B & C units are the best deal. Rooms ending in 03–06 overlook the pool, which may be a bit noisy in the summer. Overall, it's a very nice place to stay. Most are rented through Maui Condo. Rates are a very reasonable $115–$215.

MANA KAI RESORT
(800) 367–5242 OR (808) 879–2778
WEB REVIEW

MAUI OCEANFRONT INN
(808) 879–7744

85 units. An overpriced dump. The name and brochure might lead you to think you'll get good views, but only building F has them. Others have no

view at all. Tiny 200 sq. ft. rooms, (the ones we looked at smelled foul to us), tiny TVs (I didn't know they still made them that small), microscopic a/c (perfect—if you're staying in a phone booth). How odd that a high end restaurant (Sarento's) is next door. At press time its new owners were quoted in the newspaper as saying they were fixing it up. Good, because it's got nowhere to go but up. Rates are $94–$184.

HALE HUI KAI
(800) 809–6284 OR (808) 879–1219
WEB REVIEW

Wailea Accommodations

Many people consider Wailea the most desirable place to stay on Maui. Gorgeous beach after gorgeous beach along with almost perfect weather make it a vacationer's paradise. The only downside is the price. If you look around for packages, however, paradise can be had even if your last name isn't Gates.

PALMS AT WAILEA
(800) 688–7444 OR (808) 879–5800
WEB REVIEW

WAILEA EKAHI VILLAGE
(800) 367–5246 OR (808) 879–1595
WEB REVIEW

RENAISSANCE WAILEA BEACH RESORT
(800) 992–4532 OR (808) 879–4900

345 units, 2 pools, 2 spas, fitness center, room service, massage room, valet parking, lu'au, child care services, 3 restaurants. Here's one of those occasions

Web address for all accommodation reviews is www.wizardpub.com

where the resort's motto matches reality. "Barefoot elegance" really sums it up. The resort is one of the quieter Wailea resorts and the grounds are lush and immaculately landscaped, creating a very serene atmosphere.

A Real Gem

Rooms are nicely furnished and reasonably sized at 500 sq. ft. (including lanai). Bathrooms are nice and come with deep tubs. There are lots of freebies, such as free room safe, coffee in the rooms and free videos. (Only the 90¢ local call fee and the $5 per day parking, even if you park it yourself, seems at odds with this philosophy.) The staff is very professional and service here is exemplary. Their lu'au is the best in South Maui. Beach toys are pricey ($7 *per hour* for snorkel gear), so get 'em elsewhere. By the way, the room balconies aren't *private,* and if you're not careful, others may see *yours* from the Sunset Terrace. The oceanfront Mokapu Wing comes with greater services in the form of dedicated personnel, a small pool for Mokapu guests only and free continental breakfast.

Check out the impressive bromeliad "tree" that greets you in the lobby. Rates are $330–$430, Mokapu rooms are $530, suites are $1,000–$3,800. If you're booking direct, ask for a leisure rate.

Wailea Elua Village
(800) 367–5246 OR (808) 879–1595
WEB REVIEW

Grand Champions
(800) 367–5246 OR (808) 879–1595
WEB REVIEW

Outrigger Wailea Resort
(800) 688–7444 OR (808) 879–1922
WEB REVIEW

Wailea Ekolu Village
(800) 367–5246 OR (808) 879–1595
WEB REVIEW

Grand Wailea Resort Hotel & Spa
(800) 888–6100 OR (808) 875–1234
WEB REVIEW ◆

Four Seasons Resort Maui at Wailea
(800) 334–6284 OR (808) 874–8000

380 rooms, 2 pools, 2 spas, health spa, fitness center, valet parking, child care service, 2 lighted tennis courts, 3 restaurants. Oh, my, where do we start? We're fearful of sounding like drooling stooges for the Four Seasons, but we are deeply impressed

A Real Gem with this resort. This is, without question, the class of the island. When you walk in, you can actually feel the tension falling from your limbs. It soon becomes evident why. Here, they do everything right. The resort is immaculate and lovingly cared for. The smallest details seem to have been anticipated. The grounds are impeccable. No dead leaf or blade of grass in sight. The staff here is the most professional we've seen and seem genuinely concerned for your happiness. There are 1⅔ employees for every room. (It's getting harder and harder to find those ⅔ employees.) While you're at the pool, they'll come by and spritz you with Evian water, offer chilled towels and even water the beach sand so you don't toast your tootsies. Oh, yes, you have arrived. And you'll weep when you have to leave.

The number of complementary services is way too long to list, but includes *free* child care service, free valet parking, free cabana chairs at the beach (other resorts charge up to $40 *per day* for that), free snorkel gear for an hour at the beach each day, free SCUBA lessons, free business center with Internet and computer time, free daily aerobics and yoga classes, etc. It goes on and on. It's clear that they've made a decision to not nickel and dime their guests.

Rooms are very large (650 sq. ft. including lanai) and the bathrooms are fit for a king—lots of marble, deep tub, separate shower and tons of wiggle room. Rooms are elegantly furnished in keeping with the rest of the resort. Housekeeping would make an operating room nurse proud. Dirt is simply not tolerated and dispatched with extreme prejudice.

Their beach, Wailea Beach, is one of the best on the island, an absolute dream.

If you have kids, they'll ask for their names and spell them out in colored sponges in the bathroom, and they'll kidproof the rooms if you like. The free child care service lasts all day.

The Four Seasons doesn't give many discounts, even to the numerous celebrities who come to visit. Rates are $310–$625. Suites are $585–$6,200.

The $310 mountain view rooms are actually a very good deal because the rates increase *a lot* with better views.

KEA LANI HOTEL
(800) 882–4100 OR (808) 875-4100
WEB REVIEW ◆

POLO BEACH CLUB
(800) 367–5246 OR (808) 879–1595
WEB REVIEW

DIAMOND RESORT
(800) 800–0720 OR (808) 874-0500
WEB REVIEW

MAKENA SURF
(800) 367–5246 OR (808) 879–1595
WEB REVIEW

MAUI PRINCE
(800) 321–6248 OR (808) 874–1111
WEB REVIEW

Kahului Accommodations

There are really only two reasons to stay in Kahului: cheap rooms and closeness to the airport. Few would come here to lounge around the pool. All three large hotels are in a line on Ka'ahumanu Avenue.

MAUI SEASIDE
(800) 560–5552 OR (808) 877–3311
WEB REVIEW

MAUI BEACH HOTEL
(888) 649–3222 OR (808) 877–0051
WEB REVIEW

MAUI PALMS
(888) 649–3222 OR (808) 877–0071
WEB REVIEW

Other Accommodations

OLD WAILUKU INN
(800) 305–4899 OR (808) 244–5897
WEB REVIEW ◆

MAMA'S BEACHFRONT COTTAGES
(800) 860–4852 OR (808) 579–9764
WEB REVIEW ◆

KULA LODGE
(800) 233–1535 OR (808) 878–1535
WEB REVIEW

Hana Accommodations

It's surprising that a place as glorious as Hana has fewer than 200 rooms available. And that includes private homes for rent. There are only two sizable resorts.

HOTEL HANA MAUI
(800) 321–4262 or (808) 248–8211

95 rooms (⅓ unused) 2 pools, spa, restaurant. This was a hard one to review. This hotel has a grand past and was, at one time, the crown jewel of East Maui. But years of poor financial results and a previous owner who was carrying a staggering debt allowed the place to fall into disrepair. (An example—a Jacuzzi in a suite breaks, so instead of fixing it, they just extend the deck over it.) At the turn of the new century, Hotel Hana Maui got new owners pledging to bring the old girl back to her former glory. Only time will tell. It still needed lots of work at press time, and morale was poor among the staff. The room prices are appallingly expensive, but they have one glorious thing going for them—*they're in Hana.* The newer Sea Ranch Cottages have some nice views. We like rooms 217 & 218 best—outrageous ocean views and private Jacuzzis. Also excellent are 215 & 216 (no private Jacuzzis but you pay the same). Also nice are 407 & 408. Overall, Hotel Hana Maui is undoubtedly overpriced, but it's the kind of place that will soothe your soul. Just don't expect the quality of the rooms to be commensurate with the prices. Though these same rooms would be half this price in other parts of Maui, this ain't any other part. It's heavenly Hana. $235–$655.

HANA KAI MAUI RESORT
(800) 346–2772 OR (808) 248–8426

17 units. Not a real *ooh-aah* place, but dependable and they usually have vacancies. Pretty good Hana Bay views from most units. Studios are a decent deal. All rooms have complete kitchens. No phones or TVs, and sound carries a bit too efficiently. Studios are $125-$135, 1/1 units are $145-$165.

Other than these two, you have some of the following choices:

HANA ALI'I HOLIDAYS (800) 548-0478 or (808) 248-7742 is a rental agency in Hana. They represent 20 or so private houses for rent. The homes we've seen tend to be pretty clean and some are decent deals. Houses include:

POPOLANA—Right next to the ocean—so close we've seen turtles literally outside the window. Outrageous and expansive views. Small 2/2 with full kitchen for $130. Good deal.

KAUAMANU COTTAGE—Nicely furnished 2/1 on large lot. Near Hana Airport but quiet. Good deal at $135.

KEANINI HALE—So-so deal, large, worn, poor views through power wires. $150.

WAI'ANAPANAPA COTTAGE—At $100 it's priced well. Nice full kitchen, fairly well kept.

HAMOA BEACH HOUSE—Wow, what a place! It's $295 per night, but it's a *huge* two-story house and right on the water (though not Hamoa Beach). Nicely furnished. You can hear the surf pounding. Good for large groups. Even for a couple, you're better off here for the money than Hotel Hana Maui.

HAMOA HALE KAI—2/1, could use some refurbishing. $95.

HALE WAIKOLOA—Though close to the water, the views aren't that great since you're downstairs. (They owner is upstairs but sometimes rents it.) $140. You can do better. Studio also available for $75.

PLANTATION HOUSE—Set among a coconut grove. Near Venus Pool. Small but functional. $140 is so-so deal.

Other places in Hana on our web site.

Rental Agents on Maui

AA Oceanfront Condo Rentals	(800) 488-6004 or (808) 879-7288
Bello Realty	(800) 541-3060 or (808) 879-3328
Chase 'n Rainbows	(800) 367-6092 or (808) 667-7088
Classic Resorts	(800) 628-6699 or (808) 667-1666
Condominium Rentals Hawai'i	(800) 367-5242 or (808) 879-2778
Destination Resorts Hawai'i	(800) 367-5246 or (808) 879-1595
Elite Properties	(800) 448-9222 or (808) 665-0561
Hana Ali'i Holidays	(800) 548-0478 or (808) 248-7742
Kapalua Villas	(800) 545-0018 or (808) 669-8088
Kihei Maui Vacations	(800) 541-6284 or (808) 879-7581
Kumulani Vacations	(800) 367-2954 or (808) 879-9272
Leisure Properties	(800) 888-6284 or (808) 879-6770
Ma'alaea Bay Rentals	(800) 367-6084 or (808) 244-5627
Maui Condominium & Home	(800) 822-4409 or (808) 879-5445
Maui Beachfront Rentals	(888) 661-7200 or (808) 661-3500
Nai'a Properties	(800) 487-6002 or (808) 669-2531

Index

Index

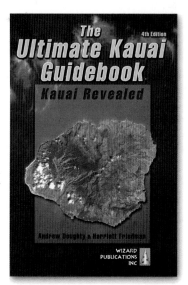
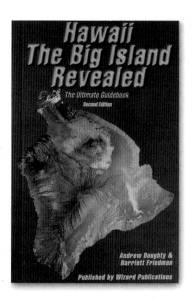